HAWAII

END OF THE RAINBOW

HAWAII
END OF THE RAINBOW

by Kazuo Miyamoto

CHARLES E. TUTTLE COMPANY, INC.
Rutland, Vermont & Tokyo, Japan

Published by the Charles E. Tuttle Company, Inc.
of Rutland, Vermont & Tokyo, Japan
with editorial offices at
Suido 1-chome, 2-6, Bunkyo-ku, Tokyo, Japan

Copyright in Japan, 1964, by Charles E. Tuttle Co., Inc.

Library of Congress Catalog Card No. 63-20213

International Standard Book No. 0-8048-0233-5

First edition, 1964
First Tut Book edition, 1968
Eleventh Printing, 1991

PRINTED IN THE UNITED STATES

Table of Contents

Preface 7

BOOK I: The Pioneers
Prologue 13
Chapter 1: Kauai is a Beautiful Island 15
Chapter 2: Transition to a Mercantile Trade 24
Chapter 3: Proxy Marriage 38
Chapter 4: Picture Bride Arrives........................... 43
Chapter 5: Picnic at Waikiki 52
Chapter 6: The People Make Merry 56
Chapter 7: The Eldest Son 63

BOOK II: The Early Days
Prologue 75
Chapter 8: Farm Life in Japan.............................. 77
Chapter 9: Contract Labor Years 91
Chapter 10: Escape from Waipunalei......................... 97
Chapter 11: A Bride Comes to the Plantation 117
Chapter 12: The First Born is Ambitious 135

BOOK III: The Second Generation
Prologue 159
Chapter 13: The Children Grow Up 161
Chapter 14: Sadao Leaves Home 192
Chapter 15: Minoru Matures 204
Chapter 16: California Interlude........................... 216
Chapter 17: A Farmer's Life 237
Chapter 18: Medical School................................. 252

Chapter 19: Hospital Internship 281

BOOK IV: Internment Camp
Prologue 295
Chapter 20: Pearl Harbor and Confinement 297
Chapter 21: Sand Island 314
Chapter 22: Hearing Board 335
Chapter 23: Transfer to the Mainland 346
Chapter 24: To Wisconsin 354
Chapter 25: At Camp McCoy............................. 358
Chapter 26: In the South................................. 371
Chapter 27: A Soldier Visits His Grandfather 392
Chapter 28: A Free Man Again 398

BOOK V: Homeward Bound
Prologue 405
Chapter 29: Tule Lake Relocation Center.................... 407
Chapter 30: Segregation of Evacuees....................... 445
Chapter 31: Turbulence and Martial Law.................... 458
Chapter 32: The Interlude in Arkansas 467
Chapter 33: A Visit to St. Louis........................... 481
Chapter 34: A Reunion of Friends.......................... 486
Chapter 35: The Return to Hawaii.......................... 500

Preface

Giants in the Earth by O. E. Rolvaag, a novel depicting the life of Norwegian fishermen struggling to homestead in the Dakota Territory. I was so impressed by this narrative that I said to myself, "Some day I'll tell our story!"

During the war years I found myself moved from one camp to another as a civilian internee and then as a relocatee, a victim of World War II when my ancestral country aligned herself with the Axis nations. That I was so treated was not for the same reason that the 100,000 persons of Japanese ancestry residing in the Pacific coastal states had to endure three years behind barbed wire fences.

Prior to the war, I lived in Tokyo for two years, doing research work at a medical school and exploring the countryside leisurely. It was a vacation for me and my family after practicing medicine for ten years in Honolulu. Japan was then engaged in a war against China and was in control of most of the strategic coastal cities of the Chinese mainland. There was an opportunity to visit these occupied areas in the company of two elderly members of the Japanese Diet. These men belonged to the Silkworm Farmers' Association and their aim was to uncover enough material first-hand to help end the war if it were at all possible. The cost of war was materially impoverishing the nation, and the silkworm industry in the Shanghai area, improved by Japanese variety, was posing a serious threat to farmers in Japan. This trip was, therefore, a serious study in statesmanship and I listened in at the daily conferences with the Japanese leaders, both military and civilian, from Canton to Peiping. A diary that I kept later became a monograph, "Glimpses of Formosa and China under Japanese occupation in 1939."

On December 7, 1941, I spent the day at Tripler Hospital, attending to the wounded from Hickam Field. But that night I was among the three hundred persons of Japanese ancestry rounded up as potentially dangerous characters by the FBI on the island of Oahu. Until November 15, 1942, I was interned in spite of my citizenship and honorable discharge papers from the US Army in 1918. After eleven months of incarceration I was released, but was exiled with my family to a relocation center on the mainland. The only crime I had committed was to write the aforementioned book. I spent three years in relocation centers with people evacuated from the Pacific coast states. I could have settled anywhere outside of the hundred mile strip along the Pacific coast, but I chose to remain with the people in the camp because, as a physician, I was most needed there.

The life in the concentration camps and relocation centers as depicted in this story is factual and is one man's experience. There is neither exaggeration nor bitterness. One of the characteristics of any people, inured to natural calamities for generations, is a resignation to holocaust and an attempt to make life endurable. The Japanese are such a race because their country is in the path of typhoons and is periodically beset with violent earthquakes. There was much laughter in the camp. Educational projects for the young and old enriched many oldsters who learned the finer things in life. For the young the experience was not welcome or wholesome, but it gave them a taste of pioneering life.

For Americans of Japanese ancestry, the end of the war in 1945 marks the end of the first era, which is made up of a half century of struggle against persecution and unacceptance by the majority group. The culmination of this harrassment was the wartime concentration camp. The second era is characterized by acceptance. This change in attitude was brought about by the model behavior of the 100,000 people in relocation centers and also by the gallantry of the Nisei soldiers in Europe and in the jungles of the South Pacific. Now job opportunities have become numerous in all fields of industry. Our sons are being accepted at West Point and Annapolis. Before the war there was not a single citizen with Japanese blood employed at Pearl Harbor. The Hawaiian National Guard limited its enrollment of Nisei to not more than ten percent of its roster.

Having experienced this half century of travail by a minority group in America, I am sending this manuscript to press with a feeling of relief. A segment of the American people will read it and I hope a vast majority of the Japanese Americans of future generations will be reminded of the thorny years of their ancestors. In any case, had I not written this story there is perhaps no one else who could have presented it to the world as it actually happened in the concentration camps and relocation centers. I may sound bombastic, but it may be the truth. I do not wish for another *Andersonville* to be written one hundred years from now by a writer highly gifted with imagination, using for his materials memoranda of the War Relocation Centers of 1942–1945 found in dusty, faded files long buried in a forgotten corner in Washington. I did not write in an indictive mood and I did not materially deviate from the truth. What happened is important history and, as such, is recorded so that in the future—in the handling of her minorities—America may not repeat the gross mistakes of the past.

The first half of the novel deals with the sugar plantation life of the immigrant Japanese in Hawaii at the turn of the century. The Americanization of the second generation in an environment that was itself peculiar and unique is depicted. Monarchy had just ended by forced abdication of the Queen and Hawaii became a territory of the United States. The aura of monarchy was everywhere. The deposed queen was still living. Even in such an atmosphere, the process of Americanization in the schools was a success. Physiognomy could not be changed, but the heart was captured for American ideals. The characters in the story are composite and thus resemble no one in particular. But some of the minor characters that appear incidentally are identified by their real names. I hope that their names will survive, and if I shall have contributed in a small measure to this tribute for their good work to my people and also to humanity, then I shall feel amply rewarded.

KAZUO MIYAMOTO

June, 1963
Honolulu, Hawaii

BOOK I

The Pioneers

Prologue

THE TELEPHONE RANG RAUCOUSLY. DR. *Minoru Murayama laid down the* Journal of the American Medical Association *and sauntered over to lift up the receiver. "Hello, this is Dr. Murayama."*

"Oh hello doctor. This is Arata—Sadao Arata. The old man is having a severe pain in the chest. Can you come over?" Extraneous voices of excited people at the other end could be heard through the receiver.

"OK. I'll be right over."

Night call in Hawaii was not hard on the doctor. The climate was balmy all the year round and at ten o'clock the traffic was not heavy. In ten minutes the doctor arrived at his destination.

An elderly man was lying on his right side, face ashen gray, and beads of cold sweat stood out on his forehead. Spasmodic pain of a crushing nature seemed to come and go and he stoically endured the onrush of these waves of agony. He gasped for air. His daughter-in-law was bending over behind him, rubbing his back along the spine. Whether or not this maneuver was helping the patient she was not certain, but at least she was deriving satisfaction from having something to do. Not knowing what to do, a half a dozen members of the family milled around in the parlor.

Without saying anything, Dr. Murayama laid bare the elderly chest and applied his stethoscope. There was no murmur or leaking heart sound. The rhythm was regular, but the heart sounds were somewhat weak. Blood pressure was normal. The symptoms were without question those of acute damage to the heart muscle.

"Arata-san, I am going to give you an injection to make this pain easier."

He took out an ampoule of demerol, emptied the contents into a sterile syringe, and injected it slowly into a vein of the old man's forearm. It was done very, very slowly. Meanwhile, the doctor kept his eyes glued on the patient's face. Apparent relief from pain could be discerned by the relaxation of the face muscles, deeper respiration, and limpness of the extremities. The patient seemed to lapse into sleep. After making sure that the patient was easier, the doctor turned to the middle aged son.

"Sadao, I think your father has had a heart attack. This pain will come back tonight and I wish to have him in a hospital where we can give him oxygen continuously to fortify the heart and injections to ease the pain if it should return. There are certain tests that must be carried out to make the diagnosis certain. If you have no objection, I'll call the hospital to send for an ambulance." The tone of the doctor's voice tolerated no argument and only acquiescence was expected.

"Do the best you can for him. We know that he has got something serious. He is 85 and he never was really sick up to now. And you know how he can stand any sort of pain."

"That I know very well indeed."

After seeing to the details of putting this man in an oxygen tent, arranging for a special nurse, and writing orders on the chart, Dr. Murayama returned home at midnight. He drank a glass of milk and ensconced himself in a deep chair. He could not sleep. During the war, Seikichi Arata came out of the Santa Fe Internment Camp and sojourned at the Arkansas Relocation Center until the end of the war. The doctor later discovered that his friend of high school days, Sadao Arata, was this man's son. During the waiting months of ennui, for the majority of elderly relocatees had nothing to do, details of the man's life were retold many times. Dr. Minoru Murayama could close his eyes and review the exploits of this pioneer of Hawaii.

CHAPTER 1

Kauai is a Beautiful Island

AMONG THE IMMIGRANTS TO HAWAII IN 1891, there was a young man of twenty-two named Seikichi Arata. His forefathers had been professional warriors in Japan for generations and Seikichi had a fierce family pride, for it was only twenty-four years since the abolition of the feudal system in Japan which had flourished for at least seven centuries. Young Seikichi's ambition was to become an officer in the new Westernized army of the Japanese Empire—no longer a mere warrior of the Choshu clan as his forebears had been. He studied hard and in competitive examinations passed every subject, but at the last hurdle he was rejected because of his stature which lacked half an inch of the minimum requirement. Disgruntled and disappointed, it was pathetic to see him and also an ordeal to endure him. He was not the type to lose himself in dissipation to forget his frustrated hopes. He was silent and seemed infinitely unhappy. To console him, friends suggested he enter the police force, but he was not interested. In his mind, bigger dreams were taking shape. Rumors of emigration to Hawaii reached him. It was the talk of the countryside. Used to two and a half centuries of isolation from the outside world, banned under the penalty of death from leaving their homeland, this was extraordinary news to the people. True, several sons of Choshu had been sent abroad to study the arts and sciences of Europe and America, but that privilege was reserved for the selected and the elite. Now the rank and file had a chance to leave the country and seek their fortune in distant climes. To Seikichi, a big horizon of activity seemed to have been pried open. Denied entry into the army, he would be compensated by finding adventure and fortune in a foreign country. However, the entire family was opposed to this proposition. To leave the country of the gods for an unknown world was in itself an unthinkable revolutionary notion; to go as an immigrant laborer was a disgrace to the family name. If go he must, then he had to depart without the blessing of his parents and endure being disowned by the family. Balked by such ignorance and false family pride, he became more resolved in his determination to proceed to Hawaii.

In the Hawaiian Archipelago, the northernmost island is called Kauai, and is the oldest from a geological viewpoint. The topography is therefore less harsh than the other volcanic islands of more recent formation. The mountains are heavily wooded as only tropical lands can be vegetated and the bare and forbidding lava flows, common on other islands, are absent. In the center of this oval island is Mt. Waialeale, the second wettest spot on earth. (First place is conceded to a spot on the Himalaya Range in Assam, India.) Because of this abundant rainfall and the cool trade winds that continuously blow from Northern Canada and Alaska, the climate is moderated to ideal physical comfort in spite of its geographical position of 20° north latitude, which ought to make this a torrid climate. With Waialeale as its highest peak, a range of mountains form a wind-break against the northeasterly trades and so the windward slopes are steep and inaccessible. The moisture-bearing clouds, upon contact with the range of mountains, unload their cargo, producing almost daily rain. The angry waves of the Pacific keep up their incessant battering against the crumbling rocks of aging volcanic formation, and have produced a wild but picturesque coastline. Only wild pigs and goats roam on this inhospitable terrain called the Napali Coast.

On the leeward side, however, a virtual paradise has come into being. Here, protected and aging slowly, the lava had disintegrated to finer particles and the soil has become ideal for lush tropical vegetation. The gentle slopes of the mountains, though made irregular by the original flows of lava from the now extinct craters and subsequently chiseled off by gradual erosion by the elements, have produced a coastline of exquisite beauty with many inlets, coves, and sandy beaches. The contour of hills and mountains are rounded off, crowned with forests and vegetation so that an impression of gentleness is conveyed to onlookers. Not without cause is this island called the "Garden Island."

People have been coming to this and other islands of the archipelago for the past several centuries. First the Tahitians, inspired with adventurous yearnings developed by generations of cruising in the south seas, headed north in their search for habitable lands as population increases made their native habitat too crowded. They accidentally discovered these islands, settled there, and then sent for their kin. Many voyages were made back and forth in the following centuries. In their double canoes, they were guided by stars, wave and wind patterns, birds, and cloud formations. Especially in the voyages that were undertaken later, a pinpoint navigation was imperative in their northern cruise. Without natural enemies, a salubrious climate, rich soil, and abundant fishing in the surrounding sea, the population increased rapidly and it is chronicled that when Captain Cook visited Kealakekua Bay in the late eighteenth century, the native population numbered well over a quarter of a million happy and contented people. There was enough to eat for everybody.

Just a little work sufficed for the simple needs of the people. Nature was in her most beneficent mood and they multiplied accordingly, not plagued with any of the disease so rife among civilized men. Being in an isolated community, there were no epidemic diseases. A famous historical fact in epidemiology is that when Capt. Cook visited Kona, there was a case of measles among the sailors. From this focus, the virus of measles spread rapidly among the natives and thereafter it overran the islands like wildfire, causing thousands of deaths in its wake. A childhood disease, considered dangerous enough in some epidemics but usually innocuous and a relatively mild ordeal for civilized populations, it proved to be a scourge among the Hawaiians who had never been exposed to this malady and therefore had no racial immunity to protect them. Estimates were made later that perhaps one third of the population was carried off as a result of this epidemic, and finally, when every infectable one was affected, the virulence of the disease waned and it died out. The present day Hawaiians are prone to get tuberculosis when huddled together in city tenements, but their forefathers did not know that such a disease existed. Then came the venereal diseases. South Sea islanders have never been known to be prudes. For many decades whaling vessels found haven in the Hawaiian waters during winter months, and their sailors contributed their share to the Hawaiian downfall. Some cynic has coined the caustic phrase, "civilization is syphilization." Blessings of civilization are not always happy and beneficial.

The Hawaiian branch of the Polynesians prospered and multiplied, but as the earth became smaller with increased knowledge and improved means of navigation and as the greed of men drove adventurers to unknown corners of the world in search of fabulous riches, these somnolent islands could not long remain isolated, and were soon opened up to immigration from Europe and Asia. The factor that facilitated this migration of races to this out-of-the-way spot was the sugar industry that found native labor undependable and looked for workers of the old world that had been inured to centuries of uncomplaining toil. Natives did not know what real labor meant. The Portuguese were recruited in the Madeira and Azores Islands. Germans, Spaniards, Russians, Chinese, and finally Japanese were brought in to work on the sugar plantations. The Portuguese were industrious and obedient. They settled permanently, but did not like the low-waged indentured labor in the canefields and soon left the plantations to buy small farms and homestead. As independent farmers they might raise their own milk-cows, and chickens. For money to buy necessities of life, they worked on the neighboring plantation. Experiments with Germans, a boatload of whom came to Lihue, Kauai, and Spaniards that followed were equally unsuccessful from the sugar planters' viewpoint. They sought greener pastures in the continental United States and migrated further on from Hawaii.

The more successful immigrants for the needs of the sugar planters were the Chinese. They came from the province of Canton in southern China where the climate is much like that of the tropics, and had been used to long hours of hard labor. To construct the Southern Pacific Railroad, they were imported by the thousands as contract laborers to California and similarly thousands were brought to the Hawaiian Kingdom. As the custom of China forbade marriage of anyone not able to provide for a wife, young coolies that came to these islands for the most part were single. Very few females accompanied them. As a result they intermarried freely among the natives and a steady mixture of races came into being.

Despite the fact that the islands were under the rule of absolute monarchs of the line of the Kamehamehas, the power of the judiciary, executive, and military was in the hands of the Anglo-Saxons. These represented the moneyed sugar planters, and they were responsible for the introduction of new races into the community. The days of the New England whaling fleet which had found refuge in Lahaina and Honolulu during the winter off-season months were history, and the spiritual power wielded over the throne by the New England missionaries metamorphosed into a new generation of established capitalists who were sons and sons-in-law of these well-meaning but fanatical religious enthusiasts. The days of religious fervor were succeeded by the greed of a capitalistic generation. A treaty of reciprocity was concluded with the United States. In return for the American use of Pearl Harbor as a coaling station for the Navy, Hawaii's sugar was to have preferential tariff rates when landed at San Francisco. Though an independent monarchy, Hawaii was a mere appendage of the United States economically. British and German interests were jealous but powerless. Therefore, when the United States passed laws forbidding entry of Chinese into her ports and across her boundaries, Hawaii voluntarily followed suit. She was sensitive to the pendulum of American sentiment and forbade further recruiting of Cantonese labor to work in her sugarcane fields, because her sugar had to be sold in the markets of the mainland.

Deprived of this profitable fountain of cheap labor, a new source had to be tapped in order to keep the plantation going at a profit so that dividends would go to shareholders. Whatever may be said about the avariciousness and cold-bloodedness of these pioneers—their exploitation of native ignorance and in the appropriation and robbing of their lands, credit must be given to their farsighted empire-building schemes. They built for generations ahead, not merely for tomorrow. So when King Kalakaua made a trip around the world in the 1880's, his itinerary included a visit to Japan. In the annals of the history of the Island Empire, Kalakaua was the first foreign sovereign to visit the empire and he was enthusiastically received. This royal visit paved the way for a conclusion of a treaty and revived migration of Japanese to the sugarcane fields of Hawaii. Previously, in 1865, such an experiment had been made but was soon given up after one shipload. A vigorous protest was made by the Japanese government when it learned that the immigrants were harshly treated and the provisions of the treaty not lived up to by the plantations. From 1885 on, a steady stream of immigrant ships plied between the ports of Japan and Honolulu and brought young men and women to the kingdom.

Thus we find young Seikichi Arata among the several hundred workers destined for the canefields for three years under contract (in other words, indentured labor) at twelve and a half dollars per month. The plantations were to furnish housing, fuel, and medical care, but the men had to feed themselves on this meager stipend. Seikichi was sent with fifty others to the Makaweli Plantation on the Island of Kauai. They were received as "new men" in a row of old, dilapidated bunk houses that had been used for a few decades by Chinese laborers. Built of the roughest 1 by 12 lumber, with galvanized iron for roofing, and painted with a white lime mixture, the external appearance of these barracks was neither inviting nor hospitable. The interior consisted of a platform about two feet above the floor extending the entire length of the room. On this platform, a thin straw matting was spread and tacked on. Blankets were to be spread for the night and folded against the wall during the daytime so that the room could serve as a living room. The walls were painted with whitewash, but having been done years ago, the bare boards exposed their ugly texture underneath the thin coating which was peeling off. Here and there, rectangular pieces of red paper on which Chinese ideographic characters were written were found pasted on the wall. These were legible and comprehensible to the newcomers and they had to admire the exquisite line in the strokes of the brush, but they could not help smiling at the meaning of the phrases. They were prompted by prayers for health, the keeping out of demons and bad luck, prayers for the coming of an ample harvest etc., and were written at New Year's time, just as Westerners would make New Year's resolutions.

How to clean up the place so that maximum pleasure might be derived even in such surroundings, was a problem to be met and solved immediately. Compatriots who had arrived earlier and were already established came instantly to meet the new arrivals. They were eager for news of their homeland, hoping to see familiar faces from their own villages, or men with whom friendships had been struck up in the ports of Kobe and Nagasaki while waiting for transportation. These men took the problem out of the newcomers' hands and tidied the room. They went to the store to buy straw mats to cover the platform and brought old magazines and newspapers to paste on the ugly walls. In a few hours the new arrivals were made to feel more at home. Breaking the ice by self-introduction, people were soon like old friends and news and experiences were exchanged. Of special interest was information regarding plantation life—what to expect and what was required of them. It was a relief to learn that the Makaweli Plantation was run by a manager with just and humane tendencies. The treatment of laborers on this plantation was incomparably better than on others, where horrid stories of inconceivable brutality were circulated throughout the islands. This brutality made the whole system of contract labor not unlike slavery.

The next day was allotted them to do as they wished in adjusting themselves to the new environment. In the red dirt of Makaweli, in the dusty leaves of the keawe tree, in the fluttering mynah birds, and in the green exuberance of the irrigated sugar cane, they discovered the richness of the tropics. The satiation of their curiosity regarding this strange land was partially attained. As a rebound reaction, a homesickness for their native villages and pine-clad hills of Japan assailed everyone as the curtain of dusk descended and enshrouded everything. But they were to be here for three years. At the expiration of the contract there would be a maximum lump sum of nearly two hundred dollars. One could return with some pride to the native village. The only thing to do now was to take care of one's health, work hard, and save as much as possible. Toward evening, the "luna," or overseer, came around and stood the newcomers in a single row. After scrutinizing them carefully, he began assigning men to different types of work. Not all were to work in the fields. The aptitude and intelligence of each man was determined at once by the experienced eyes of the overseer. Through an interpreter, Seikichi was told to report to the sugar mill the following morning.

At five o'clock the siren from the mill announced reveille and hurriedly they got up, performed their morning ablutions, and repaired to the mess room run by one of the wives, Mrs. Fukuda, and intimately called "Obasan" by all. Meals were extremely frugal, for the materials used were cheap. Monthly board to be paid for three meals a day was four and a half dollars. By any stretch of the imagination, it would be impossible to visualize anything appetizing or substantial at this price. There was just food enough to sustain the needs of the body, and perhaps the truth of the situation was that with the amount of energy expended in daily labor and toil, it did not matter very much as to how food was prepared or what variety there was: quantity was the prime requisite and the feeling of satiation was the only thing everyone asked for. To work, a man must have a full stomach. So a couple of bowls of rice were washed down with soybean soup, prepared with the addition of green vegetables or taro, and seasoned with dried, stony-hard, smoked tuna meat or dried shrimp. For the noon meal the tin lunch box contained about a pint measure of boiled rice and in a lesser compartment boiled dried fish and pickled vegetables or plum. A pint bottle of tea completed the daily lunch on work days.

The sugar mill was an object of wonder to young Seikichi who had never been inside a factory. Beyond the village water-wheel, he knew nothing of machinery. Mechanical devices were a novelty and a source of never-ending wonder. The huge flywheels, the long strips of revolving leather that kept the different machineries in motion, and the incessant din of pounding noises that issued from steel in action, filled him with an awe and fear that did not leave him for some time as he stood in the engine room. The millhands who worked nonchalantly amongst these monstrosities appeared superior and courageous to him in every respect. He wished to be like them, to be at ease in this fearsome surrounding and feel himself the master of these monstrous and intricate devices. For these were in the final analysis, products of human imagination and creation. If the white men had produced such portentous slaves of labor, then he too must study hard to learn the secret of these objects and return to Japan equipped with a new knowledge of engineering. He had come to the islands simply to make money, but here was something additional and unexpected. To have become assigned to a place in the mill was providential indeed. He would make the most of it.

He was awakened from his ruminations in the big engine room by a summons to go to the next wing of the building. Here he was confronted by a pot-bellied white man, ruddy faced and double chinned, but with kindly blue eyes. "So, you are my new help. What is your name? Arata? Easy to remember. Sakimoto, take him around and show him the ropes."

George Weiman was the sugar boiler. Most plantations had, as chemists and sugar boilers, men trained in the technical schools of Germany. He was in charge of the most important job of seeing to it that the sugary syrup was properly boiled in large vats to bring about crystallization of sugar from the crude molasses. A corps of assistants kept up a twenty-four hour vigil over these vats, maintaining a constant optimum temperature of the syrup.

Arata was taken around by Sakimoto and taught what to do. "Young man, you are lucky to be given this job. In the first place it is easy. No back-breaking toil as your friends will have to do in the canefields. You will not even get dirty. But you must not sleep on the job. You have to be wide awake."

"Oh, I shall try my best. But frankly I am scared. I never saw such large over-powering machinery in action."

"That is correct. In Japan there are no such factories. These Germans are smart. Mr. Weiman is a very good man at heart. We are all behind him and will work to our bones not to disappoint him. I hope you will likewise do your best. Your job is to keep an eye on these thermometers and regulate the steam that heats the vats of cane sugar. When the mercury in this glass tubing goes beyond this line, turn the faucet this way and when it is below this line let in some more steam by turning the faucet the other way. To slip up on this job means thousands of dollars of loss." Only intelligent and responsible men could be entrusted with the job, Sakimoto told him. Seikichi should be honored to be picked by the overseer for this particular assignment. Even if it were an empty compliment, to be accorded a favorable opinion was not unpleasant.

For the ensuing three years Seikichi Arata worked hard and conscientiously. He mastered his job and was dependable. But, however hard he tried he could not come to love it. Perhaps his inability to understand the basic theory of sugar manufacture, its chemistry and application, and the lack of books in his vernacular to read and study, were the reasons why he could not like mill work. He determined to go into commercial fields for his life work. With the passage of the years, he came to love Kauai as a place to live and possibly raise a family. The carefree atmosphere of this new country, not tied down by century-old traditions and taboos, and an immense opportunity that existed for those that would settle and seek their fortune, changed Seikichi's original intention of returning to his homeland at the expiration of the three year contract. Being the second son, he was not obligated to look after his parents. There was no breach of filial piety if he stuck to his land of adoption. In spite of the disowning declaration that had been made by the family, this impetuous rupture was soon repaired by the nominal and formal patch-work of an uncle, and the family in Japan was thrilled to hear about this new land of opportunity. News spread fast and the stream of migration of the sons of Choshu to the Hawaiian Kingdom was steady. Many came to Kauai. Life became more congenial to the immigrants. The gregarious instinct was especially evident when different races settled in a community.

CHAPTER 2

Transition to a Mercantile Trade

ARATA'S THREE YEARS OF TENURE CAME
to an end. Now he was free to engage in any trade of his own chosing,
leave the plantation for the city, or keep on with the mill work at an
advanced rate of pay—eighteen dollars per month. He planned to work
for two more years, denied himself all luxuries, quit smoking, and
stayed away from gambling and friendly games of cards that were being
indulged in by many men. His object was to acquire five hundred dollars
and venture forth as a storekeeper. He was certain of success. All the
Japanese were obliged to do their shopping at the plantation store or at
the little store run by Afook, a Cantonese. Invariably, things were cheaper
at the Chinese store. Although stock was meager at Afook's, laborers
patronized his store with reason. What would happen if he, Seikichi
Arata, should open a store and cater to the public with an intimate
understanding of their wants and tastes? There could be no mistake.
It would be a success, as certain as the sun rises from the east every day
of the year. The only deterrent was his lack of capital. It would not do
to go into partnership with anyone. He wanted to do it alone.

But it did not take him two years to work for the necessary capital.
He had heard of Dan Yone of Lihue, an eccentric, hard man but enor-
mously rich by standards prevailing among the immigrant Japanese. He
was one of the few remaining immigrants that had come to Hawaii
during the 1860's and was commonly called "The gwan nen mono."

Most of these early immigrants went back to Japan after a government
emmissary came and investigated the working conditions of the plantations. The investigators became indignant over the treatment accorded
their fellow countrymen: contrary to the agreement under which the
immigrants came to the islands. A score, however, remained. Among
these, there were a few who later prospered. Each one seemed to have

started by marrying a native woman whose dowry was land. Land was an item that came to assume added value with each passing decade as industrialization of the islands increased. Yone's first wife had died and he married again, this time a Portuguese woman. He has descendants who are to this day respected citizens of the islands of Kauai and Oahu. By the time Japanese immigrants began arriving in droves, Yone was owner of the largest store at Lihue and his credit among all races of people was excellent.

Yone had risen from the lowly coolie class in Japan and so was unable to acquire the three "R's" in his youth. He must have been of superior mental endowment for his success could not be accredited solely to his rich Hawaiian wife. He could not read or write but he had a prodigious memory and was full of ideas that would have been a credit to an educated man. He wanted to keep up with the current thoughts and events of the world. As he became wealthy and could entrust the routine of the store to his employees, he sought culture in his own way.

One day, while Seikichi was talking to Obasan, the cook, the conversation turned to gossip about island personages. "Arata-san, you have heard about Dan Yone?"

"Yes, like everybody else I have heard a lot about him as a successful businessman on this island, and particularly as he is also from my own province of Yamaguchi Ken."

"Do you know that he is trying to get someone who will read the newspapers to him?"

"Is that so? And how much is he going to pay for that sort of work?"

"Well, that is the funny part about this proposition. He does not want to openly hire anyone in that capacity. That is too much for his pride. He does not want to openly declare that he cannot read, although it is a public secret that he cannot even sign his name. He wants someone to come to him as a friend. Maybe he is not reluctant to pay for the service. He is just peculiar and eccentric."

"I should think there are any number of men at Lihue who can merely read the newspaper to him."

"No, it is not merely reading papers dealing with petty thievery or broken romances. He is interested in the editorials of the Tokyo papers to which he has subscribed regularly. Very few men can read the editorials intelligently, I have heard, for you know I can only sign my name. But I am a woman, and women are not supposed to be educated anyway.

Yone-san is looking for some educated man. I thought that if you came to know him he might open the way for your ambition. He may find a job for you at his store for all you know."

"It is an idea all right. Thanks for the tip."

"By the way, if you ever should see him, don't ever say 'boss.' I heard that the only way to please him and become friends with him is to address him as 'oyabun.' He must have a gambler's instinct or an admiration for the old time gangsters, for otherwise he would not want to be so called."

To Arata, this was news and it occurred to him that possibly Dan Yone might be a rung in the ladder to aid him in the ascent and realization of his dreams. There was no sense in getting the required amount of capital if he could get the same business started by getting the backing of some established personage. Perhaps his mythical benefactor might turn out to be eccentric Yone. How to make the contact, how to win his confidence and get started on his business career, required the most carefully planned approach.

After several weeks of deliberation, Seikichi took sick leave from the plantation and repaired to Lihue. He found the Yone store. It was imposing in size for a country mercantile establishment: painted green and bordered with white in contrast to the usual white washed walls of the neighboring houses. He rented a room at a cheap hotel and the next day entered the store and pretended to look over the goods on the display shelves. There were a number of workers of different nationalities. The manager was a Portuguese called "Shige" who spoke Japanese fluently. In addition, one Chinese, one Chinese-Hawaiian, and three Japanese salesmen and clerks completed the staff. They were all busy wrapping merchandise to be delivered to different camps in out-of-the-way locations. The salesmen had gone out taking orders when the plantation laborers were at home in the evenings and now were ready to deliver these purchases.

Just then a graying man of about sixty came in from the inner office. Painfully leaning on a cane, he brushed by Arata who said casually, "Oyabun, you seem to be having trouble. What is the matter?"

Yone seemed to be in good humor and civilly answered, "Oh, it is this confounded neuritis. Doctors don't seem to be able to help me much. What I need is a good old-fashioned masseur, but there is none around."

"In that case I can help, for I know something about massaging."

"Really! Come in then. Seems that I have never seen you before. You are a stranger in this town, are you not?"

On a couch in the inner office, Arata utilized his knowledge of *yawara,* the ancient term for *jujitsu.* Aspiring to become an army officer, Seikichi had been trained in the art of *yawara* for defense and attack, and as a part of that training, he was instructed in the rudiments of bone-setting, correction of joint dislocations, and massage. He used it to good advantage and Yone began to feel much easier as the circulation in the muscles increased and stagnation and soreness became alleviated.

"By your dialect, you must be from Yamaguchi," said Yone.

"Why yes, I am from Mitajiri."

"Well, well, I am from that part of the country myself and a very good one it is. Tell me how much training you have in massaging? You massage like a man; very effective."

"Not much, but I did some *yawara* training in my younger days as I wanted to join the army, but I was a little too short to become an officer."

"Too bad! And how much schooling did you get?"

"Enough of general education and an additional course or two in the Chinese classics."

"Is that so. Well, if you have time while you are in Lihue, come around every day. You have been very good in easing my pain today and you will be doing me a great favor if you will continue doctoring me. There is a pile of papers that came in the last boat which have been lying around untouched. If you can read the editorials to me while I rest here easily, I shall be much obliged."

The Tokyo *Asahi Shimbun* was a leading Japanese newspaper. It had been some time since Seikichi had perused a Japanese paper and it was a pleasure to read aloud to Yone the interesting news items and the current editorials of the leading metropolitan papers of Japan. Illiterate as Yone was, his comprehension of world events was good, and he grasped without difficulty the core of the discussions in the press. Evidently he had kept up with the changing opinions and moods of his home country better than Arata had been able to do. After the Sino-Japanese War, there was a big post-war boom. Yet the latent, subconscious tenseness of the nation which had knuckled down to a serious preparation for

27

an out-and-out struggle against the "Russian Bear" was perceived between the lines of the editorials. Yone commented now and then and Seikichi was able to discern his listener's line of thought.

"We must fight the Russians. The blood of the thousands of heroes that was spilled on the bleak hills of the Liaotung Peninsula will not be assuaged until the insult of the Tripartite Alliance, that forced the return of the hard-won spoil to China, can be returned in kind. The more we delay and vacillate, the stronger will the Russians become entrenched in Manchuria. It is win or die. We must fight."

"But you must not forget that the Russians have the largest army in the world and their Kossack cavalry is ferocious and famous. What chance would Japan have if she does not thoroughly prepare for the struggle?"

"Don't talk to me like the fools who are overcautious: the clique headed by Ito Hakubun who attempt in this day and era a reconciliation with Russia. Their intent is so clear. To think that Ito Hakubun is also from Yamaguchi Ken! You who once aspired to become an army officer ought to have more guts. The worst feature of bookworms is that they are too cautious. I am not educated but I have the most necessary fighting spirit. In other words, what shortage there might be in arms and equipment, we shall make up in the *yamato-damashii,* the fighting spirit of old Japan. My motto is 'strike and go to pieces if necessary,' just as the Americans say, 'do or die.' Anyway this is the topic of talk in Tokyo at the present moment. There is a lot of pro and con in the papers. Come tomorrow and continue the discussion and argument."

In this manner, Seikichi became acquainted with a historical character and a Japanese pioneer in Hawaii. Every day he went and while massaging Yone, prodded him with questions so that he would relate his early experiences both in Japan and Kauai. To be a good listener is the acme of ingratiation and the height of diplomacy.

"We first felt we were more or less stranded in Hawaii after the government officials told us to leave. We elected to remain. I married a native girl and naturally I could not take her along. I had come to like the easy-going native way of life, so different from the fierce struggle for existence that I had to face if I returned to the old country. I would be penniless in Japan and there was no money or property from my ancestors. Not to have your own kind around was a lonely feeling, but what I missed most was the *miso* and *shoyu* condiments of Japanese cooking.

But the poi and fish and the Chinese rice formerly imported from Canton and now raised in our own Hanalei Valley by the Chinese, one can get used to after several years. However, the craving for *shoyu* cooking returns very strongly after you reach forty. It is curious, but just about that time taste for food returns to the simple fare of old Japan. Longing for *Ocha-zuke* becomes very marked. The oily dishes of the Europeans and Americans, and the more oily chop suey lose their former glamor. It was hard to live among strangers; among newly made friends who had no common background with you. You felt so lost. Only in dreams could you relive happy childhood days and events, such as the festivals and games that were indulged in the villages. We were exiles, for there was no regular steamship service between Honolulu and Japan until the immigrant ships began going back and forth. A fact to be learned only after getting old is that one misses most in old age the things that he had been accustomed to in his boyhood."

"Is it true about the women too?" Seikichi ventured to ask, for Yone seemed to like frank talk and despised a fawning attitude.

"Yes, that is so too. I came from Japan when I was twenty and have been here forty years. I left the old country after knowing Japanese women. I was precocious. In any nationality there are strong and weak points, and many times these opposite traits counterbalance each other. But I feel that Japanese women are the best wives that can be obtained on earth. They are trained to serve their husbands and parents. I am old and can talk without mixing sex and passion in my talk. Anyone, be it man or woman, if service is the motive of his or her action, that service will be returned in kind. Therefore, the trained, cultured woman of old Japan is perhaps the most contented woman in the world. I ought to know.

"My first wife was a native of the upper class in Kauai. She was beautiful in face and physique. We were happy in our own way, living childishly from day to day. She sang when we were happy, quarrelled when anything got in her way, and cried like a spoiled child. She had no inhibition. She certainly was a child of nature and there is a lot of fun in this type of companion when one is young and with no responsibility. I have heard many accusations that I married her for her land. That is a dirty lie. It is true she had money and land, but that was just coincidental.

"There is a basis for that kind of talk, however, for that is the way many stranded white sailors from whaling schooners settled down to become huge land owners. On the island of Kauai you can count a dozen men on your fingers who are in this category. I pity the Kanaka wives of these unscrupulous men. For these men are the ones that are keeping mistresses more attractive than their legitimate mates, and these are the ones that are despoiling natives of their lands under one pretext or another. For a bottle of wine, a few acres of land, the only property of the native, has been known to have been signed away. On technicalities of Anglo-Saxon law, quite different than the ancient tribal and konohiki laws, lands were expropriated by those in power. My wife brought me parcels of land, but I can honestly say that whatever I have today, I made myself in business.

"My present wife, as you may know, is Portuguese and she is an excellent wife; a good mother for my children. The Portuguese seem to have no racial discrimination as you will soon find out if you live in Hawaii. They are a very hardworking, decent lot except for the good-for-nothings that have come from the Azores and Madeira Islands. They were penal colonies for the Protuguese kingdom. The only flaw in my marriage is the fact that I cannot get used to the religion. You know they are very good church-goers, although I cannot see anything good that comes from their attending churches except that they clear their conscience of sins committed during the preceding week. There is not the inside urge that makes them religious and seek the priest for consolation. They go just because they are used to going. I am dragged along sometimes but I cannot see anything in their teachings. I will stick to my own *Namu Amida Butsu*."

Bit by bit, Yone told his life history to Seikichi Arata as he massaged and rubbed every day. After living nearly four years among the illiterate common laborers, the talk of this old man was not only novel but also enlightening, for in him the cosmopolitanism of Hawaii found voice. Not only was this a voice, but the plain expression of one who was practicing and living its doctrine of equality and miscegenation. His outlook on life was bigger; he grasped its essentials and tolerated its existence, but was individualistic enough not to be overwhelmed by it. His longing was still to spend his dying days on the pine tree lined shores of Japan's Inland Sea. To the core, he was still proud of his heritage and refused to trade with the Hackfelds, one of the largest of the wholesale houses of Honolulu, because the concern was German in capital. Yone could not forgive the German participation in the Tripartite Alliance that high-jacked the Liaotung Peninsula from Japan. The peninsula had legally been ceded to Japan by the Manchu government of China as spoils of war. He would not talk to the Hackfeld salesmen, even when they happened to be Japanese. On the other hand, he patronized Theo. H. Davies and Company. It was English and England was allied to Japan.

To the recently arrived Japanese immigrants, this old timer seemed very native and at the same time very feudalistically Japanese. He was hard to approach because their ideas were so far apart. Practically all the laborers came with the idea of making a couple of hundred dollars and then returning to the home country. Yone had been there forty years and considered this land his home and the home of his children. Being materially successful, he was the victim of any number of promotional schemes, and his store was also the place where all sorts of sob stories were taken, in order to get donations for one cause or another. His gruffness to the rank and file was in a sense a defensive mechanism. He did not relish the idea of being considered "soft" for after all he was a hard-boiled businessman.

"Arata, what are your plans for the future? Are you returning to Makaweli to grow sugar cane?"

"I have no desire to remain a farmer or a millhand. I want to go into retail store work. I can see the greatest future in merchandise retailing if done right in the plantations. Can you offer any suggestions as to how to start?"

"My way is the harder way, and I must recommend to you that the hard way is the shortest way. You must learn the taste of the people you deal with. You must learn to utilize the capital you possess in the most effective manner. The best way is to go about peddling among the camps. Carry articles that will incite the urge to spend among the luxury hungry workers. Except for downright misers, all human beings love beauty and would like to use or wear something attractive. Carry different scented soaps, tooth brushes, powder, mirrors, pocket-knives etc., that you can carry in the back of a horse cart. Spread your wares at night at some friend's house and the people will come to you merely to inspect the goods out of curiosity because they have nothing else to do. You will be surprised at what your sales will amount to. Transactions will necessarily be in cash. Your expense will be the original cost of the horse and buggy, and the maintenance cost will consist of the capital to invest in the merchandise and some little present for the housekeeper where you spread your wares. You can have seven or eight camps to which you can go twice a month. If you have a mind to do it, I can stock you with the appropriate goods to start this business, and I shall give you the most favored rates, for I want to see you succeed."

For two years Arata followed Yone's advice and worked hard at retailing among the camps at night. Varieties of stock increased and soon he was carrying goods equivalent to those that lined the shelves of a small country store. It was a very good apprenticeship for him, for he had never had any business experience. He learned to mix with strangers, to make friends, to become above all a good listener to trivial talk and gossip. He learned quickly how important the last accomplishment was in winning boosters and friends. For many illiterates he wrote letters to their homes in Japan. He became a confidant to many in this way. In return, he bore them news of the world: news that he had gleaned through reading papers at Yone's. He still continued to read to the old man and to keep up with the world's movements himself. In time, country people bored with ennui at eventide came to look forward to the biweekly rounds of Arata. Business naturally improved with such a frame of mind among the customers.

One day Yone called him in the office and said, "Arata, it is about time you opened a store yourself. There is a limit to the amount of peddling you can do. The first part of your training is now over. Enter the next one as a storekeeper. Do you have in mind some locality where you would want to locate permanently? You must always bear in mind the competition, the type of customers, and the extent of patronage you are capable of getting."

"Thank you for your unfailing interest in me. By following your advice, I have not only earned quite a bit of money in the last two years, but I have learned a great deal of the world and the secrets of business success. For the latter knowledge I have had to go through a heart-aching failure or two before acquiring the knack of how to get along with the rank and file who are my prospective customers. About the place of business, I used to live at Makaweli and in that district I have a host

32

of friends. Stores are not as numerous there as on this eastern end. I shall perhaps start there."

In this manner the Arata store had its beginning. It's birth was timed to occur on the sixth anniversary of Seikichi's arrival in Kauai. The store was very humble. The exterior was painted white. The lumber used was rough 1—12 and the corrugated iron roof was red. The ten by ten room had shelves on the walls, a counter, large lockers in the business room, and a small partitioned space in the rear served as a bedroom.

The shelves were lined only with goods that would meet a ready sale. In the beginning, non-essentials and articles of luxury were avoided. To ensure a quick turnover with limited capital, he must be discriminating in the selection of merchandise and be satisfied with a small margin of profit. Reasonableness in price was his best and most effective means of advertising. It used to be the custom for Japanese wholesale houses of Honolulu to credit little country stores liberally. For payment of one hundred dollars, three hundred dollar's worth of goods were sold with a grace period of three months. The wholesale merchants themselves had a one year grace period from the export merchants of Japan. The Japanese retail merchants were yet in the kindergarten stage and the big American wholesalers of Honolulu extended no credit to them. Seikichi obtained a better bargain for himself by demanding that he get special prices for his goods as he was getting only two hundred dollar's worth of articles for his hundred in cash. Besides, he was able to rely on Yone for special articles that could be bought cheaper than from the wholesalers. He only had to work harder and make many more friends.

Soon, not only Makaweli but neighboring plantations were included in his sphere of activity. It would not long remain a one man affair; he would in a short while send for his bride, one chosen by his parents. With a wife to help him at the store, he could resume peddling to the outlying camps. A wife was a necessity now. As to her feminine charms and adaptability and capabilities as a wife, the wiser and experienced eyes of his parents and elders would be more discerning than the judgment of a love-hungry youngster. There would be children and many of them. Employed help would be obtained and he would have branch stores in strategic places over Kauai. He would eventually expand to Honolulu where he would start a wholesale department. If everything should proceed as scheduled (he had drawn up a plan in his solitary moments of day-dreaming) he would have offices in San Francisco and Kobe. All the profits enjoyed by middlemen would be eliminated and he would emerge as Seikichi Arata, the international trader. Opportunity in Hawaii was abundant. It was there for the picking. Only hard work and a little imagination were necessary requisites. Courage was the deciding factor to embark on any untried experience.

In 1898, he wrote to his father:

My Dear Father,

I hope everybody, beginning with my august parents, is well, even during this present season of oppressive heat. I am well and pray do not trouble your mind on my account. I am fortunate in having prospered in my new venture. My humble store has quadrupled in business and I believe this fact is the result of your unceasing prayers at the altar of the gods for the success of your son in Hawaii. Under the circumstances I feel keenly the want of an extra pair of hands to assist me in my work and also to add completeness to my life. I am old enough to have a wife and would beseech my beloved parents to send me a helpmate who would meet with your approval. To your wise judgment I leave the entire matter. For only with such experienced eyes can a mother to bear sturdy sons to the Aratas be selected.

Sincerely, your son

Seikichi

Four months later, an answer and a parcel post arrived:

My Dear Son,

Your mother and I were extremely glad to receive your letter. The summer months were bad but now cool autumn is here. The present is the season of "high clear sky when horses wax fat." After the harvest we are now taking life easy. The 210th day monsoon storms did not strike this region and we are all rejoicing over a bumper crop of rice.

Regarding your request, we have been more than pleased. It is high time that you thought of such serious matters. We lost no time and approached Moemon-san who is almost a professional match-maker, to see if he had on his roster of eligible girls one that would meet with your approval. It was with chagrin that they were as the ancient saying goes, "too short for obi and too long for tasuki." So I took off and made rounds of relatives in dif-

ferent villages. When I came to Mitajiri and visited with Gengoro Yamaki, he was pleased and said his second daughter, now nineteen, might be available for this match. You know the Yamakis are related to us by marriage, but there is no blood relationship. Their line is not tainted with insanity, epilepsy, leprosy, or other obnoxious diseases. She had a few years of schooling—can write and do arithmetic—is healthy. As to her feminine charms, I am sending you a recent photograph so that you may judge for yourself. Let me know your reaction. Your mother and I are enthusiastic about this match. The girl is not adverse to going to Hawaii.

Your loving Father.

Hurriedly, Seikichi opened the parcel. Under several wrappings of newspaper, a photograph of a buxom lass appeared. Under a coiffure that abruptly rose from her forehead—hair brushed up to leave both ears clear and a lump protruding at the nape of the neck—there was a rather round, plump face. She could not be called a beauty, but was by no means ugly. The full length picture showed her to be taller than the usual Japanese girl. Even the thick, many layered kimono could not hide the fact that she was well formed and strong limbed. Anyway, he wanted a helpmate, and a mother of his children. She must not be too tall, for he was not himself tall and it did not look dignified to have a wife taller than he. If her temperament, outlook on life, and womanly virtues passed the scrutiny of a jealous mother, then she must be allright. There was an irrepressible smile of satisfaction on his mouth. Life was sweet; there were many things to work for; the vista of human endeavor was unlimited.

A letter of acceptance, with a money order for two hundred dollars enclosed, was sent to his father on the following day. However, he did not breathe a word of his secret to anyone. He was too bashful to be tormented with well-intentioned but at times vulgar teasing by his friends. The arrival of his bride must be a complete surprise. Seikichi by this time was quite a businessman. As an after-thought he went around among his friends, organized a *tanomoshi,* and raised three hundred dollars under the pretext that further capital was needed for his active little shop.

When money was needed, it was obtained in a singular manner. A financial institution of mutual assistance among the common people of Japan evolved slowly during the centuries in a country without banks.

It was meant to escape the predatory menace of usurious moneylenders. In Hawaii, happily, there was as yet no man of this vampire class, but the people did not forget the blessings of the *tanomoshi* system, which worked as follows. A fellow in need of a lump sum of cash would get together with his friends and ask for help. If twelve men, a convenient number, comprised this group, they would each contribute a fixed monthly sum of about ten dollars. The first month's proceeds of one hundred and twenty dollars was to go to the fellow in need of the money. Beginning with the second month, the remaining eleven had a chance to bid for the pot. The highest bidder got the money but he had to pay the other ten dividends, equal to the figure of the bid. This "return" was at least ten percent. Sometimes it went as high as thirty percent. The longer one refrained from "taking" the *tanomoshi,* the more profitable it would be because the competition would be less keen and the dividend payment smaller towards the end. If he was the last, he would receive the one hundred twenty intact in addition to the monthly dividends he had been acquiring.

It was a convenient way of raising cash and a most profitable way of increasing funds for those that had money lying idle. The system operated so successfully that in later years other nationalities joined their Japanese friends in order to get better returns than banks were paying. Since there was no security or collateral and the system was based on credit and character only, it was not surprising to find absconders and deadbeats who betrayed their trust to the grief of trusting friends. That it continued to function in spite of these setbacks and in the face of commercial banks later on, is based on the soundness of its basic concept and simplicity of conduct to the satisfaction of all. Besides, it was a splendid way for friends to get together each month for a social affair and invariably a little refreshment was served at each meeting. There was no kow-towing to bank managers; there was no burden on the borrower in this arrangement.

Arata had two such *tanomoshi* of fifteen months each. He then sent three hundred dollars to his father with instructions to shop in the wholesale houses of Osaka and gather inexpensive articles of luxury and material suitable for male and female kimono. The material could be brought by his bride. In spite of the dusty toil that women had to endure, he knew human nature and its foibles enough to discern that attractive kimono and a desire for finery were not forgotten. To decorate and strut was not a monopoly of peacocks. To present a line of novel and attractive merchandise was the secret of commercial success. Combining marriage with business was not altogether bad. He prided himself tremendously for this masterful stroke of business acumen.

CHAPTER 3

Proxy Marriage

A MARRIAGE BY PROXY WAS PERFORMED AT his home in Japan. The bride henceforth became an Arata and came to live with his family. She could not proceed to Hawaii right away, however. The law provided that six months had to elapse after the civil marriage before a passport could be issued to an emigrant woman.

Eight months later, Seikichi received a cablegram from the Yamashiro Hotel of Honolulu announcing the arrival of his bride. He had to take the next inter-island ship to the capital city. There was to be no secrecy now. He went to the community kitchen and said to the woman who ran the place, "Obasan, my wife has arrived at Honolulu and I must go fetch her on the next boat. For the next ten days I shall have to close the store. May I ask you to keep a general look-out about the store so that nothing untoward shall happen?"

Shocked, but not unpleasantly, she retorted sharply, "What kind of a secretive man are you! To think of our mutual acquaintanceship for the past seven years and you not telling me! I have a good notion to crack your head open. But now that you are married, I shall not, for a widow would come into being without even the consummation of the first night. No, no. That won't do. Bring her along quickly. We shall become friends, I know. Don't worry about the store. But surely this *is* news!"

In a few hours the entire camp got hold of the tidings. It was a sensation. Then special orders for many small purchases to be made in the city came from Seikichi's customers. He could again combine business with pleasure.

On the following steamer day, Arata went to Port Allen and boarded the Mikahala, a rickety old ship. The trip to Honolulu took twelve hours. He travelled steerage in the ship's hold, herded together with crates of chickens and barrels of souring poi. The sweet-sour smell peculiar to such closed areas, augmented by the odor of paint, assailed his rather sensitive sense of smell. A Chinese man came around and announced, "You likee mat to sleep? One fifty cents Honolulu." He realized that he could not lie down on the dirty floor, nor could he stay erect as he was being overcome by the terrific stench. Fare was two dollars, but he wished he had paid more for comfort as a cabin passenger. He compromised and borrowed a piece of mat on which he was able to rest in a recumbent position. Holding a handkerchief over his nose, he was barely able to contain his uneasy stomach. Here and there, retching of sea-sick passengers made the situation worse.

Out in the open channel, the little tub began to dip and roll. He closed his eyes and passed in review the different events that had taken place in the seven years of his Hawaiian sojourn. Everything had proceeded favorably. Now at twenty-nine, he was to embark upon a new life. This bride of his must be a sweet young thing, but he must never spoil her. Time and again, he had been told that like a colt to be broken to the saddle, the vital question as to who was to be master in the house must be declared by act from the very start of conjugal life. Japanese girls were different from white women: they were trained to be deferential to the male sex. But feminine wile, amply demonstrated by the women on the plantation, was ever the dominant force in family life even among Japanese. It seemed by some subtle persuasion or occult power they gradually assumed the rein in family life. Wise men of old, knowing this truth about human relationships, had tried by family discipline and Confucian precepts based on *The Manual for Women* to moderate female ascendancy. In this respect, Japanese elders were more advanced than the Occidental leaders of old.

Oriental sages of yore had said, "There is no prosperity in a family where the hen crows" or "The chance to sell the family cow was bungled because the woman was too smart." He had never paid such attention to such sayings, but tonight every adage that he could recall seemed to have a weighty importance.

Even on the plantation, the way white women bossed their men around was disgraceful. A good Japanese woman would die before she would have her shoe string tied by her husband in public view, as long as she was in health. If that was Western culture, he wanted her to stay Japanese and not acquire such obnoxious notions. Yet, women were said to be funny creatures. Crazy ideas were contagious. He heard someone say, "Women are so lacking in judgment of good taste that if some leading society ladies should go naked, the majority would fall in line and go about like Eve just to be in style." He did not want her to be such a light butterfly. He must train her right. Obasan, the cook, was a good woman to emulate. In spite of her garrulousness, she had common sense and was a hard worker. She had no foolish notions about easy life. Her life revolved about her husband and children. It was fortunate that the two would be thrown together.

He fell asleep despite the pounding of the ship's machinery. Only once did he awaken to find himself lying on the hard floor and keenly aware of the engine noise. Then he knew he was on his way to Honolulu. He smiled contentedly, turned over on his side, and returned to his slumber.

Most of the immigrant hostelries were situated around Aala Park. To one of these, the Yamashiro Hotel, he proceeded in a hack—a rubber wheeled carriage drawn by a single horse. The distance was not far, the unpaved road dusty, and the day beastly hot. The exorbitant price of twenty-five cents for the ride did not seem so bad when he was spared of this walk on such a hot day. There were about a half a dozen men in the hack that were going to the same hotel. Everyone was excited and it was hard to keep still. They went back and forth to the little grocery store next door to buy soft drinks and nibble at flavored shaved ice. Ice was a commodity of luxury on the plantations. Dressed in their Sunday best, uniformly in heavy, black woolen suits, it was very uncomfortable on such a hot day. When the groom did not have a suit himself, some friend would loan his for the occasion. Even the stiff celluloid collar seemed to wrinkle and lose its shape under the drenching from perspiration. Mr. Azumi, the hotel manager, appeared and announced in a smiling tone, "There will be nothing to do until one o'clock in the afternoon. It may be best for you all to have a morning nap followed by a good bath. You all appear worn out after the night's voyage. First impressions are very important, you know. You must look your best."

"What do we do when we get to the Immigration Station?"

"You just produce her picture, identify her, and bring her here. Then we take you to a minister and have you go through a religious ceremony. Here in Hawaii, it is considered good taste to have a church marriage. Anyway, with this group I don't look for any trouble. You are all young and rather good looking. But sometimes there is the dickens to pay. The bridegroom and photograph don't match and he who tried to have some other do his long distance courting would meet his Waterloo at this critical stage. We have had several such cases. Fortunately, some girls became resigned to their fate and are good wives and mothers to-day.

"With other more spirited ones, it was not so good. Gamblers, and you know there are many in Honolulu, got scent of these unsavory cases and had pestered them like vultures would a stinking carcass. In the end their promise of an easy life in the city along a primrose path lured the women away. The fate of these women is sad and deplorable. Today, they live as prostitutes in Chinatown. So I admonish you all. In this community where women are scarce, you must treat your wives with consideration. The concept of the old country concerning women must be modified a little. Don't let them feel discontented. Don't take them for granted. You know, I am quite sure, of the number of wives that run away with other men. Seducers are everywhere. Whatever is said in the final analysis, the secret of a happy marriage is to love her well. So, now until the hot bath is ready at eleven o'clock, you had better go to bed." With such fatherly advice, the experienced hotel manager left them to masticate the contents of his message.

Among the men there was one about twenty-six years old to whom Seikichi took an instant liking. "I am Seikichi Arata from Kauai. You are evidently from another island. How was the trip?"

"Thank you. My name is Tarao Murayama and I am from the Hamakua coast of the Island of Hawaii. I came over on the Kinau this morning. It was a twenty-four hour trip and a very rough passage."

"How long have you been in Hawaii?"

"Five years. Soon after my examination for military service, from which I was exempted, I came to these islands."

"Did you know your girl in Japan?"

"Yes. She is from the same village although of a different subdivision. In fact we used to be sweethearts. She is three years my junior."

"Well, you are fortunate. You have not the fear that I have. I don't know my wife. She comes from a distance, although she is distantly related. This waiting and suspense are worse than the hour before examinations at school," Seikichi laughed wryly.

"Don't worry. I know it will be all right in your case. In the final analysis, the girls have travelled four thousand miles to come here. Something must be drastically wrong somewhere not to have things go right. Let us go up. If I am not mistaken, we are assigned to adjacent rooms. I shall be seeing you often while we are in Honolulu."

"Mr. Azumi gave us some good advice. I know of a case that was comical and tragic. This man lived on a neighboring plantation on Kauai. Like a fool, he borrowed a younger man's photograph to lure a girl. When he met her at the Immigration Station she was shocked to find that her prospective groom was almost as old as her father. In spite of all the cajoling and comforting talk, she refused to identify him as her man and she elected to be returned to Japan."

"I don't blame her. After all, to start marriage with a lie is not auspicious. We have many marriages that started this way on the Hamakua coast. They end up with the women running away with other men. A few ran off after children were born."

Arata sadly said, "It is also the situation in Kauai. Marriage may be a big gamble after all."

CHAPTER 4

Picture Bride Arrives

THE IMMIGRATION STATION WAS A TWO story frame building. There were several large halls containing rows of three-tiered steel beds. There were no mattresses. Each immigrant had to use his own blanket to soften the impact of the steel springs that sustained his recumbent body. They were forced to stay indoors except for thirty minutes after the noonday meal. Under these most trying circumstances, the women had to wait until their husbands arrived from the plantations to claim them. This picture bride system was similar in many respects to the "Tobacco brides" shipped from England to the Jamestown colony of Virginia in the early colonial days. In this instance, the women were shipped en masse to Virginia and the bachelor settlers took their pick, paying for their wives in tobacco. In a young settlement, the male element predominates. Soon, when toil is rewarded by security, the desire for a family arises. To resort to the most convenient and economical way to get the best possible girl under the circumstances is natural. Such an unusual procedure of human union sprang from necessity, and the results were not as bad as one might fear.

At one o'clock that afternoon, in a separate room, each woman was called in and introduced to her husband-to-be in the presence of the hotel man and immigration officials. Seikichi awaited his turn with a palpitating heart. With even greater curiosity and inward trepidation mixed with bashfulness, Haru, the bride, was undergoing the ordeal with unprecedented fortitude, for there was no mother or friend to lean on on this occasion. She did not have the desire to pace the floor. She merely sat still and waited the inevitable. The minute hands of the big wall clock moved forward agonizingly slow, little heeding her fear and agony. Her mouth parched easily; the salivary glands ceased functioning. It was a wonder that her heart did not stop beating also. The suspense was great.

Finally a matter-of-fact voice announced, "Arata Haru," and she came to herself. With great effort she said *hai*. Even after several attempts, it was barely audible. She stepped forward and was led to the office. With downcast eyes she entered the room, but she was aware of the presence of her man. By instinct, she knew which one he was as she fearfully raised her eyes to the men in the room.

"This is your husband, Arata Seikichi. Is the identification sufficient? If you are not satisfied, it is your privilege to decline going with him. You may both produce your photographs for comparison," the immigration official said in his routine manner.

"It is not necessary," she said in a voice that she herself was surprised to hear. For to her the striking resemblance he bore to his elder brother was evidence in itself.

"And how is it with you, Mr. Arata?" asked Mr. Azumi.

"It is all right with me," answered Seikichi automatically, marvelling at the clearcut answer the brave girl had made. It made him feel proud of her already, and at the same time he was aware of feeling flattered. She could not have said it so decisively if she did not like him. The first impression is said to be vital in matters of love. It was a good start; an auspicious omen regarding the marital voyage he was embarking upon, with Haru as copilot.

"In that case will you both step forward and sign this register? It will be kept here with the government. It concerns your marriage and entry of Mrs. Arata to the Hawaiian kingdom. You may sign in Japanese."

After signatures were affixed, the three left the office and proceeded to another room for customs inspection. Suitcases and willow trunks were in separate piles and Seikichi helped untie the ropes. As the contents were inspected by the customs official, Mr. Azumi interpreted, and Seikichi discreetly stood in the background. When the inspection was over, they went outside to the waiting hack. The luggage was to be picked up by the transfer man later. Mr. Azumi ordered the driver to go to the hotel, as he had to attend to some other affair at the immigration station.

Seated together and alone for the first time, an awkward silence ensued. Seikichi realized that he had to say something, anything.

44

"You must be tired after the long trip." She looked up, tried to smile, and shook her head. It did not much succeed. There was no verbal response. He must try another approach.

"The scenery of Honolulu and the customs of Hawaii are so different from our native land. Take this horse-drawn cart for example. In Japan only the elite ride; here it is for everybody who pays the price. See the dark street urchins going about barefooted. Everybody can dispense with footwear without incurring adverse criticism from others. You will find that practically everything is different. It is funny at first, but once you get used to it, it is a pleasant place to live in."

A flush came to her cheeks. Her eyes were shining. She was eagerly imbibing the news and information of this land of which she had been dreaming so long. Seikichi continued, "There are many men and women from Yamaguchi in these islands. Kauai is another island to the north. It is much more beautiful than what you now see." The vehicle was now on River Street and the scenery up towards Nuuanu Valley was very beautiful, but the mud flats of the stream, in full glare of the afternoon sun, were not a spectacle to rave about. The beautification of Hawaii was a project for later generations. Just then the infant community was busy with expansion upon expansion and had no time for the esthetic. They crossed the wooden bridge that spanned the river and were in front of the hotel. Hearing the wheels stop, a maid came out and led the bride upstairs to their bridal suite. It differed in no way from the other rooms: contained a double bed, a bureau, three straight-backed chairs, and a closet. The floor was covered with thin straw mats that were not new and had been burned in different places by cigarettes. The wall was decorated with a single print of an oil painting. It depicted a lake reflecting an imposing snow-capped mountain that abruptly rose from the water's edge. Other than that there was not a single ornament except for an ash tray on a rickety table. But to Haru, this was a release from the regimented life on the ship and at the immigration station. This room with its outlandish furnishings was new to her; it signified Western civilization. It was a symbol, her first contact with that which she had dreamed about in the past seven months. The maid showed her the bathroom and said that she would be back in an hour to escort them to church for the marriage ceremony. Funny to have a religious marriage, she thought, when she was already married for the past seven months. Perhaps it was a strange notion of the Hawaiian people to be married again and again; it was not a bad idea at that. It made the marriage knot tighter and tighter. Even she could recall members of the male sex who were straying rather easily from the marital fold in her native town. To make the occasion solemn was not without its good aspect, although in a strange land, among strangers, every added ritual was an ordeal. The femininity in her, seasoned for the past half year of living with in-laws, without the blessings due a bride, had steeled her to an independent view of life seldom seen in a virgin of her age.

The chapel was Congregational. The altar decorated with various symbolic paraphernalia was not like that of a Buddhist temple. It was not there to lend atmosphere. It was of a most austere simplicity. To her, accustomed to Buddhist rituals, a Roman Catholic ceremony would have been more solemn and significant and she could have felt some link to her past in the surge of a religious emotion. As it was, she was not particularly impressed. Only the solid gold ring placed on her finger during the ceremony gladdened her heart. After all, there was something concrete and tangible derived from this Western custom. Just as her mother had to shave off her eyebrows, blacken her teeth, and wear a new elaborate coiffure to show her married status, she would henceforth be wearing this simple but significant symbol to show that she was a wife; a station in life coveted by womankind all over the world.

It was early evening when they were last alone in the room. The luggage had already arrived and she began to take necessary articles from the willow trunk. Seikichi came to help with alacrity. Various toilet articles that only women use began to appear on the bureau top. Kimono and underwear came out and were laid out on the bed. An odor that issues only from such feminine wearing apparel pervaded the room. Seikichi was intoxicated with this aroma. It was a forgotten sensation. This was the same odor that filled the room when his mother had taken her kimono from the *tansu* to doll up for some festivity or visit another village. He experienced a new satisfaction of possessiveness. This was his mate. There was also the peculiar association of his mother and this woman. The woman nearest his heart had been his mother, but the entire family had to share her love and affection. Now came this woman to arouse his male instinct and he was in a position to monopolize her completely. This association was made clear by the odor emanating from the kimono. Primitive instincts long forgotten, but lying latent in evolutionary memory, arise on different occasions to assert the truth of the Darwinian concept, despite our gilded armor of civilization. Somewhere in our forgotten past, courtship must have been instigated principally by the powerful attraction of the opposite sex perceived by the olfactory mechanism. As if to end Seikichi's reverie, the maid knocked and announced, "The dining room is ready, and awaiting your presence."

At a long table, the five new couples were seated—each pair occupying places adjacent to each other. In the center of the table, covered with oil cloth, was a calabash of steaming, boiled rice. At each place was a porcelain bowl, a pair of sterilized, sanitary wooden chopsticks enclosed in wax paper, and two empty dishes, large and small. From a large communal plate, the brides were dishing out a concoction of beef and vegetables, fish cooked in plain *shoyu,* and some slices of raw fish to be eaten with *shoyu* mixed with mustard. Seikichi sat still as Haru stood up and filled his bowl with rice and his plate with the various items of food. Then she served herself. The maid came in with a tray of soup in lacquered bowls. Haru took two. As she picked up the wooden chopsticks, and placed them on his plate, she said softly, *"Oagari nasai* (please partake of it.)" Such service was almost embarrassing for an erstwhile bachelor. Only after he began eating did she start, and even then her appetite was like a canary's. He marvelled at this lack of appetite; it must be reticence and bashfulness.

The women were quiet. During their long voyage they must have become friends, but now there was no carefreeness. They did not wish to appear flippant before their mates' eyes. The men were total strangers. Under the circumstances the supper table was as solemn as a sepulchre. Each finished eating with undue haste. As he led the way out, Seikichi turned to Haru, "I am going out for a little walk. You may return to the room." She bowed obeisance and went upstairs. He went out and proceeded to the corner Chinese store across the bridge where he had noticed fruits on the counter earlier in the day. There he bought some bright colored mangoes, bananas, and oranges.

When he returned to their room, Haru was sitting on one of the straight-back chairs fanning herself, for the setting sun was fierce and there was not a sign of a breeze. She greeted him with a smile that was no longer forced. To have served him, even in a small capacity at the table, seemed to have earned her the right to claim this man as her husband. To comfort him, to be a hand or a foot for her lord, was a duty

47

to be pleasurably performed by a wife. She had been trained so at home. To have made a start in the right direction made her glad. She no longer felt, as a stranger to him. The mutual discard of the icy barrier was more speedy than the melting of late spring snow in the morning sun. She was conscious now that in this wide world there was no one to whom she could turn for help or comfort other than this man whom she had scarcely known six hours.

"Now that we have nothing to do, let me have news from home. Is everybody well? Are my parents healthy?"

"Your august parents are as well as could be. Neither of them has lost a day of work this year. The crop was coming up well. The rice plant was about two inches tall when I left. There was ample rainfall in May to assure good irrigation. The wheat crop was normal in its yield during the spring, so there is no acute want among the villagers. Your brother's wife recently gave birth to her second son and both are doing well. Our sister-in-law is fortunate."

"And how are your parents at Mitajiri? I have only a faint memory of how they look, but we shall get acquainted even if the best we could do was a photograph."

"Thank you. They are also well and send their most sincere greetings to you. Oh yes, I have a letter written by my father." She rose and from among her writing materials she produced a long envelope on which his name was written boldly with brush and India ink.

He broke open the seal and the contents read in part: *By the curious turn of the wheel of Karma our families have become intimately linked together again by this marriage. She may not have been brought up sufficiently well to suit your taste. If she has faults and is lacking in feminine virtues, we her parents are to blame for such shortcomings. Pray be patient and lead her to a loftier plane of womanhood. As a loving husband and protector you will be able to mould her character according to your wish and ideal. This we do not doubt, for she is still pliable. Where we have failed as disciplinarians, you will succeed with your love. In a strange land, her husband will be her sole support and counselor. My wife and I entrust you with her future happiness. May you both prosper and live happily, long after we two shall have departed from this earthly existence.*

Seikichi was deeply moved. He saw that this father-in-law was no ordinary farmer or merchant. After reading the letter and folding it slowly and carefully, he said to her feelingly, "I shall answer this letter myself, but when you write home, convey my message also—how I have been deeply moved. It seems what I wanted to tell you, your father has told me. At your leisure, tomorrow, you had better read this message also. It is a message both of us should heed. I have gained a very wise father-in-law."

Haru blushed deeply and was grateful for the consideration of this man for uttering such sentiments. Japanese males are usually reticent about showing their feelings. This spontaneous gesture won her over to him completely.

Just then, there was a knock and the maid announced that the hot bath was ready. Haru got to her feet and said, "Please take off your clothes." She began looking among his things for his *yukata*, a kimono of cotton fabric worn in the summer months. This she put over his back as he began taking his trousers off, and as he pushed his arms through the sleeves, her arms were around his waist tying the sash for him.

She followed him to the bathroom. As he sank his body up to his chin in the steaming hot water, she was tying her long sleeves behind her back, and tucking up the lower hem of her kimono. "Now, let me scrub your back."

He emerged from the water as red as a lobster and sat on a low wooden stool, turning his back to her. Japanese baths have a space outside the tub where soap and water may be used repeatedly. She lathered his back and arms with soap thoroughly and briskly scrubbed him. Then with fresh hot water she washed him off. After saying "At your leisure," she left the bathroom. He completed washing the rest of his torso and then immersed himself again luxuriantly in the steaming water. Relaxed completely, he reviewed the day's happenings. It was an eventful day. One thing after another, but everything a happy incident. How well-bred she was! How lucky he was! He had his parents to thank for having picked a girl with attributes he had scarcely thought possible. The female sex was so thoughtful. Losing himself in reverie, he was aware of becoming faint. The heat was making him groggy. Hurriedly he got out of the bath. He poured several basinfuls of cold water over his head and dried himself with a fresh towel.

He returned to the room and after telling her to take her turn at the bath, he sauntered forth into the street in his cool *yukata*.

Honolulu was a small town of perhaps thirty thousand. The Japanese clustered about along the Nuuanu River and infiltrated into the more established Chinatown for business. Aala Park was a loitering place for the hundreds of laborers travelling back and forth from the Oahu plantations and awaiting trains, the principal means of transportation. Men turned brown by constant exposure to the sun, wearing coarse dungarees and slouching lauhala hats, stumbled from the corner saloon and made merry on the green lawn of the park. Dusk was just settling and the leaves of the ironwood trees along the western edge of the park were restling with the slight breeze that stirred with the setting sun. Prostitutes of different nationalities plied their illicit trade here, and Seikichi, as if the mere sight of these women defiled his eyes, moved away toward the railroad station. The evening train had just pulled in from the country with forty or fifty passengers. This was Friday and people were being attracted to the town for the weekend.

To Seikichi's country mind, even the laborers here seemed a little more dapper. Maybe their ways of spending money were not quite the same. He looked at the little shops that catered to this fluctuating and floating population. Certainly they were enjoying a brisk business. The soft drink parlors and fruit stands were packed with customers who came to quench their thirst and to buy something for friends or for families back on the plantations. He was interested in the way the merchandise was arranged and displayed on the counters and shelves. The clicking cash register bespoke modernization. The kimono-clad girls in the shops seemed to be an attraction in some stores. Perhaps this was essential when competition was keen. The Chinese merchants operated more substantial shops and seemed more prosperous.

He made the rounds along Aala Street, onto Beretania, and back to the hotel. It was already dark and the gas street lights illuminated the early evening. Under the shroud of fading light and encroaching darkness, the street scene took on an exotic quality of softness and quiet. He wanted to linger a while longer but in spite of himself he was drawn upstairs.

Haru was wearing a *yukata* of bright design tied firmly at the waist with an abbreviated obi, and had finished her evening toilet. Noticing this, Seikichi sat on the edge of the bed. He wanted very much to stretch and sprawl on the mat as was his wont in Japan. Inadvertently, without forethought, he fell on his back. Softly as a cat she was at the side of the bed, with a pillow for his neck.

50

"Thank you. Oh I nearly forgot. I noticed yor appetite was not much. So I bought some Hawaiian fruits that I am sure you have not yet seen or tasted. You will find them in that package on the table. Help yourself." Haru was touched. He had noticed her to the extent of gauging her wants and needs; not only noticed but took active steps to rectify and supplement them.

"Oh I am so glad! In this package? What do you call these oblong ones that are so fragrant? Mangoes? I know these are bananas because I saw them in pictures. These oranges are much larger than in Japan. I think I shall try the mangoes first." She went out and borrowed a knife and two plates from the kitchen. She peeled one, sliced it and placed it on the plate. Taking out a few toothpicks, she placed them on a plate and offered it to Seikichi.

"Don't consider me. It was meant for you."

"But you must also share it. I shan't have it alone. Oh, this is delicious. There is a pleasant odor, isn't there? Not bad, like pine oil." He smiled and she smiled. It was the first time they had smiled in unison.

Picnic at Waikiki

SEIKICHI WAS LATE IN AWAKENING. HE HAD slept like a log. It was already light outside, perhaps seven o'clock. The bed beside him was empty and the odor of her person faintly lingered on the pillow. He drew out a cigarette and was puffing leisurely, smiling to himself inwardly of what had transpired last night. She had become his wholly. Even the thought of it sent his blood surging through his body, accelerated by the feminine aroma that still remained there. Just then she slipped silently into the room. She had arisen early and had already completed her toilet. Not to let her husband catch her in a dishevelled condition from the night's rest was one of the virtues of a Japanese wife. She was to arise and wake her husband when she had made herself presentable.

" Have you been awake long? How has your sleep been?" he asked. Her eyes were averted, her cheeks colored deeply.

She answered, "I was not able to sleep for quite a while, but once I dozed off I slept well. I was out on the veranda and taking in the fresh morning air." Seikichi was relieved that she was no different. Last night's experience had not changed her any.

"By the way, do you know the bride next door, Mrs. Murayama? I happened to meet the husband yesterday and we became friends."

"Yes. She and I became fast friends on board the ship. In fact we shared adjacent bunks." She was now able to face him eye to eye. There was no shyness left in her glance. She had earned a rightful place in this unit of society that was to begin with them. The act she had been dreading inwardly for some time was consummated rather easily. She was surprised to find herself the same; her thoughts and bodily condition were the same and there was no momentous subjective change, either mental or physical, that she could feel. Such had been her thoughts, introspection, and self analysis this morning as she had stood outside and inhaled the fresh breeze blowing from the Nuuanu Pali. But as she faced the man she was conscious of an inner metamorphosis; to feel that she was the same as yesterday was a delusion. There was a change, subtle but definite. She belonged to this male to whom she was mated. The biological aim of her being and her existence had just begun and in time would bear fruit. She no longer was afraid of him. In fact, she was aware of a desire to monopolize him, to make him hers solely and she was able to say calmly, "It is time you got up; I saw the maids were busy in the kitchen. The call for breakfast may come any minute."

The street car was horse drawn and extended to the Waikiki district. The Arata and Murayama couples boarded the car on King St. and were taken into downtown Honolulu. The sights on the streets were not only novel to the women, but also to the men, for in spite of the fact that they had been living in Hawaii for a number of years, their knowledge of Honolulu was practically nil. They had been sent to the other islands directly from the immigration station. Therefore the imposing stone and brick buildings of the main business section about Fort St., the new Young Hotel, the Palace of the King, the Legislature, the Opera House, and the executive buildings were sights to impress these young country people. The dusty road that was King St., lined with residences and interspersing shopping districts, impressed upon them the size of Honolulu.

Turning to the right at Pawaa Junction, the view changed to a rural scene different from anything they had yet laid eyes upon. Pond upon pond extended as far as they could see and myriads of domestic ducks leisurely floated in droves, busily ducking their necks into the water for morsels of food. The surface of the stagnant water was green with scum and algae. Near the homes of the Chinese who owned these ponds were wire corrals within which the birds took shelter at night. It was then that Seikichi remembered the Chinese were great duck eaters, preferring duck eggs even to those laid by chickens.

As they neared Waikiki, banana farms took the place of duck ponds. In geometrical rows the stunted variety of so-called Chinese bananas were planted and heavy bunches of green fruit dotted the roadside. The immaculately white Moana Hotel and cottages of the Seaside Hotel came into view. Waikiki Beach was then a stretch of white sand in its natural state, untarnished by stone walls or eating places. From the outer reef's edge, against which the billowy waves battered, waves of gigantic height and extent raced towards the shore like white crested steeds. More than a dozen native boys were riding these turbulent waves sitting astride, lying or standing on, long wooden boards. They approached the shore at breakneck speed, only to be stopped in the shallows as the waves lost their original impact and force. In the bright sun the deep blue of the Pacific, the numerous streaks of white crests of onrushing waves, and the white sandy shore fringed by curving coconut palms, was a scene unique to Haru who had been raised on the shores of the Inland Sea, shores of which are lined with quaint villages and numerous islands crowned with pine trees.

They got off the street car in front of the aquarium and proceeded to the beach. Kapiolani Park, as this part at Waikiki was called, lay at the foot of Diamond Head, an extinct volcanic crater. It was a spacious, well kept ground with rows of ironwood trees along the road. In another section there was a huge banyan tree with its many roots supporting the spreading branches. Peacocks roamed about unmolested on the green, nestling in the branches of the banyan tree at night. Peacocks connoted royalty and their presence imparted to the young people an impression of wealth and distinction.

Another place that left a lasting impression on the young folks was the aquarium that housed the exotic, fantastically colored tropical fish. It was continuous "ahs" and "ohs" on the part of the girls. The contrast in the primitive colors on a single fish was so marked and decided that a painter could not have been so bold in his selection of colors. Unless one actually saw the fish, he would not believe that such creatures existed at all. From the beautiful Zebra-like *manini* to the ferocious sea-reptiles, the *puhi*, which showed their rows of jagged teeth on yawning, they wandered forth around the glass compartments like Alices in Wonderland.

"Now I know this fish," said Seikichi proudly to the crowd. "These are called *ulua* and make the best eating fish raw or cooked. They are the Hawaiian counterpart of *tai*."

The two girls said in unison pointing at the next tank, "This fish we know. It is called a turtle." All laughed together in loud childish glee.

They spread their luncheon on the green lawn underneath the coconut trees and as Seikichi wandered away to buy some soda water from the push-cart vendor of fruit and soft drinks, the edibles prepared by the maid that morning were being dished out. It was a jolly picnic, away from prying eyes and non-familiar faces. Being a week day, very few people loitered in the park. They felt as if they owned the vast playground. After partaking of the light lunch, the men sprawled on the ground and the girls sat with their legs stretched comfortably.

"Murayama-san," said Seikichi "you will be leaving for Hawaii tomorrow, and it may be a long time before we shall ever see each other again. But since our acquaintance began with our wives being on the same boat coming over, let us keep up our correspondence."

"I shall be only too glad to hear from you. You can depend upon my punctuality in answering. We are both trying to make our stay in Hawaii productive. I shall try my best to forge ahead. I hear that you have become a storekeeper already and I wish you all success. For my part, I have no proclivities in that line and must stick to farming. But the country is full of opportunities and I intend to succeed. Originally, I had the idea of returning to Japan on the expiration of the three year contract, but now I feel differently. I am going to make enough money here to retire on in my old age."

Saying so much in the presence and hearing of his wife and her friend seemed both good and bad for Murayama. It appeared to be bombastic and boastful, an impression he did not want to create, but man to man it was an expression born of intimate camaraderie and understandable. As for his wife he did not much care. They had been sweethearts and knew each other's shortcomings and strong points as much as every lover pretends to know. Their first night they had mutually confessed that after five long years of waiting they both had matured physically, but on talking and exchanging views they discovered that they were the same. They both were children at heart.

So he continued, "But some day we shall come together again, I am sure. With money at our command, distance will shrink. We must see every island with our own eyes and it will be very convenient indeed when there is someone you know on the other islands. Be sure to look us up, as we shall expect to visit you in our turn." They talked and planned for the future, for they were young and optimistic. Hopefulness is synonymous with youth.

CHAPTER 6

The People Make Merry

THUS, A WEEK LATER, SEIKICHI AND HIS bride were landed at Port Allen, near Waimea. The arrival of the boat was not greeted with any gala throng as at Honolulu, for everyone was busy making a living. There were no lei girls with garlands of flowers. Only the few carriage drivers that made regular runs to different points on neighboring plantations were there to accommodate passengers. So, loading the luggage on the back of the vehicle the couple boarded for Makaweli.

As usual, Waimea was simmering with heat. The kiawe trees drooped heavily in the morning sun and the muddy Waimea River looked even dirtier. Only the towering mountains of Kokee that rose abruptly from the shoreland looked cool under the low clouds that seemed to perpetually cloak the summit. Little children, principally Hawaiian, were playing on the vacant ground near the river, while a few were intent on scooping *opae,* fresh water shrimp, in the shallow part of the stream. The winding government road meandered its way among tall, well-kept sugar cane that was about a year old. Cane did well. Heat, sunlight, and rainfall helped create a most prosperous farming community.

The carriage halted in front of Seikichi's store and they got off. The front approach had been swept clean by Obasan who had anticipated their arrival. After the houses and stores in Honolulu, this shop was unpretentious indeed. There was no ornament, no display, color, or devices to stimulate the urge to buy among his customers. The empty spaces near the shop could be improved with flower beds. A new coat of paint, probably green, might enhance the dignity and render the external appearance more pleasing. Furthermore, now that there was an extra member in the household there must be an extension to the rear of the store.

As soon as the carriage stopped, Obasan came running, along with her grinning three year old daughter. She immediately came to Seikichi and bowed slightly, "Welcome home," she greeted. Then turning to Haru, she made a formal bow, her hand reaching down to her knees. "This is my first meeting with you. I have been deeply obliged to Arata-san these many years. To you, I look forward to be favored in like manner." So saying, she bowed three times; once for each sentence.

Haru returned each bow with much bending and mumbled inaudible phrases; she could not manage to match this woman of thirty who was an old timer and more wordly wise. Even if she could outdo her in the art of formal greetings, it was best to appear and act demurely. Such tact is inborn in womankind.

To the shrewd woman, this helpless creature was likeable. There seemed to be no haughtiness. She could only sense bewilderment in the almost frightened eyes.

To Haru, the realization that here was a female with whom she had to become neighbors, made her a bit afraid. Words froze on her lips. No ingratiating smile would come to soften her taut facial expression. She was afraid her first impression was not good, but the Obasan liked her and took it upon herself to show her the ropes of plantation life. This newcomer was to be her protégé. She led her inside the house and helped her get settled. Like an elder sister she bustled around the place. In a short while, Haru began to feel at ease with her. She discerned that under the coarse exterior this woman had a considerate heart and a genuine fondness for her. At least there seemed to be no attempt at fault-finding and critical scrutiny.

That evening a stream of men and women made their way to the Arata Store to extend their welcome, but chiefly to catch a glimpse of the bride. It was a great event in the monotonous existence. Every new face in the established community was a new topic and became a subject about which gossip and conjecture spread far and wide, like a ripple on the water's surface.

Therefore, according to custom, an announcement party had to be held by Arata for his many friends and customers to make a formal presentation of his wife. Financially, such a party would not set him back very much as everyone invited was expected to bring some sort of gift, usually money. Custom decreed that this gift was mandatory, usually a dollar, whether they came or not. By using his head, Seikichi could make the expenditure low without impairing the quantity or quality of food served. He could ask Hawaiian natives to catch fish: several large ones to prepare as sliced raw fish and a dozen or so medium ones to cook intact would be sufficient. *Opihi* or shell fish and *limu*, the Hawaiian edible seaweed, would complete the necessary material from Neptune's domain. From the mountains or land, a medium sized pig might be procured for less than ten dollars and be prepared in the native style. He had seen it done and the taste was delicious.

Contrary to the usual orthodox manner of cooking, a hole was dug in the ground. On the previous evening the pig was slaughtered and dipped in scalding water. The entire surface was then scraped of hair and thick coarse integument. The carcass was eviscerated and the entire surface rubbed with coarse salt. In this condition the pig was hung during the night. On the next morning kiawe wood was burned to produce a great quantity of live coal. A large collection of porous rock was placed on these coals and became red hot. The hole in the ground was then filled with these hot rocks, as was the abdominal cavity of the animal. The body was covered with green ti leaves and wrapped with wet gunny-sacks. It was then lowered into the rock-lined hole. Additional rocks were thrown in the space around the pig and the hole was covered with hot ash and soil and left for two hours. During this time, heat penetrated slowly through the animal and the resulting meat was delicious beyond description. Sweet potatoes and yams were placed around the pig and these were baked intact.

When Seikichi had once eaten it, he was surprised that he found even the fat appetizing. In no other way could he relish fat. He was certain that the novelty of this "stone cooked pig" or as the Hawaiian called it "kalua pig" would be a big hit among his friends and ensure the success of the coming event. For compensation, the natives would be content with getting the head of the animal, which was too grotesque for Japanese taste. For a gallon of "swipe" the Hawaiians would gladly go out fishing for him.

In anticipation of this gala event, he had asked Obasan to prepare some home brew, made of potato mash, sugar, and hops. To make any party lively, liquor must flow in unstinted streams. Japanese liked this beverage hot. The accessory food items would be prepared by the men and women pitching in that morning, which would be Sunday. Materials from Japan were scarce, but enough variety could be gotten together to gladden the gustatory sensibilities of the men whose taste buds had become numbed by the monotony of the daily fare. There would be *sushi,* the pickled rice prepared in several ways, *tempura,* consisting of vegetables, small fish, or shrimps, fried in specially prepared batter requiring a secret art, and *kanten* the pink and white jello-like substance made from dried seaweed or agar-agar.

On Sunday, a corps of men and women were busy from early morning, willingly lending their skill and labor for the occasion. Luckily, fish were plentiful and to have been able to get the red snapper-like *uhu* and *kumu* was indeed fortunate. It lent not only color to the table but symbolized an auspicious omen. From the large ones, the skin was carefully dissected to make a flap, and the underlying white flesh was excised en masse and cut obliquely in thin slices. The carved meat was then replaced and to casual observers the fish did not appear to be mutilated at all. The tail was tied taut to the head with a string so that the fish looked as if it were leaping out of the water. Radish was sliced artistically so that the end product became a mesh or net and this was spread like a shawl over the fish.

The display of colors, contrasting one against the other, was a part of Japanese cooking technique. To feast with the eyes was important. Expert seasoning with *shoyu* and sugar to effect culinary perfection was necessary from the standpoint of taste.

For the banquet, the barrack was converted into a huge hall. Partitions were torn down. Three 12 by 1 lumbers were placed side by side about a foot and a half above the matted floor the entire length of the room. These tables were covered with fresh wrapping paper. The plates were set at intervals and loaded with different foods. Separately, each guest took as much as he could take care of in several mouthfuls on a smaller plate. This was replenished time and again. No waste took place by this procedure. A drinking cup of glazed china, shaped like an inverted cone and capable of holding about an ounce of liquid, was placed alongside plate and chopsticks.

Guests began arriving at about four o'clock and by five they took their seats, squatting on the matted floor. Women dressed gaily for the occasion came in with earthenware bottles of heated "swipes" and passed the liquor around. The tiny cups were usually held between the fingers of the left hand for pouring, and were passed around from one to another. Such exchange of cups was considered conducive to good fellowship, and woe to the one who refused a proffered cup! The women with the steaming liquor floated about here and there urging the men to imbibe more freely by filling empty receptacles. Food was taken liberally as it was supper time. They were well satisfied with the rare, tasteful products of the mountain and sea and everyone marvelled at the "kalua pig." Almost all who had tasted pig prepared in this manner for the first time nodded approval. Contrary to reports that natives ate only poi and salted salmon, this dish was a whole lot more appetizing than their own way of eating pork. They would henceforth "live seventy-five days longer" now that they had eaten something novel.

At a moment when everyone had the edge of his hunger dulled, and the bride and groom had taken their seats, the toastmaster of the evening stood up and announced amidst hand claps, "We are convened tonight to celebrate the wedding of our community leader, Mr. Seikichi Arata. That so many have assembled from varied distances bespeaks well the sentiments with which his friends regard him. On this happy occasion that comes only once in the lifetime of a man and woman, we shall begin the formal part of the ceremony with the time-honored chant of the *Takasago* by our venerable Mr. Saito."

Gray-haired and solemn-faced for the occasion, Saito straightened his curving back, and in a sitting posture roared out from the depth of his abdomen, a monotonous chant the rhythm of which had been handed down almost without alteration for seven hundred years.

> *"Waves of the four seas are stilled,*
> *Even the branches of trees fail to bend,*
> *Peace eternal reigns undisturbed,*
> *The twin pines of Aioi symbolically stand,*
> *To bless the good fortune and prosperity of people,*
> *Who dwell under a sovereign so beneficent."*

Saito was not very good. His facial muscles worked in contortions. He became flushed and his words were hardly intelligible. But the deep tone of his voice was different from the ordinary, and it did lend dignity to the program.

Like the *Tannenbaum* of Germany, the evergreen pine stood for longevity and everlasting troth among the common people. The twin pines of Aioi symbolized eternal faith. The legend is that this ballad was written by a priest from the famous shrine of Aso in Kumamoto who made a pilgrimage to Yedo in prehistoric or mythological Japan and on his way came to a place called Aioi. Here he met a gray-haired, dignified man and his wife. The two had apparently aged gracefully, for while they swept the grounds cleanly around the two gigantic pine trees that stood near the highway, they exuded a feeling of calm and peace to the passersby. The priest was filled with reverence and talked to the aged people. He was commended for his piety in return and was instructed to make a pilgrimage to the shrine nearby on his return trip. After bidding them goodbye and going a short way, the priest looked back and discovered the couple gone from the scene. They were, he concluded, the spirits of the twin pines that graced the roadside. In deep awe, he incorporated this incident in his travelogue which he called Takasago.

The above excerpt had been chanted for many centuries at weddings in order to wish peace, happiness, and conjugal faith to the newlyweds. Young people starting on a new voyage of life would need a happily married pair like the couple of Aioi to act as preceptors and advisors. For to "become gray together" signified a mellow marital state after raising a brood of healthy children and enjoying the remaining span of life leisurely and wisely. For this purpose, an old pair happily married for many years would be the ideal. But in a village such as Makaweli, Obasan and her husband would perhaps fill the requirement. So at this announcement they acted as the official "go-between" in Hawaii. It fell to Mr. Fukuda as the official matchmaker to present the bride and groom. With a short biographical narrative he introduced the bride and groom amidst the resounding applause of the assembled throng.

Standing with her husband as they were being presented, Haru felt embarrassed and small, and the tight obi seemed to stifle her breathing. She was conscious of the hundreds of eyes being curiously fastened upon her. Never in her life had she felt such stage fright. It seemed an eternity until she automatically bowed her upper torso in sincere humility and all was over. She sat down but kept her eyes fixed on the table. She half listened to the rather lengthy speech of congratulations by a deep-voiced man who spoke in behalf of the guests. Disclosing his past as a student of the Chinese classics, he profusely used words not in common usage. The speech of thanks rendered by one of Arata's intimate friends in behalf of the host was crisp, short, and to the point.

After this formal portion of the program came to an end and the men began making merry, Mrs. Fukuda led Haru back to her room and let her lie down in a more comfortable kimono. That part being over it was not necessary for her to appear in the midst of the drunken orgy for some were sure to get really drunk and behave in an unruly manner. Those men not used to drinking regularly fell under the influence of alcohol rather quickly. The groom had to stand his ground against the barrage of drinking cups that had to be emptied and returned. Thoughtfully, a woman shoved a bowl under his table and he poured the greater part of the proffered liquor into it. Meanwhile a housewife brought along a *samisen,* the three-stringed Japanese guitar, and singing started. The latest song hits about the China War were sung lustily, with the whole party joining in with rhythmical clapping to keep up the fervor and cadence.

> *Japan has declared war on China,*
> *The Imperial fleet out of Shinagawa steam,*
> *Leading is Azuma, the flagship,*
> *Followed by Kongo and Naniwa.*

CHAPTER 7

The Eldest Son

ALMOST EVERY TWO OR THREE YEARS, Mrs. Arata was with child and she was a mother of five in no time. Being of sturdy stock, the dual role of storekeeper and mother did not affect her very much. From morning till night she worked hard. There was little time for her to relax or enjoy herself. Like all pioneering women, her life was swamped and buried under the daily routine of cooking, washing, and attending to customers. She was active and pleasant. She was happy with the growing children, and the expanding business gave her impetus and the will to work. More and more people came to Kauai, for wages on the plantations increased and money floated about freely. Occasionally, she would become homesick for her native Mitajiri and its seasonal festive gaiety, but lately there was much activity in Kauai which made her forget such nostalgic cravings. All in all, she adapted herself to Hawaiian life very quickly and considered herself fortunate in having made the decision to come to this distant land.

Her eldest and pride of her flock was her son Sadao. To have had a son for the first child was not the best arrangement she could have wished for as a busy mother. A girl would have rendered her life much easier as she would have had a helper about the house to aid her in the daily routine and in the care of little ones that arrived regularly. But as the first child was a boy (aside from the natural attachment between mother and son, there seems to be a biological affinity between parents and off-spring of different sexes) there was the peculiar satisfaction she felt during her initial puerperal period. One has to be an Oriental mother to bask in this contentment: a feeling like riding atop the world. Next to a barren wife, life was most miserable for one who could not bring forth a male child to perpetuate the family name. She earned for herself a rightful place in the eyes of the ancestors.

To her, the red-faced, wrinkled infant that lay so helpless at her side was more than her flesh and blood. He seemed to incarnate in his wriggling body the hopes and frustrations of myriads of his ancestors. And she was the medium through which this link was forged. He nursed well and cried lustily when hungry. She had plenty of milk. To suckle was sometimes painful because of the force with which the infant nursed, but it was not unpleasant or bothersome. There seemed to be nothing wrong with his physical makeup. It was funny, she thought, that she should feel so wrapped up in this tiny child, but by his arrival she knew that in Japan the old in-laws and her parents would be immensely proud. A special offering of thanks would be offered to the village shrine, the gods of which watched over the sons and daughters of the villagers, no matter where they happened to be domiciled. Not only would there be much rejoicing by relatives in Japan, but there would be a feast again in Hawaii, and the credit would come to her. She could not help feeling contented: she was in fact filled with a glow of satisfaction. These were perhaps the happiest days of her life.

For thirty days she was supposed to take care of herself according to custom. Had she been in the old country, on the thirty-first day she would have taken the infant, clad in resplendent kimono, to the shrine to exhibit to the gods, present offerings of thanks, and beseech further protection from evil in the life that was then beginning. At the same time she could fold up her bedding and enter conjugal life without fear of untoward consequences. Such restrictions were wise regulations, born of experience governing post-partum care and sex relations, to avoid infections and damage to the maternal body. But such leisurely precautions and care were workable only in a family with many spare hands. In Hawaii, things must be done differently. Out of necessity, she was up and working on the fourteenth day and was none the worse for her early activity.

A Chinese neighbor brought her a potful of duck cooked over a slow fire for many hours, so that the essence of the fowl was collected in the thick extract. This she was urged to drink to facilitate and speed her convalescence. Obediently she took it daily and seemed to feel much stronger each day. Her lactation seemed to be favorably influenced and the infant waxed fat.

During the intervening years, Sadao did not suffer from the usual childhood diseases—except for measles. The other childhood ailments were of later importation to this isolated Paradise of the Pacific. The Aratas prospered.

In the meantime, the Hawaiian kingdom was abolished and the islands were incorporated as an integral part of the United States. Modernization programs in all fields of industrial and cultural endeavors became marked. Great strides were made. Public schools were opened in the remotest villages of the islands and attendance was made compulsory. According to the terms of the Annexation Protocol, all citizens of the monarchy and succeeding Republic and Provisional Governments were to become American citizens automatically with the raising of the Stars and Stripes over the archipelago. Children born in the islands naturally were citizens according to the constitution of the United States. They were therefore being educated as American citizens. Teachers were being trained at the Territorial Normal Training School at Honolulu and the shortage was supplemented by teachers from the mainland.

The district school had an enrollment of about two hundred pupils. Cosmopolitan in makeup, the student body was composed of Japanese, Chinese, Hawaiians, Portuguese, Spanish, and Koreans. The teaching staff was almost as representative of the conglomeration of racial extractions that made up the population—Portuguese, Chinese, Part-Hawaiian, and Caucasians. Japanese and Koreans did not appear on the list as their arrival had been recent and none of the children were old enough to have attained that age group.

The melting-pot process was a success. Youngsters were being instilled with the ideals of democracy without letup and each was made to feel that he was just as good an American as the direct descendants of the passengers on the *Mayflower*. Considering the fact that annexation of the islands was effected only a dozen or so years previously, it was a startling achievement that the children could be so Americanized. Surrounded by elders who spoke pidgin English enunciated with a peculiar accent, the children's enunciation might not have been the equal of a New England child's, his diction was limited and relatively poor, yet his line of thought and his convictions were typically American after several years of schooling.

Since their parents were immigrants from the old world, the children had to speak in a different tongue to their elders. But they were handicapped in the usage of the mother tongue at home. In other words, the children could neither speak good English nor use the language of their parents correctly. As years went by there evolved in Hawaii a new jargon—a conglomeration of English, Japanese, and Hawaiian, with a pronounced intonation like the Portuguese language. This became the popular colloquial medium through which the elders of different racial strains made themselves understood to each other, and was prevalent on all plantations. The children had a difficult time speaking any form of language in its pure form.

Among the common people, racial barriers were minimal, and one person was as good as another. Only the ruling race, the Anglo-Saxons, held themselves haughty and aloof, priding themselves on racial superiority. Yet even they were not averse to taking native women for wives: perhaps out of necessity due to the scarcity of white women. Anyway many "hapa-haoles" or half-breeds came into being from these unions. The easy-going seductiveness of Hawaiian existence made all people tolerant and a spirit of "live and let live" seemed to be the guiding motif. Whatever contrary feelings one might have harbored regarding racial equality and intermarriage prior to his arrival in the islands, he soon changed his ideas about humanity. According to the Hawaiian mode of reasoning, as long as one was intrinsically good, just, and capable, he was welcome as one of the family, irrespective of his racial extraction. Thus intermarriage was a common occurrence and usually ended happily.

In such an environment, children grew up as Hawaiian citizens—Neo-Pacific nationals—as some preferred to designate them. Many had half a dozen strains of blood running in their veins, but the pure stock felt the same way. A healthy sort of camaraderie that lasted to manhood sprang up among the boys and survived the change in the world's outlook. It was a result of mature experience and judgment.

Sadao Arata was no exception and he grew to be a strapping youngster with a mode of thought typical of this growing generation. Just as vegetation grows smoothly and rapidly, man matures rapidly in the sub-tropics. Some girls begin menstruating at nine or ten. This is a phenomenon not only encountered among the Hawaiian natives, but among second generation girls whose cousins in colder latitudes would not reach adolescence until fourteen to sixteen.

An episode without any sequel occurred at this time and its meshes threatened to involve young Sadao. Miss Miriam Kealoha was a Chinese-Hawaiian school teacher who had inherited the good features of her dual ancestry. In her, harshness in her original ancestral strains were softened and moderated and produced a harmonious blend in her charming personality. Of medium height and seductively beautiful, her large, dreamy eyes, characteristic of the Polynesians, enhanced her loveliness. Used to urban life with much entertainment and many friends to make life exciting, existence at a Kauai district school was tame and monotonous, especially to a full-blooded young woman in her prime.

Among her pupils, she noticed at once the artistic inclination and aptitude of Sadao Arata who not only could sing well, an accomplishment so dear to Hawaiian hearts, but could draw remarkably well in spite of his lack of training. Lacking this talent herself, it was not long before she asked the assistance of twelve-year-old Sadao to illustrate stories and biology lessons. Well developed for his age on account of his constant outdoor life and vigorous exercise, Sadao was a young man in stature, but the somatic portion of his development outdid his germinal cells. As far as his sexual life was concerned, he was relatively retarded in spite of the climatic factor. In this respect he was different from the other children who matured early. His artistic temperament also tended to paint the universe in beautiful colors and human relationship in childish romanticism. His dream world was of the knights of old and fairy-like damsels were to be looked at, but beyond reach. The inner urge was not there. Libido as yet lay dormant within this half-developed man.

Miriam Kealoha had had an escapade or two during Normal School days. Few maids of Polynesian blood ever escaped being involved in such romances in their late 'teens and early twenties: especially one as attractive as Miriam. She was by no means over-sexed. To the contrary she would be classed as a "hypo" among her racial sisters. She was nevertheless lonely. She was a teacher, a respectable person in a gossipy countryside. Eligible young men were scarce and she did not relish being tied down as a wife to a country swain. She had to watch her step and do nothing impulsive. Yet emotions kept her vaguely restless. Nights were long: the cool Trade Wind rustling the green fronds of coconut palms, the bright moon, and the distant strumming of ukulele and guitar, made her homesick for the life of Honolulu and its people. The lot of a young country teacher was not without its handicaps.

"Sadao, will you stay after school please. I have something I should like to have you do for me." So he remained after two o'clock alone with his teacher to draw pictures for story lessons for the following day. It occurred once or twice every week. One afternoon he was drawing the scene depicting Washington crossing the Delaware while Miriam added color with crayons. Working side by side, she was conscious of a certain vague excitement. She tried to suppress it but it was not unpleasant. Intent on his work of making a faithful copy of the general in the open boat Sadao was aware of his body touching his teacher's. He was frightened and bashful and he squirmed away. Her reactions were different and she could contain herself no longer.

"Sadao, I have some candy for you. Let us take a rest—plenty of time and there is no sense in overworking ourselves." So saying, she beckoned him to come to her desk after she seated herself in the chair. He was hesitant to take the proffered candy. Laughingly, she grabbed his hand and pulled him in front of her and forced him to sit on her chair between her thighs, holding on to his body as if in an embrace. He was quiet and as still as a mouse. She was excited but afraid. An electric shock raced through her body up and down her spine. The physical contact was pleasant: the beardless face was smooth against her cheek. This sensation was different from that experienced when she was in the passive role of a woman.

"Have some candy," and she pushed a piece of her favorite hard candy into his mouth. He was very uncomfortable, but dared not refuse. Obediently he received the candy between parted lips. The sensation was a ticklish one but no more meaning could be perceived by this half-grown man. Her hands went to his forehead, brushing his hair back and to his ears. Still no response was experienced by the boy other than a squirming uncomfortableness. Sadao was extremely happy when Miriam agreed that they should contine work on the drawing.

As Christmas drew near, the classes began preparing for a simple ceremony before school closed for vacation. The blackboards on the four walls were to be decorated with drawings appropriate for the season. The three wise men on camels led by the guiding star and the scene of the stable and manger were drawn. As the final touch, a Santa Claus riding a sleigh drawn by six reindeer was to ornament the front blackboard. In the midst of her class, Miriam announced, "I am leaving you all alone for a short while. I am going back to my cottage for a post card of Santa. While I am gone, you must all be quiet and read your lessons. I don't want to have Miss Smith in the next room complain of your noisiness later on. Now, Sadao, you come along with me to select a good picture of Santa Claus."

The teacher's cottage was an ordinary cottage with a parlor, kitchen, bathroom, and two bedrooms. She entered her bedroom and motioned to Sadao to follow. Awkwardly the boy stood by while she opened her trunk and produced a bundle tied with a red ribbon. It was a collection of Christmas cards that she had received in previous years. She sat on the edge of the bed and motioned for him to sit next to her. Then putting an arm about his shoulders, she began to examine each card carefully, evaluating each for its appropriateness. He was earnestly scrutinizing each picture with an inborn sense of artistic appreciation, apparently oblivious to the olfactory seductiveness emanating from the teacher. The shades were drawn to shut out the noon-day sun. They were alone. But it was not to be . . .

As he grew older and understood more of life, Sadao had cause to regret his adolescence, but his memory of Miriam Kealoha was always a pleasant one long after she left the plantation for another district. Even after she was caught in a scandal that forced her to resign from the teaching profession, Sadao always cherished her memory.

In 1912, when Sadao was thirteen, he was sent to Honolulu to acquire a big-town education and to learn the Japanese language. His parents found their son was becoming too Americanized and could hardly speak Japanese, in spite of the years spent at the plantation language school. The Japanese school, where an hour a day was spent devoted to the language of the mother country, could not stem the natural tendency of the second generation children to converse in the language of their country. This seemed to indicate a gloomy future for Sadao as far as his folks were concerned.

To the Aratas, no man could get above the common herd unless he was equipped with an education that would put him above the level of his contemporaries. In a community predominantly Japanese, the English language was important, but it alone was not enough. If proficiency of the prevailing language was the sole requisite for success in life, then Orientals were out of luck. Those born where English was spoken at home were the most qualified. But in a cosmopolitan community, anyone armed with the command of two or more languages was sure to be rewarded with an important job. For interpreters and liaison officers, such attainments were in demand on the plantations and in the big commercial houses and banks of Honolulu. The American executives were also loud in demanding such qualified men.

Aside from the concrete social and pecuniary advantages to be derived from a Japanese education, the parents longed to see their son pick up some Japanese traits prized by all compatriots—faithfulness to tradition of "Giri and Ninjo," a peculiarly Japanese custom of moral obligation or indebtedness to acts of kindness or social ties that at times may demand a sacrificial response in terms of material or even life. It was a code of honor gradually evolved in the centuries of an inbreeding civilization of a hermit nation. To persons of the first generation, the happy-go-lucky, self-centered, irresponsible tendencies of their offspring were sources of worry and concern. To them, a man is measured in the degree of responsibility he takes in his uttered promises and in his willingness to devote himself to communal welfare—not the egotistic betterment of one's lot alone. From this viewpoint the family must be the unit of society and as such stand or fall together: in contra-distinction to the individualistic way of looking after oneself alone, which was the attitude of the Hawaiian community.

As a successful grocer of the countryside, as a leader of the Japanese community of Makaweli, Seikichi Arata had his prestigé to look after. The Consulate General in Honolulu appointed him, without compensation, to help fill out applications from the illiterate, to interpret orders, and in general help the official Japanese representative keep the immigrants orderly. He was involved in all the major activities of the plantation and was consulted about anything that happened, good or bad. Nothing would enhance his position more than to send his son to Honolulu. It would set him aside as a far-seeing man, as a well-to-do personage in the eyes of his friends. To his own selfish interests, there was the promise of perpetuating a prosperous line of Aratas in the land of his adoption.

A Japanese High School in Honolulu had been operated for the past five years and the pick of the students from the country schools were heading for Honolulu. The school taught advanced Japanese, and was headed by well-educated teachers. The students attending this school attended the American School in Honolulu as well. Thither proceeded Sadao in September 1912.

BOOK II

The Early Days

Prologue

April 8, Sunday   *Honolulu*

AT BREAKFAST, DR. MINORU MURAYAMA *met his mother. She was now in her late seventies but well preserved. Like many women of her race, she did not put on weight as she grew old. Gray haired and straight backed, she was able to move about freely and was a great help to the family. Only the wrinkles in her face revealed that she no longer was young, but even these seemed to be at a standstill since her husband's demise four years ago.*

"When did you last see Mr. Arata, I mean the elder Arata who used to be in Arkansas?" questioned the doctor.

"Let me see. Not lately anyway. I think it was at father's funeral. Unless there is something like that happening, we do not often see each other. Is there something wrong?" Her mental faculty was very keen.

"Yes. Last night he had a heart attack and is now at the Kuakini Hospital. I hope he makes it, but it is hard to know at this stage just how he will end up."

"Now, that was a fine man. You got to know him in Arkansas didn't you? I first met him when I landed in Honolulu as a bride almost sixty years ago. Mrs. Arata was on the same boat coming over. We four went to Waikiki to see the aquarium. His wife is dead, my husband is gone for four years, and now he is sick. Maybe not to recover. Looks like I am the last to survive of the four carefree youngsters from Japan that picnicked at Waikiki that day." Minoru looked up and searchingly gazed at his mother. It was not like her to talk sentimentally of the past.

While his father, Torao Murayama, was alive, Minoru used to spend many hours listening to the stories of the early plantation days on the

75

North Hilo coast and probe into the obscure aspects of the contract labor days that he could not understand. When he was fortunate enough to meet any oldtimer among his patients, he spent extra hours gathering more information. Much of his boyhood, he remembered comparatively well. He sat in deep reverie as this was a Sunday morning and he could loaf.

CHAPTER 8

Farm Life in Japan

ON THE OTHER SIDE OF THE WORLD, Napoleon Bonaparte had risen and fallen and Europe was in the grip of a fierce struggle for a realignment of powers. In the New World an infant nation was in the throes of putting her house in order over states rights and the burning question of human rights to freedom. What about the hermit kingdom of Cipangu, the fabled land of Marco Polo?

In the fertile plains of Kumamoto in Kyushu, southwest Japan, Torao Murayama's ancestors had lived as sturdy peasants, tilling the rice patches in the rich delta regions of the Midorikawa. On the hilly sides of the Peninsula of Uto they had their village homes for countless generations. The nation was in hermetic seclusion and everything seemed to be at a standstill. After three centuries of continued peace, the warrior caste had lost its original initiative, physical prowess, endurance, and every martial aptitude that had set this class apart and had permitted its ascendancy over the peasantry in the remote past in feudal history.

In the main, long accustomed to life of leisure and bureaucratic office work, the *samurai* had degenerated into peaceful citizens delving in the gentler arts of music, tea ceremony, and dancing, rather than pursuing the Spartan ways of their fierce ancestors who had lived by the sword. The hegemony of the Tokugawa Shogunate over the island empire was numbered. Revolutionary sentiment was strong among the lower stratum *samurai* who were destined to continue in their down-trodden life should the status quo continue. Young blood clamored for the restoration of the emperor to his rightful office as sovereign in fact, as well as in name. It was a convenient rallying point for the dissidents. It had mass appeal, especially to the underprivileged artisans and peasants. Thoughtful shogunate officials saw the words of doom concerning their future written on the wall.

The external pressure of the Russians from the north, iron fleets of America, England, and the Dutch pounding at the gates of the southern seaports, hastened the downfall of the then existing government by climaxing the struggle of the conflicting forces within the country. But this foreign threat merely hastened the end of the feudal system, for inevitable doom was imminent. Attempts to save the system were naturally made, but the core of the feudal system was like a termite-eaten edifice. Leaders saw through the danger and attempting to reenforce the structure at the eleventh hour, tried blood transfusion in its literal sense. Infusing new blood of sturdy young peasant sons of superior stock was the only solution to prolong the failing tide of destiny.

Thus, Lord Hosokawa of Kumamoto looked among his peasantry for young, dependable soldier material. Edicts were promulgated to recruit second and third sons of farmers and artisans who wished to seek advancement in life in the profession of arms. It was to be a life-long job with prospects of attaining rank of the *samurai* and privileges appertaining to it. It was a tremendous opportunity for those who qualified. Examinations as to physical, mental, and moral stamina were most rigid. To have passed this obstacle was an attainment of incalculable merit, for it meant "passing" over into a higher, more respected caste than the one they had been born into. Since the law of primogeniture prevailed and all or most property holdings passed to the eldest male child, the lot of the second and other sons was not enviable. Only in wealthier families did they have any chance for a decent existence. The best they could do was to become adopted into childless families or marry into families blessed only with girl offsprings. But the future prospects of the man married by such an arrangement was not always smooth sailing. A hen-pecked husband is not a happy situation in any community, and a wife with a large dowry was apt to "wear the pants in the family." There was a saying therefore: "If you have three pints of rice polishings to your name, never become an adopted son."

These volunteer soldiers were, therefore, the pick of the land. The rejuvenation of the governing class was thus belatedly attempted. Sadaki Mayeda was among these and by his knack of getting along with people he was soon promoted to the rank of the present-day sergeant and was stationed at Kyoto when the restoration of the emperor came. Japan was split into two camps on the question of opening its country to foreign commerce. The Tokugawa group was willy-nilly forced to accede to the demands of the foreign powers, especially to Commodore Perry. The group that rallied around the emperor saw the opportunity to overthrow the shogunate and restore the emperor to his rightful place on the throne. This latter group was against anything that the Tokugawa Shogunate proposed to do. The Hosokawa clan was pro-Tokugawa but did not get involved in the bloody flare-ups near the suburbs of the Capital when the opposing forces clashed at Toba and Fushimi. So Sadaki did not get into actual battle but was awarded a crest-emblazoned sword by Lord Hosokawa for meritorious service.

Soon the restoration became a fact, following the resignation of the shogun, and everybody in Japan became equal before the law. The caste system dividing the masses into *samurai*, farmers, artisans, and merchants was abolished and every avenue of professional or vocational advancement was opened to the ambitious and industrious. But the sudden release of an enormous number of *samurai* from the security of lifelong tenure and assurance of livelihood, created a tremendous social problem. As a professional soldier and retainer of a feudal lord, the life of a *samurai* was easy as long as he was loyal and his good faith reciprocated by the master. He would be fed and his descendants looked after by the *daimyo*.

This convenient arrangement was terminated and a new order prevailed. Each had to shift for himself in competition with men of other classes who were independent, diligent, and self-reliant. When the abolition of the feudal system took effect, the lords opened up their vaults and produced the reserve funds that had been stored to be used in case of emergencies and wars. Out of these monies a lump sum was distributed among the retainers so that their immediate needs might be taken care of. As is usually the case in these circumstances, the unscrupulous hatched out wild investment schemes with prospects of easy, fat returns. Gullibly, the *samurai* fell victim to these vultures and many lost their cash and government bonds that had been given them by their erstwhile lords and new government respectively.

The new government had issued bonds to the *samurai* to help them adjust to the sudden change in livelihood. Untrained in earning money, and brought up with the philosophy that even to touch money was disdainful, it was not long before many were reduced to a pitiful lot. Too proud either to work or to beg, the best they could do was to enter the police force or to join the new Westernized army in which they gradually adjusted their mode of thinking to the new era, but the aged and past middle age group suffered most with the advent of the restoration.

Sadaki Mayeda was among these retainers who had lost the promise of the future. He had to return either to farming or carpentry. In the meantime, he had married a daughter of a *samurai* who had seen in this sturdy son of the soil a caliber of manhood that could not be found in sons of hereditary warriors. This marriage was a tremendous boost to Sadaki's prestige in the days of feudal bigotry, but would be a handicap after the restoration if his bride were not adaptable to the new era. They went to live with his elder brother, a farmer, but the lot of a second son, especially burdened with a wife and son, was not a happy one.

The burgomaster, the *shoya* of the village, one day accosted Sadaki who was helping his brother on the farm. "You are working pretty hard. That, I can see by your sweat-soaked clothes. Have you got used to farmwork?"

"Yes. I am now used to working in the fields. Anyway I was born a farmer and it is merely picking up things I left ten years ago before I joined the forces of the Lord of Uto."

"Well it is good to see you content with your work. Many of your friends have joined the police, but many have been forced to steal and commit crimes for which they are caught and brought to trial by their erstwhile friends. I am glad to see that you are happy with the lot of a farmer. But we must think of you as an independent farmer and not as a dependent of your brother. I am thinking of old Mosaku. He is getting along in years and soon will not be able to tend to his crops. His acreage is among the best and there is a good balance between fields for rice and that of the dry crops of sweet potatoes and vegetables. What do you think about becoming an adopted son, *yoshi*. Since you are married and have a son, your case will be a *fufuyoshi*. Personally, I think it is a very good move if you can make up your mind to do it."

"I have never thought much about the role of an adopted son. I shall have to talk it over with my wife and brother. But since my return I heard that old Mosaku had two adopted sons already. What became of them?"

"Well, Mosaku is quite a slave driver. His holdings have been accumulated by hard work and self-denial, even to the point of miserliness. He drove the two young men too hard and they simply could

80

not take it. But I am betting on you. You ought to be able to make the grade."

Mosaku was famous for being a very hard man to get along with. Bent with life-long toil in the rice patches, his face was wrinkled and sunburnt. He was like thousands of peasants with no distinguishing peculiarilty. There was a hardness and slyness in his assumed humility before authority, but ready to break into a fury when there was no retaliation. To his wife ten children were born, but all died in either infancy or early childhood. This was a calamity. The ancient house had to have a successor, and they were getting old. At his deathbed, there must be someone to offer the last cup of water to speed him on to the nether world. The ancestors' graves must be tended and their souls at the time of *bon*, the monthly and annual day of demise, must be properly observed with the lighting of candles and adornment of the shrine with flowers.

On the 3rd, 7th, 13th, 20th, and 33rd anniversary, priests had to be summoned and sutras chanted. Mosaku had his own soul to be looked after as well as to answer to the reproaches of his ancestors if he did not leave someone to do the proper things after he was gone.

Therefore, when he became certain that the procreating days were over for his wife, he looked about for some suitable young couple that might be prevailed upon to come and live with them to carry on after his days should come to an end. It was not hard to find a man willing to accept the proposition because the acreage he cultivated was better than the average in the locality, but to endure the exacting Mosaku was a different matter.

The first young man did not last a year. Another tried to be amiable to the old man in order to become master of the farm and property, because the wiry man could not live forever, but he too could not survive the test. It was this that Sadaki faced. But people did not laugh. They said that if Sadaki could not please the old miser, there was no one that could ever suit him. He was known to his fellow villagers as being patient and good natured, and a good mixer. The sterner part of his character that had enabled him to rise swiftly in the army was allowed to remain hidden under the mask of his smiling exterior.

Sadaki was twenty-four and of average height. His carriage was straight for he had gotten away from stooping farm work and had practiced the feat of arms such as fencing and *jujitsu*. Cleanly shaven and composed, he looked different from other peasants even when he was dressed for the field.

The arrangement for adoption into the Mosaku Murayama family was speedily concluded. Sadaki decided to make this arrangement endure. Under no harsh or unreasonable treatment would he show his temper. He would be the epitome of good manners and placate the ire of old Mosaku. The arrangement was not easy, especially for his bride who had been used to expect respect from her foster parents. But she knew too well that the present forbearance was for their future security, and especially for their little son Torao.

"Mosaku-san, it is a nice day."

"Shoya-san, good day to you. I am deeply indebted to you again and again for all the trouble you went through for my *yoshi* arrangement."

"Well, how is the young man getting used to the work as a farmer?"

"He is all right. He works hard and does not show any disrespect. He is a good son. My daughter-in-law is above reproach. I am satisfied and happy. I feel secure knowing that my ancestors' souls will be dutifully served and on their anniversaries priests will be summoned to have sutras read."

Sadaki, try as he might, could not become a true farmer. He lacked the peculiar inborn trait and sagacity that makes one a good, successful farmer and the next door neighbor a failure, although the two might be equally industrious. After a few years, the old man stopped trying to teach him and doted on the little grandchild. He concluded that perhaps the only way to get a good farmer out of the trio was to educate this little boy in the art of tilling the soil when he was young.

But the little one received an altogether different training from his mother, for she insisted that he talk and act the little gentlemen that a *samurai* son was expected to do. Unlike the sons of regular farmers, Torao had to strictly observe at home the salutations of morning, night, coming and going, with all the etiquette attending these greetings. Due respect in speech and mannerism had to be shown his elders, in contrast to the free, easy going approach his playmates paid the village elders. Soon there was a brother born and later a sister.

With the restoration of the emperor came different improvements

82

to raise the status of the undertrodden peasantry. Universal education was one. A grammar school was erected in the village next to the burgomaster's house. Textbooks were not adequate and the old classics of Chinese derivation were taught to instill the age old maxims and aphorisms that every educated person was expected to know by heart.

Every morning before he started out to school, Torao was given a cup of rice wine by his grandfather. To be a man, one had to take his liquor well and that training might as well start early. It was a peculiar notion from later standards, but in the eyes of the Japanese, heated rice wine is usually weak in alcoholic content, and was not devastating in its effect like the distilled spirits of the West. Besides, it was used in all the religious and formal rituals. Only on the departure for an under-taking that presages sudden or certin death is wine substituted by plain water. Plain water exchanged in drinking connotes death and a will-ingness to enter into such a contract. Rice wine is drunk in Japan by the men just like wine is freely taken in France or in Italy. Thus, Torao was trained to drink from his childhood, but this training was destined to cause heartbreak and loneliness in his later years.

About once a month Mrs. Murayama used to take her children to Amizu where her ancestral home was situated and proceed to the hill in back of the village where the family cemetery was located. The purpose behind this monthly pilgrimage was to impress upon her youngsters that though the world she had been brought up into had changed and was replaced by a more enlightened era under the direct rule of the emperor, it was still important to learn and feel proud of their lineage.

Not far from her father's home was a trail that led up to the hill. The approach to the cemetery was well kept for it led to the Fudo Temple which was cared for by the village but had originally been built by her own direct ancestors as a family shrine of worship and piety. It was a tiny structure built along the traditional lines of temples, but had a leading to it. In other words, it was a mixture of Shinto and Budd-hist worship and had been cared for as the village guardian deity since the temple had been adopted by the village as a whole.

Fudo-san, of Indian origin, was looked upon in Japan as a special benefactor against all catastrophies and calamities and as a guardian for the villagers. It was perhaps an appropriate god. From the *torii* to the temple there was a rather steep climb with steps cut into the slope and buttressed by wooden reenforcements. The approach was always kept free of weeds and swept clean. Cherry trees lined the road.

Her father had been the burgomaster of this region for generations. This class was peculiar in that although farmers, they were allowed the distinction of having a surname and privileged to wear two swords like any *samurai*. Lately too much drinking and inattention to details of farming had made the fortune of the family rather precarious. Just as the old order was giving way to the new, so were many established families losing out to the more aggressive element that was riding with the new tide of social and economic progress. This temple was merely a relic and reminder of her family's past splendor.

From this building the trail led up to tall weeds that bloomed in the fall and were known as the "seven shrubs of autumn," to the open area where graveyards were arranged in little compounds for different families. Perched on the side of this hill it commanded the magnificent view of the large Ariake Sea that lay quietly between the main island and the Shimabara Peninsula.

The Unzen Mountains towered majestically across the Sea, the summits usually covered by a veil of clouds. The tip of the Shimabara Peninsula, on which Unzen was located, seemed to merge with the large islands of the Amakusa group to the left. The silvery line in the plain lying in front was the Midorikawa River and the shallow shore receded for miles with the ebb of the tide, leaving sandy stretches as far as the eye could see. The mountain rising abruptly from the other end of the vast Higo Plain was the Kimbosan, behind which the active volcano Aso sent up its smoky column on quiet, windless days. Just in front of them, not more than two miles away, placed like a cone on the bay shore, was the hill of Sumiyoshi surrounded by a fishing village.

The village cemetery overlooked this beautiful, majestic landscape. Among the tombstones, the most conspicuous was her ancestors'; especially the stone of the ancestor about two hundred and fifty years dead who had contributed most to the villagers while he was alive. A stone monument over his grave towered above the other markers and under his posthumous Buddhist name there were fifty-seven names of his disciples engraved upon the face of the rock: those that would have followed him into battle and died for him if necessary.

When they arrived, panting, they stopped for a short while and became fascinated with the view that unfolded before them. Mrs. Murayama would have the children pull weeds and tidy the immediate neighborhood of the tomb, change the water in the vases that were placed in front of it, and place new greens and flowers that they brought from home. Then, lighting a bundle of incense, each child was given several to stick into the soft ground beside the vase. As the thin lines of smoke rose from individual incense sticks to merge higher up, Mrs. Murayama assumed a squatting position and with hands brought together before her face, led her three children in the intonation of praise of the Buddha, "*Namu, Amida Butsu, Namu, Amida Butsu.*" Each child held a tiny rosary in his hand and squatting alongside his mother would silently bow following her every move from the corner of his eye and repeat the "Namu Amida Butsu, Namu Amida Butsu." Then she would get up and pour water over the moss-covered tombstone.

She did not know why this was done but by so doing felt that the right thing was done for the departed ones. Perhaps the departed one was thirsty. Anyway, water was pure and it was an act of purification. Tradition and custom usually had some rational purpose when analyzed. After this was done they proceeded to clean the neighboring graveyards. Some graves had no one to care for them; the line had died out or the survivor had moved away. They felt so much better after this was done. It made them feel that they were not only doing something for their own, but also serving others.

"This world," Mrs. Murayama would tell her children, "is not to be lived in alone selfishly. One must be willing to help others whether the act is noted or not. The time may come when you will be the recipient of a kindly act. If you do good to others, it is natural that others will be good to you. But you must not expect reward. It makes one feel good to be doing good."

About the time of the Bon Festival, care of the family graves took on additional significance. During late August or early September when the moon was full and most beautiful, the departed spirits were supposed to return to their former mortal abodes. It was a season when spirits hovered in the atmosphere. Even the dead could not stay quiet. The lure of the lunar beauty was overwhelming. Every household which had a case of death in the preceding year would receive presents of fancy paper lanterns from friends. The departed spirit on its first

85

return from the nether world would find that his erstwhile mortal friends remembered him on this occasion. The mistress of the house had the house ready for the return of the departed souls. Every nook and corner of the house had to be spick and span; the graveyard weeded and cleanly swept. The room in which the Buddhist altar was placed was decorated with fancy lanterns, and before the image of Buddha flowers, fresh greens, and the produce of the fields were placed. There would be carrots, eggplants, and cucumbers piled high on plates. Candies, cakes, and the special favorite of the recently departed one were placed especially for him. A pair of huge lanterns bearing the family crest were hung from the ceiling in front of the altar. At the graveyard similar lanterns were hung and were lighted nightly during the Bon period. The cemetery put on a festive air. No colored flower was used to decorate the graveyard. All plants were branches of green foliage.

The festival began on the thirteenth of the lunar month. Next to New Year's day, this day was of extreme importance to the common people. On this night, the boys that were apprenticed to farms, shops, or mercantile houses, or the girls that served as maids in other homes, returned home and all proceeded together to the family grave attired in their best. They would go to pay reverence to the ancestral spirits. In the Murayama family, Shinshu was the family religion and Bon was merely an occasion to think of their ancestors. The living were to be aware of the vicissitudes of life and the ever-present mercy of Buddha that responded to those who sought salvation.

In other sects of Buddhism, this procession signified the welcoming home of spirits that were loose in their native countryside. This was known as "The welcoming of the sacred spirits" to the family, and for three days the departed ones were to live with their mortal relatives. This occasion was not a period of mourning and so there was no grieving. To the contrary, there was a certain element of rejoicing in the reunion and although there would be no actual merrymaking, people did not deny themselves luxuries or good food. Meat and fish tabooed at mourning would be partaken freely. In good Buddhist families the elder members usually could recite sutras and there would be recitation of these as usual in the presence of the assembled family, but no special effort was made to increase the religious services by the invitation of the priest.

When there was a recent death or "first bon" for the family, friends and relatives usually came to the house in order to lighten the sorrow of the family. For three days the family would be joined in spirit by the departed ones and on the night of the sixteenth day the spirits were to return where they came from. The ritual of "god-speeding the spirits" was performed. Where there was a creek or river a good-sized boat was fashioned out of straw. This was loaded with the seasonal produce that had adorned the altar. At a signal, all the assembled straw boats had their candles lighted simultaneously, and they were let loose to float down the river. The little fleet silently glided and eventually, one by one, disappeared to the bottom. The scene was eerie and mystic.

In regions where there was no river or stream, a horse would be constructed out of an eggplant or cucumber and the rest of the sweets and vegetables would be piled on his back. The horse would then be set down at the turn of the road and a safe journey to the nether world wished for him. In this manner the annual visit of the souls to earthly brethren was made. The annual festival in which the living and the dead both had a part was over, and people went back to the dreary routine of daily life.

The dead, therefore, were not considered in the fearful way that is the case in other countries. On the contrary, a sense of familiarity and the sensation of proximity of the departed ones was fostered in the minds of the children so that the conception of fearful spirits would be foreign to upbringing. It was natural that all should wend their way to ancestral graves to report anything momentous that was to be undertaken in the family, whether joyful or sad, or report in person when they returned from distant lands after a long journey.

As Torao grew up, he joined the young men's club. In a community where elders have absolute say, and age is a factor to be reckoned with, the young people naturally got together socially to relax. Leaders encouraged such a gathering to prevent delinquency among the teenagers. Wholesome fun was a natural development. The club had its meetings at night and played their pranks on the younger and newly initiated members. Typical was the event that occurred on the night of December 14, to test the nerve of the boys and have fun at their expense.

The leader rose and faced the younger boys. "Three hundred years ago, the forty-seven *samurai* of Akoh went out in the midst of the night to chop Kira Kozuke's head off. Kira was the enemy of their dead lord. Tonight you will be asked to show that you too are not afraid. You will not be asked to take any villain's head, but as a sign of your courage, you will be asked to bring back certain articles or erect a flag at some spot. Are you afraid of the dark? You, Kosuke?"

"No. Of course not."

"Have you been to the shrine on the Todoroki Road? You will bring back the *gohei* that is on the altar. I heard that there is a pair of old foxes living in the bushes in back of the old building, and they sometimes come out at night in the guise of a young woman. You, Yosaku!"

"Yes."

"You are to go to the cemetery, to the grave of the newly dead and buried Tanaka woman. Bring back the branch of greens that is in the vase and plant this flag in the new mound. Goichi, you will proceed to the *jizo-san* near the river. Leave this red flag on the steps of the *jizo*. You must take the road that goes under the tree from which the crazy old woman Omoyo hanged herself two years ago."

As the lone boys proceeded, tremulously whistling to hide their inner quavering, there would be a rustling noise in the nearby bushes or eerie hooting or howling from the roadside. A special detachment of older boys were there to frighten the youngsters. After the boys returned to the clubhouse, a check would be made to ascertain whether the marker was actually stuck where it was intended. Then there would be a frugal feast on homemade noodles to emulate the example of the forty-seven *samurai* who had similarly filled their stomachs before they started out on their memorable expedition of vendetta.

Torao was brought up in such an atmosphere. He was taught to revere his ancestors, to take pride in his heritage, and to be brave. Next to loyalty to the emperor, parents came first in the consideration of his everyday conduct. Filial piety was stressed with the utmost emphasis, and he loved his mother above everybody else. But there was an epidemic of dysentery in the countryside and his mother fell ill. Within a short time she was laid at rest not within the family graveyard, but in an isolated spot because the disease was contagious. The ignorant bureaucrats thought it necessary to quarantine the corpse, lest it might contaminate the graves of the non-infectious dead. Western ideas of sanitation and epidemic diseases had just been adopted and in the knowing application of these sciences, the health official was considered to be enlightened and modern.

To the three children it was like the end of the world. There were no more pleasant sorties than those to their ancestral home at Amizu village, and there was no more delightful storytelling than the many folk tales and ancient historical epics handed down among the villagers. The effect on Sadaki was equally great. By that time old Mosaku and his wife had died and Sadaki was master of the Murayama holdings.

Bereft of a helpmate, the farm was hard to maintain without some hired help, but Sadaki was not in a position to pay for help. The most natural thing for him to do was to marry again. In any country, to get married to a widower with three children was not the best marriage that a girl could wish to make, and the man himself did not look for his ideal of womanhood. If she were good enough to take care of his family and be good to the motherless children, then he must consider himself lucky.

The woman he took for his second wife came from typical farmer stock. She had been taught the art of farming but knew little or nothing of the finer training that a girl should have had. She worked hard from morning till night. That she had remained single until past twenty-five showed that she had no physical charm and had not been overlooked by the village swains without reason. For Sadaki it was fortunate that she was such a proficient worker as he was a poor farmer himself and now could rely on her better judgment in the choice and management of the crops.

But the children could not forget their deceased mother and could not make themselves like this intruder. Even in their immature minds— perhaps more so because of their simplicity—they would compare the merits of the two women. Their feeling could not remain hidden from her and she resented their disrespect. The atmosphere in the home was continuously strained and life was miserable for all.

Torao, now fifteen, was cognizant of the open breach and tried to repair it by being nice to her, but the gap was unbridgeable and finally he gave it up and openly rebelled. Time and again he would take his sister Osada to Amizu, their maternal grandfather's home, and stay for weeks: until someone came for them. Their maternal relatives naturally took sides and the talk was lively at Amizu. Their ancient family pride asserted itself. The children felt the satisfaction of basking in the lime-light of a controversy in which they were the chief participants.

Even to the illiterate woman, the conduct of these step-children was irritating, for she had to think of her reputation. This outward flaunting of her authority did not win sympathy for her and did not improve her station among the village women, who had a high regard for the deceased wife and were naturally semi-hostile to her even under the best arrangement. Gossipy women spread rumors which, in a distorted form, came back to her. Chagrined, she would complain to her husband who naturally did nothing, being the patient man he was, and kept the mental agony a man had to endure under these circumstances all to himself: stoically. Thus the only avenue left to her to dispel her pentup feelings was to pick on and be harsh to Osada, the youngest daughter.

The little girl, now grown to adolescence, was worked to death. In a farmer's life the lot of the women is not easy and with a slave-driver at her heels, there would never be a day when her work would be finished. Her only comfort was the understanding help that was rendered by Torao, and as a result their relationship became all the more intimate.

It was no wonder, therefore, that we find Torao volunteering to labor in the canefields of Hawaii when immigration companies recruited laborers. His life had become unbearable. His father, understanding his feeling, did not stand in his way. Only Osada was very grieved and wept most pitifully. In view of what happened, many old women stated years later that somehow Osada must have felt that the parting was going to be the last for her and her brother on this earth, for she was destined to die two years later from an epidemic of dysentery.

CHAPTER 9

Contract Labor Years

THE RECRUITING AGENTS OF AN EMIGRATION
company went from village to village in Kumamoto Prefecture, painting
a rosy picture of distant Hawaii. They were trying to get farmers to
sign up for work in the sugar cane fields. Laborers were to work ten
hours a day in the hot sun. But there was a day of rest every seven
days, and certainly this was an improvement over farms in Japan,
where only on national holidays, Bon, and New Years would work automatically cease. As long as there was work, it had to be accomplished far
into the night. No conception of work hours was entertained. Of course
there were days of rest, off and on, depending on the weather.

"You young fellows should think of the future. Hawaii is in that part
of the world where there is no winter. Spring all the year around. No
warm clothes needed. After a contract of three years, you can do as you
please. Hawaii is not crowded like Japan and you will make plenty of
money. If you wish to return to Japan, you can do so after three years.
But I tell you, once you get there you will not want to return to this hard-
to-exist-in country of ours."

"But mister, is Hawaii not a barbarous country, so different from our
homeland?"

"What of it? It is not as far away as *Tenjiku* (India). No wild
head-hunters are there to molest you. I know because I talked to those
who went there in early Meiji years and returned with hard-earned cash.
Think of the wages! Why, in one month you will earn what you can
make in one whole year slaving in the rice paddies." Many men from the
villages and towns were persuaded to sign up for this eventful journey
and adventure; each had his own reason.

Thus on a slow, self-propelled steamer, the *SS China*, which belched
out black smoke, ninety emigrants from different parts of western Japan

embarked at Nagasaki. Torao Murayama found himself among these people. At Yokohama, two hundred more were taken aboard and of these forty were women. It became cramped and crowded. The diet was monotonous and unpalatable. Board was a contract business and the enterprising steward was out to make money, feeding the passengers subsistence rations only. Every day it was pink or black beans, small dried fish, dried chopped turnips cooked with canned salmon, *miso* soup that barely smelt of *miso*, and a measured amount of rice.

Usually in such a crowd, to pass ennui, there would be organized entertainment amongst the passengers; but not with these people. They were too seasick or too hungry to stir out of their bunks.

Twenty-two days without a bath! Everyone began scratching. Fleas everywhere. The clothing was what they had had in the village: kimonos of tough home-spun *kasuri* (design of white specks on black or blue background) and the quasi-western attire of *momo-hiki* (tight fitting trousers).

But the day came when the sea birds from Hawaii visited the incoming ship. A bath for the steerage passengers was announced, but it consisted of live steam from a hose. Even for those who boasted of their ability to remain in the hottest mineral springs of their province, this unusual bath made them hesitate, and they decided to postpone cleansing their bodies until they landed.

"Let us have a funeral for the lice."

"What do you mean?"

"We shall dump our underwear when we land and call it the water burial of our fellow travellers from Japan. I am sure they will not be welcomed at Honolulu."

The sea was rough, and the small steamer rolled and pitched incessantly for three weeks until the bare mountain called Diamond Head met the immigrants' eager gaze. But to land and enjoy the city was not to be their lot. They were herded via the long six hundred foot bridge to the Immigration Station on Sand Island. There was a large, ramshackle building called by the Japanese *sen nin goya* which literally meant "a large house capable of accommodating a thousand people." It was in the center of an enclosure. Next to it was a smaller compound where the

92

quarantined cases were held. A large, tall chimney over a brick building was a crematory to dispose of the deceased.

After the long voyage, the feel of ground under the feet was welcome. The luxury of a shower with fresh water was met with huzzahs, even though it was in cold water.

"All you newcomers line up for inspection!" yelled the Emigration Company's official. He assembled the new arrivals on the bare ground in front of the building. "No sickness was found among you fellows by the quarantine doctor and so you will soon be assigned to different plantations. Until then, rest and take it easy. Make yourself at home. I am available every day to look after your wants if you need me." He was a humorous man of thirty or thereabouts and according to rumor a veterinarian and master of the English language.

There were about two hundred that had been waiting at this station for their dispersal to outlying islands. To pass their ennui, nothing was done, at least in an organized way. Soon however, an impromptu talent show was held and it was an instant success. It was a hilarious three hour show and a self-appointed master of ceremonies kept the meeting well balanced. Each ship contingent knew its artists and there seemed to be a friendly rivalry among the three shiploads already there. The latest arrivals on the SS China soon got into the spirit and produced comedians, singers, and dancers from their midst. Folk dances and country songs of each province were richly represented and a spirit of camaraderie was born among all.

Sand Island was barren of vegetation. It was situated to the left of the channel that led into Honolulu Harbor, dredged for ocean liners. The side that fronted the harbor was a mud-containing sandy shoreline, and the part that fronted the Pacific Ocean extended to the breakers beyond a stretch of coral reef. When the wind veered to the south the humidity was high, much like the summer days of Japan. During the day, the sun's reflection on the sandy surface made the atmosphere hot, in spite of the breeze that came from the mountains.

Without anybody taking visible leadership, a wrestling tournament began. Young muscular men were aching for a chance to let off steam. Improvised loin cloths served as *fundoshi* like the "malo" of the natives. The arena was a circle on the sandy ground, a relic from former contingents and sojourners, and a match was soon in full swing. A referee, or *gyoji,* soon found himself deciding each tussle. A comedian bellowed forth in a sing-song refrain the name of the contestants. The gallery of spectators were shouting encouragement and clapping their approval of a dexterous throw. They groaned, swayed, and sweated with the evenly matched contestants. It did not take long to end each contest. To win, one had to either throw his opponent to the ground, push him out of the ring, or force him to touch the ground first when both their bodies were headed for a fall. To touch the earth with a hand or a knee once the contest started, spelled defeat.

"Now, look into each other's eyes. Take your time, and get started," said the low, admonishing voice of the referee. He held a wooden fan between the faces of the two low-crouching, naked bodies pivoted on all fours. Four eyes glared. With suppressed breath, each was sizing up the other. With the words "get started," the fan was withdrawn and the wrestlers continued to eye each other until the opportune moment for combat was sensed. One had the right to say *matta,* wait, should he not find himself just ready, or he could delay the fight as a means of strategy. But the spectators booed if the delay was too frequent. Once on their feet, the struggle was indeed fast. There was nothing to grasp except the waist cloth. No judo holds were allowed. The outcome was not dependent solely on strength or weight, for small clever men could vanquish a much bigger man without much trouble. The expenditure of energy was tremendous, for in matter of two seconds to three minutes on the average, an opponent was usually disposed of.

Torao considered himself a good village wrestler, but he soon discovered that in such company there were many who had aspired to becoming professionals in either Osaka or Tokyo, but had failed to make the grade. These failures of the metropolitan *sumo* wrestling stables were formidable in Hawaii, and were destined to become either semi-professional wrestlers or bouncers and body-guards for gamblers and racketeers.

In groups of twenties and thirties, these recruits were at last shipped to sugar plantations on Oahu or on different islands. Considerable luck accompanied this distribution, for sooner or later they were to find that there was a great difference in the topographical characteristics of the different islands, and more important, the management of the different plantations. Indentured labor of three years, chained to a bleak existence, overrun and driven by merciless slave drivers at the end of a horse whip, was veritable hell. On the other hand, under merciful management in which humanity was a consideration in the achievement of efficiency, life was bearable even though the work was hard under a scorching midday sun. Trade winds eased the burning sun, and cool tranquil nights all the year round assuaged the loneliness of a transplanted life.

Torao's turn came. His companions were mostly made up of fellow voyagers of the *SS China* and among them were Okawa and Hirano who came from his native village. Twenty young men with their willow trunks were transported to the deck of the *SS Kinau*. This steamer was a three thousand ton luxury liner of the Inter-island Navigation Company, but in the rough waters of the channels between the islands, the rolling was terrific. Even good sailors fell victims to mal-de-mer and the peasant farmers could not lift themselves from the hard deck on which they were sprawled. Food was out of the question, and perhaps just as well, for there was none available for the passengers. A barrel of poi covered by a gunny sack stood near the stairway. Burly, good-natured seamen with pieces of salt salmon in their left hands, came to dip two fingers of their right hands into the barrel for the pasty substance and deftly slid the food into their mouths. This constituted a snack for them when they returned from their rowing assignment at the way stops. The voyage lasted eighteen hours.

At Lahaina, Maalae, Mahukona, and Kawaihae the steamer stopped to load and unload passengers and cargo. About five in the morning, the *Kinau* lowered her anchor off Laupahoehoe to disgorge some of her passengers. The Emigration Company official awakened the twenty men to get ready for the whaleboat that was being lowered. The side hatch was opened. Waves were high and with each billow the boat rose and fell. The crest of the wave was utilized to let a passenger step into the craft.

In contrast to the sun-parched Diamond Head and Punchbowl that confronted them at Honolulu, the northeast coast of the island of Hawaii was dripping with moisture and verdure. The half dozen waterfalls that emptied from the gulches of Papaaloa added a beauty scarcely dreamed of even by this group of boys who came from a country that was full of trees.

"What beautiful, gorgeous scenery!"

"It is beautiful and wild all right. Look at the white waves battering against the black rocky shoreline. I hope there is no mishap in our landing."

"Don't worry. Look at the muscles of these native oarsmen. They are big too. I bet they could easily join the professional *sumo* stables if they were in Japan."

"No, I don't think they could. I heard that these people have weak legs. Without strong legs and a tough back, you can never attain the *makuuchi* class." This meant the upper strata of professional wrestling.

The boat was deftly steered into a cove where a boathouse was built to receive freight from the boats. Laupahoehoe was a promontory, a tongue of lava flow jutting out into the ocean; a picturesque little fishing village with many coconut trees planted along the roadside and gardens.

A pock-marked little man about five feet two inches with flashing gold teeth, gold rimmed glasses, and well over forty, was there to greet these recruits. He wore a suit in contrast to the majority of Orientals who were in blue jeans. A sparse mustache and his asthenic stooping stature marked him as a scholar rather than a man from a pioneering community of coarse men.

"I am Yamada, from the Waipunalei Sugar Company. You are welcome. Your voyage must have been trying. All these trips are hard because of the small steamers. Anyway, you will not have to take another boat ride for a long time. Two wagons are awaiting you and we shall soon be on our way."

His mild manner and good standard Japanese (Mr. Yamada came from Yokohama), impressed these country bumpkins. In his youth, he was employed by foreign firms in that seaport town in menial capacities and gradually picked up sufficient English to get along. He next boarded a sailing vessel as mess boy and went around the world. As he got along in years, he became tired of sea-life and elected to settle somewhere. Of all the ports he had touched in his wanderings, he felt this mid-pacific station most ideal to spend an easy-going life's eventide. While loafing a few months in Honolulu, he was approached by the sugar planters' association to interpret on some of the plantations. Proficiency in the English language was scarce and commanded a premium. Of all places, however, this gentleman had to be assigned to Waipunalei, the worst of the plantations. It was not an enviable position to be a witness to brutality and then mediate, to settle affairs in the way his employers' wanted, at the expense of his helpless countrymen.

CHAPTER 10

Escape from Waipunalei

THE TOPOGRAPHY OF THE COUNTRY WAS majestic in spite of the fact that this was an island—just a speck of land on the map of the Pacific. The highest mountain in the world for an island, the snow-capped Mauna Kea towered in the center of the island and sloped gently towards the sea. Numerous lava flows must have occurred in the formative stages of the geological past for the slopes were cut by deep ravines accentuated by the subsequent effects of erosion. Being on the windward side and exposed to the constant northeasterly trade winds, the coast line was very wild. Precipitous cliffs about five hundred feet high rose abruptly above the water's edge making it almost impossible, or at best extremely hazardous, for the fishermen to clamber down the narrow trail.

The sea was always rough. The plantation was situated at the junction between the North Hilo and Hamakua districts and at this part of the island there was no water-bearing stratum in the ground and the crops had to depend on rainwater for moisture. It rained frequently and no matter how clear the day a shower was in the offing at unexpected moments and in order not to be caught unawares a raincoat or an umbrella had to be carried all the time. The saying went, "Even if you forget your lunch box, do not forget your raincoat." All drinking water came from rainwater collected from roofs of houses and stored in underground cisterns or huge tanks.

Usually there was enough rainfall to ensure a good crop of sugar cane and supply the needs of men and beasts. When there was no rain, drought continued for two or three months. It was then that the sugar cane turned yellow, roads became dusty, and the people suffered from lack of drinking water and had to go for weeks without taking a bath.

The Douglas Plantation was a private enterprise run by Mr. Douglas who was a well-to-do man having holdings not only in this sugar plantation but also in a gold mine in California. He was of Scottish descent like most of the Hamakua coast planters and his overseers, called "luna," were mostly from Scotland too. Apparently the plantation was not a very profitable one because the success of the crops depended so much on the uncertain weather, which could be very finicky. Because water was not abundant, the cane did not grow as tall, and compared to the neighboring plantations in the Hilo district, the transportation cost of cane to the mill was high. In the latter region cane was transported to the grinding mill by a flume. Miles and miles of this conduit would extend from the fields to the mill and sugar cane cut to about two foot lengths would flow to its destination.

At Waipunalei this convenient and cheap mode of conveyance could not be utilized and a train had to be used. But here again, because land was not flat like that on the Oahu plantations another method was used. An ingenious device called the "wire rope" was invented to transport cane from the fields to a railway track which coursed the shoreline. For miles the steel wire cable extended up the slope supported at regular intervals by posts and crossbars about twenty to forty feet high, depending on the irregularity of the surface. A revolving wheel with a suspension hook onto which a bundle of cane was hitched would be sent down from the higher fields. Some wheels would turn faster than others and there was a tendency for certain ones to be bunched together in their downward coursing. Therefore, at certain intervals depending on the slope and grade, there were relay stations where a respacing of the downward flow of cane bundles was effected. Also at certain intervals there were signal posts where flags flew to transmit messages from the platform to regulate the flow of cane, for the procedure had to be adjusted according to the available number of empty loading cars.

Torao was sent to this plantation with two members from his native village, Umekichi Okawa and Yusaku Hirano, and seventeen other men. These three were about the same age and they had vowed to stick together in all the privations and tribulations they had to face in the new land. On arrival, they were taken to a camp near the factory which was called the "mill camp."

The accommodations that awaited them were much the same as on other plantations. Because of frequent rains, the barracks were built about eight feet above ground. A rectangular hall thirty by ten feet accommodated eight men. Each was accorded about four feet on the sleeping platform. They hung their work clothes and other apparel on the wall of the walking space.

The stories concerning life and treatment to be accorded them that they heard from men already working there were most disheartening. It happened that the "big luna" or the general overseer of the plantation was a virtual czar of this domain as the manager-owner left the running of the plantation completely in the hands of this brutal Scotsman, Frank MacCracken. He must have had a streak of sadism in his nature for the treatment of laborers was brutal in the extreme. The cruelty must have been unprecedented and unparalleled for there was an unenviable appellation attached to this "devil's plantation." All who came to this place considered it an act of fate. *"Shikataga nai"* (it can't be helped) was muttered under a sigh.

For three years they were bound to this spot by the contract they had signed. In effect, it was slavery pure and simple for they could not leave the farm. Policemen of the Hawaiian kingdom were nothing more than guards whose duty was to track down runaway laborers and bring them back to their employers.

All contract laborers were to receive twelve and a half dollars a month. Housing and medical attention were to be provided by the employer. Ten percent was subtracted each pay day and this amount filled the coffers of the Emigration Company that had recruited them in Japan. There were two ways to eat. The majority of single men boarded at six dollars a month at some kitchen run by an enterprising couple, or did the cooking themselves. Examples of commodity prices were:

100 lb. sack of rice	$3.00
1 lb. of small fish (opelu)	.12
1 lb. beef	.12
1 sack 50 lb. flour	.60
1 good-sized chicken	.20

In order for the cook to be able to prepare breakfast and fill the lunch cans, she had to get up at three o'clock in the morning. Unless her husband supplemented the larder with homegrown vegetables, and raised a pig on the slop that came from the kitchen, there was not much profit to show. A little pig was obtainable at five dollars and after four or five months it was worth twenty-five to thirty dollars which was really clear money.

A single man who denied himself in the extreme by preparing his own meals could not do much better. There was an exception now and then. Mohei Sato was from Fukushima-ken and was more literate than the average immigrant since he came from the snowy north. It was said that in the northeast provinces, the winters were so cold that the children were forced to remain indoors and obtain book learning. Be that as it may, he was above average intelligence, but his conduct was ludicrous. His nickname was "sugar bag." For working clothes, he cut himself a shirt and pants out of gunny sack. It was a strange sight to see him in this coarse brown apparel hobbling along in feet turbaned with the same material. The coarse fabrics must have irritated his skin terribly, but he endured it much like the medieval monks did. He lived on, according to gossip, rice, *shoyu,* and small dried fish called *iriko.* He was a wealthy man judging by the yardstick of the workers, although nobody envied him. He was made the butt of jokes by even small children. He showed no outward annoyance and seemed to live in a world all his own. But everyone was ashamed ten years later when he was the biggest contributor to the language school that was built by popular subscription. He was miserly but knew how to spend money when the cause was a worthy one.

Back in the old country there was an authentic story of a returnee from Hawaii who had two hundred and fifty dollars after the completion of three contract years. How one could save this sum in three years, from ten dollars a month before board was subtracted, was almost impossible to conceive, but facts were there and there was no factor of gambling as a possible outside source of income for this man.

The work began the morning following their arrival. Without a raincoat they were ordered out with the other hands to go "hoe hana-ing" —hoeing weeds and grass between the rows of young sugar cane. Luckily, it was a season of comparatively little rain and they hoped the weather would hold until the raincoats would be sewed and oiled by the woman who took the orders to make these for the new arrivals.

They started out at four-forty-five and labored until eleven when they were permitted to have lunch and a thirty minute rest. Then at four o'clock they were released from their toil. They had to walk home from the field which sometimes was three to four miles away. When the days were short it was almost dark when they returned.

There was a "luna" over them who directed their work and saw that nobody loafed. He was a Portuguese and not a bad sort, although in the presence of his superiors he tried to act hard-boiled to curry their favor. His softness and considerateness were only in a comparative and relative sense and the whole setup on the plantation was that of inhuman slave-driving tactics to get the most out of these human creatures.

Little heed was given to the human element, such as inequality in physique and endurance that existed among the different working men. Maximum work was to be exacted from all concerned. To see that each worked hard, a peculiar practice was in vogue. If a man did not soak his shirt with sweat by nine a.m., he might be sent home and the day did not count as a day worked. On wintry days one had to work very hard in order to sweat. Scottish thrift and meanness were extreme in their application.

After several weeks, it began to rain. Every day showers might be expected. It got cold in the winter months when Mauna Kea was capped with snow and the winds that blew from that direction were chilly. It seemed incongruous to be working in a tropical sugar cane field and be in constant view of a long range of mountains clad snowy white. In the early morning, the need of warm clothing was keenly felt.

On these wet days the men were sent out to the fields to do "holy-holy work"—pulling dried cane leaves that kept clinging to the stalk. The moisture made the detachment easy and the fine sticky cilia-like bristles at the edges of the leaves were soft and not damaging to the bare hands. The dried leaves were piled high between the rows of the sugar cane stalks which looked fresh and clean, stripped of their dried leaves.

On these cool mornings the work was brisk. Competitive spirit was keen among the men, and the going was rapid. The only thing that occasionally bothered them was the attack of yellow jackets that had their nests in the dry leaves, but even these were rendered less vicious by the rain. This work got to be very hot and wearisome as soon as the rain ceased and the afternoon sun beat heavily, for among the tall rows of cane there was no cooling relief from any refreshing breeze.

One morning a newcomer who did not appear very robust was taken sick and did not report to work. As was the usual routine, MacCracken made his rounds of the camps at about eight thirty in the morning to see if there were any malingerers. The really sick were to report for sick call at the dispensary, where castor oil and quinine were dispensed. On this rainy morning he found this newcomer in bed and to his casual lay observation, prejudiced by a slave-driver's mental attitude, the man did not look either feverish or sickly. His only conclusion was that the man was a shirker. In his ignorant blind rage, he yanked this poor man from his bed, did not even give him time to dress, kicked him in the posterior, and drove him to work riding just behind him on a horse. Thus at a trot he drove this sick man to the field two miles away in his underwear. It was raining off and on. Ignorant of the English language, the laborer could not explain that he had a stabbing pain in his chest, the recurrence of an old pleurisy. When they got to the working place, MacCracken gave special orders to the Portuguese luna in charge of the gang to see that this man did not loaf. The toadying luna had neither imagination nor the intelligence to smooth out ruffles without causing general alarm. Told to do a certain thing he considered it loyalty to adhere to it literally without questioning its justice, and attempted to carry the order out to the letter.

Therefore, when this man began working, he followed him and saw to it that he kept up the pace of other healthy men. Not being of a strong constitution to start with and now wracked with fever, lassitude began to assail him. He could not keep up the work without feeling a faintness coming on. He stood up often to take a breath. The luna goaded him on. There came a time that he could not continue and he worked mechanically and listlessly. In blind rage, the luna kicked him across a vital organ as the man stooped over to gather dry leaves. He keeled over and went into shock.

Ignorant of the actual state of injury, the luna tried to get the injured laborer to his feet but was aghast when he saw the color of his face. There was no one present who might have given him first aid. The working men convened around the stricken man. Some slapped his face, some shouted into his ears, but he soon turned cyanotic, the color draining from his cheeks. When the terrible fact dawned upon the men that their friend had been kicked to death by this Portuguese, they turned on the horror stricken stooge and beat him relentlessly until he was no longer able to stand and cried for mercy. Luckily in this work of "holy-

holy" no implement was used or else the result might have been fatal for him also.

All work ceased. The fighting blood of the men was up. They carried the corpse to the camp and had a grand demonstration of grief, anger, and much talk. There was much jabbering and gesticulating, but without adequate leadership nothing could be accomplished. Torao took charge of the occasion. He told them that the first thing to do was to have some sort of religious service for the dead man and give him a decent burial. On the following day they could have a delegation sent to the manager and remonstrate to their heart's content concerning the wrong done and ensure that such inhuman acts not be repeated ever again on the plantation. All agreed as it was getting dark.

That night there was a very sad vigil in the dead man's room. The talk, over repeated cups of tea, recounted stories and anecdotes experienced in the old country and all tried to avoid the topic of the day's wrong that culminated in this tragedy. Torao volunteered to perform the Buddhist ritual of chanting the sutra which he knew by heart. It had been taught him at the village temple whose priest happened to be his cousin.

The following day the gang that worked with the dead man did not report to work and all went along to the cemetery located in a grove of eucalyptus trees about a mile away, where about two dozen other compatriots who had fallen victim to various traumatic injuries or sickness lay interred; unsung and unmourned in this living hell of a plantation, thousands of miles away from their native country. They bore the casket made of rough pine lumber slung on a long pole which was carried by two men in relays. Each gladly volunteered. It was a last friendly service to an erstwhile fellow-worker. A hole was dug in the ground, and the casket was slowly lowered as the men stood with bowed heads. As each helped throw in handfuls of dirt, there was a glistening in every pair of eyes that was transfixed to the spot where all life's aspiration and hope were being interred under three shallow feet of sod. As the hole was being filled, Torao stood by and again chanted the verses from the sutra that he knew by heart. A wooden marker with the name of the dead, his age, the date of demise, and his home-place in Japan was placed at the head of the mound.

Mr. Yamada worked at the store conducted by the plantation. When they returned from the burial, the entire delegation repaired to the store and asked to see this man to transmit their grievances to the manager. Used to such demonstrations, Mr. Yamada had seen the manager about it and had an answer to the remonstrances of the laborers. According to him, the manager was extremely sorry for what had occurred and had discharged the man responsible for the accident. The plantation was going to see to it that such repetition would not recur.

As to the crux of the question of punishment of the murderer, assurance was very vague. It was an act done in line of duty and according to existing Hawaiian law there was no recourse to the courts. The courts were in the hands of the white planters. The Hawaiian judges and police were mere stooges in the employ of the moneyed faction that had representation in the courts of the native king. In fact, they were advisers to the king. As to the protection of sick men not able to work, here again guarantee of humane consideration was very feeble. After all they were, in fact, indentured contract laborers. Their civil rights had been taken away and for three years they were to be victims of the exploiters of their labor whose voice was law even unto matters concerning life and death.

Yamada was a sincere man and the young laborers did not doubt for a moment that he spoke from a detached third party standpoint with their interest at heart and not behaving as a mere tool of the management. But his counsel for moderation and forbearance was prompted from a desire to settle everything peacefully. He knew full well the futility of resistance but feared that the aroused spirit of the men was not to be easily quelled. To back down at this moment meant giving in to brutality and surrendering everything considered decent in human heritage.

The attitude of the laborers became menacing. The predicament Yamada was in was perceived by his superiors and by order of the men in the office of the Hawaiian policeman, Kaihue, came out with a drawn pistol and ordered them back. Torao was enraged. To settle anything within reason could and ought to be done by persuasion. To be threatened by a pistol was an insult that he could not take lying down and so he stepped forward and yelled out in Japanese to Mr. Yamada, "It is a cowardly act to resort to 'flying weapons.' Why can't things be talked over by representatives in a human way?"

The policeman fired a shot into the air to cower the crowd. Instead, it incited them into a frenzy. They rushed forward to be met by two shots this time. Luckily, no one was seriously hurt. Torao received a grazing wound in his thigh and another got a bullet in his leg. But this deadly demonstration of might was enough to sober them. Sullenly, they retreated to their barracks. They were made to realize more than ever before that they were virtual slaves during the period of their contract. The next day they went to work with sick hearts, but the vigilence of the "lunas" was increased. In the course of time their spiritual hurt was gradually assuaged. Time seemed to be the most efficient healer of the wounds that stabbed deep.

But this unfortunate incident was not easily forgotten. Those that were looked upon as the ringleaders or anyone who took an active part in the protest were black-listed, and a systematic persecution took place. The worst type of work was sent their way; they had to go to the remotest fields so that when they returned to the barracks in the evening, others already had had their bath and supper. To be picked upon in such a discriminating way usually sours anyone. Soon, Torao got fed up with the life at this plantation and plans to escape from this living hell began to take shape in his mind. He conferred with his two buddies from the same village, Okawa and Hirano. They were willing and decided to skip this place for Kohala about sixty miles away. The latter was reputed to be a paradise compared to Waipunalei and was far enough to escape detection once they got there.

One night, therefore, when everybody was sound asleep, they gathered their meager possessions and slipped out of camp. They traveled on the government road during the night and at dawn got as far as the adjoining plantation of Kukaiau. Beyond this point, the terrain was unknown to them. When people began to stir at dawn they crawled into the canefields and slept. The food and water lasted a day. When dusk came, they got out of hiding and followed the road but not on the road itself. Where the cane was young they walked in the canefield.

Their escape was already a known fact and without delay policemen on neighboring plantations were notified. Usually, a cash prize was posted for capture and return of fugitives, and the native policemen were bent on making the capture for obvious reasons. Where the cane was tall, they were forced to step out on the road, but they walked along the edge of the highway so that they could jump into the canefield as soon as they heard approaching hoofbeats. When they came to the village of

Paauilo they made a wide detour and proceeded northward. Nothing untoward happened and they got to the middle of the Paauhau Plantation at dawn the next morning.

"This is when we sleep the day again. This will be the last of the rice we brought. Luckily in Hawaii the cane will give us both food and water. So let's chew on this ripe cane," said Torao.

Hirano replied, "We shouldn't complain. Every mile we get away from Waipunalei, I feel freer and better. A few days without food is nothing. We must be between Paauilo and Honokaa. I heard that the Paauhau Plantation camp is not on the highway but we are on the plantation now. The next village we come to will be Honokaa."

Okawa was thoughtful. "Would it be wise to try to get some food when we get to Honokaa? I heard that once you get to Waimea Plateau, there will be no sugar cane to chew. Only cattle grazing ground is found there."

Torao was more optimistic. "This is an adventure and adventure is always attended with some risk. When we get to Honokaa, we'll reconnoiter and then decide what to do. Meanwhile, let's get some sleep."

The dried cane leaves made a nice soft bed. Several rows of cane away from the highway a little snoring would not invite attention. There were very few travelers anyway. Mosquitoes did not bother them.

When it became dark, the three men stepped out of this hiding place and headed north, exercising a cautious single file march and doing most of their walking before the moon came out. Because there were no houses along this stretch, they did not meet anyone on the road.

About midnight of the third night they reached Honokaa. By this time they were so hungry they decided without much arguing to run that certain risk and seek help from friendly compatriots. Wary of barking dogs, they came to a small house on the fringe of the town. By looking at the general layout of the surroundings of the house they concluded it must be the abode of a Japanese, for there was the outdoor cooking place and the more tell-tale wooden bathtub. They knocked repeatedly. A sleepy-eyed man answered the rap on the door and cautiously opened the entrance. He was clad in kimono with a lantern in his hand. Relieved to find that it was indeed a countryman, Hirano said, "We are extremely sorry to disturb you at this hour of the night but we are seeking mercy. We have not eaten for two days."

Suspiciously, the man inquired, "Where are you from and where are you bound for?"

"We are from Waipunalei and are on our way to Niuli, Kohala."
Then everything seemed clear to the man and he let them into the hous.

"If I am not mistaken, you three are running away from the 'devil's plantation?' You have not been the first to come this way from Waipunalei. You must be hungry. Let me fix you something to eat." There was some leftover cold rice and he hurriedly boiled some water and prepared tea. With some pickled radish the three men devoured several bowls of rice and felt alive again. As the men were eating, the host prepared some two dozen pancakes.

"You had better take these along in case you run out of food again. But remember, the Waimea Plateau you will have to cross is practically uninhabited up to where the cowboys live and that is a village called Kamuela. Perhaps you had better give the Kanakas a wide berth, for they are apt to turn you over for the cash prize that hangs around your neck. Only eat these pancakes when there is absolutely no other food in sight. Now you had better get started again and reach the forest lands that start on that hill about two miles away. It is never safe in the village. Hope you have luck in your venture." He divided the pancakes into three packages. "Let each carry his own. You may become parted. Nobody can foretell what will happen."

"May we ask your name and home address in Japan? There may be a chance for us to return your hospitality in kind," said Torao.

"Oh, forget about it! Between us men from the same country everyone is like a brother as far as I am concerned. You would have done the same for me had I been in your shoes. Just watch the roads carefully. The first part of the forest road seems to be the most dangerous. In the cattle ranches beware of the bulls and play possum at night when they come to sniff at you."

They thanked this kindly man from the bottom of their hearts and took to the road again, climbing uphill towards the Waimea Plateau. In the dead of the night there was no one stirring, so the men followed the road and made good progress. Up and up they climbed. There was no conversation for everyone was intent on getting out of the danger zone. The fine dust of the road was like flour and impeded their progress. Recently, wagons heavily laden with harvested cane had used this road extensively and ground the dirt road to this pulverized state, for there had been no rain for the past three weeks. Had there been rain the road would have been well nigh impassable.

The moon came out at about two o'clock and the going was made relatively easy as the countryside came plainly into view. The lofty peak of Mauna Kea seemed to tower immediately in front of them. The cane fields, bathed in the soft glow of the silvery moon, shimmered like the surface of the sea and extended in undulating waves to the ocean miles away. They came to the end of the plantation and the scenery changed to the typical wild wooded sections of the subtropics. Large ohia trees abounded and in the underbrush giant tree ferns flourished to form an almost impassable barrier. They sighed with relief but their feeling of safety was destined to be short-lived.

The policeman at Honokaa had been notified of the three fugitives. Traces of their hiding place in the cane field at Kukaiau Plantation had been discovered by working men in the fields and the police further on had been duly notified. The native policeman at Honokaa needed the cash prize of ten dollars per head for his growing family. He figured the runaway Japanese would head through Honokaa that night and so he kept vigil at the junction of the plantation and the forest lands. The hilly terrain there would make the capture easier.

He lay recumbent on the ground and was patiently awaiting his prey to appear. As the night wore on and he became sleepy, his horse began pricking his ears and restlessly pulled on the rein which wound around the policeman's wrist. He became alert and on looking down the road he espied three forms in the moonlight. There was no mistake. To get them all was his ambition. He tightened the girth of the saddle and mounted. He used to work as a cowboy on the Parker Ranch at Waimea in his youth and lassoing was a specialty of his. He untied the cowhide rope and carefully made a big ring of it with his right hand.

When the approaching fugitives hove into sight within fifty feet, he applied spurs to his mount and made a dash for the unsuspecting men. Completely taken by surprise, they dispersed and took to the little mound on the roadside. They intended to separate but instinctively two got bunched together while the other went by himself. The lasso flew to its mark and the two men were ensnared in one attempt. Brought violently together, they suddenly realized that they were captured and their cause lost. Having heard that the Hawaiian cowboys made a practice of dragging their victims when there was resistance, the two men stopped running and felt the cowhide rope tighten around their waists. Holding the rope taut, the policeman approached them with a drawn revolver and handcuffed them together. In the meantime the third member, Okawa, had made good his escape.

Torao and Hirano were handcuffed together. The policeman held the rope that was tied to the metal handcuffs and commanded the fugitives to head downhill. He followed behind on his horse and locked them in a cell at the county jail.

"Oh, what a disgrace! I would rather die than be taken back to Waipunalei," wailed Hirano.

"Yes, I feel the same way. But not enough to commit suicide. Maybe there'll be another chance. Maybe we'll get a beating at the hands of the Jackass head luna. I can't stand that: to be kicked about by the giant. It hurts to be kicked but the indignity of being booted will make me feel so small spiritually that I surely will lose my self-respect as a human being. Why did I ever come to Hawaii!"

Fitfully, they snatched two hours of sleep and were then given a cup of coffee and two pieces of hardtack. At seven o'clock the fat khaki-clad policeman appeared. He displayed a star on his coat, wore a broad-rimmed hat with another star in front, and spurs jingled from his knee-high boots. "I think you run away from Waipunalei. I take you back to the plantation now," and he led the two prisoners out of the cell.

The two captives were taken back, retracing the twenty miles of weary hike to the plantation which they had vowed they would never lay eyes on again. It was a dusty and weary hike because the gait and pace of the policeman's horse was uniform and steady. Onlookers at the roadside had expressions of mingled emotion or plain apathy when they saw the trio. Pity, contempt, or sympathy depended on each one of the crowd, but only resignation and shame were the feelings left for the prisoners. How were the onlookers to know that they were not criminals or murderers and only men who had sought liberty? The fate of a loser was a shameful one.

"Oh, why did you have to get caught?" were the first words uttered by the interpreter Yamada, who was genuinely sorry when the policeman brought the prisoners back at night. There was no Caucasian overseer around then and he could blurt out his true feelings.

"We tried to escape but fate was against us. Coming back, we had ample time to think. We are young and can take whatever is dished out to us. We will stick it out to the end of the contract."

"Just as well. It may be harder now that you are marked men and

109

you will be segregated in a different camp as punishment but it will be for three months only. You can then rejoin your old friends."

They were thrown in the calaboose and fed only bread and water for two days as punishment, and then they were sent to a special camp where incorrigibles were quartered and those who were used for the most detestable work. Torao was very unhappy about his capture. But by this experience he evolved a new philosophy of life. He had tried escape and failed. It was perhaps inevitable that he should try to explain and console himself regarding this recent escapade and its accompanying failure.

That Okawa did finally succeed in getting to Kohala was evident by a letter received by a man in camp from an assumed name prearranged before their departure. Torao felt that there was some sort of fate linking him to this odious plantation. Perhaps he was predestined to stick to this place and it was not meant that he, a mortal, should say anything about any arrangement that was surely beyond his ken and ability to alter. Therefore he became reconciled to his fate and thereafter acted like a good obedient laborer no matter what the nature of his work turned out to be.

The work assigned to this disciplinary group was the dirtiest and the hardest on the plantation. After three months of this convict camp he was paroled back to his original gang. It is a universal truth that any act, either good or bad, significant enough to be noticed by others, will be remembered by the superiors.

He was soon promoted to be a mule-driver. He was assigned to a mule, holding the handles of a single cultivator with the long rein around his shoulders, and walked between rows of young cane. This was a promotion from the ranks of "hoe-hanamen" as the hoe-wielding laborers were derisively called. His wages remained the same during the term of the contract, but as soon as the period of indenture should end his pay was going to be boosted ten cents a day above that of the hoeing men.

After he had decided to endure whatever befell him his lot became much easier and he was able to have some fun even in this desolate place away from civilization and its comforts. It was during this time that the sad news announcing the death of his only sister, Osada, arrived in a letter that took three months in transit. He kept this news to himself for there was no respite from work for the men and no church to go to. All by himself he repaired to some unfrequented corner near the camp and said prayers for the departed soul of his only sister. Without the understanding comfort of their mother, Osada's lot as the only woman in the house besides her step-mother had not been easy and to have died without marrying seemed very unfortunate and pitiful in Torao's conception.

Three years elapsed in due course of time. It was a long three years: yet when it expired it did not seem to have been too long. At last he was a free man to do with his life as he pleased. The death of Osada seemed to have given him the opportunity to take stock of his future—the opportunities back home in Japan in contrast to what this new land of Hawaii seemed to offer. His father seemed to be making good under the capable management of his second wife. The other brother was too young to remember his real mother and seemed to be happy with his half brothers and sisters. The pioneering sturdy blood that enabled his father to do well in the peasant army during the last days of the feudal system was coursing strongly in his young veins. The mental aspiration crushed during the three years of servitude was still there; the energy of the free man was welling up inside his powerful body of twenty-five years.

The third member of this party, Okawa, on that fatal night at Honokaa, ran as fast as his legs would carry him and plunged into the cane field. As he lay flat on the ground feeling his heart pounding wildly against his shirt and the rise and fall of his breath that shook his entire body, he had time to figure things out and the fate of his comrades became his next concern. The ominous quiet and the cessation of the pounding hoofbeats meant either the stalking maneuver of the policeman or his withdrawal empty-handed. In that event he wanted to find out what became of his two companions. Carefully he peered out between the cane stalks from his hiding place and interpreted the plain story in the three figures delineated clearly in the moonlight. The agreement among the trio had been that in case of a happening such as this the surviving one was to make the trip by himself to the destination and establish contact with the ones left behind. Therefore, although tremendously shaken by this sudden turn of events he decided to proceed alone.

When the policeman and his two friends disappeared down the hill he came out of hiding and directed his course in the opposite direction. The road became narrower. In fact, except for the ruts of passing wagons, grass covered the roadbed. The trees were so tall they obstructed the moonlight and dismal darkness lay in his path. There were no wild animals to fear but many cats roamed about the countryside and their bright eyes sent a chill up and down his spine until he discovered what they were. He took five days to cross the plateau. He avoided the highway and in doing this he had to take to the cattle range where the untamed beef cattle of the Parker Estate roamed over the vast rolling grassland by the hundreds.

Not accustomed to cattle either wild or domestic, he had the usual fear of men for the horned beasts. The presence of bulls among them made his adventure more precarious. One night in particular as he lay under an eucalyptus tree and was fast asleep, he felt on his face the breath of a beast nudging against his body. He opened his eyes to discover an inquisitive cow hovering over him. He pretended to be dead and remained motionless and breathless. He had once heard that northerners would act dead when they accidently met a bear in the woods. Wild animals if not carnivorous were not supposed to attack unless they themselves were afraid. A dead man would not be considered dangerous even by the most stupid animal.

Luckily, in the woods there were thimble berries and passion fruit to fill his stomach and he was fortunate to stumble across a banana tree with ripe fruit on it. Once out of the wooded region and onto the grassy land, ripe guava trees dotted the plain but drinking water was a problem. This he solved by scooping up water found in cattle hoofprints. Cowboys were not in attendance on these cattle as the Parker Estate comprised hundreds of thousands of acres and was one of the largest cattle ranches of the world. There were no fences for miles and miles.

Okawa was very careful in conserving the precious pancakes he had been given at Honokaa and decided to keep them until no fruit was obtainable. When he saw the village of Kamuela in the distance among the groves of eucalyptus trees he made a wide detour and skirted the base of the hill to the east. Then he found himself in the drier section of the plateau and headed for Kohala which he figured would be toward the sea to his right. The terrain took on a sudden change in appearance and there was no longer the abundance of moisture and luxuriance of vegetation. Grass was sparse and cacti and lantana dotted the landscape. He had to be careful about discovery as natural obstacles behind which

112

he might hide became scarce. He sheered away from the highway and travelled in the heart of the cattle ranch heading downward toward the seashore. He became accustomed to the glassy stare of cattle and had learned that they were harmless unless he had aggressive intentions against them.

Finally, he came to a gulch and followed it toward the sea. Then he came to cultivated cane fields. On looking down further, he espied the red corrugated iron roofs of a laborers' camp amidst the green fields in the distance and approached this site carefully. He hid himself for about half an hour until he saw a woman come out of the house and he was certain that his countrymen dwelled here. It was near noon and men were out to work. He came out of hiding after making sure that no one was approaching the camp. He knocked at the door of the kitchen where the woman was working. She was taken aback at his strange appearance, but on finding out the story she hurriedly prepared for him an impromptu meal of canned salmon and cold rice. It was then that Okawa pulled out his bundle of precious pancakes. They were as hard as rocks and he tried to eat one of them but try as he might, he could not swallow it.

So, of the three fugitives, one got safely to Niuli Kohala and was given work on the plantation without any questions being asked. Perhaps because of the distance and the fact that they belonged to altogether different political districts there was no close cooperation between the Hamakua and Kohala plantations. He wrote to his friends at Waipunalei about what he found at this new place where the laborer's lot was much easier but the latter had already resigned themselves to their fate and did not relish going through the same grueling experience again. Okawa worked here for about a year and then went out to Honolulu.

At the expiration of the labor contract, a certificate of such fulfillment was given the laborers. These graduates were called "non shipped men" in contrast to "shipped men" for contract laborers. Everybody looked forward to the day when he would be graduated from the lowly status.

In later days when his son grew up, acquired a college education, and sent him a photograph of himself in cap and gown and holding a real sheepskin diploma, Torao wept and in some of his rare moments of sentimental exposé related that there had been only two really happy moments in his life. The first was the time when he received this certificate releasing him from bondage and the second was when

113

his son received a degree from a reputable institution of learning. The first was an emergence of his sunken self to that of a normal free being; the second was the advancement of his son, who was in a sense a continuation and fulfillment of his ideals and frustrated hopes in life into the group of the elite.

Because his attempt to escape made him a marked man, he had to watch his step very closely. His industry was genuine. He not only worked as best as he could, he was thrifty. He did not smoke and for the duration of his contract he cut out his drinking altogether. Therefore at the end of the three years he was in possession of about one hundred and fifty dollars. As soon as he became "non shipped man" his wages became eighteen dollars per month, and he continued to work with the animals, which were mostly imported Oregon mules.

The treatment of free men was not as harsh as in contract days and so he no longer wanted to move away although he was at liberty to do so if he so desired. The thing he had most in mind then was to find a mate. Therefore he wrote to his father that he wished to marry and asked him to find a suitable bride, preferably from among the belles of the village he had known, if they were still available. In three years' time, naturally, many had settled down to raise families, but there were a few still in circulation. His father sent him a list of such young women plus a few from neighboring towns and villages. Among these he came across the name of Chizu Omura and he lingered long over the image and reminiscences resurrected by her name.

He had met her many times when he used to go to Amizu to his mother's home. Chizu lived on the way thither and as her brother was in his class at school, he spent many an afternoon at her home. Her family had once been prosperous farmers and owned the choicest rice-fields near the spring of water which irrigated the villagers' fields. Naturally, proximity to this source of irrigation water enhanced the value of the land.

Her eldest brother was a good fellow but not extra bright, and even before he became of age was led astray by the dandies of the village and tasted the cheap pleasures of the night life at teahouses and could not forget the caresses of the painted women of these establishments. His friends were playing him for a sucker, catered to his whims, and encouraged his wild spendings. His father had died when he was still a

114

boy and now being of age he was master of his house. His mother was powerless to prevent his squandering.

Finally it came to pass that a general meeting of relatives had to be called to discuss and remedy the situation, but at this stage there was left only a few of the choice lands that had been handed down from the ancestors. Most of the rice patches had been signed off to the money-lenders at ridiculous prices. Their intervention was too late. The damage was already done. They only retained the family residence and half an acre of rice land which was not enough to feed the family of four. The mother was sickly and her vision was failing. The second brother was dependable but was in service with the army as a conscript. For this reason, Chizu had not married and remained at home to look after her disappointed mother. Being the last child and an only girl, she had been babied and used to sleep with her mother until she was fourteen. But in those days of early marriages twenty-two was considered very old for a bride and although she did not mind it, even her mother became concerned and asked friends to be on the lookout for a suitable match for her daughter.

Then out of a clear sky a proposition came to the family. Torao Murayama had asked for her hand. Would the family consider it? The aged mother did not give it a thought. "Hawaii? How can Chizu go to such a far-off corner of the world! When my deathbed comes Chizu must stay nearby to give me the last cup of water. Chizu herself would hardly give it a thought. I am sure of this."

"But, mother, you must not be so hasty. You are not the one who is going to get married. Let us hear what Chizu has to say. The Murayama family is a reputable family and with their connection with Amizu, this match is not one to be just passed off casually."

To their profound surprise, Chizu's answer was in the affirmative and she would even chance the four thousand miles of perilous voyage if it was to go to the side of Torao-san. Enough had been written home by the different emigrants to Hawaii to give the villagers some definite picture of the far-off islands. Besides, there were some men who had returned from overseas with their pockets lined with hard-earned cash. The picture these men painted did not seem wholly gloomy and fearsome. In her make-up there was an adventuresome strain and a hard common horse-sense that was lacking in her elder brother who squandered the family fortune. Neighboring old women used to say, "Chizu has inherited all the brains of the family. It is a pity that she was not born a boy."

Now that such a proposition had come from Torao she recalled all she could remember of him and was surprised to discover that she did have some secret longing for him. It was a dormant sentiment and lay deep, undetected even by herself. Simply, there had been no occasion to make her realize her submerged sentiment. A triggering was necessary for the emergence of this feeling.

There was a day when she was about fifteen when her second brother urged her to go shellfish gathering on the shore off the Sumiyoshi Hill. At the fishing village of Kasaiwa there was a married aunt and they could go there and spend the day on the sandy beach. It was a warm day in late summer or early autumn and she was glad to get away from home. In this party there were Torao and his sister Osada. The entire morning they went wading into shallow pools left by the ebbing tide, where fish swam and crabs darted away. With rakes they went back and forth on the sandy surface of the exposed bay bottom. The boys pulled on the huge heavy rakes and the girls followed in the wake of this receding implement and gathered the shrimps and crabs that were turned up from their buried recesses. Then they dug into the soft sandy loam and obtained many clams that seemed to be abundant in that particular season. At noon they repaired to their aunt's home and had their fun cooking what they had caught. It was a delightful day and she recalled it with fond remembrance.

When the negotiation for the marriage was finally arranged, two hundred yen was forwarded by the Murayama family so that she might arrange and prepare for the coming marriage. This custom of presenting the bride with money was called "sending the *yuino kin*." With this money presentation, there was usually a small party. There was a return from the bride's family to the groom's, again usually a fraction of the *yuino*. This amount was only nominal, but this gesture formally concluded the engagement.

Knowing the reduced circumstances of the family, Sadaki told them that she might remain with her mother to perform her share of filial piety as long as she was in Japan and need not come to live with them as the custom decreed for brides. She could stay with her mother until the six months' period elapsed before she could start on her trip to Hawaii.

116

She was somewhat reticent to leave her aging mother behind, but since the second brother was sensible and now was about to get married, she could entrust her mother's care to her new sister-in-law. She had her own life to live. She knew full well the kind of life a spinster might expect for her future, especially in such reduced circumstances as hers were. So after many nights wherein mother and daughter wept together, the day arrived when she was to start the first lap of her long journey to her husband.

CHAPTER 11

A Bride Comes to the Plantation

THUS IN THE YEAR 1899, WE FIND CHIZU united with Torao in the Immigration Station and subsequently at the Yamashiro Hotel in Honolulu. They struck up an acquaintance with the Arata family of Kauai during their sojourn in Honolulu. From the Inter-Island wharf, Pier 13, they boarded the *SS Mauna Kea*. The men had come to see them off and as they stood on the wharf waiting for the side door to the steerage quarters to open they looked around with interest on the bustling scene that characterized the waterfront on a steamer day. There was a pungent odor of gunny sacks that were piled high at one corner awaiting loading. Boxes and crates of merchandise were pyramided high with ports of export printed on the sides—Hong-kong, Yokohama, Kobe, Calcutta, New York, New Orleans, etc., and consigned to the big wholesale houses of Davies, Hackfield, etc. The excited mass of humanity on the scene was equally varied regarding their place of origin: Polynesians, Malayans, Orientals, and Caucasians.

As in all parting scenes at wharves, different from hurried farewells at railroad stations, there was a festive air mixed with a touch of sadness. There was a group talking in monotones; there was another group hilarious and back-slapping. There were numerous bows among the Orientals and much kissing among the whites and Hawaiians. To Chizu and no less to Torao, these sights were novel and exotic. Most queer and in a way beautiful were the garlands of flowers that friends hung about the necks of friends and travelers.

The most impressive of all was a scene enacted by two aged Hawaiians. They both must have been over sixty. One was traveling for he was bedecked with "leis" around his neck and on his hat. He was clad in a faded blue shirt, white linen pants, and wore no shoes. He only had a single friend to see him off—a friend similarly clad. Nobody paid any attention to this pair, for there was no distinguishing mark about them to set them apart from the ordinary natives on the streets and on the pier. But soon they began an old native singsong, undulating chant. There was an immediate hush and people crowded around this pair. The lei bedecked native was standing with bowed head and hat in hand raised to his breast. With the steamer as his background, his friend stood in front of him about seven feet away rendering this ancient chant to his friend who was on the brink of crossing an ocean infested with many sharks. Evidently such a chant was offered in ancient days to the maritime gods to propitiate any wrath and ensure a safe voyage in the days when the largest seagoing vessel was a double outrigger canoe.

Torao did not understand the language. Yet the chant almost half-wailing and half-beseeching possessed a deep element of the mysterious which was so akin to the *utai* of ancient Japan that he was spellbound and watched intently this scene which bespoke so much of male friendship. There were tears in the eyes of the two old men, and as the song ended the two approached each other and went into a tight embrace. Torao thought he saw nothing more moving than the friendship between these two of the old order of Hawaiian natives who were oblivious to surroundings and expressed their innermost feelings so beautifully and nobly.

The door to the steerage quarters was opened and each passenger carried his luggage into the hold. The Murayama's found a suitable nook where there would be no passing sailors stepping on the extended feet of reclining figures. Soon a Chinese man peddling mats came around and Torao procured two. The stench was overpowering. Chizu was a very poor sailor but luckily her husband was a very good one. She kept orange peelings in front of her nose to modify the odoriferous unpleasantness which assailed her and brought her repeatedly to the verge of vomiting.

The SS *Mauna Kea* began to roll and dip as soon as she got out of the harbor. Off Diamond Head the rolling became so pronounced that even Torao had to lie down for the moment. In the Molokai Channel the swells were larger and the motion of the ship became more regular and not so hard on the passengers. Toward evening the Chinese came around and took orders for evening meals. Twenty-five cents for a plate of stew or curried rice on a tin plate plus ten cents for a cup of coffee. Torao ordered the meal for himself only, for to his wife even the mere mention of food was nauseating.

It was a restless night. The steamer made many stops; Kaunakakai, Lahaina, Malae, Mahukona, and Kawaihae were touched before they got to Laupahoehoe, where they were to land.

The next day dawned when they came to the region off the wild coast between Kohala and Waipio. The green rugged countryside was broken into many sections of isolated, uninhabited woodland by deep ravines at the bottom of which many swift streams that came thundering to their terminus and entered the ocean from a height of five hundred feet or more. These beautiful waterfalls were arranged like ribbons of white against the green panorama.

After they sighted the village of Waipio where the pattern of rice fields cultivated by Chinese could be easily discerned even from the distance, they could see the sugar plantations of Kukuihaele and Honokaa and Torao was queerly moved when his eyes roved over the sugar cane fields toward the wooded section at the upper part of the plantation. There lay the site where he was captured in his ill-fated escape three years previously. What would have happened had he succeeded in his flight? It surely could not have been any better than now. It was a grueling three years that followed, no doubt, but he was rewarded for his silent uncomplaining acquiescence to the dictates of fate. He was now married, a status every respectable and honest woman or man covets.

Off Paauhau Plantation there was loading of sugar going on at the landing. A cargo ship was anchored off shore and a large boat approached the platform built on the rocks at the base of the precipitous cliff. A cable car went up and down the cliffs bearing sacks of sugar and carrying supplies for the plantation. On the platform stood a stationary derrick which hoisted the bundles of sugar sacks and deposited them in the boats and unloaded the vessels of their sacks of fertilizer and lumber and merchandise crates. This landing was unique along the Hilo-Hamakua coast. Most plantations had a wire cable connecting the landing on top of the cliff with the cargo vessel's deck and the cargo was sent down or hauled up on this wire rope, the motive power being furnished by the cable hoist in the landing house on the land.

The sight of the Hamakua coast from the sea in the early hours of the morning, especially for those who know the country was always an exciting and picturesque scenery—the imposing massive mountain chain in the center, sometimes snowcapped and reflecting the morning rays of the sun—fringed around the base by a green forest belt that gave way to the greener acreage that constituted the cultivated portion of sugar cane. Here and there were areas of young sugar cane. At other places, yellow dried leaves of recently harvested fields altered the generally uniform green pattern of the plantations. Everything was green and refreshing. Even the deep gulches were not bare. The steep sides were forested with groves of yellowish-green kukui trees. The sea was always rough, especially off the Ookala coast, and the waves battering against the rocky shore broke up into fine sprays of white that glistened in the morning sun.

The port of Laupahoehoe was reached at about eleven o'clock in the morning and the *S.S. Mauna Kea* stopped her engines. She just drifted while a whaleboat was lowered to accommodate passengers and freight. Down the ladder went the passengers to board the boat. The little craft rose and fell with each of the waves that passed underneath. A huge native sailor held on to the ladder to keep the boat from drifting away from the mother ship while another sailor helped each passenger as he stepped from the ladder into the boat. Thus boarding was accomplished trickily when the boat rode on the crest of the wave and the distance between the two ships became opportune for the novice to step down. It was a precarious step to take for any landsman, and the sailor was there just for the purpose of lending a helping hand. This whaleboat was then rowed to the shore by four stalwart native seamen and there again was the precarious leap one had to make to jump onto the land when the boat rose with the incoming surf to the highest point. The landing place was situated in a little inlet, but the waves were high even in this cove. To the seasick Chizu this was a grueling experience and made her subsequently so sick of the sea that thereafter the mere sight of a steamer brought on a psychic reaction simulating mal-de-mer.

After gathering their luggage Torao decided to spend the day and night at a hostelry at the port rather than proceed immediately to the plantation, as his wife had had such a miserable experience coming over. They went to the Omon Hotel on the government highway to rest.

Mr. Omon combined his hotel business with fish peddling. To Waipunalei he came with fish every time the fishing boat that went out of Laupahoehoe made port with a catch. This fish was of the lowly sort such as "akule" and "opelu," for the more expensive variety was beyond the purchasing power of his clientele and the fishermen specialized in the fish which were more abundant and easily caught in this section.

Torao could ask him to take them out the next day to the plantation in case there was no other means of transportation in that direction.

There were quite a few lodgers at the hotel. These had been domiciled in Hawaii for some years and were men who detested work and chose to live by using their wits and nimble fingers. This parasitic class was considerable in number and even the remotest plantations were not overlooked in their systematic scheme of exploitation. On pay days they would swarm to the plantations and gather in the silvers from the laborers. There was a famous gangleader in Hilo, Funakoshi Tatsugoro by name, who had twenty or more henchmen to do the business in the different plantations on the Hamakua coast. The island of Hawaii was divided up into different spheres of interest among the gang leaders and gambling games could not be held unless sponsored by this gangster.

On the afternoon of the monthly pay day, in order not to be caught by the manager, the gamblers infiltrated into the camps by twos and threes. Wada was a representative of the gang at Waipunalei and towards evening, would open the game in his bunk and see to its orderly conduct. He was a gambler from Japan, and to attest to his former exploits his body was covered by a tattooed dragon. He was from Kobe and there was a rumor that he had escaped capture by the police after a murder case in which suspicion was directed his way. He had a year more of his contract to serve.

On the matted floor, the players sat cross-legged in a circle. Two dice were placed in a smooth tea cup without a handle, and after jiggling, the cup was placed face down on the floor. The dice were thus covered and betting followed. The winner was the one who guessed the sum total of the face on the dice. The game was fast and stakes could reach enormous figures. Wada had a wooden box which was padlocked and had a hole big enough to admit a silver dollar. This was the "kitty" and went to Funakoshi of Hilo, a tribute he exacted from the sporting element of plantation workers. Such games might continue for several nights on a plantation and the intervening idle days between pay days in different plantations were spent by the professionals at a neutral zone such as Laupahoehoe or Hilo, where they lived peacefully in hotels away from the capitalistic scrutiny of plantation policemen.

Torao knew some of them who came to Waipunalei regularly. Since they traveled a great deal, they were up-to-date concerning inside information about any development on the island of Hawaii. He asked them about the new industrial project at Olaa of which he had heard in Honolulu. He learned in the city that there was considerable clearing of virgin forests at Olaa with the idea of planting coffee. Some capitalists wanted Olaa to be a second Kona. He got further news from one of them that there was a hostelry in Olaa, which the owner, a Mr. Uyeda, wanted to sell to a suitable buyer. The gambler added that in addition to the money that would be spent by these laborers working on the clearing project, there was a steady source of business income to be derived from travelers who were crossing from Hilo to Kau, a distance of sixty miles, and he knew the proprietor well because he not only was a frequent lodger there, but he was from the same village in the old country. Torao got Mr. Uyeda's address and thanked the gambler for the information. Some scheme was brewing in his mind. The next day he took his bride to the Douglas Plantation at Waipunalei.

Women were employed at thirty-five cents a day in the fields hoeing weeds in the young cane. There were about two dozen women who were in this "wahine gang." It was a pity, Torao thought, that his wife should be working in the hot sun. Of course she did not mind the work because she had worked in the fields while in Japan, but to him it did not seem right that his wife should be working so hard. So while he was in Honolulu, he was interested in the news that was circulating and discussed around Aala Park.

The Dillingham interests which had been singularly successful in the construction and maintenance of the Oahu Railway were interested in opening up the Hilo Railroad and forming a sugar plantation in the region of Olaa among the lava fields that had served only as grazing ground for cattle. It was talked about in town that thousands of people would be employed and the pay would be immensely better than on the sugar plantations. One gang boss by the name of Onome Bunichiro was given the job of recruiting and supervising labor in the clearing of this vast acreage of land. In a pioneering work of that sort there would be chances for profit a lot more substantial than the paltry sum paid on the sugar estates.

Now that Torao was married, he had to plan for the future which would involve a family. Some bold attempt to break away from the path of the common laborer must be made or else he could visualize himself a graying man with back-breaking toil to perform every day, burdened with half-dozen children, with no prospect of ever giving them a decent education and chance in life, and no hope of ever returning to his native village with something to be proud of. His future did not seem too bright. At Waipunalei, with the prevailing system of tenure, there was no chance whatever of going into contract work. At some plantation, contract work was let out to enterprising men who would care for the growing cane until harvest. He had heard that such a system of contract work would be adopted at Olaa.

The chance encounter at the hotel at Laupahoehoe that resulted in the information about a hotel at Olaa being on sale was a stroke of luck. If he and Chizu could make some money at this sort of vocation, then she need not toil in the fields exposed to the elements ten hours a day. Even if he could not purchase this hostelry, writing to this Mr. Uyeda would not be for naught for thereby he would be able to learn more specific facts about the development scheme of that particular region.

There was an answer to his inquiry immediately and he was asked if he could not come to Olaa, as such a negotiation ought to be done and could be done much more profitably and smoothly by the two parties coming face to face. He saw the point and at once decided to make the trip. After getting permission from the head overseer on the pretext of going to see a cousin in Hilo who was desperately ill and on the verge of death, he departed and legged the fifty miles to Olaa.

It took him two days to get to Hilo. The roads were poor and muddy when it rained. At certain stretches there were unsavory and fearful rumors. For instance at the Maalua Gulch, Puerto Ricans were said to ambush pedestrians and strip them naked. Such sites were better negotiated in the day time. As he approached Hilo, he was stopped on the bridge of Wainaku by a Japanese who was fat and tanned like a native. He wore a mustache, a khaki uniform, and a pair of leather putties. He showed Torao a tin badge and announced that he was a representative of the Tax Office. Asked what he wanted, Torao was ordered to show his poll tax receipt. Torao had been told that such a testimony was necessary in boarding an inter-island ship, but did not think it necessary to carry it on his person on an overland travel. He had, therefore, nothing to show that he had paid his annual poll tax of five dollars.

"Then you have to work it off."

"How?"

"By working ten days on a farm where such delinquency is made up by actual labor. At fifty cents a day, you will work it out in ten days."

Having no friends in Hilo to put up the five dollars, he had to follow what this officer told him to do. Used to following orders of uniformed men without questioning since boyhood, he was docile and was led up toward the mountain where clearing of forest lands was in progress. There was a man by the name of Hieda who ran this place. There were two men already there and Torao had to share the bunk house with them.

Their work consisted of hoeing hono-hono, the green prolific wandering-Jew, and burying this grass in a hole dug in the ground. In the days when chemical spray was not in use this was the only way to rid the fields of this pest because it rained every day. There was not enough sunshine to kill off this plant even when the root was severed and uprooted. Even from a cut stem, roots emerged to survive and multiply.

The food was atrocious but they did not complain—realizing the fact that they were prisoners and working off their indebtedness to the government. The tax office man had told Torao that if he produced this year's receipt later on, the work he had to do now would be credited to the following year's tax payment. It seemed rational and as he had a wholesome respect for the law, he complied without a murmur, because this was better than being locked up. The truth was bared later however when he went to Olaa and related this experience.

Mr. Uyeda said, "The whole setup is a racket. That tax office man Nakata is in 'cahoots' with Hieda and is getting innocent workers to work on that land near Hilo for nothing. He gets ten days' labor out of the men and the receipt he issues is a phony. There have been dozens of men passing here to Kau that have been so victimized."

"Well, of all the low-down tricks this takes the cake! Who would ever suspect that a fellow countryman in this distant land would be so mean and heartless as to actually indenture another man underhandedly Something ought to be done about it."

"Certainly, something ought to be done about it. It is a most stinking racket and the talk of the town. But who has the nerve to openly tackle it? Like all other big business it is under the protection of the gambler Funakoshi, and today he is the lord of the Japanese community of Hilo until better days arrive when the good people can raise their voice. For the time being we must remain dumb and watch the evil men have their fling at soft and easy living. But you know the old proverb, 'The boisterous, bragging one does not last long.' Our turn will soon come around, sooner than you think."

The epilogue to this little incident did come around soon. A huge amount of dynamite was being used in the pioneering work of railroad construction and clearing of jungle land at Olaa. To store these dangerous explosives, the basement of Hieda's house was rented by the contractor for storage. Two hundred of these cases were stored under the house. In this rainy region houses were built about ten feet above the ground, and the basements were spacious enough to hang washing. One night when his wife and children had left for Hilo to take in an itinerant show, there was a terrific explosion that sent the entire establishment into a thousand pieces. Only fragments of the avaricious Hieda could be gathered in the charred wreckage. There was not a clue to be found to unravel the probable perpetrator of the crime. It pointed toward an incendiary act and he had created so many enemies that even a cat could not survive their wrath.

Because he had not been on very good terms with his sister-in-law, his brother was taken into custody for questioning. The police had to do something and picked on this man who was the epitome of good behavior. Because he was such a good man, it troubled him greatly. To be even suspected of killing his own brother was such a shock to him, he could not possibly explain the thing to his parents and friends even though he was sure to be proved innocent. At the end of a week of brooding he could stand the strain no longer and hanged himself in the detention cell. The police did not act further. The case was closed.

The meeting with Mr. Uyeda progressed very smoothly. The elder man took an instant liking to the youngster who was not spoiled by city life and had the straightforwardness that was characteristic of the men of his prefecture. Incidentally, Mr. Uyeda himself hailed from the same province. Torao told him that he wanted to build up something for himself and his prospective family and that he had come to the conclusion that such a thing could not be accomplished by mere toiling on a plantation, and, frankly, he had not much cash to offer him for the hotel.

Sometimes it happens that business is conducted purely on the basis of mutual liking and trust. It is conducted between men on a plane above the usual considerations attendant upon such transactions. Such a feeling prevailed when the two discussed the transaction over a glass of beer. Mrs. Uyeda suffered from an intractable asthma and the principal cause of her paroxysms seemed to lie in the atmospheric condition—wet and pollen-laden—for she was completely free of the attacks when she visited Honolulu where it was dry. Therefore, to the Uyedas, it was not a matter of making a profit by this sale. A business that they two had begun and fostered over a period of years was an institution symbolizing their joint effort and they would rather see it in the hands of a person who was agreeable rather than transfer it only for a higher bid.

Torao remained there for two days and inspected the influx of new men from the old country, as well as the amount of traffic over the volcano way to the districts of Kau and Kona. At best, it was a country hostelry and unimposing, and with his meager capital and total lack of experience, he could not hope for much. At least, here was something that he could engage in as his own and not be subject to the whims of other men and be forced to curry their favor. The prospects for the future seemed much brighter and more enticing here in this young community. He decided to chance buying this hotel.

There were two hotels at the eighteenth mile post on the way to Kau from Hilo. One was owned by Mr. Inouye and was patronized mostly by gamblers. Working men of neighboring plantations who wanted to increase their hard earned cash the easy way filtered into this frontier where there was no head luna to go after their games. Games were held day and night. The more respectable element who made up the itinerant peddlers and ordinary travelers took their lodging at the Uyeda Hotel now run by the Murayamas. Chizu adapted herself to this new life quickly and from Mrs. Uyeda learned the secret of institutional cooking. She was coached for a month in the gentle art of handling coarse frontier men. It required some real art to keep them in place.

This whole region produced coffee grown by homesteaders inspired by the singular success of pioneers in Kona who had been rewarded for their foresight and industry. The slopes of the Kona coast were extensively planted with coffee and the coffee berries were of a very high quality. At Olaa, homestead lots had been surveyed and allotted to independent farmers and many white families were actively engaged in enlarging their holdings in the region of the hotel.

But it was soon discovered that this district was too wet for coffee. The trees grew to immense heights like all vegetation but the trees did not bear well and the berries lacked the necessary sugar ingredient to make them first class products. But the Olaa Sugar Company was organized and it bought up the coffee lands to add to the sugar acreage that had been opened up in the lower altitudes. There were three thousand Japanese laborers under Mr. Onome engaged in this work of starting a new plantation. These laborers came in by the hundreds and were quartered in hastily constructed bunk houses along the road between Hilo and the Volcano.

There was a set routine with which the plantation welcomed these workers the moment they landed at Hilo. All their scant luggage was piled on wagons and the men were made to walk sixteen to eighteen miles to their destination whether it rained or shined. For food they were each given three pieces of hardtack and a can of salmon. Without any forethought and little suspecting that their provisions would consist only of the aforesaid articles for the ensuing two days, they would all devour them in the first meal. Their trek of six or more hours made them extremely hungry and they were afraid to eat any of the edible fruits that were there on the side of the road for the picking. Arriving at the camp toward evening there would neither be a welcoming committee nor any warm meal awaiting them.

Usually each new contingent was sent to a new camp to avoid the corrupting influence of the old-timers on the new arrivals. They would have to lie down on the dust covered floor drenched to the skin when they were wet. They could consider themselves lucky if they could start cooking on the following day, and they were fortunate if some kindhearted neighbors were near to lend them cooking utensils and some food.

However, despite all the hardships, the immigrant workers managed to get by. In the work of felling huge ohia trees, digging up the roots of giant tree-ferns, and then gathering these into stacks to burn, they found plenty to do. It was hard, rough, and rather hazardous work.

A memorable incident connected with the labor situation took place in this place. At the twentieth mile from Hilo near the pond of water that gathered in a hollow left by volcanic flow on the Puna side of the main highway, there was a mixed gang of about one hundred and fifty men. It was made up of Portuguese, Hawaiians, Spaniards, Puerto Ricans, and about thirty-five Japanese. The work was contract or piece work. More work accomplished meant more money. Therefore the struggle to be assigned to a good piece of land or one easier to work on was constantly arising among the workers.

To make matters worse, a certain luna, Holland by name, showed marked partiality to the non-Japanese and was always bearing hard on the Japanese. He would find fault with the result of the work, always allot to the Japanese the worst piece of land, and even find fault in the way their work was being done. Since work was done on a sub-contract system there was no ground to interfere with the way men worked. Whether they loafed or worked doubly hard should have been no concern of Holland's, but he did make it his business to show his authority. He would come riding on his white horse and crack a horsewhip over the back of the toiling men if he was in a bad humor. Finally, the men were seized with a fear complex and they associated it with the white horse. Not being able to converse in the language of the country, they were not able to answer back, and having no recourse to civil courts since they were under contract, they had to bear this brutality silently. The crisis, however, arrived and in a most violent way.

One day the water boy was beaten without any provocation whatsoever by the man on the white horse when he was sitting down during his rounds of supplying the men with drinking water. He had to convalesce in the barracks as the result of this injury and when the salesman from the Onome Store came to take orders, he heard the details of this outrage. He reported the incident to his employer. Mr. B. Onome was about five feet ten inches and large for a Japanese. He was an educated man of forty-two and was bewhiskered. This added dignity and prestige among his countrymen who were mostly clean shaven. He was on his way to the mainland United States but chose to remain in the islands for he saw vast opportunities for a properly qualified man. He contracted to supply and oversee laborers for the newly formed Olaa Plantation and ran a store as his own enterprise.

Mr. Onome had been hearing about this brutal handling of men that he had helped secure employment and had been groaning to himself at the inhumanity and injustice of it all. This story was the spark that kindled within his mind a scheme that had been brewing for some time. Secretly, he sent runners to all influential men of the Japanese communities as far as Papaikou and enlisted all men versed in the arts of Jujitsu.

Fifty-two experts were recruited. In addition, young men good in wrestling were gathered, bringing the total number to about eighty. These men could fight with bare hands and were promised five dollars apiece for this new venture.

The wrestlers arrived at eighteen miles toward evening, and were lodged in the two hotels. About twenty came to the hotel run by the Murayamas. Torao sensed something ominous, but the nature of their undertaking was not divulged. On the following forenoon the other contingent arrived in several wagon loads and went into conference. The war council was presided over by a representative of Mr. Onome, as he himself could not openly show his involvement in this uprising.

"You are assembled here from distant localities for a specific purpose. I am sure you have a vague idea as to what the problem is and what is expected of you. In a nutshell I am going to explain to you the condition of this place. We have a luna—a white man on a white horse by the name of Holland. He is a brutal beast. He seems to derive pleasure in beating innocent workers. He is particularly harsh to our fellow countrymen, and this partiality is beyond reason and common sense. The other nationalities are more favored. Bodily injury at the hand of this Holland person has been incurred by about half a dozen men and we can no longer brook this insult. The other nationalities will probably take sides with Holland. They outnumber us three to one. With their bigger physique, they will be over-confident. You are picked men and trained to fight bare handed. Let us show them of what mettle we sons of the Far East are made. The floor is now open for discussion as to the best strategy for tomorrow's fight."

The final strategy adopted was as follows. The smaller stature of the combatants compared to that of the opponents and the greater strength of the hips and nimbleness of the footwork of the Japanese were taken into consideration and they planned to attack from the lower region. To avoid legal troubles, no weapon of any sort was allowed. However, it was permissible to use any captured implement of combat.

Somehow the plantation officials got wind of this plot. Their suspicion could not but be aroused when four scores of strong men loaded in several wagons passed the government road toward a region where labor trouble had been no secret to the authorities. At about eleven o'clock, two wagons sped up the road toward the mixed camp loaded with pickax and hoe handles in addition to machete-like cane knives. From this information, the Japanese men knew that their foe would be armed, but they did not care. They were confident that an inexperienced mob relying solely on brute strength would be mere child's play.

They ate their fill of rice cakes and broiled dried squids and each was given one cupful of rice wine to bless this martial undertaking. At one o'clock they advanced toward the twenty mile district. The terrain above eighteen miles was a steady, steep climb. The road was full of holes and ruts of wheels made by the numerous wagons and carts engaged in this clearance work. The land outside the road was barren as it was only recently cleared of its large trees and underbrush of ferns. It was a big, extensive field for maneuvering although very irregular and sloping. The scouts of the mixed gang evidently spotted the approach of the Japanese.

Led by the luna on his white charger, the cosmopolitan group advanced with the handles of implements as weapons, confident that they would make quick work of these little men who never did impress them much by their meek subjection to the overlording tactics of the overseer. Foreigners unable to speak the language are always looked down upon as inferior in all respects. They had broad grins on their faces. They numbered two hundred fifty to the enemy's eighty. Head-on they clashed.

The ensuing fight was a melee of yells, curses and painful cries. The weapons wielded by the mixed group did not find their mark for brute strength, primitive and strong, could not stand against a seasoned and well-trained group of men whose art of fighting emphasized the counter-use of the enemy's strength. Their weapons were soon snatched away from them and they got the brunt of the punishment.

The fight was very one-sided. Advancing down hill, the advancing cosmopolitan army had their legs scooped from under them, and when they tangled with the little men they found themselves sprawling flat on the ground, the victims of beautifully executed flying-mares. Soon they found the weight of their opponents on their backs and felt the raining fists on their faces and heads. When the attackers caught sight of the luna, Holland, on his famous white horse, several of them concentrated on him. He came charging headlong wielding the vicious cowhide whip, but was soon overpowered, dragged down, and beaten so badly that it was said he lay in his bed for weeks afterwards. There were numerous arms broken by vicious Jujitsu holds and several were knocked cold after being struck in vital spots known to these experts. The battle lasted for about two hours. The men reassembled at three o'clock after routing the mixed group.

After taking a hot bath to wash away the dirt and grime, the combatants felt refreshed and clean and were in high spirits. There was a grand celebration at the two hotels that night. Several barrels of rice wine and food good enough for the table of a prince came from the Onome store. Each recounted the story of the fight and his part in it amidst roars of laughter for there were many funny episodes. The casualties suffered by the Japanese consisted of bruises and minor cuts, whereas in the opposing camp a Portuguese died the following day and several days later two others died of injuries. It was a very exciting night for the Murayama couple, and they could scarcely sleep. Mr. Onome had sent word that no expense be spared in the entertaining of the participants of the fray and they did their best to cater to these young fighters.

The crowd was orderly. There was no rowdyism. They had to remain sober and were prepared for a possible counterattack during the night and on the alert for a police raid. Nothing happened. The next day they departed together toward Hilo in an orderly, inconspicuous manner but in a way to be able to quickly assemble for an emergency if the occasion demanded.

There was nobody to stop their return march. The police elected to do nothing. The plantation officials were told by Mr. Onome that the best policy was to do nothing about the whole episode. His argument was that probing of the unfortunate affair would only incite unrest among the three thousand laborers on the Olaa Plantation and also cause a sympathetic response on all the neighboring plantations along the Hilo region. This situation was surely something which the planters wanted to avoid if they possibly could. It was Onome who began the whole fight, and Onome who became the mediator. Thanks to this timely display of force, the treatment of laborers became much improved and overseers like the brutal Holland were cashiered.

In the meantime, Chizu became pregnant, but her sturdy heritage and healthy past stood her in good stead and the busy daily routine work at the hotel did not give her the luxury of taking to bed because of the slight nauseating feeling and indisposition that characterized the physiological change that comes to most women with the harboring of a new

132

life in their body. She kept on doggedly and in a month or two she became accustomed to her condition and the morning sickness left her too. She was careful in going up and down stairs and walking on slippery planks and boards outdoors. Torao was very solicitous concerning her condition, but there were many things about the work of running a hotel that only women could perform best and he had to let her do it, knowing perfectly well that she should not be. Torao said he did not mind whether it turned out to be a girl or a boy, but Chizu insisted that it was going to be a boy.

One morning in April just as the sun came out from the east, with only the help of a middle-aged woman of the neighborhood, she gave birth to a son. Both mother and infant did well and there was great rejoicing. The gamblers came around and for good-luck's sake deposited silver around the bed of the infant son. Torao traveled to Hilo to buy the famous Serrao wine to celebrate the occasion. This first son was named Minoru, literally meaning fruition or success.

The hotel business was progressing rather well considering the fact that it was an amateur's first endeavor in business. There was not yet the meanness among the rural folks to capitalize on the innocence and ignorance of the two. Their income was several times that of what they used to get at the plantation and with the birth of the son there seemed to be joy and carefreeness in the household that was infectious. Chizu did not lack nursemaids. The gamblers who had nothing to do in the daytime offered to mind the infant while his mother was busy with the various duties of the hotel. Besides, there was a superstition that to be carrying around a chubby boy was conducive to good luck in all sorts of games. It must have been so, for there was never a lack of men offering to carry the baby around. He was fat and chubby. He was a contented baby for there was abundant milk.

This happy start in business for the young couple was not destined to last long, however. Just about this time, Honolulu was visited by a terrible scourge. Rats infected with the virus of bubonic plague got a footing, probably from ships that came in from Hongkong or some other port of southern China where there had recently been an epidemic. There were many cases in Honolulu. In order to check the spread of the epidemic, Chinatown was ordered burned by an edict of the governor.

Next to the measles epidemic after Captain Cook visited the islands and carried off one third of the population, this black plague was most memorable in the history of Hawaii from a public health standpoint. Naturally the port of Honolulu was quarantined and the ships plying the Pacific avoided this pest hole. Being dependent largely on the outside world for her food supply and necessary daily articles, the hardship entailed upon the community was enormous. The stores were not prepared for such an eventuality, and shortage of food and other articles became very acute in a short while. This was especially so in the rural districts which were lowest on the priority column of the wholesale houses.

To run a restaurant or hotel under these circumstances was very difficult. Rice could not be had. Imports from the Orient stopped. The only rice producing community on the Island of Hawaii was Waipio and the amount produced there was limited. No condiments to produce tasty Japanese food could be bought. The daily menu consisted of dumplings made of flour with whatever vegetables could be had from local growers and vendors.

Torao ransacked the neighboring forests for edible shoots of ferns of which there were two varieties. One type was the curved shoots of the giant ferns which made very good eating after soaking in water and boiling in order to get the toxic material out of the fibers. After this preliminary treatment they made a very tasty dish cooked either with pork or beef. It looked like rhubarb and tasted like asparagus. Then there was the new shoots out of smaller ferns which might be cooked forthwith without preliminary treatment. The Hawaiian jungle offered mushrooms, an edible growth that grew parasitically on decaying guava and ohia trunks. These looked very much like animal ears and grew in layers, colored brown and almost transparent, and sprouted soon after a downpour in the cooler season. They made a tasty salad when treated with vinegar or when used as ordinary vegetables in cooking. Torao searched the forest far and wide for these things in order to produce a variation in the monotonous menu. His efforts were rewarded with an increase in permanent boarders, but the effect was of adverse benefit.

These permanent roomers consisted mostly of gamblers who would have been good customers in boom time, but when the financial condition of the countryside was critically affected by the plague epidemic, an increase in clientele of this class meant only a rising store bill. The amount of profit on the books increased but he actually went into the red with each day and the figure increased with the passing months. The

134

day finally came when they were forced to close shop and return to the plantation life that they vowed never to take up again.

CHAPTER 12

The First Born is Ambitious

AFTER LIQUIDATING THE BUSINESS AT OLAA, saddened but wiser by their recent reverses in independent enterprise, they returned to their old haunt, the Waipunalei Plantation. It seemed destiny had already prescribed that they should return and persist to eke out an existence on the dreary coast of Hamakua where even drinking water was a precarious proposition and the supply depended solely on an unpredictable rainfall. Habit was a wonderful thing and they headed for the erstwhile "demon plantation" for an indefinite sojourn. They could very easily have located themselves on one of the other sugar plantations. These had better reputations with ample water and the lunas were not so notoriously bad. Yet like children returning to their parents and home where they were born, even if it were located in the most desolate of places, they sought relief and a chance for new start at this place they knew as their first home in Hawaii.

Something different awaited them. Mr. Douglas, on hearing that Torao had returned, called him in to his office and told him that he was to become his yardman to look after his spacious grounds and to tend his horses. Torao was immensely pleased. This meant promotion for there was only one gardener to work there. It was clean work compared to laboring in the fields. In contrast to the dirty, roughly constructed bunk houses of the workers, the manager's house was a place with an extensive sloping green lawn, numerous fruit trees, luxuriant flowering vines, and magnificent silver oaks and monkey pods.

The cook was called Ah Chu, a very generous soul, with whom Torao got along famously. The maids of the residence were two Japanese women who took care of the Douglas' twin daughters. These four had no difficulties and they cooperated very well. He got to eat many different kinds of foodstuff that Ah Chu prepared and the Chinese even offered to teach him how to cook. He might have acquired the art if it had not been for the low perspective quality of his sensation of smell.

The mansion was built on an elevation and had a sweeping view of the entire camp site of the laborers. Beyond that the sugar mill near the sea could be taken in at a glance. In the morning, Torao's work consisted of going down to the stable near the mill and returning with the saddle horse for Mr. Douglas to ride for the day. Then he attended to the yard work all day and at three o'clock took the horse back to the stable so that it would be fed and bedded for the night. Since he had his quarters near the manager's home, he could return home for lunch. The work was very congenial.

Although his pay remained low, he considered his life significant and full of meaning. Daily it seemed, his son was growing and becoming more intelligent. He could now walk and was the cutest thing Torao had ever known. He had hardly dreamed or imagined that he could become so wrapped up in a child, for in general he was not particularly fond of children. This male child was going to perpetuate his family tree and was an indispensable link in the genealogy of the Murayama family. According to the tradition of the old country, this infant was the one to look after the ageing parents when he reached manhood. In other words, the birth, education, and attainment of adulthood of his male child was an insurance against want in his old age.

It was a selfish concept, but such was the tradition and the eldest son was looked upon in that light. No matter how many children might be born into the family later on, custom provided that the parents be cared for in the eldest family's home and in return the whole or the bulk of the estate was inherited by the first son. Transcending this selfish concept, there was always a spontaneous primitive parental bliss that overcame him whenever he held the child to his bosom and looked into its chubby face. Still, he was so filled with the old country idea of depending upon the eldest son for his old age support that he could not wholly feel that this bliss experienced spontaneously and unselfishly was ample compensation for all the worries and care that a parent had to go through in the rearing of a child.

Several years went by peacefully. The little son Minoru was a lovable child and being plump was petted by everyone. He had a ready smile for all and the older people nicknamed him "Ebesu-san," the jovial god of commerce and fishery and one of the seven gods of good luck, portrayed in pictures and statues as a laughing old man sitting cross-legged over sacks of rice and tucking a large red snapper under his arm. Being fat and laughing all the time earned Minoru that appellation.

When he was five years old—and he remembered the incident well in later life—the Russo-Japanese War was being fought in the Far East. The Japanese in Hawaii were deeply stirred, for they were all young men and many had to return to join the home regiment and proceed to the battle grounds of Manchuria. When the news of the surrender of the impregnable fortress of Port Arthur reached the islands there was a tremendous celebration on all the plantations. On the Hamakua Coast where the Scots had their plantation, the jubilation did not confine itself to the Japanese. It was welcome news to the managers and foreman and they were glad that their allies of the Far East were blocking the southward advance of the Russian Bear.

A holiday was declared by the manager and the entire plantation was in a festive mood. After a solemn gathering in which the prayer for the soldiers and sailors undergoing privations in the cold battle fronts of Manchuria and the Japan Sea and an eulogy for the dead was read by a leading citizen, Mr. Yamada of the store, the three "banzais" were chorused for the perpetuity of the Imperial House and another three for the success of the armed forces, the people broke loose to have some fun. A wrestling match had been announced and the young men vied with each other for the various prizes that had been donated by the plantation for the occasion.

After the *sumo* matches were over there was a costume parade. There were several attired in ancient national costume, some masquerading as natives doing the hula, some dressed as soldiers with wooden muskets, and to make the occasion one befitting the fall of Port Arthur, there were several Russian soldiers and officers bearing a white flag and surrounded by a group of Japanese soldiers whose commanding officer rode a white horse. This man must have been most proud to play the part for he was continuously twirling his mustache as he rode by on his charger amidst the applause of the onlookers.

There were several barrels of free rice wine for all who were thirsty. Being just after New Year, the climate was still cold and the men folk became festive and tipsy, but there was no brawling.

Almost every two years there was an addition to the Murayama family. The wages that the breadwinner earned were fixed at thirty dollars per month with little prospect of ever increasing, but there was no rent to pay, fuel was free, and medical care was guaranteed if one was satisfied with the rather indifferent medical service that was being rendered by the plantation doctor who treated his patients with quinine and castor oil. This plantation being a small one, the physician from the Paauilo Sugar Company took care of the patients of the Waipunalei region also. He came to the dispensary twice a week, and during the interim, Tanaka, who had acquired some smattering knowledge of nursing while he had been in the medical branch of the Japanese army, was stationed in the hospital that had ten beds. He cared for the in-patients, attended the simple medical cases, and performed first aid treatment for the injured in the out-patient department. Luckily, there were no serious cases occurring there as the inhabitants were mostly young and vigorous or perhaps the real sick got their death certificates signed before many knew about it.

Inadequate as the medical facilities were, the climate was healthy and even on the meager stipend that they were getting the Murayamas were able to get along. However, just to feed the increasing number of mouths was all they could manage and in order to earn some money to help buy necessities for the children, Chizu learned to use a sewing machine and she began sewing shirts, pants, and cloth sandals for the laborers. She managed to earn some fifteen additional dollars in this manner. It helped a great deal.

To raise children, there was no place like Hawaii, thought Chizu, for her children had nothing on their bodies except their outer garments the year round and went perennially barefoot. The childhood diseases so common in the temperate zone were absent in the equable climate of Hawaii. The only disease that her children had was measles. All her children, now four equally divided in sex, were healthy and strong. After Minoru there was a girl, Yae, and then came the second son. He was named Nichiro as he was born during the Russo-Japanese War. On the spur of the moment, Torao thought it was a fitting way to commemorate the historical happenings in the Far East by naming this son Nichiro which meant literally "Japan-Russia." This name was well lived up to for this boy was very pugnacious and independent. As soon as he was able to walk around, he showed his prowess by attacking everyone that came walking on two legs, and soon became the terror of the neighborhood. Never did a day pass that Chizu did not have to apologize to other mothers for the aggressiveness of her son. He tackled his equals with the weight of his body and the strength of his tiny arms, but when the opponent was bigger and stronger he did not hesitate on that score, and went into the fray literally with teeth and nails.

Chizu was getting fed up with the daily excuses and apologies she had to make to other women, and when the climax finally came she knew she had to radically change her routine. There was a rather nervous woman in the neighborhood whose children were equally frail and spoiled. One evening as the family was at supper, this woman suddenly appeared in the doorway: "Today, your Nichiro bit my son on no provocation at all. I am a peaceful woman and will not come to you concerning fights among children, but to bite anyone is an act I have never heard of before. He must be a dog to do such a thing!"

Torao had put down his bowl of rice and chopsticks and was politely listening to this fuss about the unsavory exploits of his son, but about which he was inwardly glad and a little bit proud. He wanted his sons to fight and win. Minoru was quiet and liked by all for his cheerfulness, but this second son was hated by all the mothers and he felt a peculiar attachment to this unruly offspring for his cussed pugnacity. Now this neurasthenic neighbor was calling his pet son "a dog." Livid in countenance, he stood up and slowly approached her in measured steps, and to her utter astonishment, there was a sharp resounding retort and a stinging slap went across her mouth. "Go and call your husband!" was the only thing he said.

Chizu was also astonished but not entirely taken off guard. She knew the temper of her man. Diplomatically, she got to her feet and escorted the now weeping woman out of the room. "I am extremely sorry for all that has happened. It is all my fault that such has come to pass. For all Nichiro's acts are my responsibility as his mother. I apologize to you and your husband. Let us go to your husband because I must explain and beg forgiveness."

The other man listened to Chizu's account frozen like a stone; not a muscle in his face moved. The silent, weeping wife confirmed the veracity of the story. For three minutes he did not utter a word nor move; then he got up and proceeded to the Murayama kitchen. "Mr. Murayama, I do not know how to make up for what my wife said. I know how angry you must have felt concerning the slip of tongue on the part of my wife, but please forget it. Women are so rash and thoughtless in what they say. As a man I apologize for the shortcomings of my wife." Torao rose to the speech of this man and with glistening eyes stretched out his hand. In the clasp of the two hands a mutual understanding and respect between them was established and they became fast friends.

Chizu began thinking. When she sewed all day at her machine making garments and work shoes for the field workers she would be stationed near the window in order to make the most of the sunlight. Every fight and mischief committed by Nichiro would be brought to her attention. If she could find something else to do that would take her away from her window, perhaps there would be less occasion to become involved in her son's daily exploits.

From the above motive and desire the Murayamas began to manufacture *tofu*, a custard-like preparation from ground soya beans. In order to make it, Chizu had to get up at three o'clock every morning to grind the beans that had been soaked in water and cooked the night before between two grindstones. The ground beans were then expressed through cheese cloth and the soluble portion saved and poured into square wooden receptacles. The addition of certain chemicals to the filtrate brought about a sedimentation of the protein substance and on letting it stand, the fluid portion drained away, leaving a semi-solid, white custard-like substance that was rich in nutritious protein and could be eaten either as it was or cooked with meats or vegetables.

There was another *tofu* maker on the plantation from many years before, so it was difficult for the Murayamas to compete against this established business and succeed. The bulk of the sale and distribution of the manufactured article became Chizu's responsibility. As she had no enemies, she was able to make considerable inroads upon her competitor. To capture the trade of the single men, she prevailed upon the women in the different camps to put in a good word on her behalf. Many such men, being too lazy to cook a decent meal, made it a practice to buy two large cubes of *tofu* for a nickel, pour *shoyu* on it, and eat it with hot rice. It was the simplest way to prepare a meal and the bachelors were a profitable group to trade with.

Since the camps were rather far apart, she could not go to all of them as there were little ones at home to attend to, and thus it became Minoru's job to deliver orders. For a child of eight to carry this soft, easily crumbling merchandise partially immersed in water in a big dishpan was rather difficult. The only way to safely carry it was to place the pan on top of the head, just like the women of Latin countries and Korea carry their burden. After spilling and spoiling the goods several times, Minoru acquired the easy swinging gait that was necessary in order not to jar the fragile, easily crumbling merchandise. He did not mind very much the deprivation of playing hours that this work demanded. On the contrary, it was a novelty and he felt proud to be entrusted with regular work that involved actual transaction of money. Sometimes there was cash payment but usually on pay days he had to make a special round to collect for the month's sale. He was given a small pocket-sized notebook to jot down his sales, but one pay day this memorandum book was nowhere to be found. It was a real blow to the prestige of this businessman of eight and his mother reproached him for his lack of responsibility. "When you cannot keep good care of your account book, how do you expect to become a businessman when you grow up?"

"Oh, then the account book will be so large that it will not be lost so easily."

In this manner, two years went by. To the people toiling on the isolated plantation, the horizon of their endeavors and subsequent achievement was very limited. There were only two classes of people. The white people who represented the capitalists and their hirelings, and the workers who toiled month after month, year after year, at a fixed subsistence income. There was no middle class, and no individual engaged in his own business. Not even a store was allowed to operate on the plantation. All owed their existence to the sufferance of the plantation officials. In this remote section of undeveloped Hawaii, communication with the outside world was very restricted due principally to the poor road leading to Hilo, the only town on this island. It was only in terms of wages earned that laborers gauged the success of their fellow men and the most a Japanese could earn under existing condition was fifty dollars a month.

It was especially true with the children, whose experience was limited to that of the plantation. They thought if they grew up to be carpenters or locomotive operators, they were successful artisans, and those not so gifted and mechanically inclined dreamed of the day when they would be driving a five mule team hitched to a wagon and get thirty dollars a month. But the height of success, the white collar job—and there were only a few of these available in the office and plantation store—was a position that all parents wished for their sons. These positions earned them forty to fifty dollars per month, but it carried a great amount of prestige. Parents with children that showed any promise above the average, dreamed of the day when they could be placed in jobs other than in the mill or field.

Life on the plantation for the children was not all dreary, however. On reminiscence, Minoru pleasantly recalled in his later life the rather happy childhood he had spent on the coast of Hamakua even where there was so little that children could call fun. There were no rivers where they could go swimming, and most of the children grew up unable to take care of themselves in the water. Only after the rainy season when the deep volcanic gulches got yellow with muddy torrents in their bottoms coursing angrily towards the sea, did they know what the rivers were like.

They longingly waited for the rains to stop. Then they would go to the many ponds where there was enough water to swim, but these swimming holes did not last long. As good weather continued for a few weeks, the water evaporated and only sandy depressions remained in the river bed until the next rainy season approached.

Of fishing, the children knew almost nothing. These gulches that dried up in the dry season would necessarily have no living creatures except wrigglers and the young pupae of dragon flies. To go fishing in the ocean which lay before their eyes was hazardous because the cliffs were precipitous, the descent was perilous, and the water's edge was assailed by ceaseless high waves that dashed their might against the rocky shoreline. Every year, there would be victims sacrificed to the angry sea and its denizens—the sharks—infested the region in great numbers. These amateur fishermen would clamber down the precipice by following the narrow trail and lower themselves down to the water's edge by means of rope ladders and go shell collecting. The conical "opihi" was attached to the seaweed-covered ledge in great numbers and, because human visitation was infrequent, grew to a large size. As these collectors were intent on prying shells from their attachment, monstrous waves that came every once in a great while would catch the men unawares

143

and carry them off into the water. Only the most fortunate or the ablest swimmers ever reached safety again. Many went pole fishing. Bamboo poles with a tough line were used in trying to lure and catch the large, wild fish of the deep. The catch was usually good for these fish had not been used to nibbling bait. But all these excursions were limited to grown-ups and the boys did not have the fun or the thrill of the tugging and pulling.

Once Minoru went on a picnic to a place called the Kawili Gulch about three miles away. The gulch was so deep that its bottom was level with the surface of the sea. Most gulches ended high above sea level and poured as waterfalls into the ocean. There was an inlet of the sea into the gulch and here one could swim in the salt water with perfect safety from sharks. Many tiny fishes also abounded in the water, and all the children had fishhooks, pieces of lead, and thread from mother's sewing kit.

Minoru rushed to the water's edge and dipped his line with the fish-hook weighed down by a piece of lead. Wait as he might and with full view of the many fish swimming about in the neighborhood of the wicked hook, none paid the slightest attention to the glistening metal. Then the teacher came around, "What are you doing, Minoru?"

To this silly question, the boy answered rather coldly, "Fishing."

"Then you must be the reincarnation of Ebesu-san for he only is reputed to have fished without bait. You must have some tasty morsel at the tip of the hook in order to lure the fish."

On many nights, especially when there was a moon, the children played out in the open late into the night. Since all the children were young—the oldest were only in their early teens—there was not much romance involved and parents were not much concerned over the escapades of their children. They would play hide and seek, but the most entrancing mass play was "run sheep run" which was a game of war strategy and helped the children plan and execute strategy. This was a very exciting pastime. There would be two teams with two leaders in each group. From a starting point the two leaders of one team would take the children on a devious path to a certain hiding place. One of the leaders would then retrace his steps to the opposing team that remained waiting. Then before the eyes of the enemy, he drew a map of the course he had used in taking his team into hiding. The enemy then would go out searching en masse, deciphering the course to the most probable place of hiding. As this group advanced, the leader of the hidden team, accompanying the searching army, would yell out code messages directing his hidden army to do various maneuvers in order to avoid detection and lead them nearer the goal. When his army would be on the verge of detection or when they were near the goal, he would yell out "Run sheep run" and there would be a race for the goal by the members of the two teams and the side that got to the goal first would be the winner. In the stillness of a country night, when mysticism seemed to lurk at every corner, to hide, run, and yell seemed thrilling indeed in the children's minds.

Once or twice a year there would be a shortage of water for the plantation workers due to the continuous drought. Huge tanks and underground cisterns that collected rain water would get dry and people had to depend on water conveyed from a mountain spring about five miles away. There was only a one-inch pipe supplying drinking water for some three hundred people, and even this water came in dribbles. During the entire day and far into the night, people stood in line awaiting their turn to get some water for the morrow. For containers, the empty Standard Oil Company's five gallon kerosene cans were used and in order to fill these, it took about twenty to thirty minutes.

The tempo of life was extremely slow and monotonous but it was not without pleasurable aspects. On moonlit nights, to be standing in line or finally sitting down to await one's turn, was a sort of carefree rendezvous for many of the young people and children. Jokes, stories, and gossip flew wild and it was a sort of social gathering for the people who had no organized entertainment and no reading material for diversion. Storytellers retold their experience and stocks of funny anecdotes for the twentieth time. A venerable and impassive man of Japan would follow a talkative and gesticulating Portuguese who related thrilling stories of Madeira and the Azores. But as night deepened, stories usually turned to those of ghosts and spirits. Hair-raising accounts of the "old countries" were swallowed by the youngsters as "ghost stories" but the local ones concerning the Hawaiians were different. Not only was there local color but there was the possibility of it being real and their running into them some night. The story realistically related was as follows:

"One rainy night a Portuguese luna was returning on his horse and as he was proceeding along a lonely road near a shallow gulch, there came a man on a white horse from the opposite direction. The hoof beats and dangling spurs were definitely heard, and he was queerly aware of the outline of the beast and man that stood out too clearly for a pitch dark night. The rider was discerned to be an aged native. He was beaten to the greetings of 'hello' by the other. As soon as he passed the horseman, he turned back to gaze at the rider, impelled by some sort of supernatural, involuntary urge, and to his consternation there was neither horse nor man. A chill went up and down his spine; he was drenched with a cold perspiration and sped home. He could not get out of bed for three days following that experience."

To rise above mediocrity for themselves, to give their children a "break" in life with brighter prospects than they themselves had had, were secret longings of the Murayamas as well as countless millions of downtrodden people scattered all over the world. It seemed hopeless to them. To continue making a living from hand to mouth was all they could envision for their future, for easy as it was to raise children in the mild climate, it was another story to educate them properly. The plantation system as it was then operated at Waipunalei was serfdom pure and simple, and no matter how long one worked he could not get beyond thirty dollars a month. There was no old age pension to ease his declining years. Yet many thrifty ones with less mouths to feed had succeeded in accumulating several hundred dollars; a few, several thousand dollars on these meager earnings, by sheer denial of comfort, and even deprivation of necessary health-sustaining foods.

These practices were eventually followed by a disastrous undermining of health. Deficiency eye diseases and beri-beri abounded among these miserly ones. They turned moneylender, charging usurious rates of one to one-and-a-half percent per month, and in some instances the rate went as high as two percent. The needy ones with large families who seemed never to have enough or those faced with some misfortune in the "old country," were forced to go to them for help to tide them over the emergency. The Murayamas had also undergone the bitter experience of seeing their loan principals doubling in the course of three to four years. Their lot seemed hopeless.

A turning point in their lives came, however, when Mr. Douglas died and this plantation changed hands. The managing personnel remained the same and each was promoted to a higher position as far as the Caucasian employees were concerned, but the same work at the same pay remained for the mass of mill and field workers. MacCracken, the cruel head luna, took charge of the plantation for about two years. Due to his aging and to his assumption of a responsible position, his harshness became somewhat moderated and he no longer personally dealt out blows to the laborers. To compensate for his humane evolution, he satisfied his blood-lust by shooting mynah birds as they swarmed about the stables looking for and feeding on barley strewn on the ground. He had a dog called "Nigger," which was trained to go after these birds as they dropped out of the sky, shot from the veranda of a woodshed. As these birds were not good eating, the shooting was pure sport and there was no justification for this wanton killing.

One day, MacCracken called Torao into his office and said, "Before Mr. Douglas sold this plantation, he asked me to look after you. He must have liked you a lot, for he said in case there was contract work to be let out among the Japanese by the new management, he wanted me to offer you the first chance. Now, I have here orders from Honolulu to start such a system at this place. So if you want to lease land to grow sugar cane on a contract basis, you will be given the opportunity of starting such a camp. I can let you have three hundred acres. Conditions of the contract are to plant the cane, keep the fields clear of weeds, cultivate with a single plow and cultivator, fertilize with bone meal twice, and 'hole-hole' twice. The cutting is to be done under a separate agreement. For the care of the cane land including the above labor, you will be paid one dollar per ton of cane as it is weighed in at the mill."

"Where will such a camp be located?"

"You can take the Kawili camp that is now empty."

"I must then go out to other plantations to recruit labor. To do that I need some money to advance to new men for traveling expenses and special inducement. Will you grant me this advance?"

"That I will fix up for you. We can let you have two hundred dollars. You may gather twenty working men."

Torao walked out of the office as if in a trance. More than anything else, the special consideration that the late manager had for him touched him deeply. He would, he resolved, succeed in this venture if for no other reason than to live up to the trust and faith Mr. Douglas had in him. Then there was the dormant feeling that had prompted him in starting the hotel business at Olaa nearly ten years previously. The fervor was rekindled in a maturer mind and heart. He realized what a test this was. If he were to amount to anything this was his chance.

147

The young couple did not sleep that night. Deep into the night they discussed the approach to the pressing problem of recruiting workers from other plantations. Naturally, the management of other firms did not relish the loss of their workers and guarded against poachers. Yet in the city of Hilo, likely cane field workers were hard to get, and they had to go to the sugar plantations to secure real workers. Finally, Chizu remembered a letter they had received several years ago from a fellow villager who had announced that he was at Honomu at a Christian boarding house conducted by the Rev. Sokabe. The reputation of the Sokabe Home was a very enviable one even in those early days. Rev. Sokabe attempted evangelization by living with these young men. By daily guidance he tried to convert them to Christianity. She reasoned that inasmuch as this was a religiously conducted place the boarder would be serious and perhaps of the picked variety as far as honesty and hard work were concerned. Anyway that was a place to go and see what could be done.

Rev. Sokabe listened with interest to this news. Since he was not working for the Honomu Plantation, he was not averse to his boarders moving to better fields of endeavor on other plantations and gave his consent for several men to leave. These were single men lately come from Japan. Two had seen service in the Manchurian campaign of the Russo-Japanese War. Torao then proceeded to Hilo and to Olaa and met many old-time acquaintances. He was introduced to many prospective workers who might be induced to go to Waipunalei. After two weeks' activity, he got promises from about thirty people willing to make a change.

The day finally came when the Murayama family moved to the Kawili camp and awaited the arrival of the recruits from other plantations. The house was tremendously large. Chinese workers had lived there in the past. There was a central partition longitudinally, and on each side of this wall there was a width of about twenty feet. Raised platforms about seven feet wide faced each other with a middle catwalk of five feet.

Minoru remembered well the first day at this camp, and moving into this large house left uninhabited for many years. Just off the government road with many huge trees on the empty lot and surrounded on all sides by sugar cane fields, the area seemed a spooky place from a distance. On getting a little closer, the picture looked more dismal. The ground was covered with waist-high weeds and grass, and empty beer bottles and rusted tin cans littered the premises. Amidst this depressing surrounding, giant pink oleanders were in full bloom, and an aged orange tree was loaded with white, fragrant blossoms. There were two large mango trees in bearing and clusters of tiny green fruits weighed the branches down heavily. The children were delighted at the prospect of the summer with these luscious fruits ripening. Two large monkey pod trees with spreading branches shaded the approaches from the road to this ancient, dilapidated house, and on the eastern side there was a row of eucalyptus trees that served as a windbreak against the prevailing winds from the northeast.

A huge underground cistern collected the rainwater that fell on the roof of the huge house. Stagnant and foul smelling, the water had to be lifted out and a general cleaning applied to this reservoir.

While the grown ups swept and washed the interior of the house, or cleared the immediate vicinity of the dwelling of its accumulated debris, the children had fun climbing trees and exploring the neighborhood gulch. The Cardozo family was Portuguese and lived nearby on their little three acre homestead. Their women raised chickens and cows for their use while the men folk worked on the plantation regularly to earn cash. With the Cardozo children, they roamed about. There were many different trees where bird nests, rose apples, and mountain apples could be found in abundance.

Within a week, new men from Honomu and other plantations began to arrive with their luggage. There was to be a central kitchen where workers were to have their meals, and the cooking and washing were to be Chizu's part of the undertaking. For three meals a day and weekly washings of dirty, tough-fibered working clothes, she was to get eight dollars a month from each laborer.

The planting of cane went into full swing. Three hundred fifty acres of cultivated land recently plowed under and fertilized were allotted to this gang of workers. A ten mule team pulling a big plow made deep furrows into the soft ground at regular intervals across the breadth of the field. Little mules with pack saddles loaded with gunny sacks filled with "pula pula," or seedlings, dumped the seeds onto the ground. These seedlings were ten inches of cane taken at the junction of the stalk and leaves. Along both sides, diametrically opposite each other, were rows of "eyes" and in this upper section of the stalk these were very close to each other. When buried under the sod, new shoots came up from these "eyes." A few men carried these cuts in a sack hung around their neck and distributed them equally spaced in the furrows. A man followed in each furrow and carefully rearranged them so that the "eyes" lay on each side and covered them with soft crumbling loam. It was an easy and rapidly progressing work especially on clear, dry days. About once every two hours or so, depending on the temperature of the day, a water boy went around to quench the thirst of the workers.

Two weeks later, two rows of green shoots came up through the soil and after that it was fun to watch the cane grow. After another two weeks, hoeing work had to begin for the weeds began to carpet the brown sod. A cultivator with an old mule was sent in to take care of the obnoxious pest between the furrows, and hoeing men tackled the weeds growing in and about the young cane as well as cutting those missed by the cultivator. Since rain and sunshine were abundant and rather optimum in spacing for vegetative growth in this subtropical climate, Torao and his men were occupied with the weeds for the next half year, until the cane became waist high.

Having been through the mill as an actual field worker in the past, Torao knew the psychology of the workers and used this knowledge to good advantage in their handling. He saw to it that those prone to argumentation were not placed next to each other as they might forget the work in hand. He placed a fast worker in a lead position so that his pace would be adopted by the rest and, finally, while supervising the gang he lent a hand to the slow ones so that the gang's work would not be retarded. To incite competition among the workers and also create an incentive, he resorted to piecework which was occasionally used to good advantage, especially on rainy days. An allotment of work in the early afternoon, the completion of which gave them the privilege of an early return home, was an effective way to get work out of them and at the same time add zest to their dull routine work.

When the cane was about five feet high there was no further work to do. Even if weeds grew tall they were ignored, but it was customary to go in and pull down the dried leaves that hung on to the stalks. This was called "hole-hole" and rainy days were chosen for this type of work. It was close in the tall cane for one thing, and moisture rendered the sharp edges of the leaves less liable to injure the hands of the workers. Besides, the leaves were more easily detached from the stalk when wet. The vicious yellow jackets made their nests under the leaves, especially under the dried ones. They created a dangerous problem as they attacked the eyes of men, but on rainy days their wings were wet and the bees were reduced to comparative impotence. Still, there were several who returned with swollen eyes. The absence of snakes or other dangerous creatures made this type of work very easy for the men. When this work ended, the men turned to other work on the plantation or again repeated the planting and hoeing on new ground, for eighteen months had to elapse before the cane became mature and sweet enough for harvesting.

As in all pioneering life the vices of humankind were also rife among these simple people. Gambling took place every pay day, when the professional class infiltrated into camp and held games for those who wanted to indulge. It was the regular "cho-han" dice games of old Japan. The tempo was fast and stakes high considering the amount of money these men earned. On such nights a professional woman or two were also visiting as the gamblers usually were their pimps. The accompanying scourge of venereal diseases left its mark on the workers. Four or five days later some men would be found digging earthworms as a consequence of their visits to the altar of Venus, but now completely sobered by the acquisition of a painful ailment and willing to take anything to get rid of the shameful disease. Even crushing and swallowing earthworms, reputedly for the cure of gonorrhea, was not repulsive to the taste of these penitent men.

School life was a very happy one for Minoru because he loved it and learning came naturally for him. Both at the American and Japanese schools, he led the classes without much effort. Lessons alone were not enough for him. Surreptitiously, he would spend hours reading cheap dime novels in Japanese concerning the exploits of the ancient popular *samurai* heroes. These novels were plentiful as they constituted the only source of entertainment and relaxation for the laborers. The men were strict about the more modern love stories and romances and kept the books away from the children, but there were ways of getting access to them when one really wanted. He was precocious in many ways. Delving into these books incited the budding curiosity of the boy. He began longing for the day when he could go to a temperate climate where there were four seasons. Even for a small boy the monotony of the perennial summer was irksome and confinement to a small locale was making him restless. Many a night, he would take a walk by himself into the cool country night, and build all sorts of air castles while gazing up at the glittering dome of heaven.

The stars and constellations are nowhere as beautiful as in the tropics. It is no wonder that the Egyptians knew so much about astronomy, for the stars of the tropics are never cold. There is a sensation of a warm camaraderie engendered between the twinkling celestial bodies and the onlooker. Then again the clouds of the tropics are beautiful. Not only are the shapes bizarre against the turquoise sky, but the changing hue and color at both sunrise and sunset are so fantastic and exotic that, especially to a growing boy, the ever-changing clouds are a never-ending source of delight and wonder. At times he thought he could discern palaces and ramparts, then again shapes of animals were depicted by the roving cumulus. There would be human forms of different ages and contour.

Whatever he wanted to have appear, he sooner or later believed he could visualize them in the mass of shifting clouds. Looking up into the vast expanse of heavenly creations, he discovered for the first time how small a country he was born into and began to dream of bigger horizons. To become a muleteer or to work in the plantation store at a white collar job no longer seemed to be the acme of success. He longed to own such a plantation himself, and if that be impossible then there must be some new country where opportunity still awaited young boys eager to make headway and fulfill their dreams. He could then ride a big white horse and the acres he would own would not be covered in a single day.

Just about this time, Halley's Comet appeared and created a sensation the world over. For quite a long time it was visible from earth and it was from time immemorial believed that the appearance of a comet preceded the occurrence of something eventful; good or bad. There was a rumor that the earth was in imminent danger of being swept to smithereens by the tail of this huge comet. There was talk current in the country-side that there was a monster called *kudan,* half human and half cow, born in Honolulu. Being such an abnormal creature, it did not survive very long, but in the few hours that it lived, it prophesied that a devastating epidemic would visit this earth and carry off the greater part of humankind. To avoid becoming a victim of this catastrophe was very simple. One only had to eat rice cooked with tiny red beans called *azuki* and somehow he would be spared. As a consequence, the stores were soon depleted of their stocks of this lowly bean.

One morning at two o'clock, Minoru was awakened to view the imposing and glorious spectacle of this comet. It was very near the earth and the immense collection of stars seemed to be within reach of the extended hand—a scene never to be forgotten.

In the summer of 1911, the small school was host to a group of promising young men who had just been graduated from the recently established Japanese High School at Honolulu. Led by their scholarly principal, they were making a lecture tour of the island of Hawaii. It was an educational and cultural campaign for the laborers on the plantation and at the same time it was an advertisement of the new school. Recruiting students was its chief aim. To the graduates, it was a grand tour of fun and excitement and a chance to display their achievement to their country cousins for, at this stage in life, they naturally considered themselves the embodiment of knowledge and wisdom. After they concluded their program of individual orations, a talk by the principal, and an impressive hymn of the alma mater, they were extolled by the local teacher who expressed the hope that even from such a humble out-of-the-way school, candidates for higher learning would emerge to emulate the splendid young men that were guests that night. To the country boys, these city graduates were the exalted symbols of culture and learning. Everyone old enough wanted to be like them, but to go out to Honolulu was an event in itself of no light undertaking, let alone the cost of such schooling.

There was one boy about eighteen years old who left for the school in September. He was Tatsuo Machida and his father was a man of means and well able to stand the expense. One year elapsed. Summer vacation rolled around and Tatsuo returned from the metropolis. His appearance was news and it spread quickly among the boys and girls. Minoru caught sight of him from a distance. It was impossible to tell what changes city life and higher education had wrought on Tatsuo, but one thing was apparent even from a distance. He was wearing long white trousers. To a child of twelve, this fact was outstanding and impressive and he asked himself when would he ever wear such clean white pants. Considering life in the country where everything was dusty and dirty, where boys and girls went around barefooted all the year round, and where everybody wore soiled working clothes, anyone wearing spotless white trousers was indeed like a person from another planet. His mind was full of this one thing and that night when he was alone with his mother, he shyly asked her if he might not go to Honolulu with Tatsuo when the latter returned in September.

"Why, you are only a child! How can you go alone?"

"I won't be alone. Tatsuo-san has already made the trip. He is much older than I am and I know I'll be all right."

"But you have only finished the fifth grade. I understand that only those who finished the sixth grade would be taken by the school."

Minoru became silent. He was not aware of this ruling. Thus his dream of going to the big city, of wearing white trousers and shoes, of enrolling in a large school—all these exciting daydreams of the afternoon—were rudely shattered and he went to sleep with disappointment in his breast.

That night when her husband returned Chizu spoke to him concerning the wish of her first born. It was with a certain amount of pride and satisfaction at the realization that Minoru was growing up and being ambitious that she imparted the news to Torao as they prepared to retire for the night. "Of course, we have just started out in this contract work and we are not out of debt yet. In fact we are in worse debt than we ever have been, but people seem to trust our honesty for I do not have much trouble in borrowing money. They always bank on us returning the loan with ample interest when the cane is harvested. I heard that the cost to maintain a boy at the boarding school is eight dollars per month in addition to the cost of books and clothing. We ought to somehow manage it."

Torao was silent. As a man and a father his mind was racing and his emotion was worked up. "So, Minoru wants to go to Honolulu! To confess, I have always felt that no matter how poor I was, my sons were not to be denied a high school education. I want them to acquire something I missed in my youth. Since he was the one to propose it, I feel jubilant. We have a good son and an ambitious one. We cannot disappoint him; we shall somehow manage the financial end."

The following day was Sunday and he went to see the school teacher who said kindly after listening to the story, "In the matter of credentials, you need not worry. I shall issue a certificate to the effect that he has finished the sixth grade. I know he will not be second to anyone coming from any school in the territory even if he is to skip one grade in this way."

In this manner, Minoru found himself preparing for the trip to Honolulu. As the days passed and the weeks crawled by, a certain feeling of apprehension assailed him. One night, his mother asked him, "Do you really want to go to Honolulu? You know you can change your mind anytime and nobody will think anything of it. You can go next year when you are older."

When he was talked to in this vein, he was shamefaced for his little manhood was put to the test. "No, mother. I am going this year. You know, I was not thinking about myself. I was wondering how you will take care of the old mare that father rides and which brings him safely home even when he gets drunk? Sometimes, on Sundays, the water boy gets drunk and forgets to feed her."

"Oh, I shall personally attend to that, and next year when you return for the summer vacation, you will find her even sleeker and fatter than she is now."

The final week drew nigh. Torao by this time was a man of some distinction. He was pioneering as a contractor, and employed some thirty men. There was only one other man that had risen to this station on the plantation. Although he was in debt up to his neck, he had to observe the formalities according to age-old custom of the "old country." On an occasion such as this, it was befitting that he throw a party, not for friends of the boy, but a real banquet for grown-up friends of the family. Torao himself was not loath to be such a host, because he himself enjoyed such gaudy affairs, and was vain enough to strut his delight before his friends. Friends came with cash gifts, and so in the long run it would not set him back very much. And so on a Saturday night, a drinking orgy was staged; the men made merry and the women urged them on to imbibe more *saké*. The boy was forgotten after the formal opening ceremony during which he was presented and his future blessed by a loud handclapping and three "banzais" for the prosperity and success of the Murayama family.

On the Tuesday that was to be the starting day for Minoru, two carriages, each with a capacity of ten persons and drawn by two horses, were chartered. Men from camp and intimate friends of the family boarded them to accompany the boy to Laupahoehoe, a quaint village at the bottom of a volcanic ravine and situated on a promontory jutting out into the sea. The *SS Mauna Kea* from Hilo was scheduled to arrive at two o'clock and so the party had their noonday meal at the same hotel that the newlyweds had spent the night thirteen years previously.

At one o'clock they started toward the boat landing. Leading this little procession was a young man from the camp who whisked out of hiding a white linen flag one foot wide and five feet long attached to a pole. There was inscribed boldly in India ink, "Bon Voyage, Master Minoru Murayama." Another banner was inscribed, "Hopes for success —Kawili camp." These were done in the traditional style of the "old country" when friends saw their conscripts off to military service or soldiers off to war.

Minoru, surrounded by these friends, had a ticklish feeling to find himself the center of so much attention and to-do. To him, going to school was an ordinary act of no particular merit and it was all strange why so much pomposity should attend it. Yet it was not altogether an unpleasant sensation to be gazed at and wondered about by the cosmopolitan population of this seaport village. The steamer had anchored offshore and the whaleboat was already halfway over. The men got into a circle; it was to be the "last cup of farewell." A quart bottle of wine was produced. Each had a sip. Minoru was made to take a mouthful, and following an impromptu leader they all joined in a resounding cheer of three "banzais." Torao bowed and thanked them all. He then led his son to the landing place where a burly Kanaka in the boat caught the lad's hand and deposited him at the bottom of the skiff.

The boat was rowed out to the open sea. Minoru sat on the side plank and intently watched the receding group of men who kept waving to him. They were his people—his father and friends of the family. There were a few among them who had been his good companions and kindly souls who acted like big brothers in the camp. Now they were being left behind and he was heading for a new environment and the unknown. He felt a tugging sensation at his throat; he felt tears trickle down his cheeks.

BOOK III

The Second Generation

Prologue

April 8, Sunday   *At Kuakini Hospital, Honolulu*

BY PREARRANGEMENT THE MEMBERS OF *the Arata family remained after visiting hours to talk with their doctor. Sadao Arata, now nearing sixty, had become obese—perhaps twenty pounds overweight. An outdoor life had imparted to him a tan almost as dark as a pure-blooded Hawaiian and the receding hairline on his forehead gave him a benevolent look like the Laughing Buddha. The clear brown eyes could still twinkle and dance when occasion arose suggesting the youthful ardor and energy that lay dormant in his powerful physique. He was still the envy of Minoru Murayama's introspective hesitant nature. Just as in their high school days, the happy-go-lucky, aggressive carefreeness of Sadao brought results if he were moved to exert himself. The two friends shook hands.*

"Well Doc, what do you think of the old man now?" inquired Sadao.

"Pain is controlled. He is quiet. Oxygen is helping his damaged heart. Electrocardiogram shows there is a change in the wave pattern pointing to damage in one of the three arteries of the heart wall. Blood chemistry study shows a high figure indicating moderately extensive heart muscle damage. The most critical period will be about two weeks from now. Sometimes the weakened area of the heart cannot withstand even slight exertion and rupture and instant death can come."

"Well, we'll leave everything up to you. Try to give him a few more years on this earth. He has had a very eventful life, as you know. Compared to his, mine has been tame," smiled Sadao as he looked at his friend who looked older than his actual age.

Perhaps doctoring was not a very pleasant life if it made one age faster, in spite of the knowledge of health that must be in possession of all doctors.

Maybe he studies too hard; he always was a bookworm even in high school. When other boys were engrossed in playing baseball every day, he used to bury his nose in library books.

While they were teenagers in Honolulu, the lot of boys with Japanese names was not a comfortable one, especially from an economic aspect. Per capita wealth was very low in their families. The third generation now attending schools or starting to work have everything smoothed out for them. The middle class is largely made up of their parents. But it was the generation preceding the present one that won—with their blood on the beaches of Cassino, the mountains of France and Italy—the respect and trust of fellow Americans. His own son who went with the 100th Infantry Combat Unit never returned. For that sacrifice and many thousands more, young men with Japanese names are regularly appointed to West Point and Annapolis. Nobody could have dreamed, much less prophesied, such a change in the mid-thirties. Now men and women of Japanese descent can proudly claim their place in the American commonwealth.

The young generation acts as if it had always been so in Cosmopolitan Hawaii. Human nature prefers to remember only the good and pleasant experiences and tends to forget and bury the unpleasant and sad episodes. Perhaps the rising generation refuses to listen to the trials and tribulations of their progenitors because they think they are moralized as examples to be emulated. The young claim that times have changed. "This is the jet age and Honolulu is the hub of the jet-flying Pacific." But when old timers meet, then nostalgic memories are relived and they feel young again. Sadao and Minoru have a treasured past to share and enjoy whenever the opportunity arises.

CHAPTER 13

The Children Grow Up

IT WAS IN THE YEAR 1912. SEPTEMBER IN Honolulu was hot. Beginning on the first day of the month, with each incoming inter-island steamer, new country boys arrived for matriculation at the Japanese High School. Some were accompanied by their parents. Most were in the company of older returning students who had gone back to their homes for summer vacation, but there were quite a few that came alone. Their ages ranged anywhere from twelve to twenty.

Among the boys in their late teens, there were two categories into which they might be divided. One group was made up of the really conscientious and ambitious ones who had been working in the canefields or at the sugar mills after finishing their grammar school curriculum and found themselves dissatisfied with the menial work. They were stimulated to dream of bigger horizons by reading the advertisements and circulars of the new school and had decided to enroll in order to better their lot in life. There was an American high school on each island, but no higher institution of learning in the Japanese language. To Honolulu they came.

The second group, by no means large in number, was comprised of young men from rather better-than-average families. Their parents became concerned about their boys growing up without being able to speak or read Japanese. Their worry in this regard was egotistic in a way because, in the first place, they realized after the boys had grown up that there could be no real understanding between them due to the language barrier if the youngsters did not become more proficient in their mother tongue. They themselves were too old to master an alien speech. They hoped that by entrusting the school with the care of their not-too-industrious sons and paying a handsome tuition, these young men would return home accomplished linguists. Unfortunately such was not to be the case. These grown up boys had an intense dislike for serious study; especially digging into elementary subjects which were not easy to master. This group came mostly from cities and towns and very few from the plantations.

The majority of the young boys from twelve to fifteen had come directly from the grades and constituted the regular enrollment of the school. A new dormitory had been constructed in a vacant lot across from the school on Fort Street during the vacation months and it was to be occupied for the first time that fall. It was a two-storied wooden building with two large sleeping quarters at each end, making four such halls. On the upper story, there was a large study hall that occupied the entire mid-section, while the storage, business, and teachers' rooms were located on the first floor underneath the study room. Two rows of army iron cots were arranged head to head, making a total of twenty to twenty-four in each sleeping quarter. Trunks were placed at the foot of each bed and books were piled on two wooden shelves tacked to the wall. There was a lavatory and a wash basin adjoining each sleeping hall. In the rear of the dormitory there was a separate building where a shower room and laundry were installed. In the yard of this dormitory huge mango trees majestically graced the green lawn.

The adjoining lot was occupied by a part-Hawaiian family whose children soon became very friendly with the boys and right next to this residence was a large three acre lot devoted to carnation growing by several aged Chinese bachelors. This farm supplied the floral shops of the city, and some native lei sellers of the waterfront bought their flowers from these old farmers. Every morning, the boys later found out, these men got up at four o'clock and by means of hand sprinklers watered these flower beds going about barefooted and in shorts.

The students soon discovered that once it rained, walking on an unpaved, uncovered walk was the most annoying experience imaginable as shoes were soon loaded with gluey mud. Locally, it was known as "taro-patch dirt."

The eighty-some-odd boys that convened for the opening of the new fall term were divided into eight squads with ten members each. Each squad occupied one longitudinal half of the sleeping quarters and was under the care of a leader, usually of the junior or senior class. These boys were to serve as models of behavior and scholarship and were the cream of the school student body. Almost all in the dormitory hailed from outlying Oahu plantations and other islands and far surpassed in scholarship and other activities the city bred boys who commuted from their homes.

Minoru found himself placed in Squad No. 2 which was under the leadership of Susumu Yoshida, a boy from the district of Kohala. He was about eighteen and was in the junior class. Quiet of disposition, not overly aggressive, but nevertheless burning with a seething ambition under the belying exterior of almost feminine gentleness, he was a good friend and monitor to have. His goal was to become a doctor. In the next bed Minoru found a Kauai boy by the name of Sadao Arata. He was of the same age as Minoru, but he was bigger in physique and much more tanned. Compared to the cool highland of Hamakua, the Makaweli region of Kauai was hot and dry and, as a result, the people were darker in complexion. As they crawled into their respective beds for the first night in Honolulu, both away from home for the first time in their lives, they could not sleep in spite of the hectic excitement of the day.

Tossing in bed, Minoru realized that Sadao was also in the same predicament. In an undertone he began the conversation. "Say, Sadao, what are you thinking about?"

"Oh nothing. I just couldn't sleep."

"Well, you know what I was thinking about? I was thinking of home. Everything seems like a dream. One month ago, it never entered my poor brain that I was ever going to travel away from Waipunalei. Not only did I travel but I took a steamer ride and here I am in Honolulu in this strange bed. Sure is a funny world."

"To tell you the truth I was thinking of home too. Small things that happened before I left Kauai now come to my mind. The old woman next door brought me her homemade *manju* with the sweetened red bean paste in the center, my favorite. She must have made those because I liked them and because I was leaving and she knew that was farewell for one year. Then father took me and the family down to the beach and we had a *sukiyaki* party on the sand. It was a sort of family farewell party. Gee, everybody seemed so nice and went out of the way to be nice in the last few days."

"Can you swim at the beach?"

"Sure. And there is a lot of good fishing too."

Then Yoshida came around to tuck the boys in bed. "You'd better stop talking and go to sleep. You have to get up at six in the morning."

The boys had to attend the Japanese school from seven to eight in the morning and between three and four in the afternoon. Two hours of study a day included the study of Japanese language, ethics, composition, calligraphy, English translation into Japanese, and Japanese history and culture. Between the hours of nine and two in the afternoon classes at the regular American school were attended according to the educational system compulsory in the Territory. For two solid hours at night everyone had to take his seat in the study hall and devote this period to study and preparation for the morrow. No letter writing or story reading was permitted and under the scrutiny of squad leaders boys had to confine their study and reading to textbooks. No talking except for consultation of school work was allowed.

Most of the boys had been accustomed to a free, easy-going life at home and had never really studied. This regimented, regular barracks life was really good for these youngsters, and it was no wonder that they carried away honors both at the Japanese and American schools. Being above normal in native intellect and under favorable environment with sufficient competitive stimulation, results showed in their improved scholarship. The oft-heard rebuke that children's minds were overworked by dual language training did not seem to hold water according to the results shown by this group.

Minoru belonged to a group of boys who were more proficient in Japanese because of the singular reason that he had been brought up in the backward part of the islands where the population was predominantly Oriental and the language spoken was mostly Japanese. Whereas the Japanese language school teacher was a very efficient man, the teachers who came to the public school—never the same person for two years— were either recent graduates of the Normal School or incompetent old ones. This situation was only natural for it was too much to expect good teachers at a country school of forty pupils in as primitive surroundings as could be found on the island. The Territory of Hawaii had become an integral part of the United States only twelve years earlier. As a result, Minoru was almost as bad from the English language standpoint as the boys who had come from Japan. His spoken English was poor. More than anyone else he realized his shortcomings and began to concentrate on the study of the English language. The Japanese language came naturally and easily to him and he was able to stand stiff competition even from boys who were recently from Japan.

Sadao Arata on the other hand was better in English because his home was a store and people of many nationalities who came there naturally spoke English albeit "pidgin." Besides, Makaweli was more populous; the school student body larger, and the teachers were more numerous and of better quality and training. The Americanization process there had proceeded much more effectively.

The menu was monotonous and the variety limited. As a result, beri-beri was rampant. It was blamed on the poor water supply that came from the Nuuanu Reservoirs and a sudden change to its use by the boys from outlying islands. The teachers blamed the predilection of certain boys to this disease following the consumption of polished rice. The then current medical thought tried to ascribe the cause of this malady to polished rice as if there were an inherent toxic element causing beri-beri rather than recognizing the deficiency element. The advice of the school physician was to feed bread to these ambulatory boys whose legs were swollen from the water-logging type of beri-beri without adding any other greens or nourishing food in the diet. As an empirical after-thought, he dosed the boys with a weak solution of bitter-tasting nux vomica and dosed them weekly with epsom salts.

Beri-beri had been a deficiency disease among the Japanese race ever since the polishing process of rice became common practice. Rightly or wrongly, the laity had their own ideas about its treatment. The eating of *azuki,* small pea-sized red beans, was thought to be beneficial and from modern ideas this seems rational. It was also believed that morning dew was especially efficacious to the numb and swollen lower extremities. So during the winter months when the lawn became sparkling white with morning dew and almost frosty in appearance, there would be half a dozen boys getting up at five in the morning to tramp up and down barefooted on the dewy grass before the sun brought light and warmth. It was exhilarating to get up that early, breathe in the fresh morning air, and trudge in the heavy wet grass. The sensation was much the same when a skier would exult in the breaking of a new trail in the virgin snow that fell overnight. If there was any benefit derived from this practice it was probably psychic.

To make up for the poor food, once a month there was a *sukiyaki* party of beef and vegetables and occasionally *tofu.* The boys did their own cooking over charcoal burners and ate until they could no longer move. Once a month they got all they could hold, but this happened *only once a month.* It was against regulations to eat outside of meal hours and absolutely forbidden to keep edibles at the dormitory. Just the same, the corner Chinese grocery stores did a thriving business in selling bananas, soda crackers, cans of pork and beans, and deviled ham. In the mango season little boys would get up before the town stirred to make rounds of neighboring yards and pick up the windfalls on the ground.

Once a month, on the first Saturday night, dormitory students were allowed to spend the night downtown until ten o'clock. Each was allowed fifteen cents spending money, and this money the boys usually spent at the movies which cost ten cents. On the way back they proceeded to Chinatown to eat a bowl of *saimin* or noodles at five cents. It was a luxury and everyone looked forward to the first weekend of each month. Yoshida usually took Sadao and Minoru along on such nights, and the trio became fast friends.

The cost to the parents to maintain a child in Honolulu was eight dollars a month. This included one dollar and a quarter for tuition, two and a half for a room and the rest for board. In addition, to defray expenses for laundry, toilet articles, and other necessities, the entire cost might have gone up to twelve dollars. The regulations specified that all monies be deposited with the treasurer, but there were many who secretly received extra spending money from indulgent mothers. The loose living habits of these boys was a constant source of envy to the group of country boys whose parents lived up to the regulations of the school and sent no money except through the regular channels. No matter what salutary effect this Spartan frugality might seem to bring about in the course of time, the immediate reaction was a longing for material comfort and an envy of those who possessed it. To make matters worse, Minoru's account book was always in the red. His parents were always one month behind in remitting their money order and were probably unaware of the deep anguish their son had to endure whenever he appeared before the teacher on disbursing day to have cash advanced in order to have a haircut or to buy a pencil and tablet.

Although monthly remittances were in arrears, Minoru was surprised to find that his father signified his willingness to let him join an excursion party to Japan during the summer vacation of the following year. A plan had been put forth by the school authorities in the spring months to organize such a group to tour Japan so that, as the first group of foreign-born Japanese boys, they would attract the attention of the thinking element of the old country that the sugar plantation immigrants in Hawaii had evolved into something substantial. That the offspring of the immigrant laborers were husky young men who were proficient bilingually and eventually would serve to interpret one country to the other and become real factors in the maintenance and promotion of harmonious relationships between the two races across the Pacific was a fact that any educator would be proud to exhibit and advertise to his compatriots.

Only a year previously, in 1912, the first sightseeing party to the homeland had been organized among the immigrants of the plantations. Those who had accumulated some cash but had no time to visit their homeland in decades had joined this group and toured the country, visiting places and seeing national treasures to which only such organized parties could gain access. As the first of such groups to visit the mother country from settlements outside the empire, this excursion group was royally treated and feted and the reports they brought back became the incentive for annual excursions. Thereafter, every trans-Pacific steamer between middle March and late April and again during the autumn was filled to capacity. All flocked to be in Japan in time to witness the budding and the glory of the cherry blossoms in full bloom or enjoy the grandeur of autumn foliage.

The second excursion party of older people from Hawaii had left for Japan that spring. The Japanese High School of Honolulu was sending her first student touring group in the last week in June and a circular had been sent out to the homes of students. The cost of the tour was one hundred and twenty-five dollars. This amount included a third class fare on ship and train and hotel expenses in Japan. While in Japan, temples were to be utilized for lodgings as much as possible and this arrangement would lower the cost of travel.

Torao Murayama perceived in this undertaking an opportunity of vicariously satisfying his ego and fulfilling a filial duty. His father had died two years previously but there were his brothers and cousins and other relations back in the native village. With a growing and increasing family, there was little prospect that he could extricate himself from the growing debt even if the crops of sugar cane turned out good year after year. Somehow, with a greater income than he had gotten previously, he ought to save more now, but his lack of economic sense and his predilection to vainglory merely increased expenditures. To return to his homeland even for a short visit was well nigh impossible. Yet the eldest son, now that he was the legal head of the family, ought to return at least once and settle the estate. By the law of primogeniture, he was the sole owner of the estate, and his brother and half-brother working on the farm were there on sufferance. Therefore, he owed it to them to settle the accounts fairly and apportion to them their just share. He reasoned that if Minoru should make this trip, it would not only be of immense educational value to the boy, but it would satisfy his relatives to a certain degree, as his son would represent him in paying respect to the ancestral tombs and particularly to his late father's grave and spirit. Lastly, he would be proud to display his half-grown son to the villagers back home. They would appreciate the reason of his not being able to make the trip when his father had passed away. In every farmer's eyes the possession of a good dependable son was worth far more than worldly treasures, and he knew he had this attribute in his son, Minoru. Besides, how many of his erstwhile fellow-villagers could boast of a son attending a high school, let alone speaking and writing English besides doing equally well with the mother tongue? This son of his was being uniquely educated!

There was an interim of about ten days prior to the sailing of the steamer and the time the school term closed for the summer vacation. Minoru made use of this period by returning to Waipunalei to visit his parents. It was merely a sentimental act as all instructions could very well have been written down on a sheet of paper and sent by mail. But he was glad to see them all. One year's residence in the metropolis seemed to have placed him in a separate world of thought. He was aware of a certain self-consciousness although he tried to forget and ignore it. Every time he tried to act his former self he was made to feel the change by the certain deference in action and speech applied to him by his former playmates and other grown-ups. As an illustration of what the simple laborers thought about education, one came up to him and said: "Minoru, you must have learned a lot at that school in Honolulu. I don't think your studying was limited to book learning. See what you can do with this watch. It stopped working six weeks ago, and I'll be grateful if you can do something to make it move again."

After a few days at home Minoru left for Honolulu to join the party for Japan. The railroad that was being built to Paauilo from Hilo was now completed and the inter-island steamers no longer stopped at Laupahoehoe for passengers and cargo. Traffic was centered at Hilo and thither Minoru proceeded. He somehow missed the picturesque steamer-day scene of the Laupahoehoe village near the sea.

He was the youngest of a group of sixteen boys who made up the excursion party. The eldest was twenty. There was one non-Japanese. Manuel Lopez was a dark Portuguese, a "sangre brava," who had lived at the boarding school and was trying to learn the Japanese language. He had a good fastball and was a welcome addition to the pitching staff of the baseball team. It was organized to play in Japan whenever the itinerary permitted an exhibition game.

All were in olive drab suits when they left Honolulu and on arriving in Tokyo bought straw hats for the summer trip in hot Japan. To be attired in a uniform was later discovered a great advantage when sight-seeing in Japan where excursion parties are treated with more consideration by the authorities. They were destined to find the summer weather hotter there than in their native land.

The boat selected was the *Chiyo Maru* of the TKK Line; then one of the three luxury liners that plied between the Oriental and California ports via the sunny southern route. They were assigned a corner in one of the foul-smelling steerage quarters for the trip. The ventilation system was poor and the steamer smelled of paint and a conglomeration of other things peculiar to ship's holds where the air is stagnant and sweating human beings toil and live. However, very few were seasick as June and July are about the calmest months for trans-Pacific voyages. To have such a group was a novelty for the officers of the ship too, and the captain invited them to a tea party and screened off a portion of the B deck so that the boys could do a few limbering up exercises and practice pitching. They were also invited to play softball against a team composed of cabin passengers.

Every evening after supper the group had to assemble at the stern of the ship, squatting on the deck or finding seats among the ropes and chains coiled neatly beside the railing, and listen to Mr. Tajima who was conducting the party. This teacher, in his late forties, was a unique character. He was born and nurtured in the heart of the mercantile center of Tokyo in the early years of the Meiji Era, and had imbibed fully of the resplendent and decadent atmosphere of the ripe Yedo culture in which the "Yedokko" took such pride. The carefree attitude, rejecting the idea of thrift and living by the motto, "Don't spend money carried overnight" was a trait that set the artisan class of Yedo apart as men of "spirit and braggadoccio" in contrast to the penny-pinching merchants of Osaka. They were hot-tempered, quarrel-picking workers in the different trades and vocations. In three centuries under the Feudal Shogunate there evolved a class distinction and a peculiar code of honor. In addition to these characteristics, the three hundred years of peace had moulded and mellowed the cultural side of metropolitan life and the theatres in particular were in a golden era.

Mr. Tajima apparently had little formal education of the sort that conferred certificates and degrees, but he was broadly cultured and an author of some distinction, although too lazy to tackle anything lengthy or complicated. He was particularly versed in the technique of classical *Kabuki* plays. His favorite saying—as if to excuse himself for inaction or bolster his claim to being a literary man and dramatic critic—was: "One does not have to be an artist himself in order to be a critic." That there was a foundation to his claim was verified in his later years when he became the manager and advisor to the great *Kabuki* player, Morita Kanya. Tajima's boast was that he was born and brought up in a mercantile district and in classrooms had tried to instill in his pupils and protégés the appreciation of Yedo tastes. He saw too much individualistic and materialistic evidence glaringly and disgustingly displayed by men in Hawaii.

Typical of his harangue was the peculiar trait of Yedo merchants and craftsmen who insisted on a silk inner lining when the outer garment was nothing but ordinary cotton fabric. To show off, to be vainglorious, were the most reprehensible traits in any individual. The peculiar Japanese appreciation of *Shibumi* (love for the unostentatious but truly artistic in the shades of black and white, and the rich, full maturity that might be discerned in antiques), were stressed repeatedly. One should have appreciation of art, comfort, and of good living, but it was extremely vulgar to boastfully display these to fellow men. Only the newly rich, lacking the background of culture and good breeding, would resort to such obnoxious behavior.

At these evening sessions Mr. Tajima reviewed many points of strange Japanese customs, the existence of which Hawaiian born children would not be aware of. In order not to appear boorish and countrybred, the boys ought to conform to the customs, for in the Orient one had to

170

follow these traditional rituals in order to command respect. He recited many anecdotes to emphasize his admonitions at these gatherings in the cool, lazy, dying hours of the day just above the foamy churning of the propellers. The nine days of lazy sailing on a glossy sea were too long for eager passengers, but in many instances these pleasant expectations are much sweeter than the actual attainment of the object.

They landed at Yokohama and went to a hotel, the Joshuya. The first thing they did as they entered the room with the matted floor was to fling their hats and coats onto the *tokonoma* or raised portion at the head of each room. Outwardly, to the uninitiated, this seemed to have just been planned for such a purpose, but it was the last place to be so used by the Japanese since it was the converging point of the room where only ornaments were to be placed. Thus, in spite of Mr. Tajima's admonitions and instructions, their first action in Japan was a breach of etiquette.

This group was invited by the Chamber of Commerce of Yokohama. The clubhouse was situated in a park amidst large trees that were different from those found in the tropics. For instance, pine trees did not exist in Hawaii and these grounds were covered with them. The flowers and shrubs that covered the grounds of the park were also strange. Mr. Kahei Otani, one of the leading tea exporters of this port, was the speaker on this occasion. He was in his early sixties, partially bald, with a venerable long gray beard and whiskers which gave him a Confucian look. There was a full course dinner in the approved Western manner. Having come from a land dominated by the Anglo-Saxons, the hosts reasoned that such food was to the taste of the boys, but none of them really had ever been to a formal dinner. The climax came when finger bowls were served with a piece of lemon. The cautious refrained from doing anything, while the more audacious ones made lemonade without sugar and gulped it down.

Mr. Otani stood up and solemnly spoke: "I welcome you boys from overseas. Yokohama has a special affection for you based on a geographical proximity and close commercial ties. Our ports are only nine days apart. We only have to walk up the gangplank and then descend the same on the other side. The rest of the travel is done for us. I understand that practically all of you were born in Hawaii and have been educated there. I am further told that you attend both the American and Japanese schools where you learn to read, write, and speak two languages.

You may not fully appreciate the good fortune you have in getting such an education. Being engaged in foreign trade, and belonging to a generation which had not the chance of acquiring the command of any foreign language, I envy your good fortune. Study hard and some day the mastery of languages will help you in getting started in life.

"I am further acquainted with the fact that those born on American soil are granted citizenship in the United States. In other words, you have Japanese features but you are American citizens. This arrangement is nothing new in our system of government. We had a lot of people coming from the Asiatic continent in the preceding centuries who became naturalized and contributed to the body politic of Japan. In feudal days, the system of *yoshi,* or adoption, was extensively carried out. In such arrangements, there were occasions when clans battled and the adopted son was put in a dire predicament. But there was no hesitation. *Bushido* was explicit in these instances; fealty and allegiance to leaders was clear cut. No matter what the blood heritage, the allegiance at all times belonged to the master of adoption. Therefore, I am telling you from a purely Japanese standpoint that, since you are American citizens, live and die for your country, the land of your birth, for then you will be following the precepts of *Bushido.* I intended to present you with souvenirs. I racked my brain the entire night for an appropriate 'something' to have you remember this happy get-together, but when I thought of the above there was no longer any hesitation as to what I was going to present you with today.

"On these fans, I have inscribed the characters 'Loyalty and Sincerity.' Please conduct your lives along this line serving your country with distinction so that we shall be proud of you from this side of the Pacific."

The following day, they went to Tokyo and were quartered at the old Hongwanji Temple in Tsukiji. The many large rooms in this ancient temple where such excursion parties were accommodated were well kept, but the odor of incense, peculiar to all Buddhist temples, tended to make the boys behave in spite of their exuberant energy and carefreeness. Places of interest in Tokyo were visited and many new things were seen and heard. There were no excursion buses and all sightseeing had to be done by trolley cars, jinrikishas, or on foot. The itinerary was so full, however, that after a while it was too gruelling to go walking or to take street cars from place to place under the hot July sun and oppressive humidity.

The side trip to Nikko included a hike to Chuzenji Lake. The five miles of winding trail that was then only wide enough for rikishas to pass was a very enjoyable one. The maple trees that covered the mountainside were green and did not present the gorgeously colored foliage of the autumnal season for which these mountains were noted, but the trees were so different and strange to the boys that they almost ran up the mountain—so glad were they to get away from the heat of the plains. The beautiful waterfalls that graced the trail from lower levels to the one near the lake, called Kegon Falls and noted for suicides, were sources of exclamation to the boys. Some wild monkeys in the trees on the roadside added to the charm of these mountains. A night in one of the native hostelries on the shore of the lake was really refreshing and relaxing.

The famous architectural masterpieces of Nikko were too deep a subject to be truly appreciated by Minoru and his friends. To be fully appreciative, a mature mind with artistic training was necessary "to stand gazing at the *Higurashi Mon,* forgetting the passage of hours and only suddenly becoming awake from intoxication when dusk approached." The extent of their wonderment was limited to the mystifying phenomenon of the painted dragon on the ceiling that reverberated with a buzz like a rattlesnake when one stood under its head and clapped his hands. The sleeping cat sculptured by the famous Hidari Jingoro on the wall in the court aroused boyish excitement because the cat seemed to be facing the onlooker from every direction.

Minoru was particularly impressed by the majesty of the cryptomeria trees within the compounds and rows of these towering trees that lined the avenue approaching the shrine. Large trees lined the ancient highway to Tokyo as shade for the Shoguns when they traveled back and forth from Yedo. The story of these trees was interesting and impressive.

As a masterful stroke in statesmanship, an early Tokugawa Shogun planned a shrine to deify the founder of the dynasty, Iyeyasu, and asked every feudal lord in the Empire to contribute something toward the construction of this memorial. It resulted in a mad competition, each trying to outdo his neighbors in currying goodwill and favor with the reigning Tokugawa family. This was exactly what the foxy shogun wanted. He wished to weaken the powerful warlords by encouraging them to squander money and material. There was a very poor *daimyo* whose holdings were so unproductive in taxes that he was not able to send anything of note and merely planted the precincts and approaches with

173

thousands of young cryptomeria plants. At the time, the trees were probably insignificant, but after three centuries they turned out to be the most splendid contribution.

When they returned to Tokyo they were invited to Waseda University. The institution was not so large then but was destined later to become the largest in the Orient. They were led to the private residence of Count Okuma, who was the founder and grand old man of this unique private center of higher education. Under maple trees, tables were set and cider with cracked ice was served freely.

Count Okuma, the president of the university, delivered a talk while sitting down. He was one-legged, having lost a leg in an attempted assassination when he was minister of foreign affairs. He was instrumental in concluding treaties with foreign powers, but the Western nations granted no equal rights to Japan and naturally the patriots became incensed and blamed Okuma for the humiliation. He spoke with his peculiar and characteristic tightening at one corner of his mouth, and the part of his speech that stuck in Minoru's mind was the following:

"You young men have come from the Hawaiian Islands. Those islands have been familiar to me since before you were born. When I was serving as foreign minister of the empire, I dispatched our Admiral Togo, then captain of the *Naniwa Kan,* to Honolulu when Hawaii was being annexed to the United States."

Minoru was then reminded of the fact that when he was little and played marbles, it was a "Naniwa shot" when the aim was an extraordinarily good bull's eye from a great distance.

On the way west from Tokyo, they stopped at Gotemba station at the foot of Mt. Fuji and, leaving their luggage at the station, they began the pilgrimage to the summit of the Sacred Mountain. The vast grassy slope of the mountain, called *Fuji-no-Susono,* was traversed in a miniature railway pulled by two horses. Except for groves of pine trees here and there, the hilly landscape was covered with shrubs and tall grass. Spacious and grand were the words that fitted this plateau. It was used by the cavalry and artillery regiments for maneuvering. Toward dusk, with the curtain of darkness gradually falling on the landscape, they arrived at the first station called Tarobo. The mountain was divided into ten such resting huts, the tenth being at the summit. Unfortunately, arrangements went awry and there was no supper awaiting them. Only

174

two raw eggs were distributed to each of them to appease their hunger pains. Minoru was in a quandary as he did not like eggs in any form, especially the yolk, but he was so hungry that he sucked the eggs as the other boys were doing and to his surprise found them palatable.

Riding horses were provided each member. There was a footman leading each horse by the bridle. The plan was to go to the third station and ascend as much as possible during the night in order to be above the clouds for the sunrise scene. There were clouds gathering and soon lightning was seen and distant thunder heard, but all this happened under them at a lower elevation. They were now above the clouds and a bright moon bathed the rugged volcanic mountain slope with her soft rays. Not a speck of cloud hovered above them, and the guides and footmen chanted, appropriately, a religious ode as they panted up the rather steep grade.

> *"Rokkon shojo, rokkon shojo,*
> *Oyama wa seiten."*

(Purity of the six desires, Purity of the six desires, The sacred mountain is cloudless.)

After alighting from their saddles at the third station, the party continued on foot in the brilliant moonlight up to the fifth station. It was a weird and strange experience for Minoru. All the climbers were covered by a conical straw hat and a piece of straw mat on the back to serve as a raincoat. He followed the guides and porters who kept on chanting while bathed by the mystic rays of a temperate moon.

The resthouse was an abode of rough-hewn lumber, shaped like a Mexican adobe hut, and piled and weighted down on all sides by rocks. The wind was strong at this elevation and in order to survive the snowy winter months, the rocks seemed necessary. In the interior there was an open brazier in the center of the room. A huge iron kettle hung on an angulated branch of stout wood that hung from the ceiling. The steam from the kettle imparted some coziness to the bare room. Smoke from the bamboo pipes of the men and the smoldering, half-dried wooden twigs under the kettle, produced much smoke in the interior of the hut where there was no chimney or ventilating system. Eyes smarted and could hardly be kept open. It was very chilly on the outside and there was very little for the boys to do except to crawl into the bedding spread on the raised floor. A sugarless roll called *shoku pan* was distributed among the tired and hungry boys and this turned out to be a delicacy to the famished.

The footmen who had led the horses had returned to the lowlands, but the porters and guides remained and were huddled around the fireplace jabbering about local gossip. They slung over their shoulders a thick, padded kimono for added warmth, and kept smoking and periodically pounding their bamboo pipes on the wooden sides of the fireplace to expel the ash. Minoru soon fell into a deep slumber from sheer exhaustion. If there were fleas or bed bugs which usually infested these mountain hostelries, he was too tired to be aware of their existence and annoyance.

At five o'clock they were all awakened. One cupful of water was given each to perform his morning toilet, for water was scarce and derived by melting snow which was found perennially in the crevices and sheltered nooks on the barren slope. A salty, reddish soya bean soup, with ingredients of small dried fish plus half boiled rice with a gritty core, was washed down in a hurry. At this elevation, the boiling point of water was low and the heat could not be increased enough to obtain well-cooked rice. It was not yet light outside, but hazily the universe was taking on shape and awakening for another eventful day. The sweeping outline of the broad plains, the Hakone Mountains, and Izu Peninsula that jutted out into the distant Pacific, were discernible. Just about that time, toward the east, solar rays broke forth, piercing through the embankment of clouds. As they watched, the luminosity increased with each passing moment. Soon the bank of the clouds itself was lit to a golden brilliance. Then inch by inch the sun emerged, and a new day had arrived.

From the porters and guides and fellow climbers there arose a series of hand claps, each person striking three times, and Minoru saw that their faces were turned toward the rising sun and their heads solemnly bowed after the hand claps. Minoru was reminded that the Japanese were sun worshippers from prehistoric times, much like the Incas of Peru. In spite of the influence of Buddhism for thirteen hundred years, reverence for the sun—the giver of warmth and light—was dear in the people's hearts. The *Goraiko* or "The first arrival of Light," was a sight cherished among the peasantry. To have welcomed and worshipped it from the summit of sacred Mount Fuji was something to relate with pride to people back in their villages and towns.

176

In the early morning light even the rugged volcanic outline of the summit assumed a soft welcoming contour. Now, they were able to view the crescent Lake Yamanaka lying peacefully below them. The rest of the Five Lakes of Fuji could not be seen from the south slope. To the north and west, they saw nothing but mountains. Japan was a country broken up by mountains. In order to protect shoes from the rugged lava ground, straw sandals were tied onto the shoes and the ascent began. Their straw hats had been left at the first rest house and they had cone-shaped head gear made of straw with a string around the chin to prevent it from being carried away by the strong gusts of wind. On their backs they carried a straw mat to keep away rain or excessive heat. These were good only in light rain and in a downpour their protection was dubious, but these constituted the usual paraphernalia for the pilgrims and they were similarly provided. An eight-cornered staff of wood six feet long was supplied each member to assist him in the climb. It was called *kongo zue* or "diamond staff," peculiar to this mountain.

At first the going was easy and the seventh rest house was arrived at in no time. Here they were served *amazake,* a freshly brewed, sweetened rice wine to counteract the chilling winds, and after a short rest resumed the climb. The grade became suddenly steep and after ten or fifteen steps, one had to stop to give the pounding heart a chance to quiet down.

Mr. Tajima fell ill with "mountain sickness" and he was supported by two porters as he laboriously tried to keep pace with the boys. His face was ashen and he seemed to be completely "in" after the vomiting and retching he had to go through. His headache was unbearable and he had a *hachi-maki,* a towel tied tightly around his head, as if to prevent a bursting, throbbing cranium from taking the line of least resistance.

The summit was a shallow concavity, an extinct crater, with a row of stone huts where lodging, meals or refreshments could be had. It was cold even on a summer's day and people went about in a kimono matted with cotton. Like all mountains in Japan, Fuji had her *Sengen Jinsha* and to this shrine, thousands of pilgrims that annually climbed the mountain turned their footsteps. They wore white kimono, white undergarments made like tight-fitting trousers, and were shod with white cotton *tabi* reinforced with straw sandals. Around the head, from the forehead to the occiput, a white towel folded in a band was tied. On the back of their garment, red and black seals of the various shrines visited en route were stamped. At the summit a large, conspicuous "Mark of the Summit" was placed in the place of honor, which was reserved at the center of the back and the center of headband.

The Hawaiian boys bought fans or "stamp books" at the Gotemba Hotel and were having them stamped at each station of the mountain. On the wooden staff, they got red-hot irons to brand their marks. Of course a sen or two was charged for this service but it was fun to gather these mementos.

Men and women of varying ages were among the pilgrims. To them it was sort of socio-religious jaunt. Over the course of several years they had made monthly contributions to a savings society called *Koh,* and when the summer excursion season came around, out of the tidy sum that had accumulated in the treasury, a certain number of the members started out on this tour led by an experienced co-pilgrim. Not only was this tour a satisfying act of religious fervor and obligation, it was a release from their humdrum life. Each *Koh* was organized for a different sect and each had a central Mother Church in some city or mountain. At a minimal cost, they enjoyed these excursions to regions full of beauty and tradition and became better acquainted and appreciative of the land of their birth. Hundreds of these white-robed pilgrims, making their way to the *Sengen Jinsha* in groups of thirty or fifty in single file, looked like pigeons from a distance. When they finished with Mount Fuji, they were going to other shrines built in other mountainous districts.

The view from the summit was obscured by cloud formations that skirted the lower regions, but enough was seen to impress the onlookers with the irregular mountainous nature of the country. To the east, north, and west, row upon row of peaks were visible. Not a glimpse of flat land could be seen. The southern slope tapered off to the shores of the Pacific Ocean.

On the summit, bottles of "golden brilliant water" and "silver sparkling water" with longevity and health-giving qualities were on sale. These were nothing more than melted snow; commercialism had invaded even the sacred realm of the highest spot of Japan.

The descent was made by way of the Subashiriguchi, where the sloping surface was sandy instead of the rugged lava that characterized the volcanic structure of this mountain, the last eruption of which was prehistoric. The downward course was very rapid.

By this time a thick fog had set in and obscured the entire landscape.

The trail was not visible except for the rows of discarded straw sandals that littered both sides of the much-used path. They reached Tarobo wet to the skin. Horses were there awaiting them and Minoru dozed on his mount as the party proceeded to Gotemba and to the hotel prior to catching the train to the West and to Ise.

Of all the places in Japan which are full of traditions and associations with historical events, the most sacred to the hearts of all is the small wooded tract of land that nestles against the almost feminine contour of hills that are located in the region of Ise and Toba. A beautiful mountain stream, the Isuzu, flows near this forest, and there is a wooden bridge to span this river. Nobody except the emperor is allowed to go beyond this bridge in any sort of vehicle. The excursion party chose the early morning hours before breakfast to make their pilgrimage to this shrine of shrines where Amaterasu Omikami, the Sun Goddess, has been enshrined for centuries. In the cool morning, when a low mist hung over the primeval forest that had known no ax, they made their way on smooth pebbles that were strewn on the broad walks. Several stony steps brought them down to the clear, transparent water of the Isuzu in which huge carp and trout swam leisurely. They stooped to dip their hands in the cold water, and rinsed their mouths. It was a purification ritual before mortal men entered the sacred precincts of the gods.

Without anyone giving an order, a group of about fifty young men from some interior town, who had also come that early, and having performed their purification ritual at the Isuzu River, fell into line and disappeared into the mist. Minoru and his friends somehow felt the sacredness that pervaded the atmosphere and they, too, were silent as they followed the other party. Huge cryptomeria and cypress trees lined the road on both sides. They seemed very old; many were without tops and quite a few were rotting on the ground. The stillness of the forest carried with it an awesome feeling of loneliness and sacredness and when they stood before the simple unpainted edifice that was the replica of abodes of prehistoric Japan, the truth of the verse learned at school came with poignant feeling:

> *I know not who in there is enshrined,*
> *But with surging overwhelming reverence,*
> *I feel my tears flowing unrestrained.*

At a little distance from the shrine there was a building where the ancient ritual dance called the *okagura* was being specially performed for a consideration, and the party sat in on one of these. Girls about ten or eleven years old, robed in white kimono and red skirts, with green ornaments and tinsel on their black tresses which reached down to their hips, danced to the monotonous incantations of lip flute and drum. Such must have been the music which enticed the Sun Goddess, Amaterasu Omikami, when she shut herself in a cave after becoming enraged at the brutality of her brother, Susano Ono Mikoto. In the pictures depicting this scene of mythological Japan, there is a rooster crowing to add to the noise and merrymaking of the crowd.

Minoru speculated about the number of roosters that roamed unmolested in the sacred precincts of the shrine ground. Perhaps for the part the roosters played in that event the pious people donated their best fowl to the service of the deity at Ise. As to correctness of this observation, Mr. Tajima was unable to comment.

When the party visited the Yokosuka Naval Station they saw for the first time a seaplane actually take off from the water and circle the bay. Aviation was in its infancy and these biplanes were some of the very few machines that flew the skies of Japan. This unique demonstration was specially put on for the guests from Hawaii. The navy had special consideration for the Japanese in the Hawaiian Islands because their training squadron for cadets usually spent a week or so in the ports of Hawaii in their cruise around the Pacific.

At Kyoto, in the suburb where the sixteenth division was garrisoned, the party became the guest of General Nagaoka, famed for his enormous gray mustache that reached about one foot from tip to tip and which was carefully and constantly rolled and stiffened by the wearer. He was a unique figure in the military circles as his outlandish mustache would indicate and even then he was a champion of aviation for the armed forces, but for the occasion he put on a more orthodox show for the party. Under a canopied stand where a liberal amount of Kirin cider and *sushi* and cakes were served by the soldier orderlies, the boys had a sweeping view of the parade grounds. When all were seated, General Nagaoka stood up and said in his same methodical military abruptness, "In the feudal days, our country was broken into many principalities, although all owed their allegiance to the emperor in Kyoto. There was rivalry and bloodshed and civil war was not uncommon. Many times it happened that father and sons were in opposite camps; brother met

180

brother on the battlefields, and the tears and anguish that are counterparts of warfare were intensified on account of the more private tragedies. Trivial in themselves when viewed from the larger issue, but more poignant and sad from the standpoint of the family and individuals.

"The *Bushido* of Japan taught these men plainly where they should stand and how they should act. Allegiance pledged was the determining factor and there was no swaying. The place you young men occupy in international relations is a unique one. I can tell you this much. We soldiers are the last ones that would wish for any war to come about because we are the ones to suffer most from such an unhappy development. Especially is this the case with Japan-American relations. War is the last thing that we wish to happen. But we cannot foretell the future. We must always take into consideration the most improbable and prepare for the worst so that there shall be no jam or hitch when the time should unfortunately come. Again as a soldier, I can tell you frankly that we are not depending on you to do our fighting. You have gone over to the great American nation as *Yoshi* (adopted son) and we would like to see you act as a true son to the *Yoka* (adopted family). In this way only can we be proud of our race and proclaim to the world our racial stamina. You are my guests today and I shall have some of the soldiers stage a maneuver for you. It is the simplest of military tactics, and because there are very few troops remaining in the barracks due to extensive maneuvers now taking place, the ones participating will be commissary troops attacked by cavalry. Please make yourselves at home and see what soldiers will do under fire."

From an entrance to the parade grounds farther away from the pavilion, there emerged a column of pack animals and one-horse carts covered with tarpaulin. Each of the animals was led by a trooper and when these came out into the center there were rifle shots from another entrance, and about twenty mounted men came rushing headlong at this small contingent. At a command of a mounted trooper, the foot soldiers led their animals into a circle and induced their horses to lie down on the ground. From behind the horses' flanks they began firing at the marauders. The return fire seemed fierce, for the attackers, after making an encircling movement like Indians in Western pictures, withdrew to where they came from.

Then about twenty soldiers dressed with a peculiar paraphernalia over their ordinary khaki uniforms marched into the grounds. They wore helmets with steel crossbars over their faces, black padded breast protectors, and guards over their left shoulder. Each carried a wooden gun with muzzles twice as long as the usual rifles. At the tip of the guns there was a round cloth ball. Another contingent of an equal number of troops similarly dressed and armed came out and, as they approached each other, there was a loud command of the non-commissioned officer in charge, and with a wild battle cry that was intended to chill the enemy and to add zest to the fighting spirit, they lunged at each other with realistic ferocity in hand-to-hand combat. For about five minutes it was a breath-taking scene. Bayonets were driven forward with all the strength of the men. When the cotton ball found its mark, which was the Adam's apple, the opponent staggered and reeled back. They clashed and then separated, to again come to a fierce grapple with their opponents. A shrill whistle blew and the men separated and marched back to their respective entrance.

After Kyoto, the cities of Osaka, Hiroshima, and the coal mine at Fukuoka were visited en route westward.

The party broke up at Kumamoto City and each member was given about ten days' time to visit relatives. The time for this purpose was short because the boys had to return to Hawaii for the fall term of school. Minoru was accompanied by his uncle who had come to the city to escort him to the place where his father had been born and raised. It was toward dusk that they entered the village. Instead of going to the ancestral home directly they proceeded to the village shrine where the uncle paid his respects and reported to the deity that one of the *Ujiko,* or sons of the patron deity, had returned to the native hearth. He did not ask Minoru to go through the rituals of worship. Then they retraced their steps toward home.

Meanwhile, a crowd of boys and girls had convened and now followed them out of curiosity to see this young boy who had come from a distant land. The rowdy ones had decided on giving this outsider a good thrashing should he show any sign of sauciness.

Darkness was descending when Minoru arrived at the door of an unpretentious farmer's cottage. The women folk had lined up to welcome the boy. Each one was introduced by the uncle amidst repeated bows. He was bewildered by the number of relatives he had. In Hawaii, he had no relatives except his immediate family, but here it was very complicated. He had to think twice or thrice before he realized what a second cousin meant; the term was new to him.

A simple but special repast had been prepared and the male members sat down on the matted floor in a circle. A lacquered tray containing bowls of soup, fish, chicken cooked with vegetables, raw swordfish prepared in vinegar, *miso,* and fresh sliced melons, was placed in front of each person. Minoru was made to drink a reddish, sweetish, not unpleasant tasting rice wine, locally known as *aka saké* while the adult members of the party sipped the more fiery *shochu.* Minoru felt rather tense. Like all adolescent boys at this age, he felt himself grown-up but was chagrined to be treated like a mere boy. He was tall for his age, but the farmers would not forget that he was thirteen or, according to the Japanese way of counting, fourteen. The questions put to him were childish and foolish, and, not knowing appropriate subjects on which to carry on a conversation with the boy, they naturally fell into talk about crops and local gossip, totally forgetting the main guest of the evening.

That night while he slept, he was awakened by a rustling noise up on the ceiling. It did not cease and as he was tossing in bed, his uncle was telling his wife, "Maybe it is after the eggs" Minoru was curious, and asked what it was all about.

"There is a snake, a harmless one, that lives in this house. It is a good mouser and takes care of the rodents, but now it may be trying to steal eggs from the chickens."

"Where are the chickens and their nest?"

"Oh, near the door where the sacks of rice are piled up."

"Do you mean to say, chickens and men live under the same roof?"

"Yes, on the farms when there are only a few chickens to care for, we accommodate them in the house."

Coming from a country without snakes, to sleep in the same house with a reptile was repellent enough. To sleep under the same roof with chickens was not human to Minoru.

On the following morning, Minoru was taken to the family cemetery. To him this custom meant nothing, but he did as his uncle wished. He did not want to appear ignorant of the customs, the observance of which distinguished the cultured from the ignoramus. His uncle was extremely proud of the well-kept precincts and of the existence of stone or cement tombstones which he said showed wealth and distinction compared to mere wooden markers as found in many of the neighboring graveyards. With greens and flowers, they decorated the grounds and burned incense before the tombstone.

His mother's village was adjacent to his father's, and on the following day he went thither accompanied by his uncle. A bamboo grove graced the entrance to this village which was built on terraced lots on the hillside. Most of the farmhouses were thatch-covered with several rows of tile along the eaves. A barn was built nearby where farm implements, straw, harvested rice, and grain were stored, and where the stable for horse or oxen was incorporated in the rear. In the empty lot near the house were planted fruit trees such as oranges, persimmons and peach. Camellia trees grew to great heights in this climate and oil from the nuts was used especially in the care of women's tresses.

As they climbed, a beautiful scene of verdure opened up before them. Minoru was thinking of his mother; how she must have romped up and down these steps hundreds of times in her childhood; how she must have climbed the fruit trees, and what pleasant memories must be associated with each tiny object, both animate and inanimate, strewn about the place. As he was reveling in this reminiscent mood while trudging behind his uncle, he was surprised by a shrill outburst nearby.

"Come out, all of you! and see Chizu-chan's boy from Hawaii." Startled, Minoru turned to the direction of the cry and discerned an elderly woman who was standing in a doorway along the road. With strange eyes suddenly turned on her, she seemed abashed at her own enthusiasm and curtsied, taking off her towel that was lightly entwined over her coiffure.

His uncle bowed to her. "Oh, Omasa-san. This is a very nice morning. How is everybody? Yes, this is my nephew from Hawaii. We are going to see his grandmother."

"What a big boy for his age. I heard he was fourteen, but he is really a young man. Just like Chizu-chan the way he carries his head. Please drop in on your return."

The two went up the steps. The evergreen hedge that divided the residential quarters reflected the early morning light and contributed freshness to the atmosphere, contrasting itself oddly with the brown thatched roof that conveyed the impression of poverty and frustration. Yet the green and the brown were in complete harmony. Chizu's eldest

184

brother, the good-for-nothing spendthrift and drunkard, was waiting for the two at the gateway. Little unkempt children hid themselves behind their father and peeped between his legs. As the children became troublesome, and as Minoru and his uncle approached, the father apologetically scolded, "Now, quit bothering me like that. Come out in front and greet your big cousin from Hawaii. Minoru-san, it is very good for you to come to this humble abode. We are poor and do not have much, but your grandmother has been restless all morning knowing you to be at the next village."

They entered the dark interior of a poorly kept house. The wife of his maternal uncle was no better than her spouse. She did not drink of course, for few Japanese women drink, let alone get drunk, but she was not of superior intellect. Her failure in housekeeping spoke eloquently for her achievement as mistress of the house. The earthen portion of the floor of the house, where farm implements, rice sacks, and other articles of daily use were piled, was a mess. The raised, matted floor was swept for the occasion but the mats were almost black from neglect and age. The usual practice of turning over the mats had not been done for years due to poverty and sheer laziness.

Squatting in one corner of the room where the sliding panel paper wall was removed for the day and which was, therefore, sunny and warm, an aged woman was expectantly waiting. Blind and helpless, she had not been happy since her "baby" Chizu had gone to far-off Hawaii, and to make matters worse and discouraging, the wife of her eldest son was very incompetent and careless, and shamefully neglected her mother-in-law. With the keen sensitivity of the crippled, she could sense the sad plight of the topsy-turvy household, but she could not use her prerogative as the mother-in-law, on account of her dependent, helpless condition. Verily, there was nothing like one's own daughter in the care of the aged, and she had been missing her only daughter keenly for these many years. But today, Chizu's own son was coming to visit and she was all excited. She was too old and feeble to express this rekindling of her emotions and passions by outward manifestations of ecstasy. She remained quiet and complacent, only betraying her inward restlessness by picking at the hem of her kimono. Chizu was her last child and only daughter. To say that all children are equally lovable to the mother who bore them is only a half-truth, for it was inevitable that special attachment arises with one child more than with another. The forces of heredity are beyond human control. Children are joys in some instances while in some cases even parents would feel that certain children would have been better unborn: both for the children themselves and for the grief they cause the family.

Minoru was urged to enter and he took off his shoes and stepped on the matted floor. His maternal uncle took him by the arm and led him to the old woman. They both sat in front of her.

"Baba-san, this is Minoru. He is a very big boy for his age."

"Ah so! The long trip must have tired you. Let me feel you." Then her hands and fingers slowly went over his head, forehead, eyebrows, nose, ears, and neck. She continued down his chest, arms, and legs, carefully feeling his muscles and the size of his bones. Minoru never felt so funny, and at the same time sorry and compassionate. To his experience, having been born and raised in a pioneering land, old people were rare and, frankly, not very pleasing. Now, to be so carefully and intimately palpated over his entire body was indeed a new sensation.

She did not say much more, for her heart was brimming over with awakened emotion. Her reasoning faculties were on the wane as a result of senility. Blindness in the last years of her life had left her helpless and her lot in the pattern of life run by a sloppy daughter-in-law was not a very happy one, but instead of becoming querulous and petulant, she retired into the safe haven of silence and unquestioning acquiescence. Even at this hour of emotional stress, she could not get out of her habitual enforced silence. Only the corners of her mouth twitched as she completed her tactile scrutiny. She remained silent and listened avidly to the queries and answers that went back and forth between the boy and the two uncles. Answers were in the main monosyllabic and not as detailed as she would have liked.

"Mother, Minoru is going to the Middle School. He not only speaks and writes Japanese like all of us, but he can read and write and speak English better than the officials at the government offices of Kumamoto. They cannot, I am sure, speak English sufficiently well enough to talk to any foreigner." The uncle was trying to please his mother by referring to things she wanted to find out.

"What is he trying to become when he grows up?"

"A doctor," answered Minoru, eager to supply the answer to please the old woman but unable to soften and endear the sentence with the familiar, very personal diminutive of *Obaa-san*. He would have liked more than anything else at the moment to give voice to those words, and his mother would have immensely approved of it, but he was inarticulate. Somehow, the word stuck in his throat.

"Tell your mother when you return to Hawaii that I am doing well, although I cannot see any longer. I go to the village temple regularly. Now that I cannot see, the vision of my heart is functioning and I can see Buddha with no worldly interference. I believe what the priest tells us, and I know with certainty that I am going to the blessed land and I shall be waiting there for her. Tell her not to miss the services. Now for yourself, you will be doing a lot of good for poor people when you become a good doctor. Performance of good deeds will ensure your entrance to Paradise and I shall be waiting for you there too. We all will meet again in the Pure Land of Amida Sama sooner or later."

When the excursion party returned to Honolulu, there was a great throng at the wharf to meet the *America Maru*. Everybody expected that these boys would be allowed to land right away, but they were taken to the Immigration Station for questioning in spite of their Hawaiian birth and documents to that effect. At the Immigration Station they were made to sleep on iron springs without mattresses and only a blanket to ease the pricking of the bedsprings, but on the following day they were allowed to leave and all were glad to be in their native city again.

It was September; school had already started and they had to return to classes. On Saturday evening there was a reception in the school auditorium. The boys in their olive-drab suits that they had worn during the entire trip were present en masse to explain to the student body and curious townspeople the nature and wherefrom of the hundreds of gifts that had been brought back and displayed on the tables set along the walls of the hall for the occasion.

Mr. Tajima gave a lengthy account of the itinerary: the anecdotes, the general reaction of the boys who had seen Japan for the first time, and the manner in which the people had received these foreign-born boys. He spoke humorously about the incident near Sengakuji in Tokyo when a girl came running out of the house and yelled at the top of her voice, "Mother, come out! the Manilas are coming!" Having dark complexions they were everywhere mistaken for Filipinos.

Repeatedly he was asked, "Can these boys speak Japanese?" and so once at a party there was genuine surprise when one of the boys thanked the hosts in elegant Japanese. Out of curiosity, the hosts desired to hear the same in English by someone who might be able to do it, and so he ordered the same boy to deliver the same thanks in English. With pride, he said, he heard the sincerely expressed surprise and admiration of the assembled guests at the achievement of the students in the mastery of the two languages. For in Japan, the study of English is through reading and writing. Passable written English might be expected from the best, but spoken English was beyond attainment. The teachers of English were themselves no good at conversation.

Mr. Tajima closed his report of the trip with the hope that such undertaking, being very educational, might be repeated every five years or so, in order that both undergraduates and alumni might join the excursion trip.

However, such a trip was never destined to be repeated and these boys were singularly lucky to have had the chance to go.

After a hurried trip back to Waipunalei to report his experiences and observations to his parents, Minoru resumed his studies in Honolulu. There is nothing like travel to broaden one's outlook on life and to acquire self assurance. The provincial Chugoku brogue that was prevalent in Hawaii jarred on his ears on his return because he was initiated into the crisp Japanese heard in Tokyo. He was surprised himself at the discovery that he not only had a wider vista of life, but that he had a higher criterion from which to evaluate the common things of life. In the classroom, lessons came to mean something more than a mere recital of facts and incidents; they became associated with places that he had visited. He became keenly aware of his antecedents, his heritage, and naturally a keener resolve to outdo his cousins back in Japan.

In the then current talk among the Japanese, the easy-going attitude of the Hawaiian-born children had been a subject of considerable criticism and the second generation were condescendingly and collectively classed as "Hawaiiborns" with pity and contempt. Even to Minoru this epithet was an insult. After seeing Japan and its people, he began to appreciate his advantage. The simultaneous acquiring of two languages and cultures might be hard on some boys, but he knew he could do it with credit and he was not afraid of hard work. Diligence decided how proficient one was to become in any type of work.

Susumu Yoshida, his friend and squad leader, was very curious about his travel in the Orient and plied him with innumerable questions. Minoru answered him at length and in detail. It was easy to talk to an interested and intelligent party. The little details of travel or the most trifling incident and observation were to Susumu an illuminating exposé of a country he intended to go to soon.

"What is all this talk about the smell of the countryside and the filthiness of the latrines that I hear from some of the boys that went along with you?"

"Well, I can tell you this much. The smell of the rice patches recently fertilized with night soil pervades the atmosphere at certain seasons and when you come near the locality, you will get a whiff of it and it is not very pleasant. But after a little while you will get used to it and you will take it for granted as an unavoidable unpleasantness of the rural atmosphere of Japan. Even when you are living in cities such as Kyoto, until about nine o'clock in the morning push carts bearing night soil from the residential sections out to the farms are on the streets and the smell of these carts is at first nauseating. After a while we became so used to the sight and smell that whenever we did not come across one while we were in that city, we felt that we were cheated. After all we are creatures of habit."

"I guess so, for otherwise everyone would be complaining about it. The people born in Japan don't seem to be bothered by it very much."

"Yes, that is about what it amounts to."

"Tell me frankly, would you care to live in Japan after all that you have seen?"

"I would gladly, if I had a chance to go to school there. It was a novel experience to be where everyone about you was like you in race. Here in Hawaii, your classmates are of different racial extractions. There, they are all the same. They are dressed in gray uniforms and conduct themselves with strict military precision so that their school uniform will not be disgraced. Many people do not like it. I know most of the boys that went along did not like to be so hampered in their freedom. I like that way of living better, compared to this loose, carefree way we are living in Honolulu."

"Minoru, I think I'll follow my parents' advice and go to Japan. To get a doctor's degree will be much cheaper in Japan. My father can afford to send me to a medical school in the old country. We don't have much money here in Hawaii, but what little real estate we own in the old country will see me through school, so they claim, and I am going to follow their advice."

"You are lucky, Susumu, in that respect, for I don't know what lies ahead of me. I am from a very large family with no money, so I cannot hope for much. I may yet end up in the plantation store as a bookkeeper at fifty dollars a month, or as a mechanic in the sugar mill. But I am going to try to get a higher education in America. I will have to work my way through college if I ever get that much time off from helping earn money for my family. As I understand it, America offers the best chance in the world for an ambitious boy with no money to get a college education."

Listening to this talk between his two friends, Sadao Arata was silently trying to digest the letter he had received from his mother. It was written without the knowledge of her husband. She said that Sadao's father had become restless with the monotonous life of a country storekeeper and was trying to put over a deal: a short-cut to wealth. Instead of expanding gradually and conservatively, he was planning to make a killing with Mr. Weimann, the former sugar boiler at the Makaweli plantation who had gone into his own business as a mercantile trader at Lihue. They planned to charter a schooner, load it with merchandise purchased on the mainland, and transport it to Kauai directly. In this manner they planned to eliminate the high cost of steam transportation, the expense incurred in the loading and reloading at Honolulu, and save the commission of the Honolulu jobbers. To participate in this enterprise the Aratas would have to invest beyond their means, so they persuaded friends to invest their savings. Therefore, she concluded, she was rather apprehensive.

To Sadao, however, his father's adventure was admirable and his regard for him trebled. He attributed his mother's apprehension and pessimism to natural feminine timidity and conservatism. Everything was going to be all right. It had to be. He could almost picture himself as a millionaire's son and all the adventures and fun that would go with such a station would be his. He was going to some university on the mainland to study finance or banking. Not that he liked those subjects, but going to college was expected of a rich man's son and perhaps study in the handling of money would be expected of him.

He emerged from his reverie, got into the current of the conversation, and added, "Anyway, those things concern the future. We are going to stick together at this place until next summer. Susumu will go to the Orient, Minoru and I will go to America. Our ways will part then, but the friendship that grew here must be kept alive. Susumu will graduate next year. My proposition is that before he goes to Japan let us spend about two weeks at my home. I can show Kauai to you fellows."

"Gee! That will be fun! I certainly will enjoy it I know. How about you Minoru? You will have most to travel," Susumu was enthusiastic. He had never been to the Island of Kauai and he had a secret desire to visit that beauty spot, if he could, while he was in the Hawaiian Islands.

"I should like to go too. Maybe it will be my only chance to go there. Anyway, there is a lot of time and I am going to write to my father about it."

CHAPTER 14

Sadao Leaves Home

ARATA'S ADVENTURE IN SPECULATIVE BUSI-
ness did not turn out as expected and the worst fears of Mrs. Arata became a fact that had to be faced by the family. Fifteen years of toil and
sweat turned to naught and they found their ledger deep in the red.
They discovered that their trust in a mainland agent who acted for them
had been misplaced and they were betrayed in the end. Arata's dream of
a mercantile empire, starting from a chain of grocery stores and branching out into export and import trade with agencies in the Far East and
in the seaport cities of the continental United States, became a bubble
rudely punctured. For a while, until their fortune was further recouped,
there was to be the strictest economy; even Sadao was recalled from
school to help the family in productive work.

The chief reason in getting their fourteen year old boy out of school
was a face-saving measure; a concrete and tangible act to demonstrate to
the community and to friends who had invested and lost in his commercial venture, that he had suffered the greatest blow and his family
was even being denied what little advantage it had enjoyed prior to the
unfortunate affair. In this manner the family fortune was at the lowest
ebb, but the reputation and prestige of the storekeeper was maintained,
and Seikichi Arata could hold his chin up in the community.

Sadao was given a job at the plantation store, but not having had
courses in bookkeeping at school, his status was that of a mere salesman
and a laborer in the warehouse. He discovered that he was not cut out
to catering to the whims of customers. To the great disappointment of
his father, he quit this store work and landed a job at the sugar mill.

From early morning he would report to work in his oil-soaked clothes
and on return home was too tired to seek youthful companions. Although
well-developed for his fifteen summers, he was not yet hardened and the

work at the beginning was trying to him. He was getting twenty-four dollars a month for this work. In the beginning, he was somewhat ashamed of the fact that he could not graduate from school. Especially humiliating was the fact that he could not invite his friends over to Kauai as they had planned that night at the dormitory, for now he could not spend the days hunting and fishing with them.

Meanwhile, when summer came and went, Susumu had left for Japan as planned, and only Minoru continued his studies in Honolulu. Not being of a studious make-up, Sadao fell in with his old boyhood friends and after he got inured to the toil, began to go out at night to while away the idle evening hours in their boisterous company. His mother did not exactly approve of this development and would rather have had him stay at home and watch the store. But then it was almost impossible to deny him the few pleasures that were due him after the day's hard work at the mill. A parent could not be too strict or the severity would boomerang; not be too loose, for then there would be no discipline. A happy median was indeed hard to hit.

Two years passed. Sadao became a hardened worker. Pleasures were very few in those days on the plantations. About twice a month a traveling entourage of movie men came around and showed pictures outdoors on the schoolgrounds. On such nights, the young swains would have a chance to meet the girls of the village. Among them Sadao was attracted by Aki Aoki, two years his junior, who had just finished school and was going to a seamstress of the village to learn needlework. It was nothing more than a puppy love affair, but not having any other interest to occupy them in their leisure hours, it soon became noticeable and was talked about among the younger set. About all that each felt was a keen awareness of the proximity of the other and profuse blushing when kidded by their friends. But such well-intentioned teasing only helped bring them closer.

When Mrs. Arata heard this rumor, she was not pleased at all. She had not outgrown the teachings of old Japan that followed the old Confucian concept of "When boys and girls reach their sixth year of age, they should not sit together." Perhaps precocity was a tropical phenomenon, and looseness of boundaries between the sexes the result of American education and training; still she did not like the idea of her first son becoming enamoured with the daughter of Aoki who was a chronic alcoholic. She did not dislike Aki as a person, but in marriage the family had to be taken into consideration. The Aratas, despite their recent financial setback, rated a bride from a better family and background.

So one night, Seikichi Arata, with his wife at his side, talked in an even tone to his first born. "Son, you are growing up to be a man. In old Japan when a boy reached his fifteenth year, he was considered a full-fledged man after he went through the ceremony called *genpuku*. He was allowed to carry two swords and sit in the council of men. His hairdress became different from the one he had been wearing since his boyhood. According to the Japanese way of calculation you are already eighteen, and so I am going to talk to you as a man. We have heard talk linking your name with the Aoki girl. She may be all right. I don't know enough about her to pass judgment. But I do know something about her family. Her father is a good-for-nothing. He does not work half of the time. Just raises kids. They must be fed just the same and as a result he owes every store. The sum owed us is increasing all the time, with never a gesture to reduce it. You know what will happen if there should ever be a family tie. That is too much of a risk. Therefore, before you get involved any deeper, you will see to it that this affair stops and you meet her no more."

Sadao was not able to answer. It was the first time he had to speak to his parents on a subject such as this. He was plainly embarrassed and kept quiet. To Seikichi, of the old school of thought, silence signified acquiescence.

"Now that we understand each other, we shall not refer to the matter again. But we shall be on the lookout for a girl who will be a good wife and a good daughter-in-law. Marriage is a serious matter and the balanced, wise counsel of elders should be heeded."

Sadao felt a peculiar reaction. He was an obedient son. He thought a great deal of his father and so far had obeyed him dutifully and implicitly. Now he felt a surge of emotion within him that was new, a reaction that was akin to anger. To be rebellious against parents was not new, for everyone had his scoldings and whippings in boyhood that inevitably brought about sullenness, but this anger seemed of a new character. The man in him seemed to be awakening and with it a desire for an assertion of his rights and independence, just as a fledgling would have an instinctive urge to try out its wings in the open sky.

The more he thought about it, the less did he cherish the idea of remaining at home. He did not wish to go contrary to his parents' injunctions, for to him they were both antiquated and silly. After a week's pondering, he made up his mind to leave for the pineapple cannery that was then operating at Kapaa, thirty miles away. He left suddenly without telling even his mother, but wrote the day he arrived at his destination.

Dear Parents:

Since the talk father gave me a week ago, I have given your advice the deepest thought and have come to the conclusion that perhaps my staying away from Makaweli for the time being would be the best move for me to take. This is the only way for me to follow your advice. Life here at Kapaa among strangers may not be as easy perhaps as at Makaweli, but at least I am old enough to take care of myself.

I am going to ask for a job tomorrow at the cannery. I am sure of landing a job as the season is just about beginning and the schools have not yet closed. It is not so far away from home and I can hop a ride back on my days off when the pineapple season gets slack.

Please overlook the fact that I left without your knowledge and consent for obvious reasons.

Your dutiful son,
Sadao

The pineapple cannery at Kapaa was situated in such a charming location that, had it been a more populous township, the site would have been reserved for a park or for beach homesites. Black volcanic rocks and disintegrated lava sands made up the shore. It was not suitable for swimming or wading in the surf, but the air was exhilarating with the sea that pounded against these rocks and sent the spray flying in the wind. The ironwood trees fifty to sixty feet high planted in several rows as wind-breaks along the beach became a natural park for picknickers, and the factory was located just leeward to this grove of trees. A perpetual rustle of the trees in the usually prevailing Trade Winds harmonized rather awkwardly with the din of machinery that kept on revolving day and night during the busy season about the Fourth of July. The pineapples were hauled from districts to the north and west where hundreds of acres were planted. Huge trucks with trailers were used in the transportation of these ripe fruits from the red soiled fields that were particularly suited for their culture.

The ripe fruit were with one stroke of a cylindrical knife shed of their skin and central core. They were then sliced transversely with machinery and these pieces were laid out on a conveyor belt that passed in front of many white-robed and gloved females of many races. The idea was to make the conditions as sanitary as possible so that no bare hands came in contact with the fruit itself. Standing alongside this belt the girls picked up the undamaged slices and placed them in open cans. The damaged pieces were allowed to be carried further on to be used in cans of lesser grades or to be crushed. Different belts conveyed different sizes of fruits and gradations of products were made in this manner. The cans were then taken along, the syrup poured onto the sliced fruits, covers or lids placed on them, and sterilized.

To supply these female workers with trays of empty cans and remove the filled ones was the work of "tray boys." These boys had to be husky and muscular and Sadao landed a job as one of them at seventeen cents an hour. Contrary to sugar mill work, this toiling at the pineapple factory was fun due principally to the fact that it was a mixed working crew and the presence of girls made life easier and more colorful. Time passed fast. There was a lot of bantering and kidding amongst the workers at time of rest or during lunch hours, for while the machinery was in motion they were chained to the relentless arrival of yellow slices of fruit that had to be disposed of. There were occasions when they were not so occupied. There might be a dearth of trucks arriving from the fields or some trouble with the smooth operation of the machinery at which time they were able to relax. Such intervals were apt to occur during the night shift.

Pearl Harmon was twenty-two. In her veins ran hot Irish and passionate Polynesian blood, but for reasons known only to herself she had not yet married. She lived with her brother who was on the police force and when the canning season came around she worked there as fore-woman among the female workers. Her shift was mostly at night. She was not too hard a boss and opinion concerning her among the male workers was divided. It was common knowledge that she was no angel and yet a certain amount of deference was paid in spite of the secret desire with which they viewed her supple form. Among the older male workers there seemed to be rivalry as to who might eventually win her favor but to a newcomer and youngster like Sadao, such a situation was not comprehended. Neither did he harbor such ulterior motives. For big as he was at seventeen, he was still a timid boy and blushingly submitted to the taunts of older men and women.

Sadao was on the outside leaning against one of the ironwood trees and taking the fresh air. He was puffing at a cigarette he had learned to smoke in the past year. It was quiet at one o'clock in the morning and the moonless tropical night seemed more beautiful with stars to embellish the heavenly dome. Constellations and planets were beyond his ken. He could only tell the Great Bear and the North Star, but at least he was able to recognize and appreciate the beauty of Orion with the jewelled dagger. The remoteness of these heavenly bodies and the pure brilliance of these starry creations imparted a mysterious and romantic element so different from the ugly man-made machinery that kept on turning and pounding to do man's bidding in preparing one more item to display on the grocers' shelves of the nation.

The proximity of another human being was somehow easily sensed, a sixth sense inherited from our ancestors of days when such acute sensibilities were necessary for the safety of the individual to survive, and he was doubly sure of it when a strong emanation of a feminine odor wafted near. He did not turn and he felt a hand cover his eyes from behind. "Guess," was the single word that gently came. He wound one of his forearms backward and caught her around the waist and the soft body came forward to press soft breasts against his back, and before he knew it, he felt a warm kiss on the nape of his neck.

"Now, I have started something!" with a soft giggle Pearl Harmon had her strong arms around him tightly holding him against her body.

In such a way, on such a night under the singing ironwood trees begun an episode which was soon to culminate, transforming the outlook of life from that of a diffident boy to that of an aggressive male.

Sadao and Aki were together after a separation of two months. They had broken away from the dancing crowd and were under the ironwood tree in the shade which at that hour was dark and away from prying eyes. He had his arms around her waist as they sat on the dry pine needles that carpeted the ground The rest of the young and old were dancing, swaying to the monotonous rhythm of songs that were lusty, comical and at times parts of merry episodes of historical ballads. To the country boys and girls, coming out together at night was a rare privilege granted by parents and guardians only during this season. The spirit of the *Obon* was not comprehended at all or was lost in the centuries of merry-making in villages and towns of Japan. In Hawaii, few even paid attention to the significance of the festival as deaths were few and far between and old people were a rarity. Anyway, it was an occasion when secret rendezvous between the young were surreptitiously carried out. At the end of the busy season, Sadao had returned to Makaweli and for the time being was doing nothing. He had planned to proceed to Kapaa or Lihue to find more permanent employment.

"Don't you find the dances kind of tiresome? I do. I do not care much for the endless motions with the feet and hands."

"I can dance all night. I feel like I am free like the birds. It is fun to dance together with all the girls."

"You mean with the boys, don't you? By the way, did you get to meet someone you liked better than you do me?"

"Oh don't be silly. How can you talk like that! I am going to be real hurt if you say anything like that again."

"Do you mean that I am your boy friend and there is none besides me? Really? Gee, I never thought you cared that much for me," he pressed her closer to him and she did not object. Aki got her first kiss that night and she clung tightly to him. To her it was a dream come true, but to Sadao it was not so pure. Pearl Harmon had shown the secrets of the procreating animal to the young lad but he did not have the nerve nor the heart to carry his instincts beyond the decorous boundary prescribed in the etiquettes that were taught him in books and at school. Again and again they kissed and swore everlasting troth to each other. To make the most exaggerated promises under such circumstances is not only natural but beautiful. Every dream, every act, every artistic creation is beautiful until destroyed and in life which is full of vicissitudes, there is nothing that may be called truth. Sadao's fervent expressions of love and the endearing metaphors were truly said no matter how false they might turn out later.

His adolescent tendency to put women on pedestals, the Walter Scottian concept of the relation between the opposite sexes, was rudely shattered by the realistic initiation he received at the hands of Pearl

Harmon. But there was still decency left in him and he could not but help reciprocate Aki's purity in the beginning. But the season of the *Obon* was celebrated at practically all the larger camps where there was a predominance of men from Yamaguchi or Niigata Prefectures, for it happened that these dances were not prevalent everywhere in Japan and only those that had childhood memories to revive were ardent backers of them in Hawaii.

Surreptitiously, Sadao had a chance to meet Aki almost every Saturday evening for a whole month. They traveled from one dance to another in groups and, therefore, avoided the restraining supervision of their parents and elders. Soon, Aki too became mature in both body and spirit and to her inexperienced mind, Sadao was destined to be her husband, for did he not pledge to her his ultimate intention? Then and only then did she yield wholly to his ardor. Life became sweet, as sweet as she had ever dreamed it could be. Yet, there were times in her young, inexperienced inner soul, when she doubted if everything were as it should be. The submerged racial experience of her millions of female progenitors was tormenting her quiet hours. The tears and anguish of her ancestresses were making her uneasy, but as soon as she met Sadao and felt his strong arms about her, all such fears melted away like the morning dew when bathed by the morning sun, and she was ashamed of herself and of her lack of faith in him.

"I have been doing some real thinking lately. My going to Kapaa to work at the pineapple cannery was meant just for the time being, for the summer. I cannot see any future for me in this dinky country town, where everything is owned by the haoles. My father owns that small store but I am no businessman. I cannot stoop low to please anyone. I think I would like to build things and run tractors or trucks. I know what it is to live in Honolulu and there are a few friends I made while I was there at school. I am going out after I talk over this matter with father and mother. You will remain while I make a start and then I will come and get you. Then we can get married. Be a good girl until then."

"Don't you think I want to go to the city too?"

"But you must not and cannot go until plans are made for you. The city is not a place for you until you are sure that someone will take care of you."

"Yes, that may be true, but can't I learn dressmaking or something and keep myself occupied? Maybe I can do housework. I heard that many girls have jobs as maids or nursemaids and are able to save considerable money. I do not want to remain here after you are gone."

"That may sound very well. Just the same, I don't like the idea of you going until I feel safe about your being taken care of in the city and then I shall come and get you. I think I can return in a year or two and that is not very long."

For ten minutes Aki was silent. She was in deep thought but decisively she gave her answer. "I have a few dollars with me. I will go to Honolulu and start my own life too and be near you. I am not afraid of hard work."

Seeing that there was no way of dissuading her he said, "Then you'll come with me. I know Honolulu. Let us go in different buses from here to Nawiliwili to avoid suspicion. We can meet on the steamer." She pressed his hand tightly.

The steamer day in Nawiliwili was not as colorful as in Honolulu because the passengers were few. Homemade leis bedecked the passengers surrounded by their relatives and friends. Half the travelers were "drummers" that were returning to Honolulu after making their monthly rounds of the Kauai retail stores. Sadao lingered on the wharf for an hour and tried not to appear conspicuous in the activity that was taking place. He stayed away from the crowd and stood near the stevedores loading the holds of the ship with sacks of sugar.

The hourly bus from Makaweli arrived and disgorged its passengers, and among them was the forlorn figure of Aki. She appeared relieved when she spied him but kept her distance. On such a small island people knew one another too well. She, too, mingled with the crowd until time for boarding.

The chain across the foot of the gangplank was removed and the purser stationed himself there. Sadao advanced and climbed the steps behind the "drummers." When he was almost at the top, there was a commotion and a loud voice. "Stop that girl! Stop that girl!"

He looked down and there saw Aki just mounting the gangplank, pale and shaken. Two men were running toward her. It was her father accompanied by the native policeman from the Waimea police station. She shot an appealing glance toward Sadao, but soon composed herself and descended the few steps to the wharf and walked toward her pursuers before a further scene could be enacted by her irate father.

Sadao drifted to an employment agency as soon as he got settled in a cheap hotel room on River Street in Honolulu. The reception of a city to a job seeker from the country was a chilly one compared to the smooth welcome accorded a student seeking an education. On the blackboard there were openings of housework, yardman, waiter, hotel handyman, but these did not interest him. He wanted hard, muscular work. He drifted to another agency and there he found a call for truck drivers and caterpillar operators for a construction job on a dam in Wahiawa. He had no experience but brazenly went to work on the truck. Luckily, he was put on as helper and by his glib tongue he struck up a friendship with the simple, good-natured native driver and was allowed to drive, away from prying eyes, on the open stretch of road. In a few days he was able to operate a truck. He worked for a month and in the meantime got acquainted with the storekeeper of this booming town.

"Mr. Oka, I see many trucks on the pineapple fields from where I work. Are they all company trucks?"

"Yes, many belong to the pineapple company but at the height of the harvesting season, like now, additional trucks are hired by the hour or by piecework. Those fellows make a lot of money. Why don't you try? You seem to be strong and healthy and perhaps not afraid of hard work."

"Oh, as far as work is concerned I am as strong as a horse. But where is the money to buy a truck? Nobody will lend a young man like me money to buy a truck," Sadao retorted just a trifle irritated.

"Well, if you really want to do that kind of work, maybe I can arrange it for you. You can buy a second-hand one and pay the dealer as you earn the money. It may turn out to be a very good start for an independent career in business. You young fellows should not work for others all your life." By this time the storekeeper was assuming a fatherly attitude.

It was a novel idea. Perhaps he could work in the manner advised and come out an owner of a truck. "I am game to try it. Please teach me how to go about getting a truck by that arrangement. I'll work very hard."

The second-hand four ton truck cost him fifteen hundred dollars. There was no down payment, for the storekeeper co-signed the agreement of sale. Sadao promised to pay as he received his weekly compensation for the hauling job. The short hauls of ripe pineapple from the field to the loading platform of the railroad netted him three and a half dollars on the average and he was able to make about ten trips a day. He engaged a Filipino youth as helper and paid him ninety cents per day.

It was hard work but very stimulating. There was a lot of incentive, and so by the end of the season he became complete owner of the truck and netted five hundred dollars.

When the pineapple harvest season ended, he was called to Waipahu by the chief overseer who had seen him work at Wahiawa and now offered him a job hauling pipes from the station to the mill. It was a very small piece of work, but nothing was too small for him at this stage.

"Well, young man, that's all the work here right now. I will let you know when there is more work than our own trucks can handle," said the overseer who took kindly to this young man who worked very hard.

"Thank you. I certainly can do any kind of work and I won't disappoint you," smiled Sadao as he received his pay.

"By the way, drive over to the sisal lands and see if you can clear that land of all the brush. The sisal and cactus must go. If you can do it, give me an estimate of your bid. We need one hundred acres of cleared land to build a mooring mast for the navy dirigible." He pointed as he talked. The sisal land lay beyond the sugar cane fields of Ewa plantation on the way to Waianae. He drove there and saw the rough rocky terrain covered with overgrown shrubs of acacia, cacti, and sisal. It was an abandoned sisal plantation that had been started decades earlier but was now neglected. He saw smoke rising several hundred feet from the government road. He stopped his truck and walked to the cluster of makeshift huts. Three Japanese laborers were making charcoal out of algaroba trees that abounded there.

"Good afternoon. What a hot day and you all working so hard."

"Good afternoon, young man. It's always hot and dry here at Ewa." The men all smiled. Visitors were few and a break in work was not unwelcome.

"I come here with a job for you if you care to make some money. I have a contract to clear one hundred acres of this land. Can you tell me about how much it will cost to clear an acre?"

"We are charcoal makers and only work on the large algaroba trees. We have never had anything to do with clearing such land. What is the object of this work?"

"The government is going to build a tall mooring mast to tie a large dirigible when it flies here from the coast. You know the large baloon-like aircraft the Germans have?"

"I see. We have no idea what labor is involved in such clearing work, but we can try and find out, can't we?"

"That's fine. If I can get an estimate and if I can get the work, you will profit, because I must depend on you fellows here to do the actual work. Let us mark off an area, say one hundred by one hundred feet. You work on it leisurely and the result will give us some idea as to how much labor will be necessary for an acre."

So the three men set to work and cut down the obnoxious shrubs and sisal plants. Sadao timed their work, and a rough estimate of the time required to clear an acre was arrived at. He doubled the estimated figure and submitted it as his bid for the hundred acres to the Waipahu Plantation overseer. The latter accepted the offer and a contract was issued for the work.

The charcoal burners became the nucleus for the crew and independent farmers of the vicinity were recruited at two and a half dollars a day. When these men saw that a youth had gotten this job for them, they felt glad—glad as if one of their own sons had been in his shoes. The princely sum of two and a half dollars was two and a half times the plantation pay. These laborers realized the potentiality of the second generation who could speak English in various industrial and commercial ventures in a not-too-distant future. They worked hard: much harder than if the work had been their own. They not only wanted to be worthy of the wages, they wanted the young man to feel the satisfaction of success in this his first contract work. As a result he netted five thousand dollars, and Sadao Arata was on his way as an independent contractor.

CHAPTER 15

Minoru Matures

AFTER THE PARTING OF HIS TWO ERSTWHILE friends, Minoru was left alone at school to continue his studies. As he was an avid reader, his English was improving with leaps and bounds. The inadequate training in the two room country school was reflected in his poor English, and this became more pronounced as he skipped the fifth grade and found himself enrolled in the sixth grade. This feat was accomplished by lying to the principal and saying that he was duly qualified to enter the sixth. However, by a little extra studying, he found the lessons too easy and after a lapse of four months audaciously asked to be promoted to the seventh and this permission was granted. Thus in the second year he was in the eighth grade and by sheer cramming, the entrance examination to McKinley High School was passed with flying colors and he was second among a group of eighty from the Royal School.

High school was conducted differently from the easy-going grammar school. Prof. M. M. Scott was then the principal of this, the only public high school on the island of Oahu, and its scholastic standard was very high. Students who could not survive the examinations were mercilessly asked to leave. Out of a class that started with one hundred fifty strong, only thirty-six were destined to graduate four years later. Sports were relegated to second place and McKinley High was then noted for its weak athletic teams.

Prof. Scott was unique as an educator. He was a Doctor of Philosophy and was instrumental in the organization of the educational system of Japan, where he had gone forty years previously as an expert in education. Not only had he helped establish the normal school system in the Ministry of Education, but he had taught English at the Imperial University of Tokyo. He was adviser to the Japanese consulate at Honolulu.

His interest in Oriental students was a lifelong one. At this time, the Chinese students predominated in number and the Japanese children were just beginning to arrive at high school age. This old pedagogue's conception of education was indeed the symbol of democracy and he laid the wonderful achievement of assimilation of the heterogeneous races of America at the door of her system of public education. His favorite saying—and he took every occasion to emphasize this conviction: "If I should take a Chinese boy born in Peking or in the hinterland of Hupeh and transplant him into a typical family in Mississippi, his mannerisms and modes of thought will be typically American or southern. In the same way an American boy, born in Mississippi, if transplanted into a cultured Chinese family in Nanking, will grow up no different from his Chinese playmates with whom he associates. This then is the essence of education. The Americanization of the different racial strains that are found within the boundaries of the United States will be achieved by education. Americanization transcends racial differences."

Therefore, his emphasis on the study of the English language was very strong. Only by speaking it correctly and writing it well could assimilation be expected. In the freshman year, he called the composition class "jackplaning" and the advanced classes "the finishing touches." Minoru was later to find how well he was drilled in English when he enrolled in one of the leading universities on the mainland and discovered, to his amusement, how poor the Caucasians were in their written English. In order to improve his English, he read one novel a week in addition to his usual school work and committed to memory all idioms that he came across.

Every Thursday morning for one solid hour the seventy year old principal would have his assembly hour when his announcements would be made to the student body. At the same time he would wind up the bulk of the hour with anecdotes and sage advice or admonitions, derived from his long and useful life, to the students and faculty. Sage talk flowed in these assemblies and student and teacher alike looked forward to these meetings. Silver-haired, with a far away look in his eyes, always wearing a white linen coat with high collar—like a dress uniform of a naval officer—and black serge trousers, he was a person who lingered in the memory of the young people who were fortunate to be at school under his direction.

Minoru had to make up his mind as to what he wanted to do in his adult life. The courses open to the students were college preparatory and commercial. Somehow he could no longer visualize himself as a worker on the plantation; neither could he be happy, he was pretty sure, to become a mere clerk. City life had opened greater vistas of life to him, and the significance of life and the way of living fired such an ambition in him that he began to aspire to something higher than the opportunities the Hawaiian area had to offer. He must by all means go to college no matter what line of work he should eventually pursue. In order to prepare himself for the final choice of vocation—and that selection was very difficult to make at his age—he planned to take all the sciences, mathematics, and German, since one of the natural sciences would be his choice anyway.

It later turned out to be a very logical, rational, and wise way of studying and arranging for his future life. Every subject was interesting. History had a particular fascination for him. Without much effort he led classes in all courses whether ancient or modern. However, he never intended to go into scholarly work, because his poverty-stricken family required an earning career as soon as possible. Moreover, he had no conception of any man earning his livelihood by study and research in such metaphysical sciences for the simple reason that he had never come into contact with real scholars. To become a school teacher was not to his liking as he was too well aware of his shyness, and to become didactic was never his nature.

Miss Agnew was a history teacher from Wisconsin. She taught third year history and it was a study of English parliamentary development. In particular it was a study of English common law, and the development of the Bill of Rights and *habeas corpus*. The struggle of the yeomanry against the landed gentry was not so strange, but the hanging and beheading of kings and then enthroning another ruler because of his blue blood was hard to understand. When Miss Agnew stressed the point that it was the birthright of all free men to rebel against the existing government if the trust of the people was betrayed by officialdom, it was a very difficult philosophy for the Oriental students to digest.

She used to smile and it apparently was a source of considerable interest for she used to say, "How you Japanese and Chinese, especially Japanese, hold the existing government as almost infallible is interesting to me. Much like the Germans of Wisconsin, you are apt to follow the governing body without question. To try to change a corrupt government, first by ballot and by force if necessary, is the English way of life. In fact, in that way the United States of America got its start." Minoru, try as he might, could not fully accept this political history until many years later.

When he took botany and zoology, he intended to take up agriculture and sent for catalogues from different agricultural colleges. In his junior year when he became fascinated by chemistry his future career could be nothing but chemical engineering. In his senior year when physics seemed the acme of exact science, he dreamed of becoming a marine architect. During 1917 and 1918 shipping was the talk of the press due to the submarine activity in the Atlantic. The final decision and how it was determined was to come later.

During adolescence, everything is new and every day strange vistas of life are being opened up and the world's horizon is widened before one's eyes. It was during this period that Minoru received a profound spirtual stimulus in the unravelling and comprehension of the mysteries of the universe. A glimpse into the philosophies of the ancients that are, after all, human attempts at an explanation of the meaning of our existence; especially what will become of us after the body gets cold and the heart stops beating.

He never went to church while he was in the country school. His father and mother were Buddhists and like all good followers, there was a family altar to which on days especially to be remembered by the family, special vegetable offerings would be made by his mother and his father would recite the simplest of sutras, the *Shoshin-ge*. Aside from these rituals, there was nothing in his life to make him realize that there was an invisible, all-powerful creator or a savior to whom he had to account for his behavior. In a robust colonial life where almost everyone was in the prime of youth and working for his livelihood, there was scarcely any concern about the problems of death and the future life. Religion created for the believers was not a topic discussed freely.

Once when he was about nine years old, the Hawaiian teacher who had been assigned to Minoru's country school as his first teaching job spoke of the Day of Judgment when the Creator would sit in review of all human souls. Opening the Great Register, he would sift out the good from the bad and bid them go to the right or the left according to the information gleaned from the records. The children were told that such was the arrangement of the Creator and so henceforth they should look out for their activities and behavior because the Lord in Heaven was so all-seeing that nothing would escape his scrutiny. Minoru was immensely impressed and got into a deep talk with a boy three years his senior, and together they marvelled at the justice of the arrangement because to him the Creator of the universe would beyond any doubt have sweeping power, and it was nothing but right that the good should be rewarded with everlasting paradise and the wicked go to the torture of never-ending fire. It was a logical set-up.

After he came to Honolulu, he was compelled to go to the Sunday School and attend the temple after the one hour session in which stories of Buddha's life and the basic teachings of Buddhism were systematically taught. To him these were nuisances and he concluded that better use could be made of a Sunday morning if he remained in the dormitory and read something more after his heart. The teachers at the Sunday schools were like parrots and nothing dynamic was conveyed in these lessons, because the teachers themselves lacked fire and faith. But one day at school a teacher referred to the old story of Ishido Maru, dear to the hearts of the Japanese people, as an example of folklore with a lot of pathos and human emotions that have wrung the sympathetic heart strings of the populace for many centuries in songs, drama, and sermons.

"Kato Saemon Shigeuji was the governor of Tsukushi that encompassed the extensive domain that is now known as the island of Kyushu. He had practically the power of life and death over all the people that dwelled there, but having one day seen the wickedness of one's desires and the unbelievably base extent to which one was willing to go to attain that end, he became disgusted and disillusioned with the conduct of life as it was currently lived. He deserted position and family and joined the roving band of monks and priests to seek personal salvation and the spiritual peace only the enlightened are privileged to enjoy. In the concept of the teachings of India, only by casting off all earthly ties, greed, and the carnal desires, could one ever hope to aspire to this state, but his agony over the foibles of humanity was such that he did not hesitate to take this ultimate step. Fourteen years passed. His only son, Ishido Maru, left behind with his mother and his sister, heard from some source that his father had been seen among the three thousand monks at Koya San. Bereft of the love of his father, there was an insatiable and uncontrollable longing in the heart of this fifteen year old boy to go seek this father who had only existed in his dreams.

"Accompanied by his mother, he arrived at Kamuro-juku at the foot of the sacred mountain of Koya. To their great sorrow, the ascent of women on this mountain on which three thousand monks lived under the strictest discipline of self-negation and celibacy was absolutely forbidden. Leaving his mother to wait at an inn at the foot of the mountain, Ishido Maru made his way alone toward the summit. The wayside was lined with little temples and large communal living quarters for the disciples of Kobo-Daishi, the founder of this sect. Treading his way among the nine hundred ninety temples, he failed to detect or meet any individual that fit the description of his father. In this fruitless search three days and two nights were wasted and he began to feel concern for his mother. His thoughts went flying to her and the urge to be at her side became so insistent that even the rustle of the wind among the pine trees was mistaken for her voice and the shadows of unexpected objects were imagined to be the presence of his mother. The ancient poem of Gyoki Bosatsu,

> Listening to the copper pheasant,
>   Crying horo-horo in the dale, I wonder,
>   Could it be the voice of mother,
>   Or might it be the call of father?

came to his mind and he was in the deepest abyss of despondency.

"Just then there came down the mountain trail a monk, Karukaya, with a rosary around his left wrist and a bunch of flowers in his right hand, quietly reciting the verses of the Shingon sutra. As the two met and their garments brushed each other, Ishido looked up into the wise face of the priest lined with evidence of suffering, 'Will you have the goodness to teach me something? to inform me of that which I seek?'

"Karukaya looked down and was struck at the freshness of the youth, and the urgent appeal in the eyes that tended to melt the hardest of hearts. Karukaya's eyes went down to the boy's waist and there descried a familiar sword, and with a tumultuous heart his glance returned to the face and about the region of the eyes and eyebrows he discovered a resemblance to his wife. Mystified, he answered, 'If it is someone you are seeking, then go to the central office and put up a sign to that effect.'

"To this answer, Ishido's face assumed the greatest disappointment and Karukaya was so sorry for his abrupt way of dismissal that he led the boy by the hand to his modest abode, and there asked the youngster

209

his name, where he came from, and the reason for his intense search after someone. 'I am the son of Kato Saemon Shigeuji, the former governor of the land of Tsukushi. My name is Ishido Maru.' The priest was astonished and could not hide or control the glistening of his eyes and the tears that coursed down his cheeks. Ishido seemed to sense the truth. 'If you are my father, pray speak the truth.' And he looked up so intently into Karukaya's face from the front and from the side with a longing that Karukaya would have gladly gathered up the child in his arms and said, 'Yes, you are indeed my son, my dear son, whom I have never seen these many years and have neglected so long,' but the training of his religious order prohibited such indulgence and relapses into worldly ties.

" "The man you seek died last fall when the leaves of trees turned crimson.' Ishido was stunned and then wailed so sadly that Karukaya led him by the hand to a neighboring cemetery and pointed out a fictitious grave. The child weakly knelt down before the tombstone, tears rolling down his cheeks, and burned the incense that the elder priest had brought along. Clasping his hands in prayer he intoned in anguish *Namu Amida Butsu.*

"Karukaya had weathered the trying self-negation practice for ten years or more and he believed in the vicissitudes of all living beings, that the meeting was the beginning of parting, that all living things would eventually end in death, and that impermanence was the unshakable truth of the universe. Despite this conviction and knowledge, the call of blood and the sight of the helpless child had awakened the apparently forgotten human emotions and weaknesses, and he picked up the boy who had crumpled on the ground.

" 'To waste tears is not good for the soul of the departed. Go to your mother and tell her what you have discovered. Then pray for the peace of your father's soul. Your father will surely be extremely glad to have a son so devoted to his memory.'

"Ishido was completely defeated but the thoughts of his mother waiting at the inn sped him downward, but alas, he was to find her not of this world for a virulent infection, probably modern pneumonia, had carried her off. The people took pity on the unfortunate boy and helped him cremate her remains. Bereft of his father as an infant and now robbed of his only remaining parent so suddenly, the only one to turn to was an elder sister remaining in Tsukushi. Thither he returned to report the sad tidings, but on arrival the vicissitude of life was more forcibly brought to him in the news that she also was no longer living. Ishido had no one on this earth who had any interest in him. The erstwhile governor's family was easily forgotten by men who had catered to the governor for favors. In this chilly atmosphere the boy's memory of the kindly priest of Koya became the one bright spot in his existence and prompted him to retrace his steps eastward. Again he climbed the sacred mountain to find refuge in the sanctuary of Karukaya's guidance. Karukaya never divulged the true relation between them and for many years they roamed about the countryside as pilgrims and finally at Zenkoji in the province of Shinano they settled down after building themselves a temple."

Minoru was immensely impressed with the story. Its pathos and religious discipline were one thing and the story was a fine one in which to shed many a tear, but above everything else Minoru was struck with the depth of Buddhistic thinking and philosophy. To look at life in the widest sense, to recognize the dumb animal as a possible reincarnated relative, was a way of thinking that was really all-encompassing and its magnitude was tremendous. The poem of Gyoki Bosatsu was a shining revelation to him about the "oneness" of the universe. In this mode of thinking the universe could be considered as "one." Brotherhood of mankind could be stretched to a oneness of all, both animate and inanimate, of the universe. It was at the same time very romantic and poetic.

From this time on, his selection of reading material took on a revolutionary change. He used to read a lot in order to improve his English and he found that was the only way to write fluently. His taste had run to Scott and Dickens, but he now stuck to the writings of Lafcadio Hearn and read from cover to cover all books penned by this author. They not only revealed a philosophy that was very new, and strangely near to his heart because he had been brought up in a family where talk naturally would include phrases that originated with this religion, but he enjoyed these books for the beauty of Hearn's prose. His English had a mystic ring and was very beautiful. What the Sunday School failed to convey, Hearn was able to make him understand in a very poetic way. His introduction to religion was through this channel of portrayal of an otherwise dry philosophy. *The Kokoro, Glimpses of Ghostly Japan,* and *Gleanings in Buddha Fields* were books that were read and reread. He learned more about the thoughts of the Japanese from Hearn's writings than from reading Japanese novels and writings, because they were written for people who were nurtured as Japanese with all the background of Japanese traditions. With the foreign born Japanese, Western writers were more easily understood because their elucidation of the topic was meant for such as Minoru, the uninitiated.

The dissection of Japanese character and customs, at times very flattering and perhaps undeserved, evoked and fostered in him a pride in his cultural heritage. Coupled with the short trip he had made to the Orient, the writings of Hearn accentuated this feeling which was destined never to be erased. He felt with all his conviction that to be a truly good American citizen, this pride was important, for America never would welcome a cringing individual, and in order to be a valuable member of the Commonwealth capable of contributing something to the culture, one had to be proud of his forebears and add whatever he understood was good to the sum total of the existing civilization of America, which was in essence the collection of different strains of European culture grafted upon an English trunk. There was something fine and worthy that had been evolved in twenty centuries of Japanese adaptation of Sino-Hindustani civilization, and the culture had attained a point of refinement elsewhere unseen. America would not be the loser in adding this artistic evolution to her vast variety and collection of human achievements. Who else could be a better interpreter of the East to the United States than he? How could it be accomplished if he himself could not read the originals and if he could not really understand the feelings of Japanese culture in his bones and be really proud of what he was trying to interpret?

This search into the thoughts and philosophy of the East became not cold logic and abstract philosophical elucidation, but assumed the warmth of religious faith in the chance reading of a pamphlet that told the following story.

"There was a high school girl brought up in a very devout Buddhist family in Tokyo. She attended the Chiyoda Girl's High School because of the religious affiliation of the school to the Shin sect of Buddhism. At school and at home her drilling into the tenets of the sect was thorough and she believed without reserve in the teachings of the Buddha Amitahba who had vowed, 'in the eons of lives that preceded this planetary age that until all living beings should become Buddhas or have entered the blessed realm of Nirvana, He would not rest and would continue to toil for the salvation of all living beings.' Her religious nature might have been the result of her not-too-robust constitution, for finally she contracted a lingering disease of the chest and had to spend months in bed. This confinement and solitude spurred her to read the unlimited number of writings revolving around the meaning of this transient human existence, and meditate over the vicissitudes and untrustworthiness of what we deem as secure things, and rejoice over the glory of the life that awaited the believers according to doctrine of salvation through the mercy of the Amitabha. Her belief was like a rock and it even shamed her parents in their realization of their own honest state of faith, for as frail human beings they were not able to keep their religious fervor at a high pitch in this humdrum life which had to be spent in the pursuit of earning a livelihood and at this endeavor invariably and unwittingly they committed sins and transgressions.

"To the great astonishment of the parents, their daughter one day confessed in tears that although she believed in the absolute salvation of human beings by the all embracing love of the Buddha Amitahba, and was firm in the belief that her next life would be in Nirvana, she did not want to die. She wanted to live with her loved ones in this world even if it were full of deceit and human strife.

"Her parents did not know what to do. Was she backsliding? Was her faith not sufficient? In a quandary, the mother visited the principal of the school, Reverend Izumi and reported, 'Our daughter who used to have so much faith in Amitahba's mercy has uttered strange words. She does not want to die; does not long to go to the blessed land. She would rather remain in this world. Why does she waver now when even our eyes can see that her days are numbered. We cannot bear to see her in such an undecided state of mind. She should travel to the land of bliss with more conviction than that. We simply are worried, my husband and I.'

" ' I shall visit with your daughter, for I have not seen her for some time,' Rev. Izumi answered sympathetically and he came along. At her bedside, he looked down into the emaciated face that was pale and pasty and which lacked the color of life. Only the bright, fever-ridden eyes shone with a luminosity that was intense: too intense and avid to be for her own good. Something was seething in her mind behind those bright eyes. At the sight of the venerable teacher color rose to her cheeks and

213

she smiled pleasantly 'What is this I hear from your mother? She says you do not want to die.'

" 'Yes sir, that is what I feel within me these last few days. I know that I do not have long to live. As this realization of the imminence of my end becomes acute, I feel that it is good to be alive. Death, I do not relish. Why should I feel this way?'

" 'Well, if you must know, you are not the first to be faced with this problem. Many hundred years ago when the founder of our sect had his disciples around him, there was a very bright young priest whose name was Yui En. This young priest was sickly, but his faith was firm. One day, he asked in perplexity, "Teacher, I am in my deathbed. I know that the time for my departure to the land of Lord Amitahba is nearing and I should be glad and rejoice that I should be severed from the Laws of Transmigration and become reborn into a Buddha according to the Forty-Eighth Vow of the Amitahba, but truthfully, I feel no joy. Rather I feel an attachment to this worldly existence." '

" ' "Saint Shinran took hold of his favorite disciple's hand and spoke to him compassionately and slowly. "Because of our having become accustomed to it we cannot part with pleasure from this world of change and vicissitude in spite of the promise of a rebirth into a land of eternal bliss and enlightenment. Even a hovel long accustomed to will appear more comfortable than a clean and sanitary but untried palace and one feels a hesitancy to change even for the better. It is not lack of faith that has brought this doubt in your heart; it is the manifestation of the frailities of the human mind and heart. I, too, do not like to die. I should like to keep on living. It is because of this innate weakness of the ordinary man that Amitahba had created the Easy Path of Faith for the rebirth into Nirvana and a transcendance over the Laws of Karma. It is directed for you and me who do not possess the strength of character to follow the hard way to attain enlightenment like the sages of old, like the enlightenment of Prince Shiddhartha, the Shakamuni of India. The very fact that you have such doubts entitles you to the mercy of the all-embracing love of Lord Buddha. It is no evidence of your lack of faith. Rather it shows the necessity of such teachings as embodied in the Forty-Eighth Vow of the Amitahba, which says that if anyone having heard of my name and having longed to be born into my land and having lived accordingly, will not be rewarded with a birth into Nirvana, I, too, will not accept enlightenment." '

214

" 'So you see, my dear girl, in our good predecessor, Yui En Bo, we find the same query as yours and our Teacher said that he, too, did not wish to die and that it was further proof of the necessity of such a lofty, all-embracing teaching of the Jodo-Shinshu Sect for the like of us who cannot attain enlightenment by self-denial and abnegation by our own efforts. Is this proof enough, and does this let your mind at ease?'

" 'Thank you very much. It has taken a great load off my mind and now the attachment and clinging to this life will not bother me any more.' "

When Minoru read this short anecdote in a pamphlet, he was profoundly affected: affected in a way that it was almost a shock. All his emotional balance was shaken to its foundation. So deep was his reaction that he shed copious tears about the way Saint Shinran suffered with the questioning disciple Yui En Bo and felt that the essence and core of religion was being revealed to him.

This religion was a religion that came down to the level of man and did not command from a platform "Do this, do that, and don't do that under the penalty of hell fire." It rather acknowledged and took in the weakness of human frailty of the individual as he is and suffered with him. It was sympathy literally as the Greeks meant it when they coined the word "sym-pathy." There was friendliness and intimacy to this teaching, and it seemed as if he were being enshrouded with a warm cloak made with mother love. That evening he met a teacher who had taken special interest in him and he related in detail his reaction to the reading of this story. The elder turned to him with tears in his eyes, deeply moved. "I am returning to Japan next year. After what I have heard, I shall go with a very light heart for I know that wherever you will be you will not be irreligious." This happened in his sixteenth year.

CHAPTER 16

California Interlude

ONE HUNDRED AND TWENTY-FIVE DOLLARS in gold coin was all the money Minoru possessed when he landed at San Francisco, to embark upon an eight year course in medicine.

"What! Gold coin! I haven't seen one for a long time," smiled the hotel keeper as he played with the five dollar coin between his fingers.

"Gold and silver coins are being used in the Hawaiian Islands. What have you here?"

"We have silver half dollars all right, but the rest are paper money." He drew out of the cash register several denominations of currency.

"That must be lighter and easier to carry around. I brought my money in a belt because it is safer to travel."

The innkeeper in San Francisco was kind. He ran a modest hotel on South Park, near the terminus of the Southern Pacific Railway. It was in the tough section of San Francisco, and the Japanese hostelries catering to immigrants were located in such areas all over California.

"You have over a month before college opens. Why don't you go to work on a fruit ranch? All students in California work during the summer vacation to earn part of their school expenses. Now since you come from Hawaii you must be used to hot weather. Let me see, the peach season must be in full swing in Fresno, and soon the grapes will be ready. You had better go to Fresno."

"It is not a bad idea. I am used to working manually because I was a part time gardener in my last two years of high school. I need all the money I can get."

"That is the spirit, young man. America is a land of opportunity. Opportunity is reserved for young men who are not afraid to work! Take Mr. Hoover who is now helping poor Belgium! He, I heard, worked his way through college."

"There is fully a month before the fall semester starts and I may as well earn some money."

Before going to the country to work, sightseeing in San Francisco had to be done. With Makoto Hara, who had come on the same steamer and was now staying at the South Park Hotel, he walked to Market St. Makoto was about five feet tall, pale of complexion, wore a short clipped mustache, and walked with a short, waddling gait. As an artist, he was trained in the Japanese style of brush painting. He came to the United States to study oil painting and he was going to matriculate in the fall at the San Francisco School of Fine Arts. The metropolitan immensity—the tall buildings and the four laned trolley cars on the streets—were a real surprise to the two, but more impressive than these was the tempo of life manifested by the great speed and stride of the pedestrians. Everybody was in a hurry. Nobody seemed to be leisurely sightseeing. Taking the streetcar as directed to the Golden Gate Park, they saw an orderly, well planned landscape planted with evergreens and flowers that were then blooming in profusion and were quite beautiful.

To Minoru, the Japanese Garden run by the Hagiwaras was a real treat, and Makoto did a lot of didactic explaining about the intricate garden design; that there was a purpose and reason for the placement of each rock and plant and the real source of development of this art was from the philosophy of the Zen sect of Buddhism. This inclusion of deep and subtle philosophy in garden architecture was in marked contrast to the European garden design as exemplified by the Golden Gate Park. It was spacious and beautiful and seemed to strive for one goal: visual enjoyment. The Japanese tried to produce in miniature the beauties of the mountains, rivers, and forests. It was physically cramped for space just as the country in which it developed cried for elbow room, but the aim was to achieve space and roominess by the arrangement of rocks and shrubs.

They proceeded to the Cliff House and there enjoyed and marvelled at the rare sight of sea lions on the rocks offshore. Nearby Sutro Baths excited their curiosity and they entered to view the interior, but they were politely told that Orientals were not allowed to purchase tickets for a swim. Up to that time, Minoru was not conscious of his race. He was raised in a country where there was no open discrimination in public places. Makoto Hara was older than he by eight years and having worked in a newspaper office as an artist, he was aware of many things in California that Minoru did not know.

"Don't get peeved and downhearted. In anti-Oriental California, you must expect some unpleasantness. I am afraid this is just the beginning," he consoled in a big-brother attitude, hiding the unpleasantness he felt within himself.

"It is hard for me to believe that there exists such a feeling. Look at these people all around us. There is no hostility on their faces. We are not even noticed by the children. They usually hang around and taunt you if you are not accepted. But none have even noticed that we are here."

"That is because there are many Japanese in San Francisco. Japanese are not a curiosity in this part of the country. Their presence is tolerated. But it does not mean acceptance." Hara's face was drawn.

"What other discriminations are there then?"

"Intermarriage is prohibited between the Oriental and white people. I heard you have to cross the state line and get married. Certain swiming beaches are not open to the colored races. Ordinary barber shops do not cater to Japanese. The claim is that our black hair is too coarse for their scissors, but I think the real reason is the attitude of the white customers even if the barbers were willing. So we'll be reminded of discriminatory California once every month when a haircut is needed. We have to seek a Japanese barber."

"How awful! What if there is no Oriental barber in a small town? Does one have to travel miles for a fifty cent haircut?"

"I am afraid so."

Minoru, with Makoto Hara, boarded a Fresno-bound train and for six hours passed through the rich central valleys of California.

The countryside of California in the summer time was dry. The rolling hills simmered in the reflected heat of one hundred degrees and there was no beauty here. But the orchards and vineyards were resplendent and green and were something new. The geometrically arranged row upon row of fruit trees and stunted grape vines was a gorgeous sight and a source of surprise. The huge scale of the farms impressed them and above all the air of prosperity that pervaded the countryside was a thing that one could not ignore.

Fresno city was hot and dusty. Mr. Kato had his grocery store beyond the railroad tracks. The street was unpaved and the sidewalks were wooden. Houses in the neighborhood were small frame structures that had seen better days. Umbrella trees planted along the sidewalks gave welcome shade to pedestrians. Toward evening, as if the heat of the day was forgotten, people sauntered forth from their homes to breathe, stretch their legs, and stroll along the streets to forget the heat of the day and escape the high temperature that still lingered in the interior of their homes.

When he had read the short letter of introduction, Mr. Kato turned to the two young men. "I understand you two are from Hawaii, a student and an artist. In a way, I am from Hawaii, too. Although I was in Honolulu only six months, I liked your country. Sometimes I wish I had remained there. You see how hot it is here in the summer! We have malaria too! That you do not have back home."

"But we heard you make more money in California!"

"That we do when there is work. But work is seasonal and laborers migrate from place to place following harvest, hoeing, or pruning. In Hawaii, wages may be low but there is steady work all the year round. In the long run, I am not so sure who is ahead!" Mr. Kato smiled the knowing smile of the wise. He was well preserved, for a grocer's life was sedentary compared to a farmer's and he was not exposed to the elements.

"The farms on the way from San Francisco were well cared for and looked prosperous. They must be individually owned. In Hawaii, as you know, land is cornered by the large plantations. I am sure anyone owning those farms is materially well off." Minoru was curious. His background on the plantation had moulded him as a farmer.

"No doubt about that. But there were many years of back-breaking work before a desert became that productive. Many people from Hawaii that settled in this area bought farms in their children's name and now are well-to-do farmers. The famous Yamato Colony at Livingston is the most notable example. The Japanese acquired a desert and transformed it into enviable vineyards by hard work. But these are only in the minority and the majority are migrating field hands. You will join them and see what kind of life these floating people are leading. I am going to give you fatherly advice. Those 'blanket carriers' are a good example of failures. Do not become one of them. The one thing you should not do is play pool and join the crowd that goes to Chinatown over the weekends. Sooner or later you may be drawn into games of chance." Mr. Kato was serious and apparently enjoyed giving this sage advice.

"We won't. Mr. Hara is going to become a great oil painter and return to Japan later on. I am going to study hard and get a college degree."

"Yes, many have started out like you. Hundreds of ambitious young students have been coming from Japan, but there have been too many that fell by the wayside. It is a shame! It is a pity! Stay away from Chinatown."

Reedley was a small farming district and the bunkhouse was located on Sorensen Ranch. The kitchen was erected under a tall eucalyptus tree and not far away there were two frame houses where itinerant workhands were to sleep. Since the houses were weather-beaten and appeared old, the contractor, Mr. Honjo, must have been well known and returned every year during busy seasons to supply field hands to the nearby farmers. It was dusk when the two young men arrived at this ranch with Mr. Honjo. An elderly man conducted them to the sleeping quarters.

"I hear that you are new to a California farm. I will show you how to make a comfortable bed. This space is allotted to you. You go to the barn yonder and fetch some hay. Spread the hay rather thick and you can cover it with a canvas bag if you have one, or you can get a gunny sack and spread it out."

There was an earthen floor in the middle, and running parallel on each side was a flat platform about three feet above the ground. There were not too many workers assembled yet as the season for grapes was not to start until late August. Minoru and Makoto were able to sleep side by side with a lot of elbow space.

The elderly man then conducted them to the kitchen. Again there was no wooden floor and a long rectangular table stood in the center. Benches were placed around it. It was semi-dark in the kitchen and as the boys sat down there was a low murmur audible above the table. When their eyes became adjusted to the subdued light, they found the source of noise was the sudden flight of hundreds of flies that were disturbed in their feasting over food remaining on the table. Whatever appetite they had was completely lost. After a cup of tea the boys walked out. However, this finickiness was not long to remain with them for on the morrow they were to discover how unsanitary the whole camp was. Desultory attempts at capturing these flies were made by having half rotten meat under traps of screens, but it seemed that breeding places were so numerous, any human endeavor to combat them was both too feeble and inadequate.

Work began the following day. It was easy. With a bucket and a ladder a peach orchard was their hunting ground. Leisurely and carefully ripe ones were picked, and naturally the most enticing ones were eaten by the workers. At other times they were ordered to pick fallen figs to be dried. This was easy work as they would squat on the ground and forget the passage of time in conversation.

The worst part of the entire setup was neither the living quarters nor the work, for these one could endure. The monotonous fare of rice, fish, and eggplant was more than one could bear and one Sunday the boys made their way to King City, walking two hot, dusty miles for roast beef and coffee. Prior to leaving San Francisco, Makoto had bought tubes of oil and some canvas at an art dealer on Market St. Minoru accompanied him on sketching trips to the King's River and nearby irrigation ditches where his easel was set up for a leisurely hour or so of painting poplar trees and rustic scenes new to the men from the tropics.

Between supper and bed time, there was a period that was spent pleasantly without physical effort. Gossip and story telling answered the purpose. The expert storyteller of the camp was a wiry little man who had the habit of grimacing and rolling his eyes when he waxed warm or came to the climax in his narration.

"I spent some time in the Imperial Valley in summer and winter, and I am telling you, there are a lot of stories about smugglers."

"Smugglers of what? Opium?"

"No. Not opium or any merchandise. Smugglers who smuggle themselves from Mexico into Imperial Valley."

"Oh that! Yes, even Hawaiian papers used to carry accounts of them, but I thought it concerned mostly Chinese."

"We do not have so many Japanese crossing over illegally now, but up to a few years ago there were quite a few. I met one man in a boardinghouse in Los Angeles. He was quite a chap. Not the strongman type that one would expect in such a role, but rather feminine in his appearance and ways. Anyway, according to his story there were five men in the party. They started in the desert on the Mexican side far away from the main highway. That precaution was the only way to avoid detection and capture. The attempt seemed simple because the only direction they had to follow was directly north following the needle of the compass. But the vastness of the desert was something beyond their calculation. The heat was beyond what they expected, and the lack of water was killing.

"After a few days, water ran out and their empty canteens became mere burdens. They could not discard them because they might yet come across a well. Cactus leaves were cut; some moisture was obtained for their parched throats by sucking on the cut edge. They could not be choosy as to odor or taste. To avoid heat and conserve energy they stretched themselves out in the shade of the mesquite and cacti in the daytime. Traveling was done mostly in the cool hours of the night. Five days elapsed. Two of the members simply collapsed and could raise themselves no more. The remaining three staggered on. They came to a stretch where even cactus was not too plentiful. To quench their burning thirst, they began to drink their own urine. But this could not go on for any length of time. Food had not passed their mouths for three days. No living thing was present. No lizards nor snakes which are usually found even in deserts. Nothing that could be devoured to sustain their flagging strength. Infernal heat that was literal hell dogged them. Why did they so rashly leave easygoing Mexico for this trying journey just so that a little more money might be earned? Somehow they must survive; 'somehow I must survive' was uppermost even in a heat-crazed mind. Two of the trio lagged behind and spoke in subdued tones.

" 'It looks like our friend cannot go much further. He is barely able to stand on his feet.'

" 'If he is to die anyway. . . . Are you thinking what I am?'

" 'I think so. We should not wait until he dies naturally. In order to make use of his flesh and blood to make us stronger we must go at him while he is still living. . . . '

" 'I don't think he suspects anything. Let us pounce upon him when we get to that mesquite grove.' With murder in their hearts the two followed the weakened member toward the fateful clump of vegetation.

Literally, it was going to be a survival of the fittest. Driven by hunger and thirst, there was not the faintest thought of mercy.

"Just then there was a stir behind the bush and a donkey appeared. It was not wild and probably one that had strayed away from its master. It was not very difficult to capture it. On this donkey meat they gorged themselves and drank the warm life-giving blood. Soon their minds cleared and they took stock of their whereabouts. Until then they were in a stupor, with dulled sensibilities. But now they could distinctly hear sounds that had escaped their ears. Whistle sounds were made out and they guessed that they must not be very far away from a railroad. Keeping a course parallel to this sound would eventually lead them into the United States. They succeeded."

"What a story! But why all this illegal entry?"

"It is still legally possible to immigrate to Mexico and a few still enter that country annually. But Mexico is not a prosperous country as you can see by the many Mexicans that are working in the Fresno area. Hundreds of thousands of them come to California as seasonal farm laborers. The Japanese cannot join this band and so they try this hazardous trip."

"What is this friend of yours doing now?"

"Human nature is a funny thing. You would suppose that after all this hardship he would work hard in golden California and save every dollar he earns. The smugglers endured the heat, but the three are no better than we are. They gamble away their earnings in *shiko* games in Chinatown. I must admit it is funny, for whenever and wherever the third man meets a donkey, he clasps his hands in front of chest and reverently bows his head low toward the donkey. For when the trio were finally safely settled in California a confession was made of what might have happened had not the donkey so opportunely appeared as a sacrifice. To him since then every animal of this lowly breed was a Goddess of Mercy."

Work turned out to be more scarce than expected and when the middle of September came around and time to return north to school, there was not much to show for their labor. Minoru pocketed exactly sixty-seven dollars.

Stanford University was situated in the Bay Region and the climate was most salubrious. With the advent of fall, the tang in the air was invigorating and Minoru never felt so good to be alive and doing things he liked best. The cool weather gave him zest to study and be active. His appetite knew no bounds. He put on fifteen pounds in a few months. Hawaii's equable climate was good, but the mild winters of California suited him better not only for mental activity but physically too.

On the first day at college, he was invited to the new clubhouse where Japanese students resided. This clubhouse was unique among college campuses anywhere in America. It had cost about ten thousand dollars to build and was constructed with donations from the residents of California. The students went around during their summer work and solicited donations for this clubhouse. The more fortunate ones roomed in this building. To economize on board these students took turns in cooking, washing dishes, and doing housework. Many students worked in private families for their board and room and gathered at the clubhouse over weekends for socials and Japanese food. There were about thirty enrolled at the university at this time. Minoru was the only one in his teens; the rest were much older because they had had part of their schooling in Japan.

"We at Stanford University welcome you to our campus. California was a strange country to all of us too in the beginning since we practically all came from Japan. I think you are the only American citizen in this club, but you are a stranger in California. We can help you adjust. Do not hesitate to call on us for help. By the way, what are you majoring in?" Mr. Uchizono was sociable and approached the newcomer to make him feel at home.

"In pre-med. That is, I have to major in either physiology or chemistry. Then in the 4th year I shall start my medical course."

"Then there is Takahashi, a senior, who is starting his first year in medicine this year and he will be of help to you."

"Thank you. I shall have a lot of questions to ask him. Now, the reasons I came to Stanford are: first, I wanted to get away from the Hawaiian Islands and secondly, because I heard that one has a chance of working one's way through college here. What are the opportunities for me?"

"Well, we all are self-supporting. I am working for Prof. Marshall of the Chemistry Department. Being an engineering major with lots of lab work, I find it rather hard but I manage to get along. We can ask the boys what openings there are because families that have been accustomed

224

to hire Japanese students keep the jobs open for us. We all have been aware of this aspect of things and have done our best to do a good job so that we shall be preferred and new students will inherit the jobs. Anyway, stay at the club until there is an opening."

Up to the end of World War I, all Japanese students attending colleges and universities of the United States were aliens. After finishing middle school they had crossed the ocean to get American University training in spite of the language barrier. This meant that they had to repeat high school to master English. Since job opportunities for alien Japanese University graduates were almost non-existent they planned to return to Japan after graduation. There was another group: graduates of Japanese higher technical schools and colleges of engineering and commerce. After a probationary period these students were classified as juniors or sophomores according to their showing in classrooms. As a group, it was made up of hard working and serious-minded young men. Topics of the day: the Peace Conference at Versailles, socialism as a factor in class struggle, the rise of a new type of socialism in Russia, were discussed at supper tables. Arguments pro and con on class struggle, police surveillance, and persecution of socialists in Japan made the discussion very impassioned and personal. One could sense right away how the students were divided on these topics. Those that went through American high schools could be described as leaning towards Socialism, whereas those recently from Japan, reactionaries. Some students from southern California bore the influence of the communist, Sen Katayama, who was later welcomed to Soviet Russia as a hero but was destined to die there unheeded and unsung. At this stage of history, he was a Bolshevik and at the extreme left of the socialists.

Minoru was lucky to land a job with Mrs. Harris of Palo Alto. There were only two in the family for their only daughter after graduation from the University had married and moved to Seattle. Mr. Harris was a realtor and moderately prosperous. He had a two-story house on a corner of Embarcadero Road with many large oak trees gracing the lawn. Mrs. Harris was very fond of roses, and there were many varieties in her garden carefully tended by an Italian gardener. Trellises of small roses gracefully covered the white fences and arches. Roses were hard to grow in the islands, but in California they were gorgeous and there was little care needed. The orioles in the oak trees with their beautiful songs turned this garden into a veritable paradise in spring.

Mrs. Harris was an average housekeeper, but was a most sympathetic, motherly person and Minoru was to be impressed with the common sense and well balanced outlook on life a middle class, educated Caucasian woman had. The house was almost a mansion, but life was simple and frugal. No pretension was present. Because the town was collegiate with no saloons, the inhabitants were made up of faculty members, semi-retired people, or businessmen who worked in San Francisco but preferred to raise their children in this clean, healthy environment. The social life among these people was patterned on a conservative, sensible and sedate manner.

" What are you doing? Isn't there a basketball game tonight? You can always do that later or in the morning. If I were you, I wouldn't miss this game." Having had a daughter only recently graduated, the hectic goings-on of a coed in the family still lingered and Mrs. Harris seemed to enjoy such chiding. She seemed to feel younger and enjoy a fulfillment of a certain nostalgia in these proddings. Minoru felt thankful.

"Mrs. Harris, can you teach me some cooking? The only thing I know is how to cook vegetables and boil rice."

"Indeed, you do know how to boil rice the way the Chinese do, hard and not mushy?"

"Yes, ma'm. Before I left home, mother taught me two things. Boys were not allowed in the kitchen, following the custom of the old country. We were never allowed to complain about food either. We were trained to eat with relish what we were served. But for some reason when I was to leave home, she taught me how to cook rice and how to sew buttons on my clothes."

"I think she is a wise woman. But why should you learn to cook? Let us follow the teachings of your people. Boys should not be in the kitchen too long in life. Now this work is an expediency for you. You are not going to be a cook. So why fret and try to learn something you will not use? You try and study hard to be a good doctor." Cleverly she evaded a session in culinary instruction, and the fare remained monotonously pork chop and lamb chop; lamb chop and pork chop.

One day Mr. Harris sat down at table apparently not in the best of humor. A deal in a real estate transaction must have gone awry. "What, chops again? Rotten!"

"Why, Vic! That is a very poor word to use. You should have said 'decayed'."

"Ha, ha, ha," came a resounding burst from Mr. Harris. Minoru felt shocked, and then he cast an admiring glance at the unperturbed mistress who joined in his raucous laughter.

The following day was Saturday and in the afternoon he was in the process of dusting and pushing the carpet sweeper in the livingroom when Mrs. Harris came into the room humming a tune. "Who is the boss in this family, Mrs. Harris?"

Smilingly, with a twinkle in her eyes she said, "Vic thinks he is, but really I am!"

The college work was leisurely and not as didactic as in high school, except for chemistry and physics where laboratory work was a burden on the hours of a self-supporting student. Minoru was able to relax and enjoy life. Taking notes in classes was a new experience and many times he wished he had learned shorthand. He soon discovered that there existed many gifted young men and women. To have gotten a straight A in high school did not mean much at an intellectual center like this. He marvelled at the brilliance of some of the students. In fact, he was compelled to consider himself an average scholar, with an average intelligence quotient, and a type of mentality that was suited neither for deep thinking such as philosophy nor for detailed investigative research in the sciences. Subjects which appealed to him in high school such as chemistry and physics were found not to his liking because they were too exacting. In German, however, he met with unexpected success.

Miss Tasartez was his teacher at high school and she insisted that only German should be spoken in class. She was a linguist. Of Spanish lineage, she was born in Paris, and graduated from a German Teachers' College. She was able to speak eight languages, and was learning Japanese and Chinese from her students. Minoru recalled with a smile a scene not many months old.

"What are you going to study in college, Minoru?"

"You may laugh, because I am going to study medicine."

"Why should I laugh?"

"Well, just the other day, you told some other student, 'another doctor! Hawaii will soon be over-supplied with doctors and dentists.' "

"Oh, did I? I may have said it because almost every other student seems to be aspiring to become one, but I am sure you will make a very good one. I sincerely mean it." The three years of German Minoru was grounded in by Miss Tasartez in high school had taken deep root for he was able to conduct some semblance of conversation in his contact with German patients many years later.

As there was nothing to do during the Christmas vacation, Minoru joined the University YMCA boys to spend a week at the Asilomar Camp at Pacific Grove near Monterey. It was a very worthwhile, memorable interlude that can only come in the impressionable years of exciting collegiate life. A large hall rustically constructed in a pine forest near the seashore was the meeting place of hundreds of serious college men from the ten states of the Pacific Slope. An atmosphere of youthful zeal, sincerity, and idealism hard to find anywhere else was evident. It was the end of World War I. A war "Fought to end all wars" was still a vivid memory and many had only recently returned from the European theater of war where they had been active participants. There was a camaraderie among the young men that transcended racial lines and Minoru was thrilled with the high level of aspiration of the conferees.

To crown it all, the principal speaker of this conference was James Stitts Wilson, the socialist mayor of Oakland. He was a forceful speaker. A brilliant speech is for the moment only. Substance is the essence of a speech. Mayor Wilson had a timely message. He urged that the world be reconstructed with Christian socialism. A materialistic socialism was not enough and there must be a religious warmth to soften the reforms. Bolshevism was heard of only as a new political experiment in Russia after the overthrow of the Czardom. Communism, the offspring of the Bolsheviks and Mensheviks, was yet to make its ugly appearance. Socialism was the anathema to "decent" folks.

Christian socialism seemed to Minoru either an idealistic evolution of social movement or a very clever way to deceive the religious conservatives into accepting socialistic changes proposed by the radicals. Not used to talks such as these and not having taken any courses in political science, he was not prepared to digest the mayor's talks with objective evaluation, but it was a very stirring series of speeches and supplied him abundant food for thought.

A religion must be based on this life, in the betterment of the lot of the downtrodden people. Christianity's strong points were these. Christians were active and dynamic. They took the bull by the horns. In contrast, Buddhists were satisfied with the status quo, leaving and resigning to Karma, the wheel of fate, any social injustice as an inevitable ugliness of life, the inescapability of that which was to happen despite

228

feeble human attempts to stem the inevitable things repeatedly taking place as the result of the law of "Cause and Effect." But was it right to let it go at that? Should there not be an active propulsion of religious effort to bring forth in this world an imitation of the Nirvana that is promised to the faithful?

The life for a student of Japanese descent at a California university was not a very happy one. He was an outsider. He attended lectures, performed and handed in reports in the scientific laboratories, took examinations, was graded, and in due time had a place in the commencement procession to receive a parchment of sheepskin announcing to the world that he had been awarded a bachelor's degree. He joined in the "rah rahs," shouted himself hoarse at football games, thrilled to tears watching the frenzy of a bonfire rally before the homecoming game, and wept with chagrin when the rival college won the big game. But somehow he did not belong. He might have believed that such was college life, but he later went to a midwestern professional school and then realized what the sensation of really sharing in the activity of college life was like. The reason for such a reaction was partly due to the lack of time for participation in extracurricular activities. Practically all Japanese students were self-supporting. Secondly, their natural hesitation due to the general temper of California people against their race, although the campus was singularly devoid of this attitude because of the idealism of the chancellor, made them unduly self-conscious.

Summer rolled around and the academic year came to a close. Minoru joined a group of four students experienced in the ways of summer farm work. Like other migratory workers they drifted to Sacramento and there awaited for the farmers of neighboring regions to come and hire help. June in Sacramento was hot and dusty. The section around Fourth and M streets was thronged with Mexican, Japanese, Chinese, and Hindu laborers who hung around pool halls and small shops, retailing fruit, cold drinks, and laborers' apparel. In particular, there was a very good *sushi* and noodle restaurant. Food prepared there was better than that which could be had in Honolulu or San Francisco.

Finally, after a wait of two days, they proceeded to Chico with Mr. Kodama who had hired them. A five hundred acre pear orchard was being developed right in the middle of wheat country. At this season this verdant orchard was like an oasis in a desert of yellowed stumps of harvested wheat. The job was irrigation. The rows of young trees

229

geometrically planted required a large amount of water in the rainless summer, and water was conducted by a furrow on each side of the tree rows. When water was allowed to flow into these newly constructed ditches, there was a tendency for it to break through the porous wall. With shovels the workers had to repair and strengthen these gaps and fill up gopher holes. Until the walls were once soaked and found competent to withstand leakage, there was a lot of muscle work and no time for loafing. When the rough work was done the day was spent in an inspection tour to see that there was no leak and the flow was smooth.

It was a good place to spend a summer. The farmer was considerate, food was tolerable, but the pay at three dollars a day was not too attractive. A certain amount of money was necessary before the fall session started and so, after one month, and a reluctant adieu to the pleasant farmer and his wife, the group of students headed south to Dinuba in central California and the grape harvest.

Piece-work in the muscat vineyards would bring in a tidy sum. At three and a half cents per tray, ten dollars a day would not be impossible. The only way to begin the next college year seemed to be in a new suit in addition to tuition fees. No longer was the seasonal laborers' shack and life strange to Minoru. The short sojourn at Reedley had prepared him, but the actual grape picking was a revelation. It was almost like war. Driven by the motive power of greed, one got up at four o'clock in the morning, gulped down a frugal breakfast, and trekked to the field while it was still dark. As soon as it became light enough to discern objects the picking began. A worker stooped, or if he became tired squatted, and cut the stems of the clusters of grapes so that they fell into a large tin pan that was shoved under the vine. Wooden trays were placed side by side in the middle of the row to get the full impact of the sun. A full pan was enough to spread the bunches more or less evenly for one tray.

The grape leaves were covered with a fine dust of sand and sulphur-spray. Usually there was no breeze or wind. When the trees were disturbed, these particles rose and covered the workers, irritating their eyes and choking them. Heat was intense and the temperature was at least one hundred fifteen in the field. There was no shade except that cast by the grape vines. The trees were thirty years old. The trunks were six inches in diameter and trimmed to about four feet in order to facilitate care and harvesting. The bunches of fruit therefore hung from short branches surrounding the trunks. In this tremendous heat, water from canvas bags was drunk in quantities but within a few minutes the ingested fluid poured out from the pores in streamlets of healthy abandon. There was a certain coolness that followed this profuse perspiration.

When he arrived at a point of near exhaustion, Minoru used to stretch himself in the narrow shade cast by the row of grape trees and get a semblance of rest and respite. It was no longer greed that drove him. It was competition with other workers and also a struggle within himself: a part of him was for surrendering while the other was for completing the work. But he was not destined to make the ten dollar a day mark. Try as he might, working until he could no longer see, he struggled to fill the number of trays that would add up to ten dollars. The best he was able to produce was short by two trays. It was such a small additional effort, but his physical reserve was not able to produce the necessary energy.

One of his college friends, old in the ways of grape picking, was able to pick as many as five hundred trays when the crop was good. Laborers' talk centered on the number of trays picked. It was a competitive game among them, for they did not compare notes in dollars and cents. Knowing that many of them were to squander this hard-earned cash in Chinatown or in gambling, one student casually remarked, "After all this work in dust and sweat how much will be deposited at the Shanghai Bank?"

"Oh, don't say that! If I even think of that, I lose fight. I am now concerned in picking five hundred trays," came the sad answer from a laborer.

One day Minoru found himself unable to perspire. He felt burning hot. In spite of drinking huge quantities of water, he could not perspire. His skin remained dry. It was like being in a hot oven. Not only was it very uncomfortable, but fear that he might die from this strange condition assailed him. What a way to die! He returned to camp utterly fatigued, disgusted with himself, and deeply frustrated. It was a very long one mile hike in the early afternoon heat and in deep, fine sand. He expected to feel better in the cool shade, but when he threw himself on the bench under the large cottonwood tree, there was no welcome coolness. He became panicky; he had to get away from this hell hole. He figured that once he returned to the Bay region to the north, he would very likely regain his health. There was no time to lose. Hurriedly he wrote a note to his friends, gathered his things, and took the first vehicle bound for Fresno. As evening came and he was out on the streets he felt immaesurably better, and the watermelon he ate was most delicious.

The next day was spent in the train to Palo Alto, and he repaired to the students' club where a few friends were taking summer courses. It was a restful night sleeping between clean sheets. He went to the railway station the following morning to claim his luggage, and as he was about to step out of the building a violent chill gripped him. It was so intense that his whole body shook and his teeth chattered. He had no idea what it was, but it was clear that the hospital was the only place for him at the moment. He took a taxi to the university infirmary.

Dr. Barnett smiled and evidently had a working diagnosis. A blood smear was taken and the verdict was malaria. This malady was to haunt him for three years and he learned to dose himself with quinine capsules until his ears rang, gather all available blankets, and await the spiking temperature every other day when the cycle recurred annually. It left him in a weakened condition, and he lost whatever weight he had gained immediately after his arrival in California.

For two years Minoru led a carefree college life, working and studying. Buying a second hand bicycle at twelve dollars solved his transportation problem. Whereas his high school days were a series of crammings, he learned to relax at the university and had no ambition to make Phi Beta Kappa. He soon learned that he was quick to pick and grasp the salient facts and features of a course, but could not laboriously commit to memory the mass of details and fine points one was certain to forget one month after final examinations. In order to garner an "A" such scholarly endeavor was needed and he discovered that he lacked interest in such ardent academic pursuits. Contrary to popular concept that the lot of a self-supporing student was a pitiable but heroic one, he discovered that it was enviable. Feeling no obligation to anyone, including his parents, he indeed felt he was captain of his ship. Without a nickel in his pocket for weeks, he could sing as he pedalled back and forth to the library at night for his tuition was paid and his board and room were assured. He was serene, happy, and avidly imbibing from the fountain of knowledge. He knew he was broadening the horizon of knowledge and step by step approaching the coveted goal.

The requisite courses in the pre-medical curriculum had to be taken and passed and he was glad to get a "C" in some of them. In a large university like Stanford, there were outstanding men in various departments, and some of them Minoru determined to study under if he possibly could. Unique courses were given by Professor Terman in Educational Psychology and he was privileged to attend this seminar course, after sweating through a grilling prerequisite study in statistics for which he had no liking. Dr. Terman, together with Dr. Cubberly, made Stanford a center of pedagogy on the West Coast.

It was a seminar discussion course, and Minoru was the only under graduate and a non-education major. It showed him how investigators worked and solved their questions, for the text each week was a Doctor of Philosophy treatise. He discovered that the merit of such an article did not lie in the truth of the result arrived at, but rather in the process of reasoning and the effort expended in preparation of the paper. For what appeared as truth today might be proved wrong in a few years. The professor was interested in gifted children and had a roster of such highly endowed children, the future of whom he and his co-workers were planning to follow in the ensuing decades. The Binet system of measuring human intelligence was modified by Dr. Terman and was known as the Stanford-Binet method, and naturally talk revolved around this new scientific concept.

In World War I, a great amount of data was collected in the measurement of recruit's intelligence quotients. The possibilities for classification of soldiers for different branches according to degree of intelligence were discussed. Furthermore, the peacetime application of this knowledge and method for job aptitude tests was studied. The seminar was made up of school principals, school inspectors, and educators from the Antipodes, China, Japan, and Europe. Professor Terman, clean shaven and bespectacled, did not look much older than his students and the discussion was very informal and friendly. It was a privilege just to sit and listen.

Another course that left a lasting impression was called bionomics. This word was coined by Dr. Jordan. He planned a course comprising all departments of science and even languages, and had representatives from each department lecture and demonstrate the development and evolution present in every branch of study. When evolution is discussed, one is apt to conjure up the spectacle of an ape transforming itself into a man, but evolution is present in all phases of life, for living things are ever changing for better or worse. There is no stagnation.

Dr. Jordan delivered several lectures on biology as he was a renowned ichthyologist. What Minoru thrilled to most was Professor Swain's lecture on chemical compounds. He diagramatically showed that all matter of the universe, organic or inorganic, could be broken down into hydrogen and helium. Conversely, all matter was the combination of hydrogen and helium in myriads of different proportions. There was no cleavage line between the organic and inorganic matters. The significance of protoplasm—the differentiating characteristic between the organic and inanimate—was just an unexplained phenomenon, for in time it would and could be clarified. What is not clear in the light of existing knowledge is called mystery or a supernatural phenomenon.

To Minoru's intense delight, what he was taught at home in his boyhood was being verified by men of science. In Buddhism, there is no distinction between organic and inorganic. All human beings, all animals, all vegetables, and all inorganic matter such as rocks and minerals, have Buddhahood or the potentiality of attaining the perfect state or enlightenment. The fantastic idea was hard to swallow, but a Christian scientist was lecturing on the platform in a detached manner on this religiously significant point. He knew nothing about this old Indian philosophy nor of the teaching of the bikkhus along the Ganges River. He was merely propounding a theory based on the known analytical results of chemistry, and was not aware that it had anything to do with or fortified an old Hindu philosophical concept of matter. To Minoru, Professor Swain's lecture seemed to underwrite the veractiy and feasibility of Amida Buddha's vow that "I will not enter into the land of eternal bliss until every living and inanimate object shall have attained enlightenment."

Professor Price was in his early sixties. Tall and slim and entirely gray, he wore a pair of bi-focals that he labored to adjust whenever he scrutinized or handled objects. He taught embryology. To substantiate the fact that evolution is the basis of all living beings, the development of a human being is studied by taking chicken eggs at different hours after they are laid. A human being at twenty hours after fertilization is no different from a chick at the same age. Every living object is said to relive or duplicate in its short development from the union of the sperm and egg, the entire gamut of its biological phylogenetic history. Within several hours of its early life it will go through the development of thousands of years of the evolutionary history of its species.

There was no humor in Professor Price's lectures for he rarely ever tried to entertain or make the class laugh, but he was very, very clever with his fingers. With a lump of putty he would fashion out a mass of cells and produce in animated manner the development of new parts. So sincere and so dexterous was he that Minoru was completely enthralled by his class demonstrations. Usually such a course is a dry subject, but in Price's hands it became a living, dynamic creative art. So thoroughly was he able to awaken his students' attention and curiosity and succeed in implanting the image of the embryonic development that they in turn did not have to do much studying from their textbooks. Each day seemed an unravelling of the mysteries of life. For mystery it was to watch how, from a mass of cells, all the different organs, muscles, and bones differentiated and evolved into specifically functioning parts of a zoological machine; and all of this was modelled with plastic clay by the nimble fingers of Dr. Price.

Minoru was impressed as never before by the question of the mystery of life. What was the force that directed such metabolic precision, timing, and growth? The easiest answer was to give credit to a divine power, but he could not swallow this explanation and continued to ask himself and think about it. Endocrine activity? But the mysterious force or mechanism exists before the formation of any glands. Then could Karma, the law of cause and effect, be brought in to explain this mysterious propulsive energy? This energy must be inherent in the sex cells.

Out of sheer laziness he enrolled in a course of Russian literature because it was an easy way to earn credits. It continued for a year and he was rewarded amply with an appreciation of this unique contribution to the world's literature. There was a very interesting lecturer in the person of Mr. Lanz. Gogol's "Mantle" was stressed as the beginning of true Russian literature with a unique slant on life and the deeply psychological analysis of the personages and heroes that seemed to have been the product of these writers of the snowy country. It was gloomy and ponderous, but deep and searching for the realism and tragedy of the common people. As a self-supporting student burdened with afternoon laboratory hours, there was very little time to delve into English literature. In many ways, this introduction to contemporary world literature was more practical than the studying of Chaucer's *Canterbury Tales*.

His love for geography drove him to the top floor of the main library, where books pertaining to Latin America were stacked. He spent many

Saturday afternoons browsing over travelogues of South America. In time, he became well informed about the southern hemisphere. Why he did so, he could not answer himself. There was no definite motive except curiosity, and the knowledge that in several decades to come, that continent below the equator would become the center of world activity.

CHAPTER 17

A Farmer's Life

ANTI-JAPANESE FEELING IN CALIFORNIA WAS being fanned by politicians every election year and the bungling, historic "grave consequence" utterance of the Japanese ambassador at Washington D.C. so ired the Congress that the Japanese Exclusion Act was enacted in 1924. Prior to that fateful year there was a complete hamstringing of legal residents lawfully entered and actively contributing to California economy by a law that forbade leasing of any farm land to any "person ineligible to United States citizenship." Primarily aimed at alien Japanese, the majority of whom dwelt on farms either as lessees or farm hands, this law of 1920 reduced at one stroke all of them to the status of day laborers. The sword, however, was double-edged, and the white landowners were equally hit hard. How to get around this newly enacted law (which was ruled unconstitutional in 1947 by the United States Supreme Court and also removed by a referendum in 1956) was the pressing need in the winter of 1921.

Children of California Japanese were too young to step in to utilize their legal rights to help carry on the farms that their fathers had so laboriously improved and cultivated. A year to year basis of tenure was too precarious to make any investment, and a long term agreement was desired by both landowners and tenants. To lay out a fruit ranch and plant and care for young trees, needed a lot of expenditure both in capital and work and a guarantee of a lease for at least ten years was imperative. Knowing the loyalty, industry, and ability of Japanese farmers, independent white ranchers and absentee landlords were eager to have them remain and continue as tenants. The fall of 1921 was thus a very dark, depressing, almost hopeless one for the Japanese community.

"A telephone call for you. Long distance."

"For me? I wonder who from!" Minoru was surprised for there was no particular person that he knew in California.

"This is Kawano of Oakland. You are Minoru Murayama of Waipunalei, Hawaii, and your father is Torao Murayama?"

"Yes sir."

"I am a cousin to your mother, and I left Waipunalei when you were about five years old. Lately I discovered from one of your fellow students that you are now at Stanford University. By the way, how old are you now?"

"I became twenty-one years old in April of this year."

"Can you come to my store in Oakland right away? I have a very important piece of business which may be of great interest and help to you. I heard that you are working your way through college. This proposition may solve your problem."

The summer was a very unproductive one due to low farm wages and scarcity of work. Being faced with the beginning of the fall term and increased expenses (he was beginning his first year in medicine), he was mentally debating whether it would not be a wise thing to stay out of school for a year. He was just back at the university from a frustrating three days on the island of Rindge at Stockton. He worked at onion harvesting, but the fine dust hurt his eyes so badly he had to flee. The outlook was extremely dismal. Any legitimate way to add to his scant coffer was welcome. He proceeded to Oakland immediately.

"This is Mr. Tom Tanaka of Courtland in the delta district of the Sacramento River. He is about the biggest Japanese farmer of northern California and is well known to all in that district. He is related by marriage to us. Mrs. Kawano, my wife, is first cousin to Mrs. Tanaka. Now, you being my third cousin will make this a talk among relatives and whatever can come out of this discussion will be within the family so to speak."

This introduction was made after the usual handshakes, at Mr. Kawano's fruit stand on Franklin St., Oakland. Proffering cups of green tea and delicious Japanese candies, talk dealt with generalities and Minoru instinctively sensed that he was being sized up. From his side, he was also trying to form some sort of evaluation of these people who suddenly appeared in his life. He was sure they were shaping a definite milestone in the course of his destiny. Mr. Kawano, he vaguely remembered, came to visit the family at Waipunalei just before he left for California. Only he was then much slimmer. His wife was a jolly extrovert, rare among Japanese women. Mr. Tanaka had a strong Kumamoto brogue but he seemed to be very worldly wise for he never contradicted anyone. But one could sense the strong undertone of his character even in his acquiescence and adaptation to the talk going on.

"You have no doubt read in the papers in what plight the Japanese farmers are. After the recent law that forbids even one year lease of farmland goes into effect, there can be no farming done in this state. Mr. Tanaka not only farms himself, but has several tenants who sublease acres for different crops. His present interest is in beans and he has been working about fifteen hundred acres on a new island called Holland Tract. His tenants take care of the fruit ranch, the seed crops, potato, celery, and onions. There is a need for someone to lease these lands. The landlord is a very honest man known to Mr. Tanaka after twelve years of intimate business dealings. Because he is honest and upright, he wants Tom to be protected legally by a lease. It can be legally done. The whole crux of the arrangement is in the getting of a trustworthy citizen who will not betray the Japanese farmers. Since you are twenty-one years old, you can lease these farms for us. What do you think? In return Mr. Tanaka will guarantee the expense to put you through medical school. Isn't that what you will do if you both can agree in this matter, Tom?"

Mr. Tanaka became serious and said, looking straight into Minoru's eyes, "The subject has been covered well by Mr. Kawano and there is not much for me to add, except to say that we shall be most grateful if you can sacrifice a year or two of your life and come to the farm. We have to show the neighbors that you are farming even if the actual thing is done by us farmers. You will be doing a lot for us with families, and we in turn will see to it that you will also profit by this arrangement. Please give it deep thought."

It was a very unusual turn of events and nobody could have planned anything more convenient at such an opportune time. No matter how hard he worked, it was impossible to raise enough money to finance medical school and he had already discovered that to work through the last four years was an almost impossible task. Now, out of a clear sky, he was offered a way to achieve his ambition. He could very well afford to stay out of college a few years if such a guarantee was in the offing. He might have had to do just that anyway without that assurance.

239

Tom Tanaka had cleared a sizable net that year and he decided to take a trip to Japan with his family. He planned to remain a few months but the possibility of prolonging his stay was strong. At forty-two, he was a rare individual. He had no formal education except grade school in the old country. Since his arrival in California, it was a constant struggle to keep poverty from his home, within which the children had increased every two years to a total of seven. He learned California farming the hard way, subject to the whims of the elements and market fluctuations of agricultural products. In the late 1980's, when work was scarce on farms due to a general depression, he was lucky he had a roof over his head at a Concord orchard. The wage was fifty cents a day. Food was a monotonous repetition of rice and a can of salmon.

But soon white farmers began to respect his integrity, his inborn ability to grow plants, and his open-heartedness. He was an extrovert. He was hard of hearing in one ear. The barber, according to Japanese custom, shaved the external auditory canal with a special long razor, but must have nicked Tom there, for infection set in and he was left partially deaf. Because of this handicap, he had a habit of talking loud, and when he met anyone, it was a bellowing "Hello, how are you!" This attitude was very different from the usual Oriental who, because of language difficulty, shunned conversation and tried to make his presence inconspicuous. Not Tom. He loved company. Anyone who could drink was especially welcome. He was accepted by neighboring white farmers as a good fellow who had a sense of humor.

As a practical man and from painful experience, he diagnosed the cause of the perpetual hard luck assailing Japanese farmers in spite of their ability to raise excellent crops, and formulated a remedial measure. Against the prevailing resigned attitude that "since California agriculture depended primarily on fluctuating market conditions, if you hit a good market price once in four years you are ahead," his effort was directed to minimize this factor of chance. He selected conservative crops to be assured of an income that would defray expenses. Then he was able to indulge in a little speculation. Ten to twenty percent of his acreage could then be planted to crops such as onions, celery, and potatoes. For the first category he grew seeds for the C. C. Morse Company. This work was so non-productive and dirty that other farmers were not too keen to undertake it. The income was low but dependable, and this company never let a farmer down. Onion bulbs grown for the seed company were contracted at a dollar per hundred pound sack. When the price of onions on the San Francisco market soared to three dollars it was very frustrating, but when it dropped to forty cents, he was glad he had this agreement. He further learned the wisdom of diversification and tried to vary his crops as much as he could, utilizing trusted subtenants who were experienced in that particular crop.

Adjacent to Merritt Island on which he was a tenant for twenty years, there was a large twenty thousand acres of delta land that was being reclaimed by the construction of levies. Since this protection against high water of the Sacramento River was not one hundred per cent completed there was a great element of speculation in the crop planted. Only beans could be grown with any degree of success. Tom Tanaka was quick to see the potential gain even in the face of the risk. This delta land was as a whole very rich, much like the inundated Nile delta of Egypt, but he knew which part was particularly adapted to bean culture, and, moreover, the owner of this tract was anxious to have him farm.

The European war and the subsequent participation of the United States as an active combatant meant increased demand for food. He scraped up enough money to buy two old caterpillar tractors, a 45 and a 75, and leased one thousand acres of tule land. As soon as water receded in May and even when the ground was still waterlogged, work had to be pushed to prepare for planting. It was a race against time. By July 4th, all seed had to be sown. The caterpillar tractors were at work twenty-four hours a day, plowing up the waist-high tule, cutting up the prostrate plants with heavy discs, and running a sled over the irregular ground to get some semblance of evenness for the actual planting. Teams of horses were right behind to make parallel rows and deposit beans at regular intervals and cover them with a little dirt in the same maneuver.

With the loyal help of a mixed crew of whites, Mexicans, and Japanese, the entire thousand acres were planted to beans. California sun and the moisture in the ground produced a bumper crop. War in Europe brought a cry for beans. Three cents a pound was a price that would satisfy a farmer, but the demand of war time economy raised it to an unprecedented seventeen cents. However, at harvest time, it was again a race against time and a prayer that the fall rains be a little late in coming.

As soon as the pods matured, teams of horses pulled machines that had two blades of sharp knives attached like wings. These cut the bean stalks just below the surface. There was no rock in the delta soil. Instantly the plants died and began to dry. About ten rows of these dried beans were gathered together by a side rake early in the morning when there was still dew on the plants.

The harvester began operating at about ten o'clock, when there was no moisture to prevent free splitting of the pods. This work removed the beans from the pods, conveyed them into sacks, and blew away the dried stalks from a rear exhaust. This continued far into the night with the aid of powerful lights. On a particularly good day a thousand sacks of beans lay in the tracks of the harvester to be hauled to the cleaning factories that lined the western bank of the Sacramento River. Rain would have spoiled everything.

Anxiously every morning, Tom Tanaka looked at Mount Diablo to the south. Rain usually started there and the moisture-bearing clouds would follow the Sacramento River up into the valley. It is no wonder that Tom uttered a prayer on these mornings, although he was not a religious man. All he had, all he could borrow, had been invested in this venture. But Providence was kind and was on his side, for rain did not come early that year of 1918. Both Tom and the landlord made a killing. For the first time Tom could consider himself wealthy by the yardstick of an immigrant farmer. Such sky-high prices could not be hoped for in peacetime, but Tom continued to raise beans for the next three years and he netted a modest profit and had it deposited in the bank.

Tom Tanaka was an outstanding success among Japanese farmers of the Sacramento Valley. He was five feet ten, tall for his race. His forehead showed a receding hair line, his lower jaw was protruding. His face was ruddy, but by no standard could he be described as a handsome man. He was elected President of the Japanese Association of Courtland. By temperment he was not one to take a back seat. He was not averse to flashing a diamond necktie pin and wearing one carat of the same stone on his finger. He was a well dressed man when the occasion demanded. He drove a large, seven passenger Buick and also a red Buick roadster. Notables from Japan were directed to his farm by the Japanese Consulate General or the Central Japanese Association in San Francisco. These visitors were shown what penniless immigrants from the rice patches of Kyushu were able to accomplish in a land of opportunity, and he was lavish in entertaining them. Perhaps it was vainglory, perhaps it was his natural gregariousness, but he did not feel that he was put to unnecessary expense. He enjoyed their talk and company and became a better informed man by widening his horizon of knowledge. In turn he became known to the big-wigs in Japan as an example of a progressive farmer utlizing mechanized tractors in the operation of two thousand acres of land.

There was, however, a very big void in his aspiration and longing. To be sure, he made money in California. California was kind and rewarding to those who labored and developed her natural resources. But there was discrimination in her beneficence. No matter how much he loved California, no matter how hard he tried to become an integral part of the California constituency, he was forever barred from becoming a citizen. It was a bitter pill to swallow and very disconcerting that race should play such an important part in a country that stood for equality of mankind before the law. Negroes were eligible to become citizens. Then Orientals were classed below the Negroes. Yet he saw the plight of the Negroes who were chained to servile jobs. He saw college educated Japanese men, brilliant students, reduced to waiters and window cleaners should they elect to remain in the United States after graduation. There was no job opening in the trade or profession for which one was trained if one had an Oriental physiognomy.

All his children were by birthright American citizens. What of their future? How to educate them was a real challenge! To let them continue attending schools in the land of their birth (which was the easiest thing to do) and grow up to become tillers of the soil like the rest of the first generation immigrants, or drift to cities doing menial work? There was nothing wrong in tilling the soil if one was by nature inclined to that sort of work, because it was a very rewarding life, but there was a vast difference when one was forced to do it whether one liked it or not.

The second way to solve this question was to have the children graduate from an American university and then seek an opportunity in the land of their parents. Were there not many students coming to the United States to secure higher education? He discovered from the honestly expressed opinions of his overseas guests that the Japanese industrial firms were so dominated by the so-called *gaku batsu*, or academic cliques, that when a graduate of a different college tried to wriggle himself into such a circle he felt keenly that he was an intruder. Advancement was slow for him. If a university man of Japan not from a proper university met with such a reception, what chance had an American graduate whose command of Japanese was inadequate to say the least? This second alternative then was not the best solution.

The only path he could pursue was to take his children to his country early in life and have them educated from the grade school up so that they could compete on an equal footing with the other aspirants for jobs in Japanese firms. With proper industry and luck, there was no handicap or impediment to advancement. Even presidency of any company was open to an American born, because there was no discrimination based on racial lines. Naturally his wife had to remain with their children. Theirs would be a very unnatural marital state, but under the circumstances everything had to be sacrificed for the sake of the children. The eldest son who was fourteen would remain with his father because he was too old to learn a new language and there must be a son to carry on the farm in California.

There were many people in California or Hawaii who wanted to follow this third way but could not afford it financially or did not have the will power to decide upon a path of virtual celibacy. How wise or mistaken this step would turn out to be, only history would decide. The situation in the early 1920's and events that might follow in sequence could be deduced rationally with some degree of accuracy and the conclusion was that there was very little future for the Nisei in their own country in white-color jobs unless some totally unexpected turn of events occurred to obliterate all anti-Japanese sentiment among California politicians. Such a miracle rarely happened in real life. A Jap was a Jap and destined to a servile, second rate citizenry. Children were too young to decide, and parents must do the thinking for them. Responsibility was great, but after all there was nothing in this world that was not a gamble more or less. Wise counsel had to be based on firm logic and known facts. Wishful thinking should not be used for reasoning. Tom Tanaka believed that he was doing the right and best thing for his children's future in taking them back to Japan for an education.

Thus the management of the farm was thrust into the hands of an inexperienced twenty-one year old. The actual farm work naturally had to be assumed by Tom's lieutenants, but the business end was entrusted to Minoru and for fully nine months he had to make his own decisions. He could consult Tom's elder brother, an independent farmer, when he encountered difficulty and even asked for a loan of three thousand dollars when the bank account became low. It was a new experience and sometimes bewildering. During this time there was not a letter from Japan. Tom Tanaka was such a man. When he trusted a person, he went all the way, although it must have looked almost foolhardy to a more cautious individual.

A two year experience at actual farming began for Minoru. Fall and winter months in the delta district of the Sacramento River were full of excitement for someone with a sporting inclination. Thousands of migratory ducks from the Arctic region lighted on the sloughs that surrounded the islands and plowed land. There was a sense of great expanse; fogginess and drizzling rain added a depressive note to the landscape but the cold breeze was invigorating.

There was a double-barrelled shotgun that he was tempted to try, although at home his gentle mother had forbade the use of firearms and as a consequence, he had never fired a shot in his life. He went along with a boy of seven as his guide into the asparagus field and before they proceeded fifty yards, a cock pheasant made a loud noise and took to the air. "What a shot you missed!" was the wry remark from the disappointed youngster. Cotton-tailed rabbits jumped from their hiding places. Again he was rooted to the ground and his reflexes would not function. Even had he fired, he could never have aimed at the hopping creature. Finally they came to a slough where water was still and mudhens leisurely dove for prey and swam short distances. "Try that shot. You can't miss," urged his young friend. He took careful aim and pulled the trigger. The mudhen somersaulted. It was a pleasant sensation. He felt he had somewhat regained the lost respect of his companion. To have fired a gun for the first time and be rewarded with game, albeit not worth retrieving, was not without a sense of achievement.

They entered a grove of sycamore trees and there better game was busily feeding on the bark of bare tree trunks. He aimed carefully and brought down a woodpecker. It was not dead yet and when he approached, its claws worked the air in violent motions of defense and its beak emitted hideous noises to scare away an enemy that had proved to be cruel and heartless. Minoru struck its head with the butt of the gun like a savage to which he had momentarily reverted. The bird was silenced, but he could not forget the death throes of the luckless bird, its struggles

245

from pain and fear. He could not erase this picture from his mind and he vowed never to fire a shot again at a live target as long as he lived.

Fishing was different. There was no heart-rending cry by the landed fish. Having spent a boyhood on the windward shore of Hawaii where there was practically no fishing, Minoru had had no experience with line or hook. Fish abounded in water surrounding the reclaimed islands of the Sacramento River Delta and it was a superb fishing ground for those who liked this pastime. Catfish could be caught by the sack. Large black carp were hooked easily with bread bait, but only Mexicans ate them. Japanese in their homeland prized carp as eating fish but in California would not even think of fishing for them except for sport. "Muddy smell" was the comment, but this odor could be easily eradicated by letting them live in clear water for a short week. The only real answer to such a behavior was that in California waters, there were striped bass, black bass, and sturgeon. Both as game fish and in tasteful quality, there was no comparison. No wonder the carp was left alone. In the winter season striped bass could be caught and Minoru got the thrill of his lifetime in pulling in a five pounder that fought him for about ten minutes. He required a lot of coaching to land it, but it was thrill that he remembered for many years.

These activities took up part of his time, but life on a remote farm, isolated in wintertime by bad, muddy roads was something he did not know. The ranch hands got up early in the morning because they were used to rising with the sun. At once they proceeded to the stables to attend to the horses. After the rains came it was merely sitting around the kitchen stove drinking coffee or sipping home-brewed rice wine, and telling and retelling the same stories. When the effect of liquor took hold of some of them, stories became sordid. Repetitions became more pronounced, and it was quite a strain to appear interested and pretend to enjoy the not-funny joke told for the fifth time.

There was no radio then and even mail was delayed because the road to Clarksburg was impassable on account of mud. There was no rural free delivery as yet. Later on, when he could see a certain advantage in this life that even tempted Minoru to consider changing the course of his life to one of farming, he could not forget the utter ennui and feeling of uselessness during the winter months. Life to a young, ambitious youth was too precious to idle away in such a fashion.

Sunny days were therefore welcomed. Work was resumed in the

fields. Acres devoted to bean growing were to be turned to something more permanent such as orchards or asparagus fields, since the levies surrounding the island became substantial and the drainage ditches that criss-crossed the island could keep the land permanently dry. In early spring months when the volume of the Sacramento River increased from the melting snows of the Sierras, the surface of the cultivated land was lower than that of the river, for the pumping station kept the water in the ditches of the island at a constant level.

The high price of bartlett pears had earned a lot for ranchers on older islands to the south and east, and so there was a great demand on the upland nurseries for young, grafted pear trees to plant on this new island. Trees were planted every twenty feet, geometrically, but to do this a very primitive method of laying out a rope in both directions and walking on it to mark the ground was used. Where the rope marks crossed each other were the sites for the young trees. Forty acres were planted but these trees were destined to become a total loss because pear blight was to affect them and there seemed to be no remedy except to destroy the trees.

Summer months meant toil from dawn to dusk. Minoru had to drive back and forth to Sacramento to convey laborers, buy provisions, and attend to minor details in the maintenance of a labor crew. He was in fact an errand boy. The island that was so dreary looking in the winter was now carpetted by green crops and there was vibrant activity in the air. One could see the young beans and asparagus sprout and grow before one's eyes in the intense life-giving sunlight, and the alfalfa fields were white with tiny butterflies that flew and hovered above the green carpet. There was no loafer; everything seemed to be moving or growing. The sensation of a rancher, a small capitalist, was vastly different from a wage earner, wielding a hoe or a shovel at thirty-five cents an hour. He had a larger perspective. He was concerned about the yield of the land and the cash that was to accrue from this enterprise. This was, however, only a symbol, a tangible manifestation of profit or loss, and to what degree the result showed in actual numerical figures. To a degree, he experienced the satisfaction that comes to any contracting builder or rancher of cattle or sheep. It was an intoxicating feeling.

September came and when the harvesters were ready to move in and thresh the crop of beans, Tom Tanaka returned from Japan. He had much to recount of his trip, which had educated him as only travel can do. As to the result of the farm work during his absence, he did not have any comment one way or the other.

"Why can't you have your folks come over from Hawaii and settle in this part of California? Your father may like it better than in Hawaii." Not long after his return Tom queried Minoru after supper. Evidently he had given a lot of thought to this problem. He did not want to invite any trouble by being accused of circumventing the new law that prohibited lease of land by aliens ineligible for American citizenship. He had been advised by his lawyer in San Francisco that everything was legally done, but in his own way he wanted to make doubly sure in complying with the letter of the law.

"I also have thought about that move off and on. There is certainly land for the asking here, whereas there is a scarcity of farming land in Hawaii. The best part of the move would be the independence. The sugar plantation, although it has outgrown contract labor days, still has a paternalistic hold over the workers. Looking at these farmers in California, they work much harder. I think they do because they have a stake in the crops. In Hawaii, the only requisite expected of a worker is that he put in a certain number of hours each day. I think my father would seriously consider the move if the passage can be financed."

"I think it can be arranged. If your folks can be here permanently, then your tenancy will be more realistic and convincing to the outsiders. Your absence at school will not be a cause for suspicion."

"I'll write to him tonight and explain the situation. I think it is a real advantage for him, but it is a difficult step to pull up stakes after so many years in Hawaii."

Torao Murayama was able to move to California, and find employment on Tom Tanaka's ranch. It was quite a change from sugar raising, but he was not too old to learn and this temperate climate was not too different from what he had been used to in his native country. In many ways he was glad to shed the cloak of old ties and encumbrances that had become a real burden after nearly thirty years. Social obligations among Japanese were so heavy, even in an overseas country, that after a while one went into debt to maintain respectability. For every marriage, birth, funeral, and trifling occasion, an invitation meant cash expenditure or purchase of a gift. There was a "return" to the above. Coming and going, it meant an expenditure, and in a closely knit community every family groaned and bickered but like the proverbial weather did nothing actively to remedy the situation.

Now in a new community he could start life anew among newly acquired friends. Probably in the next twenty years the burden of social obligation might be just as great, but for the time being life would be easier. In a year or two he could start on some subleasing project that could, if luck held, produce results scarcely hoped for in Hawaii. Because of his son's presence he was greeted warmly.

To add to the feeling of belonging was the fact that the people he met in the Courtland area were mostly from Kumamoto Prefecture in Japan. In fact, these people spoke almost the unadulterated dialect. Spoken Japanese in Hawaii was a mixture of all provinces, but the core was a Hiroshima dialect. To converse in a tongue accustomed to in childhood conveys a feeling of intimacy no other medium of speech can bring about.

The Murayama's became Californians in domicile but long established friends continued to play a great role in their future. Minoru was now assured of his college future. After seeing that his parents were well settled on the farm, and having remained the full two years there, he was ready to resume his interrupted studies. During this interval he struck up acquaintances with neighboring Caucasian farmers and tradesmen in nearby towns. That he was actually a dirt farmer was an established fact. But by this time many friends approached him trying to have him stay and continue as a farmer.

"Minoru, why return to college? You have a very good set-up here. You can actually expand on your own now. Your credit has been firmly established. People trust you. Such an opportunity very rarely comes to a young man at your age. When you graduate from college, you will have to work. Work for money is what we all do, no matter what field of work we get into. Money is the final objective."

"I don't know. I never have done anything halfway and I probably will return to school for my degree because there is only one-half year more to go for my sheepskin."

"You only have a few months more for your bachelor's degree, but what I am referring to is your medical degree."

"Oh that. To be frank, I am not so certain about that myself."

"Anyway, our own people are crying for men like you: dependable men of voting age having U. S. citizenship. Really there is no limit of good you can accomplish in this valley alone."

"In the last two years, I have enjoyed the life of a farmer immensely, but that is only in the summertime. The dreary winter months are not very exciting and I cannot stand around doing nothing. I'll go crazy. I have often wondered about this matter and have considered, as you say, the opportunities that lie ahead of me. Perhaps I may attend school during the winter months, but the quarter or semester systems of the colleges do not conveniently break up the academic year to make this possible."

"Anyway, give it good thought. We certainly would like you to remain in the delta district."

Not being able to decide what to do, he paid a visit to the university campus, hoping that a change of scenery would help him. He dropped in at the Harris' and since Mr. Harris knew the farming situation well (he had Japanese tenants as strawberry sharecroppers on his own land in the vicinity), Minoru explained the predicament he was in.

"Young man, you shouldn't hesitate for a minute. Your course should be one without deviation. I only went through the seventh grade, and how many times I have wished I had continued schooling! You can become a farmer any time. Mind you, I say 'anytime'. Go to school while you can." Sincere words that came from the heart could not fail to strike home deeply. There was no wavering on Minoru's part after this interview.

At Professor Ichihashi's (he was an Assistant Professor in the Department of History), he was met with open arms, for the savant and his charming wife had befriended him when he had matriculated five years earlier.

"Well, well. How does it feel to be back after toiling in the mudflats of the delta district? You look well indeed."

"I am feeling very well, thank you, and I am happy to report that I have been assured of finances that will see me through my medical course of four years."

"That is good news. To work your way even partially in the professional school is almost impossible. Where do you intend to matriculate?"

"I am in a quandry about that. The easiest thing for me to do is return and continue at Stanford, but I should like a change of scenery."

"It may not be a bad idea at that. Stanford has been a very liberal school as you know. It was until lately headed by Dr. Jordan, a scientist of the first order in his own right, widely known throughout the world for his high statesmanship advocating peace and tolerance. His influence is still with us after his retirement to emeritus status and so, on this campus, it is not like being in California. But it seems to be different in San Francisco at the medical school. One of our students was here last year and complained bitterly about the outspoken and open hostility of Professor Howell in the department of internal medicine to persons of Oriental descent. Certain patients were not assigned to Oriental students and without material one cannot learn.

"Now that you have the means to continue, and as I know you have a B average in grades, it may be a wise move to enter a Midwestern or Eastern school. It will be a broadening experience and a valuable part of your education to live in another part of this great country. You will find that America is made up of many different groups of people. Do not judge America by seeing only this state. If possible, go to the eastern seaboard, in particular Boston, for the flower of American culture is centered there. American civilization is now on the verge of maturity We do not have to take a back seat to Europe in many fields anymore."

CHAPTER 18

Medical School

"MY NAME IS METSCHER, ALFRED METSCHER. I am also a freshman," a tall blond man walked into the room as Minoru was unpacking his suitcase on the bare army cot. Taken by surprise, Minoru straightened up and smilingly received the proffered hand.

"I am also a newcomer, from Hawaii and a transfer from Stanford, California."

"I am from Enid, Oklahoma."

"Oh, where the oil-rich Indians live?"

"Yes, that's right. The Osage Indians. It's a rich country." By this time two more Oklahoma boys sauntered in and were introduced as having come from the same college. The four went out to supper at a corner restaurant. Minoru was impressed by the friendliness of these young men, quite different from the aloofness of the people he met in California. It augured well and he felt that his life in this Midwestern city was going to be enjoyable.

The dormitory was rapidly filling up with old and new students. Somehow freshmen could be spotted without difficulty, a certain eagerness, timidity, and ready-to-please attitude differed from the nonchalance and studied indifference of the upper classmen. Age differences among the new students were much more marked than at the collegiate level, for at this graduate school many possessed advanced degrees or were resuming study after working several years. Only seventy-five belonged to the incoming class and these came from the entire United States. Minoru was the only non-Caucasian. About five were women. There was an air of friendliness from the beginning among the students for everyone was serious as each realized what an arduous four years lay ahead and felt that all belonged to the same group for better or worse. It was like soldiers thrown together in a task force. There was not much rivalry among them since they had all been accepted. The problem common to all was to stay until graduation. This factor depended on one's own industry. A common travail was to dog them for four years and the friendship that was born and nurtured in this environment of hard work was going to endure.

Minoru was soon made to feel that he was accepted by the class as one of them. Many met a Japanese for the first time. Many did not know exactly where the Hawaiian Islands were, and even the Registrar classified Hawaii in the same class as China, Japan, or British Honduras.

The following morning the freshman class was assembled in the auditorium and Dean Marriott spoke at length. He was over six feet tall, on the heavy side, balding, and the large, penetrating eyes on a ruddy face precluded any undue familiarity.

"Ladies and gentlemen, you are welcome at Washington University Medical School. You are embarking upon a course that is full of significance to yourself and to your fellowmen. To yourself you will be starting a life of hard work, for it is a strenuous life both at school and after graduation. Whether you will become a great healer or a mediocre pill-peddler will be a vital concern of the community. Hence your responsibility is great. There are three courses open to you after graduation. Most of you will naturally become clinicians and take care of the sick both in mind and body. A few will become teachers and research workers to advance the torch of medical knowledge a little further. We are always trying to discover some such men in every class. Both types of men are needed and the tremendous endowment of this university is to further these ends and produce first class doctors after four years of intensive teaching. To my mind there is yet another field open to you. The vast field of foreign medical missions awaits those spiritually inclined. This school has no church affiliation but I should like to see men with this high dedication among you.

"Starting with this class, we will take pictures of you and arrange them on a single cardboard. A copy of these rogues' gallery pictures will be in front of every instructor and professor at the beginning of each course so that the teacher will associate your name and face and come to know you. Here at Washington we take pride in teaching, and all departments are headed by full-time professors. They are anxious to know you as individuals and not as a mass of faces. Buckle down to work and the entire faculty is at your disposal to guide you. My office is open to all of you. Come and confer with us before we have to send for you."

Dissection started in earnest the following day. Two students were assigned to each cadaver: each taking one half of the body. There was no time to loaf. A certain amount of work had to be done, for at the end of each afternoon a demonstration of the various tissue and structures was held on a specially dissected cadaver by a surgeon. Thus there was no excuse for not having seen the part. Every Friday, there was a written quiz to keep the class studying. With this system, there was no room for cramming for examinations. The subject matter had to be really digested and understood each day.

At college level there was much to enjoy. To round out one's cultural attainment was one of the aims of going to college, but at a professional school, especially medical, there was one aim in view and that was to cram knowledge and statistics into these aspirants. It was the German system of instilling fact after fact into the plastic minds of youngsters who could not discern the grain from the chaff. Detailed facts of anatomy and histology had to be committed to memory. Most of these details were of no earthly use, but had to be remembered. Later on there would be surgical anatomy which would be of more practical use for those who would elect surgery as their specialty, and histology would be the groundwork for abnormality in disease which would be taken up in pathology.

Of what use was the response of a guinea pig's terminal ileum to the stimulation of a certain chemical substance? The students had to memorize the way the drugs affected different organs of various experimental animals. Much unnecessary midnight oil burnt and much unimportant cramming had to be done in order to pass the examinations.

Dr. Schaefer in biochemistry frankly said, "We expect you to commit to memory the structural formulae of the sixteen amino acids. We are well aware that one week after examinations you will probably forget them. What we teach you today may not be true five years from now, but our aim is to train you in fundamentals so that you will be able to understand the advancements in medicine and allied sciences that are in store for you. To train your mind in basic medicine so that you will be able to reason and deduce when you encounter conditions that your teachers and textbooks have not taught you. If you are well grounded in the fundamentals, you will be equipped with such weapons. Some of the greatest contributions in clinical medicine have been the results of some obscure country practitioners like McKenzie, who was practicing in the English countryside, but was observant enough to leave to us priceless observations on conditions of the heart.

"The greatest dicovery in medicine in the past few years is insulin for diabetes. It was initiated and completed by Banting who was not a biochemist. Do not consider these seemingly unimportant subjects from the standpoint of clinical medicine as humbug for they are the tools with which to understand life. One student once defined life as being one chemical reaction after another. Without chemistry and physiology we cannot understand the workings of the organism large and small."

This opinion in essence epitomized the attitude of the faculty.

Minoru was soon to discover that he was good in subjects that could be visualized, but was woefully weak in abstract matters such as pharmacology where he was obliged to commit to memory the Latin names and dosage of one hundred drugs, without using them in any way. Just memorizing them in addition to the complicated experimental results of these drugs and poison on mammals was indeed a large order even to one endowed with a prodigious memory. It was during these three months of intensive grind that he did not sleep more than six hours a night and fainted early one morning from sheer exhaustion. In retrospect, he used to say that were he asked to repeat the course in medicine, those three months in pharmacology would make him hesitate to give an otherwise very easy answer in the affirmative.

The city of St. Louis had the unglamorous distinction of being one of the three dirty cities of the United States. Burning in her thousands of furnaces the cheap bituminous coal that was extensively mined in neighboring Southern Illinois, there was not one clean building in the whole city. It was made up of grey and black, or red brick buildings. When it snowed, the white flakes were grey before they hit ground.

One afternoon about Christmas time, while the class was in the midst of taking a two hour written examination, the city became suddenly dark. Lights in the classroom went on, headlights of automobiles appeared, and an instructor came into the room and advised, "Place a handkerchief over your mouth and breath." Eyes smarted and breathing was difficult. The pall of smoke that rose above the city had been gradually moving southward, but an atmospheric quirk over the Gulf of Mexico reversed the wind. This northbound wind drove the accumulated smoke and soot back to where it originated and for three hours St. Louis smothered under this blanket of polluted air.

A Midwestern autumn was gorgeous, especially to a man from the tropics. The beautiful oak trees, a mass of crimson or yellow foliage, was a sight almost staggering in beauty. Every evening the students took a walk to Delmar Street where restaurants were more numerous. On the way, huge mansions lined one side of Kings Highway and their grounds were aglow with deciduous foliage trees. The cool air necessitated a light topcoat, the leisurely walk after a hectic day in the classrooms and dissecting laboratories contributed to make these eventide strolls a most enjoyable and rewarding hour of complete relaxation.

Snowfall in St. Louis was not severe, but it happened once in a while. When it first came, Minoru spent the entire Saturday afternoon walking up and down streets and strolling in nearby Forest Park. Black birds flying in groups and searching for food in bare areas, and the glee of the polar bears in the zoo were experiences reserved for those who had been denied in their childhood days the fun and ecstasy of making snowmen and hurling snowballs.

When he recounted this afternoon adventure to his dissection partner, Mullinex, the next day, his friend responded, "I can very well understand that. I was raised in Kansas and when I went to Cuba, I roamed the beaches in bare feet and walked in the surf half of a day. Even the mountains in Colorado are new to us raised on the prairies. You see, we see neither mountains nor sea."

"Yet in the short time I have been here, I can see beauty in the grove of trees and in the undulating hills of the Missouri countryside," truthfully remarked Minoru, for he began to love the large oaks on hills along the Mississippi River.

Mullinex continued, "Especially when you have lived in the Midwest, you will have associations of childhood memories with each seasonal change and that is an added charm to us who must continue to live here. By the way, have you gone to the shows yet? No! Well, try to take in the musical comedies of the Schubert Rialto Theaters. I am sure it will be worth your while to see some of them. I have heard that there is a very famous Municipal Operetta during the summer months at the outdoor theater at Forest Park. The plays are put on by local amateur talent and supposed to be very good."

"That is an important phase of my American education," replied Minoru becoming interested and laying down his dissecting forceps. "By the way, speaking of Americanization, I've been pondering over a joke sprung on me by our friend Kane three days ago. It runs like this. A traveling salesman came to a small town in Kansas that sprung up along the railroad. He noticed a peculiar thing about the population of this place. The number of children was extraordinarily large compared to the adults. So he asked the druggist at the corner store about the possible explanation. 'Well, you see stranger, there is that railroad running alongside the town and at exactly five o'clock in the morning there is a train that lets out a shrill whistle as it races by.'"

"Ha, ha, ha. That's a good one," roared Mullinex.

"Now, Mullinex. What is the explanation? I don't see anything funny about that observation," fretted Minoru.

"You say you thought about this for three days and can't figure it out? You are worse than an Englishman," and then he proceeded to enlighten Minoru.

Everyday someone brought in a new joke. Two Irishmen led in new laughs and Kane who was working part time in a small hospital was the most guilty. Every afternoon except on quiz days there was a huddle and a "ha, ha" ensued. Then it was invariably tried on Minoru and everyone watched his reactions. The latent period of three days gradually shrank to a matter of hours as he caught on to the play on words and of thought. He soon discovered that there was a peculiar channel into which the perceptive mechanism of mind had to be directed in order to grasp the hidden meaning. In six months he was able to laugh simultaneously with the rest of them.

The humor, the open-heartedness and the geniality of his friends were really refreshing. Nobody scowled, no bickering, no back-talk or envious remarks, everybody laughed and there was goodwill among all. The humor in the phrases of "cat's meow," "rare as hen's teeth," "the H A," etc., became a part of his everyday existence and a very important phase of Minoru's Americanization was accomplished.

One day in early spring, there was a surprise visitor for Minoru. Off and on there were doctors and scientists from Japan. If he were not in class or not too busily occupied, the registrar's office used to ask him to conduct them around the medical school and hospitals. Being out of the usual lane of traffic, St. Louis was not flooded by visitors like Chicago, but there were quite a few. Sometimes it became quite a nuisance. But this visitor was an old friend of Honolulu days. When he saw the name card, he was astonished and had to look twice.

Susumu Yoshida had become skinny and his receding forehead foretold that he would soon become bald. He stooped somewhat too, and this gave him a prematurely oldish appearance. The "Charlie Chaplin" mustache did not enhance his dignity much, as his complexion was rather pale.

"This is a surprise and a very pleasant one!" Minoru grasped Susumu's hand and shook it a dozen times.

"I heard in Honolulu that you were in California and so I was on the lookout for you somewhere in the States. I am here to attend the post graduate course in pediatrics offered by your dean, Dr. Marriot." Susumu was grinning widely and sizing up Minoru. He noticed that the latter had matured and changed also, but not very much. He observed that in America, people retained their youth much longer. Society did not demand that they should act old once past majority.

"What made you come to the United States?" Minoru asked.

"After finishing medicine, I started my practice at Yokohama and was struggling for three years when suddenly the great earthquake of September first struck and I was wiped out. I was in a quandary as to whether I should return to school and work for my advanced degree in medicine or go abroad to acquire new ideas, technics, and above all the prestige of having studied in foreign countries. There would be a considerable time before reconstruction could begin in stricken Yokohama and the neighboring cities and I could not very well remain idle. I chose the latter course and here I am."

As Minoru escorted him out of the registrar's office to walk the two blocks to his dormitory room, he felt a glow in his heart as he had seldom felt before. Here were two men who had shared their boyhood experiences together, come from opposite ends of the world and about to recount stories of their lives. There must be a great difference in their viewpoints, outlook on life in general, politics, and even religion, for during their separated years which were their formative period, their characters were moulded by different schools of thought and heritage. How different, he was soon to find out. For the time being he was hungry for news. As they settled in Minoru's room and took off their coats, Minoru resumed the train of conversation. "Tell me, what happened to you after you left Honolulu for Japan to enter medical school? Tell me about medical education in Japan."

Susumu lit a cigarette and leisurely began to talk in Japanese, for this language came more easily to him and there was nobody around. "There are two classes of medical schools there. The lower class is called the *senmon gakko* and admits graduates of middle schools on the merits of competitive examination. Because of insufficient training in foreign languages, instruction is conducted in the Japanese language. The higher class of schools require three years of study at the *koto gakko*, where languages and science are taught. German is intensively taught. After five years of English in middle school it would be logical and easier on the students to continue in English, but practically all professors were trained in Germany. This system is comparable to your premedical courses in colleges. The five imperial universities belong to this class. The students are required to read the original German texts and the lecturers use German medical terms interspersed with Japanese. This is a very funny evolution of speech. It does disservice to both languages, but there is an advantage. In talking before patients a mixture of Japanese and German technical terms are used freely but the key words are not intelligible to the poor layman. I chose the former class of school because I had to get out of school as quickly as possible as my parents were getting along in years. I spent two years at a hospital in pediatrics after graduation and then started practice at Yokohama."

"How were you received when you first went there? Did you get yourself acclimated without difficulty?" queried Minoru.

"Well, you know how we were looked down upon by our elders who came from Japan. We, born outside of Japan, were thought inferior because we were offspring of emigrants. Since my Japanese pronunciation was not quite up to par, the children used to giggle when I talked to them, but I became no different from them after six months. At school I had difficulty in the Chinese classics and in math, but I was not so poor in Japanese. I really showed my mettle in English and even teachers used to come to me when there was a foreign visitor, for they were no good in conversational English. Therefore, after one year, I got along well at middle school. I was marked as somewhat different from the rest, but I wasn't treated differently by the school, nor by my schoolmates. There was a certain advantage on my part and I made many friends, perhaps not the best, but good company. Since my parents sent me money regularly from Hawaii I had more spending money and was in a position to treat my friends. It helped," smiled Susumu as he was recalling escapades and episodes of those carefree days.

Minoru's mind was actively engaged not only in listening to and digesting the answer, but in forming new queries. "I have heard and read about the recent great earthquake of Tokyo and you are a victim of it. How was it?"

"Well, you can't really appreciate a natural catastrophe of that size unless you are a part of it. We are used to quakes, you know. At times you may have four or five sizable ones a day when there is a volcanic or subterranean geological upheaval off the coast. After a few years you got used to them; just hold your breath and wait for the end of the violent shake. When the first is over you wait for another, for there is always the return quake. I think the technical names are 'foreshocks and aftershocks.' The latter may be many. The horizontal kind is not bad.

"The last catastrophe was a vertical vibration and brought havoc to the Kanto region. But the real damage was the fire that followed. Narrow streets, wooden and paper structures, and almost total lack of fire fighting apparatus and hydrants put the cities at the mercy of the raging fire. You know, Japanese wooden houses are built without nails and the ends of posts dovetail into each other. There is a resiliency of the houses to the motions of the quake and the structure can withstand quite a bit of to and fro movement, but this up and down motion caused the top-heavy tile-covered-roofs to collapse, crushing the occupants. Many people were killed by the flying tiles."

"How about your family? How did you escape?"

"Luckily my wife and child were in Kyoto with her parents. Her mother was ill and she went to help. Being a poor young doctor just starting out, I had my combined office and residence near the hills in back of Yokohama, and it was not hard for me to seek refuge in the forest. In Japan, a bamboo forest is said to be the safest spot during a quake because the intertwining network of roots prevent fissures in the ground. But I lost everything except my savings in the bank."

"That was tough, but I'm glad that that was all you lost."

"Yes, I was lucky, lucky that I was able at my age to come to the United States for a sightseeing trip as well as the opportunity to pick up something. The prestige of having seen the world is another factor that will go great with my patients. Once you are rooted in medical practice, you are chained down and cannot go on any extended tour until you become old and unable to really appreciate travel and sight-seeing.

"On the way here I stopped over in Hawaii and spent two happy, interesting weeks. Naturally I went to visit my parents at Waimanalo. Honolulu hadn't changed much, but the road over the Pali was very much improved. My most interesting experience was meeting and renewing acquaintance with Sadao Arata."

"Well, how is he? I haven't heard much from him for a long time. I have been away for five years, you know."

"Yep, he is doing all right. He is a prosperous contractor. I never saw anyone with more nerve. He is a born gambler, I guess, but that description does not fit him too well. In his seemingly intuitional risks, there seems to be very exhaustive preliminary research. His aggressiveness to acquire knowledge and his utilization of influence from the right source astounded me.

"He did not even finish the first year of high school but he contracts jobs requiring highly technical civil engineering knowledge. How does he do it? First, he knows how to handle men. He makes them feel important; 'Hoomalimali' them as the Hawaiians say. He is not proud. He stoops low to learn. He was telling me about a pipeline he had to lay for the navy. He had a subcontract job and had to dig ditches about thirty miles following the notations on the surveyor's spikes. Those numerals did not mean anything to him and yet he had declared to the general contractor that he knew everything connected with such work. That night, he betook himself to a Japanese surveyor of the Waipahu Plantation, a stranger, and humbly asked him to teach him what those figures meant. The latter was impressed by his humility and obligingly went out to the field and with the aid of a flashlight gave him a lesson in the practical application of elementary surveying." Susumu smiled with evident pride as if he had done it himself.

"Well, good for Sadao. I hear he is doing quite a bit of road construction now."

"Yes, there's another story just like the one I told you. He could not afford to engage any bona fide civil engineer, so he took the territorial engineering inspector to a tea house, wined him, and had him give practical suggestions so that the work was acceptable to the government. Anyway his work is first class, because the inspector teaches him how to construct. It's just in the means of getting information that he shows his originality and cleverness. The inspector is not asked to pass any inferior work. He is asked what the government expects and Sadao delivers, nothing wrong about that. I think he is branching out into money-making house construction. He can pay for technical knowledge, hire brains, and I'm telling you he is more of a success now than either of us can ever hope to be."

"Yes, I guess so. This hard studying is fun to us but, for Sadao, he just wasn't made this way. He had his own way of life. Which is better, I don't know. I hope he is happy. Was he married? The last time I saw him before I left, he was in love with a part Hawaiian girl."

"I met her. He married her over the objection of his father, who was very much of the old school. And, as Sadao is the first son, he was adamant. But faced with an accomplished fact the arrival of a grandson softened him and they are now reconciled."

"How did you find out that I was here?"

"I visited the students' club at Stanford University and asked about you. All of us tourists visit Palo Alto because of the beauty of its campus. There I was told of your being here. Now that I am here I'll remain for two weeks and take the course given for practitioners by Dr. Marriott."

"I don't know anything about his course as I am only a freshman, but I hear that he is a real research man and nationally known in infant feeding. He is a biochemist to begin with."

"That I have learned today. Because I had my training in Japanese, I may have some difficulty in understanding his lectures, but I know I'll get something out of the course. The atmosphere of such a gathering under so distinguished a teacher is itself a rare privilege."

"I see you have become quite Japanese in your outlook."

"Have I? Well, I should be. After all I was there ten years."

Many men have confessed what role teachers played in altering the course of their lives. They had their minds set on becoming something, but preceptors with whom they came into contact influenced them unconsciously or deliberately so that they ended up in a field totally different. Eminent men can be a decided influence upon a sensitive young man and leave an indelible imprint upon the plastic mind.

One day in 1924 a very sad event took place. The Congress of the United States passed the Immigration Act that barred from entry into the United States all people of Japanese ancestry except for a favored few such as scholars and ministers of the gospel. Not many had been allowed to cross the border anyway, so actually it did not matter much. But this congressional act left a deep, festering sore in its wake. It hurt the pride of the Japanese people most to be labelled "unwanted."

Susumu took a deep breath and shaking his head said, "I cannot really understand how this came about. When Tokyo and Yokohama were still burning last year, U.S. destroyers stationed in Manila came racing into Tokyo Bay loaded with relief supplies for the needy. The Japanese authorities were stunned and almost paralyzed and did nothing to alleviate the people's suffering. Before they woke up from their daze, foreign war vessels came into our harbor loaded with welcome medicinal supplies and food. We were very, very thankful for this merciful act. Many living today perhaps owe their health to the prompt care that was given with the material from Manila. Many were wearing clothes from the American Red Cross when I left Yokohama.

"When Ambassador Saito died at Washington, the United States Government paid the highest tribute and courtesy to the Saito family and our government by sending a battle cruiser bearing his remains to Japan. This act deeply touched our people. Never was a single act by any foreign country so penetratingly good and touching. It brought tears to our eyes just to listen to the news. Now a complete about-face and this resounding slap across our face!" Minoru saw tears glistening under his friend's spectacles. There seemed to be no anger, no hatred, only a complete resignation. He looked at Minoru searchingly for some explanation.

"In a democracy, the judiciary and executive departments can act independently. No inter-departmental correlation and consultation. The act of mercy by the Far Eastern Fleet was the typical American way of acting in such catastrophes. The courtesy shown the late Ambassador Saito was because he was well liked by the American govern-

263

ment and it was ordered by the President of the United States. Beautiful sentiments have prompted such gracious acts. I don't think this was done for diplomatic reasons.

"According to the papers, the passage of this last Exclusion Act was the result of a threat made by Ambassador Shidehara. Maybe he did not mean it as a threat but the ill chosen words 'grave consequence,' had a sinister implication if one were inclined to interpret them in that way. And I am afraid many in Washington today are ready to pick up ambiguous words to twist them into meanings suitable to their express wishes." Minoru also was not in a jovial mood. The day had passed dismally and even though he tried to rationalize, his analysis seemed hollow to his friend. He recalled the incident of the day and continued.

"Today at noon I was called into Dr. Graham's office. Dr. Graham is Professor of Surgery and he does not know me as a student yet. I entered his room and he said, 'You know, we thinking Americans are extremely sorry for what happened today at Washington. You may or may not meet unpleasant incidents at school or in this vicinity, but if you do, come to me directly.' I told him I was an American citizen, but he said people will not know the difference. I was extremely grateful to Dr. Graham and also was impressed by the stature of this man. He is a great man. Susumu, when you return to Japan, please relay this incident to the press. By so doing you may in some degree assuage the hurt and show the Japanese people that there are many Americans who do not see eye to eye with that law."

Susumu looked up and wanly smiled, "That I will do. Yes, I'll see to it that the news spreads."

Susumu's stay in St. Louis was only two weeks, but during that time he was able to observe at first hand how studious American students are compared to their medical counterparts in Japan. In Japan one did not have to attend lectures, only had to pass examinations. But in America, state laws required that a certain percentage of hours be spent in lectures and laboratories. Roll call was taken frequently to enforce this law.

Practical training in clinical work was given more extensively in the American school. At least twelve maternity cases had to be handled at patients' homes or in hospitals in the senior year and this practice gave a lot of confidence to students. In Japan, seniors only watched such deliveries at the University hospital.

Leaving St. Louis, he visited Chicago and New York, but only did sightseeing. Unless there was a special friend or an unusual occurrence a traveler did not linger long at a place, and he gained nothing by merely going through the physical plant, unless he was an architect or administrator. To learn, to evaluate and, to absorb actual medical knowledge as practiced in another country, one had to spend months in wards, dispensaries, or laboratories.

Susumu did not have the time to devote to such a leisurely tour. He saw America. Now he could return to Japan and devote several years in some medical college and do research work under the guidance of a professor. For five to seven years doing part time work, he would qualify for the degree of doctor of medical science because what he possessed now might be comparable to Bachelor of Medicine of British institutions. Only in that way could his prestige both in medical circles and among lay people become enhanced. This was a system peculiar to Japan, where title meant so much.

Months of hard work came and went, and eventually the dreary winter was gone. Pink magnolia saginatta added color to the dried up lawn. Orange breasted robins jumped here and there looking for worms, and green blades of grass began to peep from under the brown grass that covered the surface of the yard. In the land of short spring time, the heat of summer returned within a week, crickets became noisy, and the green leaves rapidly grew in size and covered the bare branches. In spite of it, a cold front from the Arctic sent a snow storm into the Mississippi Basin and there was a six inch carpet of snow on the 25th of May. But in the first week of June the temperature rose to nearly 90 and summer had really arrived.

Final examinations were at hand and students burned the traditional midnight oil. It was a serious business to pass these examinations. If one failed in these examinations it was a death knell to his aspirations as he could not be accepted at any other first class medical school. Questions of professors for the preceding ten years or more were perused as reference, for usually one could discern what sort of questions would most likely be sprung in the coming exams. Even brilliant professors had their Achilles' heels and bright young students were good strategists.

It was an anticlimax pure and simple when a half a dozen or more men congregated in one of the rooms and caroused late into the night, keeping grumbling elderly people in the next building tossing in bed until three in the morning.

"All dormitory students are requested to meet in the auditorium," Miss Kaiser of the registrar's office announced at the cafeteria that noon. All looked at each other but could only guess at what had transpired to bring about such an unusual announcement.

It was an informal gathering and Dr. Marriott, the Dean, stood in the hall among the rows of seats. When all sixty were gathered he faced the crowd. "It seems you had quite a party last night at the dormitory. I am not censuring you. After examinations perhaps it is a natural reaction to let go, but please do not throw bottles out of windows. There are wastebaskets for such. Don't keep your neighbors awake at night. They are nice people but this office has received complaints this morning. Apparently your neighbors have forgotten that they were also young once. If drink you must, drink like gentlemen. That is all, gentlemen."

During summer vacation, Minoru returned to California and spent three months helping Tom Tanaka on the farm. Many times he operated a Fordson tractor and dug ditches with the laborers. His father was getting used to this new environment but was not farming independently. His brothers and sisters were enjoying the change from Hawaiian living to a busy farm life of California. Each was given an opportunity to work and make pin money during the vacation months. Sports that children love abounded in the river and sloughs. Post war depression had come and gone and the nation's economy was on an even keel. Peace was everywhere and farm prices held. There was no enormous profit in any produce as in the recent war years, but it seemed that one's future was secure in a country of plenty.

Each year Minoru returned for the summer to California. For three months he worked out in the sun and it was good for him. After the completion of the freshman year, the second year was really not too hard, but there was an enormous amount of reading that had to be done. Courses were numerous and each required a substantial amount of preparation, but there was an attempt made to correlate the fundamental sciences with clinical medicine and each subject seemed to be of some practical use. As a result work was of interest. From the latter half of the sophomore year, physical diagnosis was taught and students began to feel that they were finally nearing their goal. Examination of patients using their five senses was stressed. Above all, observation of tell-tale signs, little clues that might lead to important hidden trouble, and to think objectively and analyze the accumulated signs to formulate a working diagnosis were didactically emphasized.

Dr. Sachs was a most effective teacher. Every Thursday at 11 a.m. there was a surgical amphitheater session for juniors. At random two students were called down into the pit of the amphitheater to be grilled by this famous neurosurgeon who loved his role of a tormentor. Students dreaded to be picked, yet could not stay away. In every session there was a point or two hammered home; an unforgettable gem in diagnosis or an anecdote that carried a lesson to remain with the men for the rest of their lives. This session was an institution at this medical school and was continued as long as Dr. Sachs remained on the faculty.

"Mr. Allen, this patient is suffering from abdominal pain. He is disrobed now. His chief complaint is in the right lower quadrant. Demonstrate to the class how you will examine him." Allen seriously started with inspection of the abdominal surface, noting any bulge or discoloration of the skin. His hand gently kneaded the abdomen to elicit any mass or point of pain.

"Now, wait a minute. Gentlemen, Mr. Allen was very good in doing a careful inspection of the surface. But you saw him begin with the right lower quadrant in palpation. Now this patient's probable pathology lies in that area. It is a cardinal point to remember never to cause unnecessary pain when examining. Once you inflict pain, the patient becomes apprehensive and tightens up and cooperation is difficult to get thereafter. Start, therefore, at some other part and leave the area of complaint to the last. Now, Mr. Allen, you are going to become a doctor, and I hope a good one. But with those nails, your digging in the soft abdomen will cause pain. So trim your nails short." Allen was red as a beet. Incidentally, he would not again be caught with untrimmed nails by Dr. Sachs or by anybody else.

"Modern surgery began not long ago. With the advent of bacteriology, the greatest boon to the sick was the development of asepsis and surgery was performed without fear of complicating infection. Can anyone tell me who was responsible for this revolutionary forward step in surgery? He used to spray the operative room with carbolic acid fumes, and soak his hands in weak carbolic acid. Any of you gentlemen know who this man was? Now there is a bright young man with his hand up. You tell the class."

"Lord Lister of England."

"Good. Now I am going to assign you work. Prepare to give a short talk next week about Lord Lister." The class giggled and Dr. Sachs grinned. Perhaps he knew that Kinney was an eccentric and the butt of many a joke among the students.

Thursday morning the surgical clinic was held in the usual manner. Two students submitted to three quarters of an hour of penetrating questions that probed into certain phases of the diseases under consideration. These revealed how utterly ignorant they were and they were gently rebuked for their lack of observation. They had a sympathetic audience for each of the class took every torment as if meant for himself. Today, however, there was a certain tension and a suppressed expectation. Suddenly, ten minutes before noon, Dr. Sachs looked up into the gallery and announced, "I shan't keep a certain person in suspense any longer. We shall have the pleasure of listening to Mr. Kinney on his dissertation on Lord Lister." The class applauded and roared. Dr. Sachs was all smiles. All were in for a brief period of entertainment: a respite from a heavy routine not often encountered at medical school.

Ray Kinney did not bat an eye. He proceeded straight to the blackboard. Out of his coat pocket he produced a picture from some book. Gravely he tacked it on the blackboard with thumbtacks, faced the class, and delivered a really brilliant resumé of the achievement of Lord Lister, the father of aseptic surgery. When he finished, there was no giggling in the gallery and a round of appreciative applause broke loose. Dr. Sachs got up, advanced to Kinney and warmly shook his hand. "Well done Mr. Kinney, very well done indeed." Ray was no longer considered condescendingly by his fellow students.

St. Louis had a good sized colored population. The migration of southern Negroes northward during the First World War to work in war plants of Chicago and Detroit found this border city between north and south as a first steppingstone. The Negroes found comparative freedom from restrictions extant in the South and found St. Louis to their liking. Many settled permanently. Minoru was very interested in these people for he was a great admirer of Booker T. Washington. *Up from Slavery* was a very inspiring book and in his limited library he had a copy that he had bought at a secondhand book store in Oakland.

While dissecting in anatomy, talk drifted to the racial question. Mullinex was a Kansan and studied at the University of Missouri for a while. "I once witnessed a Negro lynching at Columbus, Mo., and I never saw a whiter Negro. He certainly was scared!"

"You mean to say college students participated in the lynching?"

"It was not led by students, but I am sure the mob was made up of many men from the university. Anyway, even in Missouri we have to resort to such extremes to keep them in place. Once you give in there will be no bounds to their demands. The only good nigger is a dead one!"

Minoru saw that Mullinex meant it. There was no room for argument; it was like religion and better be left alone. He changed tactics and continued the talk from an oblique angle. "Don't you think that there are many Negroes well educated, capable, and worthy of respect? For instance Mr. Booker Washington, the great teacher at Tuskegee Institute is an outstanding man."

"I don't think he is."

"But President Theodore Roosevelt thought he was above the herd and had dinner with him. The King of Belgium had supper with him. A man invited by the heads of two nations surely deserves respect."

"Heck no! Who you describe as a great Negro is no better than the lowest white."

Minoru realized to what depth this prejudice had taken root in the minds of these people in spite of their education. It was beyond his comprehension. The warped ideas propounded and instilled into children were certainly firmly established. No haphazard attempt at education would lift their prejudice. In a way it was understandable. Only until recently Negroes were bought and sold and Missouri was a Southern state in affiliation. A newly arrived southern Negro, after sensing the freedom of St. Louis, was said to be first bewildered by the lack of Jim Crowism on streetcars. Later he would become cocky in his exercise of this freedom. Native Missourians and Southerners used to remark about this phenomenon and their reaction was not tolerant.

In the senior year, the class was divided into three sections to serve as ward clerks in rotation among surgical, medical, obstetric, and pediatric services. The students were assigned cases in the wards. They took exhaustive histories and followed these patients as to course and treatment while they were at the hospital. The interns and residents did the physical examinations and gave students practical teaching along with routine handling of the sick.

Ward rounds by the professor was an important occasion because the student had to present the history and be questioned regarding the patient and his ailment. Considerable reading concerning the entire aspect of the disease had to be done in preparation for the impromptu quizzes.

Minoru's section was assigned surgery and in addition to ward clerkship, the senior student became a fifth member of the operating team to hold retractors or just hover around. It was an introduction in the ritual of scrubbing hands and forearms for fifteen minutes before operation, carrying scrubbed hands in a praying position, and the sensation of being robed in sterile gowns by the operating room nurses.

In the wards, the poor patients were stuck every day with a pin to supply blood for blood counting. Urinalysis was done every day. It was very exhaustive work and rather hard on the patient, but as a whole they were not complaining and enjoyed being so very well investigated.

At the Barnes Hospital there was a Negro ward which was not too large. With the wealth of material at the outpatient dispensary the Negro sick requiring hospitalization were either taken care of at the City Hospital # 2 or in the colored ward of Barnes Hospital. It was natural for a teaching hospital to admit the more rare afflictions in this ward and as a rule each presented medically interesting conditions. The student clerks were rotated among the men's, women's, and colored surgical wards. When Minoru's section was assigned to this last pavilion, he was given about four patients. Among them was a mechanic by the name of Channing who had to have a daily dressing for a large hole in the upper jaw where a recent operation had been performed for cancer.

Minoru asked the supervisor for the use of the dressing room for this task. A student nurse came to help. Channing was a large mulatto who had apparently become thinner because of his sickness and the ordeal of the operation. He sat down in the chair and glared at this puny Oriental.

"If you hurt me, I'm gonna sock you," he declared belligerently. Minoru did not say a word while the student nurse turned astonished eyes on him. He took hold of a Kelly forcep and slowly pulled out the packing.

"Does it hurt? Tell me, when it does," and rested when about one third of the length of the iodoform pack was out. "All right grit your teeth, I am going to do it very slowly again. Don't hesitate to stop me if it hurts." There was no word from Channing during the rest of the procedure.

The next day, Minoru was in the room to take Channing's blood. He did not use an ordinary needle but used a "gun" which released a sharp needle on the pressure of a release. Channing jumped in bed and there was a roar in the ward, for every patient's eye was glued on him. "Don't get me wrong, fellows. I was not prepared for this new needle. It's none of this doctor's fault. He did not hurt me any, honest," and he gave Minoru a sheepish smile. Apparently he had been giving his fellow patients a build up of Minoru's gentleness, and now at this crucial test he failed to convince them.

Three weeks later when Channing was leaving the hospital he came to shake hands and said, "If you ever practice in St. Louis, let me know. This here is my address." It made Minoru feel very happy.

In the ward there was a very intelligent looking, clean-cut young patient assigned to another student. He was about thirty-eight, lean and tall, and registered as a Pullman waiter. He seemed anxious to start a conversation and smiled at Minoru every time the latter came into the ward. "Did you see today's paper which says that there is a large typhoon approaching Japan?"

"No, I have not yet read any paper today."

"Well, it says it is going to be bad."

"It's like your tornado here in the midwest. People are used to it. They are rather philosophical. By the way Mr. Brown, if I am not too inquisitive, will you tell me how much schooling you had?" This patient appeared different from the average Negro in St. Louis. "Did you finish high school?"

Mr. Brown smiled, and said, "Yes, and I tried to become like you."

Minoru was taken aback and blurted out, "Do you mean that you went to medical school?"

"Yes, sir, I finished at Meharry," he wryly responded.

"And you a waiter!" groaned Minoru and he became silent for wholly three minutes. "You ought to be ashamed of yourself! Look at the plight of your race in the South. I, being an Oriental, am intensely interested in the racial questions in the United States. The Negro question is the most urgent and the most pathetic in my mind. The cause of this sorry situation in my observation has been the dearth of educated

271

leaders. There must be more Booker Washingtons to guide and lead the masses. And another thing that you know more than anybody else is the inadequate medical service among your people. Now if one trained and qualified like you shirks the duty to bear the role, who will assume the task of ministering to your people? I really can't understand your being a waiter." Minoru was flushed.

"What you say is gospel truth. I had to work my way through college and at Meharry Medical College life was not soft for me. When I got my degree and license to practice medicine I went out into the world filled with the ideals of youth and the burning desire to better not only my station in life but that of my brethren. But I was confronted with the most discouraging condition in Birmingham, Alabama where I hung my shingle.

"There was no hospital where we Negro doctors could take our patients. Every sick person had to be treated at home or at a makeshift hospital. Not only that, but my class of patients were charity. I was on the verge of starving, and I would have if I hadn't turned to something else. My work as a Pullman waiter gives me two hundred a month and this is sufficient to keep the wolf away from the door. I can now raise my children decently. Can you blame me much?"

There was sadness in Mr. Brown's expression. A far away look that bespoke of many moments of self reproach and of the sense of lost opportunities clouded his eyes now that he was confessing to an utter stranger, although a sympathetic and understanding one.

"I don't know that you have done the right thing. Maybe I am too young and inexperienced in the ways of life to appreciate realities, but perhaps you should have stuck to your first love and sacrificed your life with missionary zeal. You might also have sought new opportunities in other parts of the country when Birmingham was not as good as expected." Minoru could not help but express his honest opinion.

"Well, you can't really say what you'll do until faced with the actual problem. I'll tell you a very interesting experience that I had during my first days in the slum districts of that industrial Alabama city. As I said before, I had to sit in my office day in and day out waiting for patients to drift in, but with little prospect of success.

"Getting a bit tired of this inactivity, I went out for a walk. The streets were not paved and I was walking along the wooden sidewalk, when a bulldog jumped at me on the other side of the fence. He could not bite me. I was taken unawares and so without stopping to think, I drew the revolver that I always carried for protection, and shot him. Then I realized where I was and to whom the dog might belong. I was standing in front of the house of the most powerful gangster in the colored community. Naturally I made a beeline for home, put my white gown on and waited with a thumping heart for what might follow.

"Before long there was knock at the front door. I peeped through the window and saw the cigar-munching man with the injured dog in his arms. I was dismayed. There was nothing else to do. I drew in a deep breath, straightened up, and assumed the most complacent poker face I could gather at this crisis and opened the door.

"Good evening, doctor. Some good for nothing bum took a potshot at my dog. Think you could fix him up?'

"I was visibly relieved. Luckily the dog did not recognize me in my white gown. I put a couple of stitches in the wound and collected three dollars. This was the first paying patient I treated in Birmingham."

When spring came, six weeks of obstetrics and graduation awaited Minoru's section. It was better this way, rather than to run around in this city of one million during the cold winter months. Stevens from Milwaukee approached him to team up. Students had to work in pairs. Washington University was unique in that, for out-patient home deliveries, students were sent out without the assistance of any nurse or intern. They were strictly on their own except for being in constant telephone touch with the resident surgeon at the hospital. Progress of labor had to be reported to him every thirty minutes and if indicated the latter rushed out to assist. But since all the deliveries were second babies or more, complications were few. The position of the babies had been carefully checked and followed monthly at the out-patient clinic. It was a sort of experience that doctors of the older school were doing in their daily practice. No instrument was used and the students had a chance to observe and handle a normal, natural parturition.

Each had to have twelve cases for the course but usually ended up with nearly twenty for they were assigned hospital cases as well to follow and observe the conduct of first baby deliveries. But these hospital deliveries were handled by interns and students merely assisted. In the home deliveries the students were called when the labor pains became regular. Luckily Stevens had a car, and Minoru was able to travel in

273

grand style. A delivery kit readied by a nurse was received in exchange for a used one when they returned from a delivery, and this was with one of them so that they could start without a moment's delay.

As soon as they arrived at the home, one became the obstetrician and it became his responsibility to examine and determine the exact state of progress. It was his duty to report to the resident at the hospital and to get a new addition to a happy family. The other student took charge of the arrangement of the room and selection of assistants.

Usually there were a few women assembled for the occasion. He looked at the crowd and picked the most intelligent woman as his first assistant to tidy up the room. An ironing board was placed crosswise under the mattress of the double bed to prevent any sagging. A pad of newspapers sewed together at the edges as instructed at the out-patient clinic was placed on the mattress and under the buttock to prevent blood staining. Newspapers were spread on the floor and two straight-back chairs were placed at one side of the bed to act as foot rests for the patient. The obstetrician was to work between these chairs.

After these arrangements were completed, it was a vigil of waiting until the arrival of the baby. Some babies came fast, some were slow, and some seemed never to arrive. Some mothers were stoical, others less so, and quite a few uncontrollably panicky in spite of the fact that the experience was not new.

People were cooperative. As the hours wore on coffee was brewed and pleasantries exchanged. When night progressed into the small hours of the morning, the obstetrician lay down next to the woman in labor, so that she might wake him up when the pains got severe. The assistant lay down wherever he could make himself comfortable.

When the baby was born it was handed over to the assistant who tied the cord, put the abdominal binder on, and instilled drops of silver nitrate into the eyes as was the law of the land. It was then delivered into the custody of the woman assistant who clothed the infant in a soft, warm gown. The obstetrician was busy attending to the proper expulsion of the afterbirth. Only then and no sooner was an injection of ergot given into the muscle for proper contraction of the womb.

This was the usual routine and a very satisfying experience. The first house to which the Stevens-Murayama team went was a white family from which water had been shut off that morning because of non-payment. Minoru thus went to the next house to borrow a pailful of water, as the grumbling husband of twenty-five was half drunk and of no help. Even while the delivery was in progress he was dozing in the next room, oblivious to the goings-on. It was a very discouraging experience for their first venture.

They were marooned one night in a street off Grand Ave. in a Negro home by a tornado alarm for the city of St. Louis. It was a home of decent folk, and the house was spick and span. As a whole, all students preferred Negro homes to those of poor white people. Perhaps the former were more grateful and cooperative. The student doctors had more freedom and felt at ease, and they all claimed that Negro homes were generally cleaner.

"You ladies and gentlemen will be in this section of gastroenterology for three weeks to become acquainted with this specialty. In clinical laboratory work, you were taught chemical analysis of the stomach contents. The importance of such an analysis is self-evident, but the contention and differences of opinion lie in the method of collecting this juice; fractional method of gathering the juice every fifteen minutes for two hours, versus a single aspiration about forty-five minutes following eating of shredded wheat. Each method has its merits, but I think the latter is a more practical one," Dr. Gorham lectured to the section in the section of gastroenterology at the Outpatient Department one afternoon. "Is there anyone here who wants to express his opinion regarding this point."

Minoru raised his hand, as this instructor seemed to be friendly and open minded. "For one thing, by the single method, you cannot tell the degree of secretory activity of the stomach glands at different stages. Valuable information will then be lost, and so I think the fractional method is superior."

Dr. Gorham smilingly said, "You have a point there, but we are treating these patients on an out-patient basis. If you can get sufficient information in forty-five minutes rather than two hours, I think there is sufficient reason and justification to abbreviate the test." But Minoru had other ideas regarding this stomach analysis so he now found courage to blurt out.

"Dr. Gorham, I am not at all certain that gastric analysis contributes much to diagnosis. If the amount of acidity is unfailingly high in ulcers, and always negative in cancer, then it is perhaps worthwhile to do it painstakingly. But I read somewhere that even cancer of the stomach will have normal acidity. If, after all diagnosis of a stomach ailment is going to rest on X-ray, then why subject patients to this uncomfortable ordeal?"

Dr. Gorham did not answer and concluded the interview by saying, "Medical science is ever changing. The armamentarium of diagnosis is incomplete and subject to change all the time. You will soon discover how inadequate our knowledge is."

The next day, the seven students were assigned patients, but Minoru was not given his. "What, a discriminatory measure in St. Louis! Perhaps I shouldn't have opened my mouth yesterday." He was irritated and annoyed.

Dr. Gorham came along. "Good afternoon young man. By the way what are you interested in?"

"I do not know yet. Whatever I come across, I get interested."

"That is understandable. Have you thought about research?"

"I have done a little under Dr. Loeb in pathology."

"I don't mean that type of work. Clinical research is what I have in mind. You know there is a lot of work in clinical medicine that is awaiting research workers. You seem to have an investigative mind. Sometimes foreign students are at an advantage, but many times they are left out. I know because I was one in Germany. Have you met Dr. Barr, the professor of medicine? If you haven't, let us go meet him," and he led the bewildered Minoru to the Barnes Hospital. But the professor was in the midst of a lecture, so Dr. Gorham left a message with his secretary.

Next day Minoru was summoned by Dr. Barr. "Mr. Maruyama, Dr. Gorham tells me you do not believe everything that we tell you. That is a good trait and it shows you do some thinking on your own. We are always on the lookout for men who are curious and are driven to investigate. This department is yours when you bring to us any problem for solution. Not only I, but all the department heads will welcome your problems. A very great amount of money is spent to operate this medical school, but it is considered well spent if the torch of medical knowledge can be advanced a bit further by her products."

Dr. Barr was a very distinguished man and his lectures were precise and clear. Minoru was deeply impressed and grateful. It was recognition that he did not feel he was quite worthy of. He was grateful for Dr. Gorham who evinced such a liking for him and took this trouble to further the cause of a student. As a practitioner spending several afternoons a week for charitable work, he was an extremely busy man, but he was primarily a teacher.

With the beginning of the senior year, students began to think about their hospital training after graduation. During undergraduate years, the training of the students followed a rigid line of reasoning, deduction, application of all basic scientific knowledge, and the use of recently developed diagnostic armamentarium for the proper clarification of what ails a human being. This phase of clinical medicine was stressed above everything; it was diagnosis with a capital D. How to treat a man could very well be learned later in the wards of hospitals. Therefore, the role of a good hospital to put finishing touches to a budding physician was of the greatest importance.

The type of hospital each student wanted was determined primarily by what he wanted to do, but to a greater extent was conditioned by his financial status. Those more fortunately situated could spend several years in hospital training which paid them no stipend. The better the training a hospital could offer, the less it paid. Usually the university hospitals paid nothing while other independent institutions paid twenty-five dollars above board and room. Some paid as high as seventy-five dollars a month but these were in the rural districts, away from teaching centers.

For Minoru there was not much choice. Financially he could not continue a prolonged course in hospital work, but the other more important problem that faced him was discrimination based on race and color. Since there was no Negro at school, he did not know how young physicians of this race fared. But he heard they were barred from all white hospitals.

The City Hospital #2 for Negroes in St. Louis had only Negro doctors and nurses on their staff. Several of them were excellent in any company. The resident surgeon, Dr. Thomas, was an excellent diagnostician and surgeon. The roly-poly jet black roentgenologist certainly knew his X-ray and his interpretations profoundly impressed the instructors and the class when the latter spent a weekly afternoon at this hospital to see the variety of cases, both medical and surgical, that were handled there. These Negro physicians had only a few hospitals in the country to receive their intern training and to send patients to once they went out to practice. To a lesser extent Jewish graduates were not accepted at Gentile hospitals, but there were numeous superior institutions of their own scattered throughout the nation. In fact, Gentile graduates sought internship training at Jewish hospitals because of the excellence of their staff. Jews were good teachers.

Minoru Murayama did not have any precedence by which to conduct his campaign. If he had gone to a Chicago school he would have been able to seek a Cook County Hospital berth which was dependent on the outcome of competitive examination among graduates of Illinois Medical Schools. Had he gone to school in California the university authorities would have seen to his appointment because the state law in both states required a year's internship before graduation. In Missouri the medical degree was conferred after four years of formal work and the subsequent training was left to each individual's choice and inclination. He thus sent applications to representative hospitals in many cities, but the majority did not even have the courtesy to answer an application with an Oriental name.

"Try the Jewish Hospital here. While you had your clerkship there you were liked by all. The younger instructors who are on the staff at the Jewish Hospital know you and your diligence. Since the Jews themselves know what discrimination is, they may be more tolerant. Try anyway," suggested Dr. Somogyi who was his teacher in biochemistry and was now head of the laboratory at the Jewish Hospital. Being an immigrant himself he knew what a minority member had to go through in job hunting.

The luxurious new hospital was run not by industrious young instructor-practitioners, but by businessmen who were cognizant of the possible adverse reaction of their wealthy clientele to anything but the best, even to the extent of citizenry. No doctor of second rate citizenship was to be tolerated in this new edifice, the pride of St. Louis Jewry.

Dr. Sachs took an active part in writing to some other hospitals in Detroit and New Orleans but even with his friendship with the department heads, the answers were discouraging. By mid January the majority of the class got appointments. Students with lower standings than Minoru were experiencing no difficulty in getting positions at the very best hospitals. For the first time he was being faced with an almost impossible wall of racial prejudice. Later he heard that a student with the name of Arata was accepted. Katsuki and Iseri were also able to celebrate, but the three were in for a rude jolt when their photographs were submitted. Their Italian and Jewish sounding names fooled the hospitals, but the portraits did not.

Murayama was a name not to be mistaken for any other racial extraction. The bulletin board of the medical school had new posters from many hospitals advertising for interns, and they quoted stipends. One day there was one from the Omaha, Nebraska Methodist Hospital.

"I am graduating next June and am trying to get a rotation internship. Frankly, I am having difficulty in securing a place because of my race. I am an American citizen of Japanese blood born in Hawaii. If this is considered an unwise selection by your intern committee, please do not hesitate to say frankly. It will not be taken with rancor. The silent treatment is what hurts."

Within a week, there was an answer. "The Methodist Hospital is glad to have you on its staff. In the past we had a Filipino intern and he was accepted by all without any trouble."

Thus Minoru felt relieved. He got an appointment to a good hospital, but he was thankful for the good record left by this dusky predecessor. But how did this Filipino get the appointment in the first place? Were there hospitals run in the true spirit of their professed religions in this era of money-wise boards of trustees?

The commencement exercises were held in the large gymnasium on the university campus on Skinker Road. Summer had come but it was not too hot yet. Everything was green and people's hearts were gay. Many students graduating in medicine had not been on this campus at all since they had been so busily occupied on the other side of the Forest Park where Barnes Hospital medical center was located. Robed and capped, it was the culmination of four years of hard work and an achievement of note in anyone's life.

For Minoru it was a great sense of relief; relief that there were no more nightmarish examinations to prepare for. Nobody could take away the prerogative that went along with the sheepskin that he was to obtain. If ever such an event were to take place, it was to be solely the result of an infraction of the Hippocratic oath and the fault would be his own doing. It was a sense of achievement, but there was not much

279

jubilation in his heart. A high school commencement ten years ago had been more joyous. Over a thousand graduates thronged the hall. The class presidents from each department went up to receive the diplomas from the chancellor while the respective classes stood at attention. Since there were so many out-of-staters who did not have parents or relatives at this exercise Minoru did not feel too lonesome. After the diplomas were distributed by the class presidents, groups gathered here and there to take final snapshots and bid farewell to each other, for the following day they were to scatter.

CHAPTER 19

Hospital Internship

ON JUNE 30, 1927, DR. MURAYAMA REPORTED
to the Methodist Hospital in Omaha, Nebraska to begin his one year
rotation internship. The receptionist, Miss Brubaker, was cordial and
led him into Miss Fuller's office. Since he had had correspondence with
her they were acquainted in a way. She was in her mid-forties, rotund
of figure and slightly gray, but she had a mature comeliness that set him
at ease at once. The jittery feeling he had while en route from California was gone after two minutes in her office.

"Dr. Harry Lang from Northwestern came to us three days ago and
is already working in surgery. Two Nebraska men are also working.
Have a good talk with them and arrange the work amongst yourselves.
You may have to start with medicine as there is nobody on that service."

"It is all right with me to start on any service."

"It is best that you meet Dr. Lang. He will show you around."

Miss Brubaker conducted him to the interns' quarters and soon Dr.
Lang entered the room. "My name is Lang. I came here three days
ago," he said and offered his hand. This was the beginning of a very
intimate friendship. "I started in surgery because there was no one in
this service. Seems like the former bunch left before their contracts
were over. They needed someone to scrub and so I was roped in before
I could make up my mind."

"How is the service? Much work?"

"I don't know yet. I guess there is no limit to the work you may do
because we are shorthanded. Anyway, you and I have to stick together
and work it out. Since I am on surgery you may as well start in medicine.
I have heard the medical service is good. A lot of diagnostic cases from
country practitioners are here and the staff members are top notch in
this city."

"I have no idea how the staff is made up. Do you know anything about it?" Minoru was going to learn now who his teachers in clinical medicine and surgery were going to be. Were they to be busy practitioners who would have little time to devote to teaching, or born teachers who would love to impart their knowledge, experience, and be genuinely interested in the training of interns?

Dr. Lang was Nebraska born and knew the local condition well. "Omaha has two medical schools, the University of Nebraska and Creighton University. This hospital is not affiliated with the State University, but the faculty members of that school bring their private cases here. As a result we have good men. I presume they can teach us a lot."

"How about charity cases?"

"I really don't know, but I guess some, as this is a church eleemosynary hospital. But it does not have an out-patient department. We may lose out in that respect."

"Do you get along all right with the Nebraska men? It seems we two are outsiders."

"They are good fellows. I don't think we'll have any difficulty. Let us look the hospital over," said Lang as he stood up and led the way out into the corridor which led to the large medical ward. As in all hospitals everybody, except the patients, was busily occupied and the inspection tour was short. Cursory introductions to floor superintendents was about all there was to this trip, for the guide himself did not know most of the personnel.

Just as he dropped off to sleep, the electric buzzer—2 short, 2 short —which had been assigned to him rang. He was awakened and it took about five seconds to orient himself and recognize the call as his and walk to the telephone.

"Are you the new intern on medical service?"

"Yes, ma'm."

"This is the medical floor. There is a patient of Dr. Young the neuropsychiatrist. The patient wants something for his sleep. What may I give him?" For a moment Minoru was floored. He had never prescribed anything before. At school it was only diagnosis that he was drilled in. Of drugs, he only knew the hundred with their Latin names and dosages committed to memory in his sophomore year. He knew nothing of the recent products with their trade names.

If he had sense enough he could have asked the nurse what Dr. Young usually prescribed on such an occasion, but he was now a full-fledged doctor and did not wish to look like an ignoramus. But what could he give? An answer was expected. His sleepy brain did not function too well. "Give an eighth of a grain of morphine sulphate." At least that was the correct dose of morphine and it could put the patient to sleep.

"Thank you," was the answer. Minoru felt a satisfaction of a task accomplished and went back to sleep.

Next morning when he appeared on the medical floor, he was embarrassed to see a note in the handwriting of Dr. Young. "No opiate derivatives may be given to my patients!" What an experience for the first night at a hospital and what a sock he had on the jaw! It made him feel very humble. He realized how little he knew. He also was made aware how nurses functioned in a hospital. No matter how silly doctors' orders were, they were carried out. Like in the army, discipline was maintained very strictly. Their position was not an enviable one.

Minoru became his natural student self from the second day; the apellation of "Dr." was not going to deter him from learning. There was to be no conceit. He was there to observe and learn and he realized that old time nurses could teach him a lot in their intricate art of diagnosing and healing. Such a sentiment and attitude were perceived easily by the nurses and they reciprocated in kind.

"I used to be able to smell a typhoid case," mused an elderly nurse, "and there was no need of a Widal test." She was a veteran in rural service and had spent some interesting years in the Indian Service. Besides, she was adept in Swedish massage and taught the student nurses how to allay tired muscles and lumbago aches.

Minoru plunged into work with wholehearted enthusiasm. He worked late into the night. Breakfast at 7:30 and soon morning rounds began as each attending man came onto the floors. He followed the doctors with the floor supervisor to receive further orders or to discuss the case if the attending man was in a mood to talk. He made it a rule to work up all cases on the day of admission and have the history, physical examination, and his own impressions written before the next morning. The thoroughness of the student clerkship days was still with him and it did not take long before the chief had a smile for him when he arrived every morning.

Mrs. Strong had been hospitalized with a daily temperature for a week when Minoru arrived. The cause of this fever had not been diagnosed as yet. The routine examination and laboratory work had been reported negative. On about the fifth day of his arrival he had a little spare time in the afternoon and he decided to put into practice what one young instructor at school impressed him with: "Whenever you examine urine, make a smear and stain it. By all means, stain and examine it. You will be rewarded with some gratifying discovery." Thus a drop of catheterized urine was placed on a slide, dried and chemically stained and was examined under an oil immersion lens. He was amazed to see bacteria. He wrote about this finding in the progress sheet and next day pointed it out to Dr. E.L. Bridges, the chief of service. The chief nodded and smiled, "Let us put her on urinary antiseptic. Caprokol will do."

Within four days, the fever curve descended and to all intents and purposes, Mrs. Strong was well. But she was not any better. She would not eat, and she was afraid that she might jump out of the window some night when nobody was around. Minoru was at a loss to understand this new development. Dr. Bridges, out in the corridor and away from the patient's hearing explained, "Many patients will react this way after a long seizure of fever or debilitating disease. When typhoid fever was widespread this psychosis was a rather common occurrence." Out of a rich store of practical experience, Dr. E.L. was going to impart to this young man many things not found in books or journals and reveal to him the real "Art of Medicine."

A month elapsed. Minoru worked hard but he did not know how he had fared in the eyes of the men he served. "Dr. Bridges, I have been here a month. How have I done in my work? If there is any way I may improve and produce better work please be frank and point them out. I am here to learn and am willing to eliminate any shortcoming." He was serious when he confronted his chief in the library at the end of the morning round.

Dr. E.L. smiled and patted him on the shoulder, "You are doing all right. Just continue the good work."

It was a pleasure to follow this chief in the morning rounds. There was much to learn and emulate in the way he conducted himself at the bedside. There was none of the aloof professorial attitude of the chief of staff surrounded by a retinue of residents and interns at the medical school. There was warmth and understanding here in the sickroom. Dr.

E.L. entered the room, greeted the patient with a cheerful, "Good morning." He sat down in the chair and read the nurse's report of the preceding twenty-four hours and corrected spelling and punctuation. Incidentally, nurses were careful in writing up the progress of his cases and they felt their effort well spent for they knew their work was going to be scrutinized. Then he would ask the patient questions, listen to new complaints, and check to ascertain the validity of these symptoms. Minoru was impressed and at times entertained by the adroitness with which Dr. E.L. parried an embarrassing question with a joke or an anecdote.

After two months, as they were about to finish the rounds, Minoru asked, "Dr. Bridges, I have noticed in these rounds that you always told the truth. Many times you do not answer the question but I have yet to catch you speaking a falsehood just to make a patient feel better. I heard that white lies are of therapeutic value sometimes."

Dr E.L. stopped and smilingly said, "Well, it is my policy not to tell a lie, even a white one, because once I begin it I won't be able to remember the lies. Some day I'll be caught in my lies. It is such an effort to remember everything."

Having taught at the university for many years and now being the chief of staff in medicine at the University Hospital he was used to young men and knew how to encourage their zeal and perseverance.

A traveling salesman came to his office with a general let down feeling and he was hospitalized at the Methodist for a general check up. Minoru interviewed him and made a careful physical examination that did not give much hint as to diagnosis. But as was his custom he jotted down his "impressions" as to what he guessed might be the underlying cause. Because the patient's pulse rate was rapid, felt weak, and he stuck his feet out of blankets, Minoru made a wild guess of "hyperthyroidism." The patient was rather fleshy and there were no other signs to substantiate this diagnosis.

Dr. E.L. shook his head when he read the "impressions" and ordered the routine laboratory examinations which were subsequently reported normal. Several days elapsed, the patient continued to feel weak, and pulse rate did not slow down in spite of his being in bed.

"Dr. Bridges, just to humor me, why don't we run a BMR test?" By this time Minoru felt audacious enough to venture such a suggestion.

"All right, let's order one for tomorrow," came the reply, and on the following morning a basal metabolic test was performed. It came back plus 30. Since such tests, being only adjuncts or help to make a diagnosis, are not conclusive in themselves, Dr. E.L. shook his head.

Minoru was now like a bulldog after a scent. "Why can't we order another one to check this report?"

Tolerantly, Dr. Bridges answered. "Go ahead." Back came the second report: plus 32. Still the chief was unimpressed, and rightly so, because there were no other symptoms to corroborate the meager signs of palpitation and a laboratory report.

"How about placing this patient on lugol's solution?" brazenly suggested Minoru, and to the lasting credit of Dr. E.L., he was not deaf to the urgent plea of a young intern. Like all teachers, he was ready to experiment, to learn himself, and above all to encourage and nurse along the exuberance of an intellectual curiosity.

"All right, let's put him on twenty drops of lugol's solution in half a glass of water three times a day."

After a week this patient left the hospital and Minoru lost track of him. Six months later when he was in surgery, Dr. E.L. happened to drop in at the scrub room and sat down for a chat with the surgeon. When he finished he turned aside and in a relaxed manner said, "Murayama, you remember the case I had in 218 some months ago when you were in my service? The traveling salesman you thought had hyperthyroidism is the one I mean. You may be interested to know that after he left the hospital I kept him on lugol's and after a month he came to see me. He climbed the hill and two stories to my office and I found his pulse rate to be 80. Last month Dr. Roeder did a thyroidectomy on him at the Swedish Hospital. You were correct in your diagnosis."

To give credit to others was an admirable trait in anyone; to acknowledge defeat to an inferior and an inexperienced novice was sublime and showed how great this man was. It was no wonder that Minoru had Dr. E.L's portrait on the wall of this consultation room in later years to guide and console him at moments of frustration, for he realized more and more what influence this taciturn man had on his professional career.

"Murayama, let us go and examine a woman just admitted in the surgical ward. I cannot make up my mind. She is in for a laparotomy tomorrow morning, but I have my own suspicion as to the diagnosis." Dr. Lang led the way to the third floor.

"Whose case is it?" asked Minoru.

"He is one of our big shots, Dr. Black, and I think E.L. is on the case too," answered Lang as he asked Miss Nielsen the supervisor of the floor to come along to assist them in the examination.

"Harry, do you know what I think?" After the examination and as he was drying his washed hands, Minoru spoke to his fellow intern. "I think this is pregnancy. Sometimes there is pelvic pain in pregnancy. This condition I remember having read about in Crossen's *Textbook in Gynecology*."

"That makes me feel better, because I wasn't quite sold on the idea of an ovarian cyst on a twisted pedicle. Anyway what we think will not change the diagnosis one way or the other. She will go to surgery tomorrow morning. I'll let you know then," Dr. Lang went to his work of writing up the case preparatory to next day's operation.

Ten days later, Dr. Moody who was in charge of intern training casually said, "You fellows kind of showed the old-timers a thing or two, didn't you?"

"What do you mean?"

"Oh, the case in the ward. It turned out to be pregnancy."

Then Dr. Lang gave him the details of the case and why he was not talking until then. "That case happened to be a minister's wife. The ministers think they own the hospital and so this particular one got furious because his wife was subjected to a thorough examination by lowly interns. This aspect of the case was reported to Dr. Black. He was not too pleased and spoke to Miss Nielsen who told him all we found. The fact that it turned out we were right saved our necks. He did not want to admit his mis-diagnosis and so could not censure us. It made me feel rotten to hear this and so I did not tell you." Not only censure but probably some disciplinary measure could have been instituted against these two for having treated a minister's wife as an ordinary ward patient.

"There is a patient from western Nebraska. Will you please examine him?" one of the nurses stopped Minoru as he was returning to his quarters after lunch. Without wasting any time he went to the bed of "the new admission."

"I am an intern here and would like to have a talk with you and see what I can do for you."

"I want to see Dr. Bridges. I came all the way from Kearney."

"Dr. Bridges will be here in the morning and we have to get all the dope on you so that his diagnosis will be made easy when he arrives. If there is something special to be done I'll phone him and get his opinion and orders. That is the way studies are made here."

"But I came to see Dr. Bridges and no one will see me but him."

Minoru saw that it was impossible to do anything. Dr. Bridges was notified the following morning when he came. His remarks were, "Murayama, you will in time discover that the patients that demand instant and unreasonable service are usually the charity cases. Good paying patients are as a rule very considerate of the time and comfort of the doctors."

Dr. Lang later told him how ornery the patient was and refused to be treated by a "Chink." Maybe that was the reason that he was placed on surgical service.

By this time Minoru could laugh over such an incident. Since coming to Nebraska, he found that he belonged to this large unit that was the hospital. He was a necessary cog in the wheel. His services were important and appreciated by his colleagues and respected by the nursing staff. Moreover, the people of Nebraska, Iowa, and northern Kansas, were mostly of northern European stock and he found them to be different and more tolerant than people he had so far come across. The fact that he was different in racial extraction was a factor that he forgot altogether since everbody tried his best to make him feel at home.

He was to learn months later that when a new patient entered, the student nurse that was in the room to check his belongings and prepare him to get into his hospital gown, took this opportunity to add, "In a short while a young doctor will be here to question and examine you. He is from Hawaii and we consider him very highly as a doctor." Therefore, when this doctor from the Hawaiian Islands entered the room there was a smile to greet him which made his daily work very congenial and productive.

Miss Rusk, the instructress in the nursing school, stopped him one day and asked whether he would not be good enough to teach medicine. "We know you are very busy but it would be a special favor to us if you can arrange to teach clinical medicine to the second year class. I have noticed you explaining cases to the nurses on the floor and I am sure the girls will be more than happy to have a systematic course under you. As a teacher I can assure you that you will learn a lot by teaching. The second year class is composed of bright girls but very active and prone to neglect their studies. Please teach them something."

After thinking it over a few days, he accepted the job because it was put as a challenge, but he discovered that to lecture an hour he had to prepare for about three hours. He prepared an outline of his talk and the nursing office mimeographed the syllabus for each lecture. He was thus able to talk freely on the salient points, leaving the details to the printed matter. With the aid of diagrammatic sketches on the blackboard he was able to present the basic pathology of the more interesting diseases. As Miss Rusk had prophesied, he learned tremendously while he prepared and lectured.

Noon meals at the hospital were very good. Especially on Wednesday, when they had delicious short ribs and sauerkraut. Even staff members remained to partake of this dish. But supper was very light. At times in the summer there was only corn on the cob with a side dish of some berries. Therefore, by ten o'clock the interns used to go up and eat with the nurses on the "grave yard shift." Several times when the fare was meager they raided the pantry by going through the transom, and Minoru was elected to do the climbing because of his size. But it could not be repeated too often.

Four interns to a two hundred bed hospital was not sufficient and there were no specified hours of duty. No monetary compensation was forthcoming. White uniforms of four coats, six shirts, and four pants were issued twice a year, and at Christmas time a golden key was issued to each. However, it was a grand year for Minoru; full of pleasant, fruitful experiences and the sense of belonging that was fully appreciated. He worked hard and was willing to help at all times.

As Dr. Bliss remarked at the approach of the end of the year, "You appear to have worked the hardest, and I am sure you have profited most from the service at this hospital. You are, I hear, returning to the islands soon, and some of us are glad that you are not starting out in Omaha to practice." Just like Dr. Bliss to couch his words diplomatically, but Minoru was human enough to blush and feel a glow of satisfaction.

In spite of the heavy work there was still time for non-medical reading. Now that there was no specter of examinations to haunt him, he decided to do some cultural reading. Once a week there was librarian who pushed a cart loaded with books from floor to floor to supply patients with reading material.

One day Minoru stopped her and said, "Miss Koontz, I wish to ask a favor. During my college days, I was not able to take courses in literature because I had to work my way and had to take more scientific courses. Now I have a little time and would like to catch up in my reading. Somewhere I read, 'whenever there are two new books published, read one classic.' I do not know how true this statement is but I do know that I should not waste my time on trash. Can you guide me in my reading?"

Miss Koontz's face lit up with pleasure, "I'll do it gladly. What you quote is true, but still there are many good contemporary books that that are worth reading. Have you read any European authors?"

"No ma'm, none whatsoever."

"Then I shall get you representative authors of the different countries. When I come next week, I shall have a book or two for you."

Thus for the rest of the year he read Thackeray, Wassermann, and Nobel prize winners from Poland and Norway.

Nebraska State Board Examinations were held in May and he decided to take them. There were two sets of examinations. In order to weed out the ill-prepared candidates of the unorthodox healing professions, the Basic Science Board Examinations were held preliminary to the regular medical examinations. The examinations of the basic science board were very stiff and very up-to-date. The questions were prepared by the professors of the respective branches at the medical schools, and so for a recent graduate they were not very difficult. Minoru did not have much trouble passing them.

Then came the State Board Examinations. The first examination was in physiology. An old practitioner presided and had questions passed around to the examinees but none began writing. After about ten minutes, one candidate raised his hand. "Can you explain what the first question means?"

"It is very easy. Just recall the picture on the third page of your physiology textbook."

"I cannot recall that there ever was such a picture."

"What text did you use at school?"

"Howell's *Textbook of Physiology*."

"Never heard of that one. I am referring to one that I used."

"How long ago was that?"

"In 1904."

A suppressed giggle ran through the hall and the tension was relieved. All went to question #2.

At King Fong's Chinese Restaurant, Minoru was having a rare Oriental feast with a few of the Hawaiian medical students of Nebraska University.

As the booth was open, a well dressed lady passing in the hallway popped in, "Dr. Murayama, congratulations." Minoru was nonplussed. He could not recognize her. Seeing this she added, "I am Mrs. Rosenblatt in room 218, Dr. Bliss's patient."

"Well, good evening Mrs. Rosenblatt. I couldn't recognize you in street clothes. But why the congratulations?"

"Oh, I read in tonight's paper about your having passed the state medical board examinations. Your name was on the list. Let me be your first patient when you begin practice."

"Oh, I have not read the paper yet. Thank you for the compliment and I'll certainly let you know when I hang my shingle out."

BOOK IV

Internment Camp

BOOK IV

Interdepartment Group

Prologue

THE MAJORITY OF HEART DISEASES DUE
*to occlusion of the coronary artery go on to healing without complication
after the initial stage is successfully negotiated. It is a matter of remaining
quiet, refraining from exertion, and thus complying with nature's demand
that an opportunity be given for the damaged muscle to heal and achieve
an establishment of new blood supply to this area. Sometimes, however, due
to the magnitude of damage suffered, even a slight exertion may cause a rupture of the softened heart wall.*

*Toward the end of two weeks when pain was already just a bad memory,
and everybody was breathing easier, the unexpected occurred and Seikichi
Arata ended his mortal existence after a sudden convulsive movement. He
did not suffer at all.*

*A wake service was held the night after his demise at a mortuary on
Nuuanu Street. The Buddhist altar was brightly lighted with a dozen
candles. The image of the Buddha serenely sat on a cushion of lotus flowers.
The spoke-like lines extending from his head, depicting radiation of light,
and the intricate artistic sculpture on the edifice that covered him and lotus
flowers in front of the image were of gilt gold. These objects shone in the
combined reflection of electric lights and candles. Two columns of incense rose
from the two tables placed in front of the altar. The columns wafted back
and forth from a slight disturbance of the atmosphere. Two priests, resplendent in their* kesa, *a richly decorated collar of religious order and rank worn
around their necks and shoulders, sat before the altar and were reciting a
sutra in Chinese. One rhythmically struck a wooden gong with his right hand
as the recitation of the chant progressed. After a little while, the other made*

295

a sign and the master of ceremonies went to the front seat where the relatives were seated. He bent down and whispered to Sadao who went up to one of the tables. He picked three successive pinches of the powdery incense and added it to the smoldering fire. His wife and children followed and the rest of the relatives did likewise and then bowed reverently to the lifeless remains in the casket. Incense symbolized the transiency and viscissitudes of life; every living object would eventually burn and go up in smoke just as the incense was doing.

After the relatives, the many friends went up in double file to pay their respects to the deceased. There were many friends of his youth on Kauai, but equal in number were friends that had spent the war years, 1941 to 1945, together with the deceased in the internment camps of Sand Island and the states. Most of these were in their sixties and seventies. Almost all were grey-haired and a goodly number were slow and uncertain in their gait. Each realized that his turn might not be very far off, and the group that constituted this unique casualty of World War II would dwindle with each passing year.

After their return from camp after the war, there were annual get-togethers when the teahouses were overflowing every weekend with carousing parties in the name of new year good fellowship. These parties sometimes were held as late as February. Old internees used to convene and recount old times; tears and laughter mixed with half forgotten anecdotes. Willingly, each spent the seven dollar fee for a few hours of relaxation, reminiscence, and renewed good fellowship. But now such get-togethers were seldom held. Only occasionally could these old-timers meet, and a funeral was a good excuse to convene. Most of them had lost heavily materially. To be deprived of freedom for four long years was not an experience relished by anyone, but after thirteen years since the end of hostilities, these men were enjoying their remaining years in peaceful Hawaii. The anguish and heart-breaking experiences were being pushed back in the foggy past and only the pleasant ones revived in such a reunion.

CHAPTER 20

Pearl Harbor and Confinement

SO USED TO EASY-GOING LIFE, THE PEOPLE of Hawaii continued in their routine, little disturbed by the darkening clouds of uncertainty and impending catastrophe that lurked in the Far East. In spite of seeing with their own eyes the gradual increase in armaments transforming the once languid Sandwich Islands to the "Gibraltar of the Pacific," they complacently viewed these military preparations as a mere acquiescence of the Congress to the clamor for preparedness and eventual conflict voiced by the jingoists and seconded by the army and navy. For such had been the periodic spurts for preparedness and pacificism, one following the other alternately since the turn of the century, that people were not easily influenced anymore by changing events that usually would be considered highly significant.

Prior to 1905, Japan was almost a protégé of the Anglo-Saxon nations. The Russo-Japanese War, with Japan as the victor, put a scare in some quarters and the "Yellow peril" bugaboo came into being. American-Japanese relations were strained because of California's anti-Japanese incidents centering in the school segregation question of San Francisco. The Takahira-Root Gentlemen's Agreement eased the situation. By this agreement no laboring Japanese could leave Hawaiian shores for the mainland. During World War I there was a spirit of amity across the Pacific, for the two nations were allies.

At the cessation of the war Japan had to be dealt with as a powerful naval power and the disarmament talks among the three nations—the United States, Great Britain, and Japan—were conducted with considerable bickering and ill-feeling. But for the time being anyway, Japan was compelled to maintain a ratio (5–5–3) to the naval ships of the two powers. An uneasy peace was maintained in the Far East. The spread to the Asiatic continent by the over populated inhabitants of the Japanese

Islands was in the domain of the army and its hot-headed, young, fanatical officers. The Southern Manchurian Railway became a toy of the army and the vast, sparsely populated plains of Manchuria became a sphere of influence and a place to indulge in dreams of empire-building. An autonomous state was created with the backing of the Kwantung Army of Japan. This new state and Japan's role in its creation finally led to the bolting of Japan from the League of Nations. The consolidation of the new country of Manchukuo steadily progressed in spite of Western non-recognition, and Japan became almost self-sufficient in coal, iron, and her food supply. She, however, sorely needed tin, rubber, and oil for her factories and navy.

Japan's belligerent course created a deep chasm in relations between the nations across the Pacific, for in spite of bickering they had been fundamentally friendly since the opening up of the hermit kingdom by Commodore Perry in the middle of the 19th century. The tension became worse with the years, and when Japan joined the German-Italian Axis the Rubicon seemed to have been crossed.

People in Hawaii, in particular, were intoxicated with a boom never before enjoyed in the islands' history. Millions of dollars were spent monthly in strengthening military installations. Hundreds of civilian defense workers were arriving from the mainland to further the project. Island workers were hired by the thousands. Common laborers were earning eighty cents and skilled workers were making one dollar-and-a half an hour. Spending by these workers was lavish and merchants were enjoying good business.

The Japanese population of Hawaii was no exception and little realized how near the war was. Even after the freezing order of all Japanese government assets in the United States was issued, very few, if any, realized that the final chapter was approaching. Entrenched was the belief that the Pacific Ocean would remain forever pacific. There would never be any war in spite of the rancor and bellicose fist-shaking of politicians on each side of the ocean. They felt that as long as the President of the United States persisted in his attempt to thwart the national aspiration and expansion of Japan on the Asiatic continent, the relations between the two nations would not improve. Severance of diplomatic relations was a good possibility after Japan's invasion of Indo-China, but the eventuality of the two nations becoming entangled in mortal combat was a situation not imagined or forseen.

By the end of September 1941, the authorities in Honolulu began issuing statements to the effect that in the event of war in the Pacific, the Japanese aliens legally residing in the territory would be protected and that there would be no concentration camps such as existed already in the European theater of war. This promise coming from General Short, the commanding officer of the army, helped allay the fear among the Japanese nationals. As far as the American citizens of Japanese extraction were concerned, they had implicit faith in the United States Government that they would be treated without discrimination as citizens of the United States in spite of their Japanese features.

Seikichi Arata, at 69, was spry and healthy. The night before, on Saturday, his oldest grandson, Edward, had returned from Schofield Barracks where he was taking basic training with the last draftees. He had just finished his basic training. Because Honolulu was lit up with lights anticipating a very prosperous, unprecedented Christmas sale on account of the affluence that suddenly had descended upon certain segments of the citizenry doing defense work, Edward had taken the family out in the car to see this nocturnal splendor.

Like all his friends, Arata felt that times were difficult. Every day was trying on his nerves whenever he glanced at a newspaper. There was not a day that did not carry news or commentary that was not deleterious to the amity of the two nations. But Hawaii was his home. Because of the law that barred Orientals from becoming naturalized, he had to remain an alien until his death. However, he had lived longer in Hawaii than in the land that gave him birth. He was at heart a Hawaiian and he was going to have his bones interred in this soil together with his posterity. To see Edward in a uniform of the United States Army made him happy and proud. His thoughts wandered back about 50 years to the scene in the old country when he was rejected by the army because of his stature. He no longer thought a uniform glamorous, but it was nevertheless heartwarming to see Edward assume the responsibilities and duties that must necessarily accompany citizenship.

On the night of the farewell dinner when Edward was inducted three weeks previously he had said, "Edward, you will proudly wear the uniform of a soldier from tomorrow. You owe everything to this country. Times are difficult for us with Japanese blood and you will have to work doubly hard and prove that in spite of your racial extraction you are a good American citizen. Your ancestors in the old country were *samurai*.

I know you will be a good soldier. Let us all be proud of you." And Edward, in spite of his mixed blood, for his mother was native Hawaiian, nodded and seemed to understand the meaning he wanted to convey.

This morning, December 7th, 1941, at 8 o'clock the radio stations were announcing the events that were taking place in the skies over Honolulu and at Pearl Harbor. "Oahu is under attack by an enemy air force. Keep off the streets for the military needs all traffic lanes. Do not go to the hills and mountains. You are all doing fine. Keep calm. We shall from time to time let you know about developments. Keep your radio tuned to this station." The announcer was calm. There was no trace of panic and to hear this matter of fact voice was very reassuring at a time when any smoldering anger could be fanned to hysterical intensity and mob action. Seikichi was dumbfounded. He sat down and closed his eyes. His head felt tight. The thinking faculty was at a standstill, and he could only mutter a prayer that this be a dream only!

Then the special announcement came over the radio, "All soldiers on leave over the weekend return at once to your outfit. This order applies to all men in uniform, soldiers, sailors, and marines. Return at once to your barracks." Edward Arata left at once for downtown where buses for the various military installations usually congregated—at the Army and Navy YMCA near the Palace Grounds. There was not even a farewell: he just picked up his overnight bag and rushed out.

Seikichi Arata stepped from the house. Lower Alewa Heights was a vantage point from which to see some of the action that was taking place. Toward the West the distant Waianae Range was clear in the bright morning light, and about eight columns of black smoke and doughnut-like white smoke rings that signified anti-aircraft fire were increasing in number. Incessant crackling and booming noises came from that direction. Little planes were zooming over Pearl Harbor and looked like dragon flies in the distance. Just then there was a terrific roar as two groups of fighter planes flew low down Nuuanu Valley from the Pali, evidently advancing on Honolulu from the windward side. They flew so low that the amber colored wings bearing the blood-red sun insignia showed on the under surface.

To Seikichi there was now no doubt at all that these attackers were from his own country. What a shock it was and what a shame he felt toward neighbors who were non-Japanese. Just then a terrific explosion took place at the intersection of Liliha and Kuakini Streets. He heard later that these were misfires of anti-aircraft shells. What little bombs these attacking planes carried could not be wasted on ordinary targets: they were destined for military installations and battleships lying at anchor in Pearl Harbor.

Several children were injured, some were killed from these explosions, and Seikichi felt that if these shells had injured him, an old man, he might have felt better. He might have felt in his suffering a sense of expiation, of atonement for the destruction and killing that were taking place among the soldiers and civilians of his adopted country by the planes of his Japan, for in spite of the half-century he had lived in America, he could not have severed the ties with the land of his birth because the America he loved would not legally accept him as a citizen. He was old and had lived his natural life. No matter what befell him, he had no regrets. History was replete with incidents of massacre of minority races under emergency. His children would live and survive as Americans, but under the circumstances in this emergency how would they fare? Pogroms had no precedent in America but lynching was not unthinkable when people became hysterical and the mob got out of hand. Could one develop into another? So far everything was quiet. The rushing of the army trucks to points of vantage, the activity of the police cooperating with the military police was exemplary, and the directives over the radio had a reassuring and soothing influence on the mental state of the population.

In spite of this poised state, wild rumors started. "Some enemy soldiers parachuted in the mountains. They are clad in green suits. They are poisoning the water supply. Boil your water before drinking," was the advice circulated among the neighborhoods by block wardens. Seikichi half believed this and ordered his women folk to follow the instructions. Sadao was quiet the entire morning. He was in a state of partial shock from the events that developed so swiftly after he was told by neighbors that the graduation service for Red Cross trainees was not going to take place.

"That is ridiculous. If the drinking water was poisoned, the poison will not be removed by boiling. But is there food enough for several days?" irritably asked Sadao of his wife.

"Yes, we have plenty. Weekend shopping was done yesterday."

"Then it is all right, but I'll go out walking for a while. This waiting and doing nothing is getting me jittery." He sauntered out of the house and walked the sidewalks of the almost deserted city. The streets were clear of civilian traffic and at intersections policemen and military police enforced order. Military vehicles, both trucks and touring cars, were racing back and forth. An ominous quiet pervaded the Sunday morning atmosphere. A few loitering men were inspecting something on the telephone post on Kukui Street and a half dozen were milling around.

"See that noodle restaurant over there?" pointed a man in a gray sweater to a half-burnt small store with its roof caved in. "There were seven boys eating breakfast. A shell landed on the restaurant. Three killed and four badly hurt. Amatuer boxer, Chinen, was one of the killed. Now, see the piece of flesh on the telephone post. This post is about 50 feet away from the restaurant, but with the explosion the bodies were shattered to shreds and the piece of flesh flew over here. I live over there in the lane and when the bomb fell, it was like an earthquake."

Toward one o'clock Sadao was home. Everybody was waiting for him. Silently they sat at the table for a light lunch of sandwiches and iced tea.

"What else was there different?"

"Nothing except that people remained at home and the streets were deserted."

"Yes, the sensible thing to do is not crowd the streets. The army will see to it that we are protected. But we must be prepared to be strong and cool-headed. Except for your mother and me, all of you are American citizens. You have been told at school all these years where your allegiance should be, and I have not told you anything different at home. Your son, Edward, is serving his country in uniform. Your turn to be useful to the country will come in some way. Be good citizens. It may be hard because you have Japanese faces and names. I do not know and nobody knows how hard our lot in Hawaii will be. We only have to conduct ourselves bravely. During the last war the Germans at Lihue were not molested and they lived without any trouble," solemnly lectured Seikichi.

"Oh, but they are Caucasians! They could merge with the rest, but we are of a different race," interjected Sadao.

"That may be so. It will take a longer time and the road may be more rocky for us. Because of that I am praying that you retain your calm and courage."

"I wonder if the rumor we used to hear several years ago is true.

You remember I told you when the writer, Upton Close, returned from China and on his way to the mainland he made a speech at the University Club? You remember I attended that lecture and reported to you that if ever war should start, all Japanese would be concentrated on Molokai? It seemed fantastic at that time, but I wonder!"

"Hardly possible. In the first place, if they had such a plan, they could not let us live there like animals without any housing, and no news of any such construction work has been reported on that island. You must remember too, that only two months ago the general assured us that there was going to be no concentration camp as long as we obeyed the laws and lived peacefully."

"In that case we can relax. Since there is nothing to do, I am going to water the lawn. Father, you can take a nap."

Mrs. Haru Arata was in the kitchen early. From that night on there was to be no light after sundown. A complete blackout and curfew order was out for the civilians. But no home was prepared for such an emergency measure and the only alternative was to go to bed early. It was nearing a time of the year when nights could be long even in Hawaii. The sun set at 6 P.M.

Just sandwiches or rice and tea with pickled vegetable for those that wished a light, simple dish. Nobody had much of an appetite. The day was bright and sunny but toward evening it cooled rapidly. There was no moon. In no time the entire city was dark. The streets were deserted except for official cars that silently coursed back and forth with shrouded headlights. Sporadic firing could be heard from many quarters of the city. Jittery civilian guards must be firing at any moving object. It was risky to be stirring outside.

At 7 o'clock, Seikichi Arata was in pajamas. It was early to go to bed but it was a nerve-racking day and he was very tired. Just to stretch and relax would do him good. Just then there was a knock at the front door. Sadao went to the door.

"Is Seikichi Arata at home?"

"Yes, he is."

"Please call him here." There were two men and they produced badges. They indicated that they were from the police department.

"I'll go call him," and Sadao went to the bedroom to fetch his father.

"We are from the police department and want to take you to head-quarters for questioning," explained the Caucasian member.

"For what?" asked Sadao.

"Oh, just a few questions. He will be detained only a few hours," soothingly explained the police officer.

"Then I have to change clothes," said Seikichi and turned to go to the bedroom.

"I'll go with you," said the officer as he entered the room and remained there while Seikichi dressed.

Haru Arata, instinctively felt something was wrong and followed the two. She took out his heaviest serge suit, added a few handkerchiefs, a comb and his pair of glasses. "You may or may not need any money, but just in case, I am putting two ten dollar bills in your pocket. These officers say it will only be for a few hours. We hope you will be back in the morning. Take care and be careful. Now officer, please drive slowly."

"OK mama-san. He will be all right."

Seikichi stopped to the doorway. "Sadao, I'll leave everything to you. Take good care of all." Somehow he felt it was going to be longer than a few hours. The two men helped him from each side to descend the front steps. Just to be escorted in such a manner gave him the feeling that his liberty was being curtailed: that he was being spirited away. In some inexplicable way he felt in his bones that this was like being kidnapped.

When they reached the street, there was a touring car with a man at the wheel. "All right, let's go, Joe," commanded the "haole" man.

"Papa-san, hands please," and when Seikichi raised his hand to a horizontal level he felt the cold steel of handcuffs applied to his wrist.

Shocked to his bones, Seikichi felt a cold anger rising in his chest. "Why this degradation! Can't these two giants see that a puny five footer at 70 years of age would not even consider escape? Why, in decency's name handcuffs?" He was seated between the two men on the back seat. He reclined and closed his eyes. When he opened his eyes because the car came to a stop, he found that all traffic was being scrutinized at a roadblock at the junction of Liliha and King Streets. Several men in plain clothes and military police with fixed bayonets were peeping into and inspecting cars that approached. The driver of each car stepped out to show identification badges to the sergeant in charge. Everything was done in subdued flashlight.

The touring car proceeded toward the waterfront and finally turned to the right and stopped in front of a building. It was not the Police Station. It was the Immigration Station. Seikichi was led into a room where six army enlisted men were processing arrivals. The handcuffs were removed and he was led to a desk by the detective who laid a blue card on the desk. It bore the name Arata, Seikichi, alien. This name was checked on the list of names that filled several pages.

When he entered there was a bald, timid, and whimpering man in pajamas and wrapped up in a blanket. Evidently he was not given much time before he was snatched away from his sick bed. "I am sick, I have a fever of 101. Very chilly. I must have my medicine. My blood pressure is high and I must have medicine." To this plea the sergeant said nothing. There was no consideration. His duty was to process these prisoners into this readymade prison. Sick or dying, nothing beyond handkerchiefs and glasses were allowed. Medicine was not a permissible item.

"Now go over there and face the wall. Put both hands above your head and keep your hands on the wall." Seikichi did as he was ordered, while one of the sergeants searched his pockets and took out the wallet and fountain pen. These were confiscated and placed in a large Manila envelope marked with his name.

"All right, old man. Go up the stairway. It is dark. Hold on to the side railing. It is perfectly safe," said the not unkind sergeant. Then he yelled facing the second story. "Another prisoner!" Seikichi was ordered from home with the assurance that it was going to be an interrogation lasting a few hours; the truth of the matter was that he was now a "prisoner."

Up the stairway, he was careful to cling to the metal railing. At the top a soldier took him by the arm and talked to a guard that stood outside a door. The guard opened the door and pushed him into a room that was stuffy and reeking with the odor of human bodies. There was a continuous mumbling sound and there were some bodies on the floor. When his eyes became accustomed to the darkness he was able to discern the outline of three tiers of iron beds. It occurred to him that since he was not the first, he would not be the last. He had better look for a place to sleep if he were to rest at all. Most of the beds were occupied but on the farther end, he found empty spaces on the uppermost tier. He clambered aloft warily to avoid stepping on the persons on the lower two levels. Without taking off his coat, he stretched out on the mattress.

305

It was a strange feeling. He closed his eyes. It did not matter much because even with his eyes wide open there was nothing visible in this pitch dark night. He reviewed the turn in events of the last thirty minutes.

It was a short half hour, but during that interval a revolutionary change in human status had come over him. Never had he dreamed before that he would ever run afoul of the established laws of the country. He considered prisoners a different breed of men. He was an honest and upright citizen of the community. But then, here he was with that appellation preceding his name. In the seventy years of his life this episode could be the culmination and an inglorious end: to be considered a shame by his children and grandchildren. The low voices of the people in the room were strained, but devoid of any anger or hysteria. The conversation centered on the events of the day rather than the arrest which brought them together.

Almost every quarter hour the door opened to let in new arrivals. "Mr. Kagami, how is Waialua way?" came a voice from near the door. Evidently the newcomer was recognized.

"Four of us were brought in from Waialua by the FBI. Whereas ordinarily it is a one hour travel, today we were five hours on the way. There was another attack by Japanese planes after dark. Police stopped the car and crawled under it. We four sat on the side of the ditch, but nothing happened," related the new arrival and Seikichi listened to the talk as he had nothing else to do. His mind ceased to function and he was in complete passivity. Somebody opened the windows. It was discovered the following morning that in a room built for eighty persons, one hundred and eighty had been crowded in. The stifling oppressiveness resulting from the stagnation of air was somewhat ameliorated by the open windows, but in the wee hours of the morning it became chilly.

At about two o'clock, a commotion took place as twelve barefooted fishermen wearing raincoats were thrown into the room. These men were out fishing that morning, had been machine-gunned by planes, and were glad to be alive.

With every arrival there was conversation and the continuous hushed talk prevented any sustained sleep. When day dawned at six o'clock, the outline of faces became more distinct. Remarks such as these were heard all over the room.

"You, too! What a night! When did you arrive? I was escorted by an MP in the late afternoon. The Caucasian MP's were very gentlemanly and there was no rough talk."

"I came after dark. Oriental detectives came after me. I was watering the lawn wearing tennis shoes. Because I was told that this questioning was to take only several hours I did not even change clothes. I have thin summer pants and tennis shoes. It certainly was cold this morning. I wonder how long the several hours is going to stretch out?"

"Soldiers came after me. They had fixed bayonets and appeared fearsome but they were gentle. We were having supper when they arrived but they allowed me to finish my meal. I was allowed to change into a suit and hearing what you went through, perhaps I was the best treated," smiled a groceryman from Pawaa.

With the break of dawn, people began stirring and most headed for the lavatory. It adjoined the large dormitory and was open at all times, but contained only two flush bowls and two wash basins. To economize on water a gadget usually found on steamers was attached to the faucets. One had to grab the two flaring out-turned thumbs to turn on the water. Thus to wash one's face, the left hand had to grasp these blades to let water out while washing with the right hand. While the new immigrants from ships were accustomed to such devices, why the architect installed such a miserly gadget in water-plentiful Honolulu was beyond anybody's comprehension. With one hundred eighty men to use this limited facility, the room was packed continuously.

At about 9 A.M., the door opened and an MP stuck his head in and announced, "You will be taken out of the room to have your breakfast. Form in a single line and make it snappy!" The inmates lined up and marched into the hallway and descended a long straight stairway that led into the inner court of the Immigration Station. There were three MP's with bayoneted rifles stationed along this hall and stairway to direct and keep the file of men against the wall. They used the sharp instrument at a menacingly short distance from the men urging them forward.

To Seikichi Arata, this was the most degrading and humiliating experience he had ever gone through, but this was only the first experience of such a nature he was destined to undergo. He heard one of the soldiers growl, "What the hell! Let's get a machine gun and mow these bastards down. Lot of time wasted and good food thrown away." Seikichi could not help feeling sorry about the whole situation. Perhaps this soldier

307

lost a brother or friend in the blitz. Naturally he had seen the sunken ships in Pearl Harbor. It was natural for one to become angered at the wanton destruction. Perhaps his own grandson, Edward, was feeling the same indignation as this lately arrived soldier to the islands.

The line passed a table out in the open courtyard and each was to pick an army aluminum mess kit and be given two slices of bread with strawberry jam. Each was to help himself to coffee which was in a large, thirty gallon container. The coffee was so hot it nearly burned Seikichi's lips and tongue. Most just drank coffee. Ironically, Japanese carpenters were busily constructing barbed wire extensions above the ten foot wall surrounding the inner court. The twenty minutes allowed out in the open air was a treat after the stuffy, cramped room. Men walked back and forth stretching their stiffened joints, and shaking hands with friends who were also caught in yesterday's raid. A shrill whistle blew and they were lined in single file and returned to the same room.

At about noon, Shoichi Asami's name was called and he was led downstairs. Because his name began with an A, there was a faint hope in everyone's mind that "hearings" had begun in alphabetical order and soon all would be returned home. All knew almost everyone else and there was none in the crowd that would have acted inimically to the security of the United States.

Mr. Asami returned after a short while. "There was no hearing. I was questioned about certain matters concerning the Nippu Jiji Publishing Co. But while I waited there, I overheard talk that there was a Japanese naval officer taken captive in yesterday's attack. I wonder how it happened but the talk was pretty excited about this captive." This was the group's first news concerning the operator of the midget submarine with whom they were to travel and share hardship for many months.

At about three o'clock, the door was again opened and the single file procession proceeded down to the inner court where two slices of bread, corned beef, and a cup of coffee were served. As the room could no longer admit newcomers, the men were able to arrange themselves so that as many as possible could sleep on the bunks. On Seikichi Arata's three-tier bunk, three slept in place of the regular two. Two on the edges slept with their heads in one direction and the middle person had his head at the opposite end. This arrangement was all right as far as stretching their bodies was concerned, but being kicked in the face during the night was not very pleasant. On some lower bunks four slept across two beds.

That night, December 8, there was a turmoil in the next room until dawn, just as there was with their incarceration the previous night. Germans and Italians were being hauled in and the door kept banging as a new arrival was shoved in. The following morning, Seikichi counted about sixty men and twenty women when the new arrivals were marched out for their meals. There were only a dozen Japanese women incarcerated. During the night, there were about fifty more Japanese apprehended and these were quartered in a room in the opposite wing. When these arrivals came out for their meals, the old-timers, with mixed emotions, looked down upon them from their window.

"He's come too. Well, well, we'll have company and fun too," joyfully exclaimed one observer.

"There's Yamada. He was very active in community affairs. He led the drive for the Japanese Red Cross and help for the woundeds' families. I was wondering why he was not in the 'blue card' list." His remarks were not devoid of a certain triumphant glee in seeing a mishap overtake a competitor.

"Just the same I am sorry that he has joined us, because I heard his wife is bed-ridden from apoplexy. For that matter there are several here that should have remained at home. Mr. Komeya, now eighty-four, was in bed for the last two years. Dr. Mori is also about that age. He has diabetes and can hardly walk. That man from Ewa cannot walk from joint trouble. I don't know how the FBI picked us out of the mass, but if you qualify and I am considered suspect, then there are thousands more that should be here," said Seikichi Arata. He was thoughtful. The whole pattern of procedure was not clear. How extensive was this round-up going to be and on what evidence was it based? For as long as he could remember he was never questioned once by the authorities.

A journalist nearby added, "We are all in the 'blue card' class. Those not in this category have not been invited, that's all."

"But look at some of these young men. I don't know them well. They are Nisei I am sure. Doesn't American citizenship protect them?" Seikichi was thinking aloud.

The journalist took up the thought, "Whether you heard or not I don't know, but yesterday's radio announced that Governor Poindexter conferred with Washington, D. C. and turned the government over to the military. Hawaii is now under martial law and run by General Short."

"What does this change of government mean?"

"It means that the usual protection for civilians is now suspended. You have heard of the writ of habeas corpus that was evolved in England in the people's struggle against the aristocracy? You have not? Well, it is a guarantee that we 'small potatoes' are given: that our liberties will be protected and we cannot be imprisoned without cause for any length of time. I don't know to what extent the martial law will supplant civilian law. I don't think martial law ruled any American community for a long time because Americans are very proud and jealous of the writ of habeas corpus. From a legal standpoint, the people of Hawaii will be at the mercy of the military. A dark age in Hawaii has come. Yet a military governor is an American raised with an education no different from any other civilian, and his military lawyers are grounded in Anglo-Saxon law. I cannot see how these men will defy the usual concept of human rights. But I think the courts of law will function very swiftly under martial law."

"That means then that all of us are now subject to martial law?"

"That I am pretty sure. Even without martial law enemy aliens are subject to detention and segregation. This is a customary procedure among warring nations. A country at war must look after security from within. We as enemy aliens can be detained as long as America decides to keep us behind fences."

On Tuesday morning after breakfast, the sergeant came into the room and read the names of about half of the men. These were ordered out of the room; where to nobody knew, but it was better than being locked up. Seikichi Arata's name was not on the list. For the first time in two days the remaining ones, being relieved of congestion, felt that they could at least sleep in comfort. Brooms and mops were handed to them and a general clean-up was undertaken with vigor. People were glad to do something. The atmosphere seemed to get cleaner and fresher after the sudden exodus and the common urge was to stretch at full length and catch up on sleep. Just about the time when they woke from their nap in mid-afternoon, the sergeant reappeared and called off a list of names. Seikichi was among them.

These men were taken out to the lawn in front of the side entrance facing Pier 2 amidst a drizzling rain that soaked them to their skin. Few had coats and there was no shelter. The list was checked twice. They were then ordered to board covered trucks which took them to Pier 6, the Naval Wharf. During this trip they were guarded by soldiers with fixed bayonets, three to a truck. Two armored cars were sandwiched among the vehicles. On the wharf, the men were lined up and again checked as to number and then ordered to board a large scow. A steam tugboat towed it. Fifty men that comprised this group were ordered to crouch down on the floor of the flat boat, while half a dozen soldiers with shotguns stood menacingly fore and aft with the muzzles pointed at the men huddled together in the center.

Perhaps one of the young soldiers could not help but crack a joke, in spite of the situation being anything but jocular, when he said, "You are all being taken out into the Pacific Ocean and will get scuttled to feed the sharks." This was bad enough, but the Germans had machine guns trained on them when they were ferried across later. A coast guard cutter was moored nearby, and its crew lined the rail watching these poor captives led away.

The radio of the coast guard cutter was turned on and its loud speaker blared forth President Roosevelt's message to Congress announcing the declaration of war against the three Axis Nations. It recounted the treachery of the Japanese in attacking Pearl Harbor while peaceful negotiations were being conducted at Washington. Since these men were ignorant of the events taking place in the world, this was the first news of the spread of the war to a world-wide scope. Honolulu looked like a deserted city. At the waterfront, the usual traffic at that time of day was conspicuous by its absence. It looked like a Sunday afternoon.

The tugboat pulled the barge out into the harbor and took it straight across to Sand Island which is situated on the west side of the harbor entrance. When the first contingent left the room in the morning, somebody said that they were to be shipped to an "island," and many thought it would be Molokai. Since pineapple crates are hauled from Molokai and Lanai on these barges, the destination could have been that island. When it turned out to be Sand Island everyone let out a sigh of relief.

A detachment of soldiers awaited them at the crude landing and the captives were marched two abreast. A dozen soldiers armed with shotguns flanked both sides. It was just getting dark but everything was still visible. In front of Seikichi Arata walked Mr. Komeya, eighty-four years old, who had been routed out of his sick bed. He could hardly walk, let alone keep up with the rest. Seikichi called the guard's attention to his plight. The captain came over and told the old man to step out of the line, for a truck was going to take him to the destination.

Just then a cold shower drenched them to their skin. It was a short march and a welcome exercise for most of them, but the tragic spectacle of a beaten group of men guarded with lethal weapons forlornly marching to an unknown destination in the gathering dusk was objectively and poetically felt by Seikichi even as a participant. It is said that Japanese love tragedy—love to shed tears over drama and stories—and they seem to have the peculiar quality of "enjoying pain." For any motion picture or drama to be a financial success among the Japanese there must be included in its plot scenes and episodes that wring the tear glands. Seikichi was detachedly imagining the scene of "retreat from Moscow of Napoleon's men" that he had once seen in a picture book. Surely the only common factor was the dejected manner of the marchers, but somehow he felt poetically elated. The procession ended at the headquarters of the Sand Island garrison made up of low, Spanish-type architecture.

The prisoners were lined up in single file in the hallway, which was lit by a very dim green light, for the windows were all covered by black board.

"Take off all your clothes and shoes. Hold them in your hands." As they stood without a stitch on their shivering bodies, a captain appeared and addressed them through an interpreter.

"You are now prisoners of war. I have been ordered to see that you are kept here. Strict discipline will be maintained, but I do not intend to be inhuman. Whether I shall be able to pursue this course and succeed in my purpose will depend on your behavior. I have respected the Japanese people in the past. I have studied your people a little and I think I know you. But after Sunday I know that we have a worthy opponent in the Japanese army and navy." Captain Coughlin, spare and straight, was well over six feet and his bearing was very military.

The immediate reaction to this speech of introduction was favorable and the men accepted the ensuing humiliating search of their person and belongings without resentment. It was a manly talk, straight and succinct. They were ordered to stand before several non-commissioned officers, to place their belongings on the desk. Money and valuables were placed in an envelope and after a search, clothes and shoes were returned. When ten or twelve put their clothes on, they were led outside. It was pitch dark. No light could be used and so they held on to each other's hand and followed a soldier. After walking about a quarter mile, they met their friends who had preceded them in the morning. These people had put up tents all day. The new arrivals were handed two blankets and assigned tents for the night.

When Seikichi Arata went to his tent there was no cot. Because of the rain the ground was wet and, since Sand Island is only slightly above sea level, brackish water seeped through the ground. The sergeant found cots for them and led them to the dining room for some sandwiches. The attack of mosquitoes was persistent and annoying, but before Seikichi knew it he was fast asleep. He was exhausted mentally. It was an eventful day.

CHAPTER 21

Sand Island

THE NEXT MORNING THE PRISONERS DIS-
covered that they were in an enclosure of about five acres, surrounded
by a fifteen foot fence of tough meshed wire, topped by several rows of
barbed wire on a framework of lead pipes that tipped inward. There
was a long cement sidewalk that connected the headquarters to an open
air pavilion which was also surrounded by tough meshed wire. This
pavilion served as a dining hall. A kitchen with oil stoves was under this
roof in an adjoining room. There were two latrines, one at each end of
the enclosure. Probably they were intended for the two sexes, but were
now used for the different races. These latrines were very well built
and contained showers with both hot and cold water.

It was evident that the military authority had planned an internment
of the leaders or suspicious characters in case war should come, in spite
of all the proclamations issued by the government and military spokes-
men that there would be no concentration camps because the FBI had
investigated and found the Japanese community 100% loyal. They had
prepared this site months or years ahead, for the cracks in the cement
walk betrayed the apparent age of the construction. Naturally this precaution was a necessary and efficient measure from the standpoint of
national security and the prisoners saw nothing incongruous in spite of
the proclamation to the contrary.

The first contingent that came to the island in the morning had worked
hard, not only in pitching their own tents but in erecting them for the
next group when such an order arrived in the waning hours of the day.

A new day for all and the first day in concentration camp began for
the inmates. All men were set to work at once. Volunteers for the kitchen
crew and carpentry were first taken. The rest were divided into work
gangs to clean up the enclosure and to erect more tents. Tents were put

up in geometric alignment because there were a few contractors used to sighting and measuring. It was done over and over again until it was well nigh perfect in alignment. Eventually tents capable of accommodating three-hundred-twenty persons were set up. The unskilled majority of men were set to work cleaning up the grounds. In such circumstances, leaders emerge spontaneously. They lined the men in single file at one end and had them walk across the compound, picking all the rubbish and leaves in their path. In two hours the entire area was spotless and men either sat down or congregated to talk. The guards came at once.

"Keep on moving and working."

"But the area is clean. There is nothing to work on."

"Keep on working just the same. The order from the commandant is to keep you busy. Better go back and pick up leaves," mischievously smiled the young soldier who saw himself that the area was clean.

The men again traversed the area leisurely talking, picking up a pebble and throwing it a few feet forward; picking it up and examining its contour and casting it another five feet ahead until the other end was reached. Thus it continued for the entire forenoon and afternoon. The objective of the commanding general's office was to keep these men occupied, out of mischief, and from brooding over their lot.

The original guards were soldiers and they comprised a very decent lot. The top sergeant had been an instructor of ROTC at McKinley High School and some of the inmates knew him. He appeared hardboiled and harsh, but actually he was a kind man. Soldiers at the gate and patrolling the outside of the enclosure fence carried shotguns, but those within the area had only clubs hanging from their belt. The sergeants within the enclosure were especially gentlemanly and Seikichi Arata was impelled to speak his mind one day.

"You soldiers are very good to us. I want to thank you."

"Well, you know we Americans treat anyone fairly when we are treated decently." He was a typically western type, open and frank and there was dignity in his bearing. He assumed no overbearing attitude of a captor to the less fortunate.

"I hope you stay with us all the time," countered Seikichi.

"Oh, but we have orders to move to an island next week. Where, we do not know. Just an island," he smiled wistfully. He was apparently from California and before long he and Captain Coughlin were no longer seen at Sand Island.

The entire group of about three hundred were divided into four companies. A captain elected by the group headed each company. He was usually one that could speak English. The camp spokesman was "Admiral" George Kotani. He had been in the U. S. Navy as a steward or cook, or some said in the U. S. Merchant Marine. He spoke English brokenly but rather fluently. In civilian life his glib tongue had rewarded him well and he was a successful insurance salesman. He came over with the first contingent and as everyone was more or less backward, he stepped forward and assumed the job of liaison man. In due respect to the army, he refrained from calling himself "general," and facetiously styled himself "admiral." Henceforth "admiral" became synonymous with "spokesman" or "coordinator" in this camp.

The "admiral" was invaluable in the chaotic stage at the beginning. As in all sorts of disorganized societies the type of leader suitable for an orderly peacetime community is singularly helpless and a new, bolder, buccaneering sort gets hold of the rein. As the days passed, however, and as some semblance of order emerged out of the chaos, the people became fed-up with the "admiral" because of his uncouth manner and partiality to his particular clique.

The Honolulu internees constituted the upper stratum of the Japanese community of Hawaii. Due to the preponderance of priests and language school teachers, a great number were university graduates and it was distasteful to many to be led by a man so wanting in culture and manners. It is in the Japanese character to be sensitive about his racial dignity and reputation. George Kotani was not fit to be a spokesman, although practically all acknowledged his contribution to the general welfare so far. Kotani had many good friends and some of these advised him to relinquish his job at this stage when there was some gratitude, but it was hard for him to step down.

Power is an intoxicatingly dangerous plaything. He became too friendly with the soldiers and one day he used obscene language to a non-commissioned officer which was not too offensive in colloquial English among equals or friends. This conversation was overheard by the new commandant who was a stickler for formality and dignity of rank. Thus George Kotani was thrown into a solitary cell at Fort Shafter for one week and was returned to the camp completely cowed and meek. He could no longer hold any position.

After Captain Coughlin and his men left for some "island," the

Honolulu Home Guard members were detailed to guard the camp. They were composed of mere boys: seniors in high school and freshmen in the local university. They might have had military drill, but the contrast with the seasoned soldiers that had left was so great that the internees felt very unsafe. For into the hands of these boys were placed shotguns which would fire too easily. During the night while the boys were patrolling on the outside of the fence and got sleepy—for their duty was long, arduous, and monotonous—their guns would drop from their arms and go off with subsequent commotion by the corporal of the guard. There were about three or four such mishaps every night. Luckily, no shot fell within the compound.

One sergeant in particular was nasty. He was about 19 years old, probably a senior in high school and a recent arrival from California, and to make matters worse he had lost two brothers at Pearl Harbor. His attitude was revengeful and there was nothing decent about him. The internees were told to watch their steps because these boys had "itchy trigger fingers," and would not hestitate to turn their guns within the fence. The new commandant apparently took no step to ameliorate the situation.

About a dozen teenagers arrived in camp. They were picked up at their homes and brought directly to the island. Many fishermen were also thrown in. The first group were amateur radio hams and had belonged to a club. All the members with Japanese names were picked up and thrown into camp. Most of the fishermen had been investigated by the FBI and naval intelligence long before the outbreak of the war and were arrested because they neared the Kewalo Sampan Basin where their boats were moored. These men were gradually released as the hearing cleared them. But those with the "blue cards" did not come under this scrutiny.

At sundown the city of Honolulu went into blackout and this continued for months and years after the Pearl Harbor attack. The only place that was lit was the Sand Island Internment camp. The tents were without light but there were powerful lights on the posts surrounding the enclosure in order to forestall any escape. At sundown everyone had to retire into their tents and by eight o'clock conversation had to cease. Guards came around and tapped on the tents with their clubs when they heard voices. They always roamed around in twos.

The inmates were strictly confined to the tents but no one could regulate the call of nature. They were allowed to go and return from the latrine but when they heard footsteps of soldiers nearby, they would stop ten paces away and shout, "Prisoner." "Prisoner" was a hard word for an elderly Japanese tongue to twist and enunciate correctly. Ogata with a naturally loud voice had to do this one night. He stopped short when he heard footsteps. Try as he might, he could not recall this word and shouted "Gardener."

For two weeks they were held incommunicado. Although they lived just across Honolulu Harbor, their whereabouts was a total mystery and many families were afraid they had been shot. Wild rumors had been rampant in Honolulu. Dr. T. was rumored shot in the leg because he resisted arrest, Mr. S. shot to death, and Charles H. had been caught red-handed in the act of sending short-wave radio to the Japanese Navy and shot to death instantly from behind. About ten days later when Charles H. entered the compound, he was kidded by friends that a ghost had arrived. There was also a rumor that the firing squad was busy all day at Fort Shafter in disposing of suspicious characters apprehended on the streets. But it turned out that the U.S. Army, as in their orderly patrol of the city on the day of attack, was cool and collected.

During this two week period, they were without change of clothes and tooth brushes, and everybody had grown untidy mustaches and beards. A canvas cot with two blankets were all that kept them from dampness and cold. Sand Island, being just about two feet above sea level, was white with salt crystals when the tide receded following lunar gravitation. A little rain would flood the place six inches deep, but luckily the ground was semi-sandy and there was no unpleasant mud to contend with after the showers that were frequent at this season. A tent was poor protection against December weather which is cold even in Hawaii.

How to keep warm on the canvas cot was a problem, for cold penetrated through the porous canvas. If one blanket were used under the body, the other was insufficient to keep them warm. Ex-army men taught them how to make a sleeping bag out of these two blankets, but Seikichi was heavy set and restless at night and the bag would not maintain its shape. Luckily the serge suit that Haru made him wear kept the body heat. Skinnier men had better luck in this respect. After repeated requests were made by the internee doctors, mattresses were supplied the chronically sick men confined in the hospital tents. Mosquitoes were a vexing problem. All night long sleep was prevented by persistent attacks. The only relief was in fashioning and folding a handkerchief to cover the face leaving enough airway for respiration.

Since all were taken into custody with an assurance that they would be detained for a few hours of questioning, many came with thin, flimsy trousers and sweatshirts. Some came only in house-slippers or sandals. After their removal to Sand Island, they were forced to conclude that the detention might be for the duration of the war. Some artisans were sent to the carpenter shop and they returned with wooden clogs or *geta*. This footwear was very simply made and ideal for a life such as this. And in a short while the entire camp was supplied with this footwear. An old fisherman, called Tachibana, began taking apart jute fibers of gunny sacks and from these he wove sandals. The result was a masterpiece and even the commandant had a pair made for himself. Incidentally, he began supplying all the gunny sacks Tachibana needed.

As many people as could be detailed were put to work. Some worked in the laundry on soldiers' uniforms. Those with no special training were taken out of the enclosure to cut down the algaroba trees that were abundant on the island. These were chopped down and dragged into the shallow reef water that adjoined the enclosure on the seaward side. Even while they pulled on these trees, there was a guard with a shotgun trailing at their heels, and reminded one of a scene depicting the construction of an Egyptian pyramid in which slaves by the hundreds were driven to pull on the ropes. It was a pathetic spectacle, inasmuch as these men were not used to such manual labor. They might have thus labored in their youth on the plantations, but in forty years they had become leaders of their community. Now by a turn of fate they were doing work like slaves.

Seikichi Arata knew Dr. Takata and volunteered to take care of the sick in the hospital tent. He thus shared the tent reserved for the doctor. Dr. Takata could not bear to see the men over sixty toiling in the hot sun without hats, and some were not too healthy. He begged the commandant to relieve the unfit from manual labor for humanitarian reasons. After several talks he scored his point and he was given the responsibility and task to weed out the unfit from doing hard work.

There were many "surgical cases." Hundreds of slivers had to be dug out and the lone surgical instrument was a short, straight pin from Dr. Takata's coat lapel where he had occasionally displayed a gardenia.

It was missed by the inspecting MP's when his clothes were searched on arrival at Sand Island. It was a most useful instrument. Drugs and medication available in the first two weeks consisted of epsom salt, tincture of iodine, boric acid, and aspirin. There were a few cases of homesickness. A school teacher kept on gazing toward Aiea all day long. It was apparent that he was missing his wife and children too much. A nervous breakdown was feared. Other psychosomatic cases were in the making.

"Mr. Arata. You are good in quieting people with your smooth talk. Talk to him. Give him something," said Dr. Takata.

Seikichi went to the kitchen and got some table salt in a small bottle. "Mr. Noda, Dr. Takata was able to get this nerve tonic from headquarters especially for you. Let us take a quarter teaspoonful twice a day," and he offered it in a most solemn way.

"Thank you very much. Maybe this will make me sleep better. This heaviness of head and insomnia are getting me down. Why this tastes like salt! Well, all medicines are alike, hard to take." He walked away feeling better.

The really sick ones, such as Mr. Yamamoto, and Dr. Mori were immediately accommodated in a special double-roofed tent. Several high-strung individuals on the verge of mental collapse were put in another tent and a course of special treatment was begun. Arata was quite a raconteur himself and arranged several hours a day of stories and lectures for these men. He enlisted the aid of professional storytellers and men of wide travel. What was most effective was his sympathy for the mentally depressed.

There must have been a shortage of drugs at headquarters for one day the commander came in and took Dr. Takata out of the enclosure to a barn-like structure. "Doctor, here are some drugs which may be old, but if you can use them you may. There are surgical instruments which you may have," said the commandant as he opened a weather-beaten case.

One look at the instruments and the doctor declined politely. "These are too large and cannot be of any service to us in the camp. A real sick case has to be taken out to a hospital anyway." In the days of Oriental immigration into the territory by the thousands, all were kept here for a few days. The quarantined cases were kept in a separate enclosure. If they died, these "surgical instruments" had been used in the autopsy procedure and the remains cremated in the nearby incinerator which still stood adjacent to the barn-like structure.

Daily, the elderly group with no special work policed the ground. They lined up as on the first day and walked across the compound picking up anything out of the ordinary lying around. One day, one of the men approached Dr. Takata and asked him to announce to the camp at large to refrain from spitting on the ground, not from any sanitary reason but from the fact that certain elderly people who did not have glasses with them had actually picked up expectorated phlegm mistaking it for rubbish. Everybody laughed, but for those concerned it was a repulsive matter.

At this stage of incarceration the captives were treated as war prisoners. All the metal possessions on their person had been taken away on the night of arrest, and there was a strict order forbidding anyone to shape any object that might be construed as a weapon. No printed matter was allowed to enter the compound. All pencils and fountain pens were confiscated and there was only one pencil allowed the hospital tent to keep records of sick and injured men, and a daily report was to be made on a sheet of paper supplied each day. One watch was allowed Dr. Takata so that he might take pulse rates. This watch was surreptitiously used in rousing the men in the morning.

Technically, no one was allowed to do any writing. As a group, the level of education was very high because the percentage of college men was way above the usual figure for any community. The deprivation of printed matter and newspapers was the hardest blow to endure. Only occasionally a sheet of newspaper came in accidentally with the groceries. Dr. Takata was given the sheets while several stood guard outside and the doctor sat in the latrine to read. He later reported to the camp. History was being made every day all over the world and they were denied the privilege of hearing the news. They, therefore, looked forward with anticipation to new arrivals who were being sent over from the Immigration Station after perfunctory screening. These men brought in news that was gleaned from newspapers and shortwave radio broadcasts from Japan. News of Honolulu was hungrily listened to by the prisoners.

When the gate was opened and a newcomer entered, there was delegation to greet and conduct him to a tent. He was seated and was soon surrounded by faces that he had known on the outside, but were now almost unrecognizable with the growth of beard.

"Welcome to Sand Island. These are all your erstwhile friends," ventured one of the impromptu welcoming committee.

The newcomer looked from one to another with incredulity. Such an unkempt group of humanity! There was a fearful attitude on his part as if he were a hunted animal. His voice was subdued and low when he almost whispered, "Gee, you all have changed!"

"Don't be afraid. There is no FBI here. You have sunk to the lowest here in Sand Island and cannot be further demoted. Cast away your fear," facetiously another put his hand on him. In a visible way he demonstrated under what stress the first generation Japanese lived in Honolulu since December 7.

There must have been a constant dread of a visit from the FBI investigation or imprisonment or the possibility of a neighbor turning informer against him. Even a ten day ordeal, continuous apprehension day and night, could effect a tremendous change in an individual. The few days behind barred windows at the Immigration Station applied the final touches to these cornered human beings.

"Now, let us have your report. What is the news report from the Far East. Has Singapore capitulated?"

"Not yet, but Hong Kong is now ours," his voice was almost a whisper.

"I tell you. This is Sand Island. No spy is around. You cannot sink any further. Don't be afraid to talk aloud."

In a short hour or so, the entire camp knew that Hong Kong was captured and Singapore was to be sacked in a matter of days. Many got indignant over the traitorous activity of some men who had enjoyed the respect of the community in the days of the past. These men, in order to save their hides, had become informers and turned in names of men who, any Japanese knew, were never dangerous to the security of the United States. That Nisei should be active in helping the FBI was comprehensible because they were citizens, but for certain Issei to have become renegades for selfish self-preservation and nothing else was a subject of very severe indignation. But in the course of time a peculiar psychology developed among the men. Largely perhaps to make their lot easier, they felt that they were better off in this enclosure since they did not have to go through a mental strain that all persons with

322

Japanese physiognomy had to endure under war time circumstances.

No matter how stringent regulations were, people would devise things that would unwittingly break the law. "Necessity is the mother of invention." Boxes of groceries were brought into the area and these were re-enforced at both ends with thin strips of flat steel. These strips of metal were taken from the wooden boxes, cut into pieces about a foot long and bent in a "V" shape so that in the picking of dried grass and leaves, the bare fingers need not be used. It was a clever device for leisurely work. But ingenuity did not stop there. Out of this steel someone fashioned small knives for cutting pieces of wood. Some went as far as making a handle for these sharp knives with no evil intent.

One day, about ten days following arrival, a detail of men went out of the enclosure to do some work. Everyone coming into the area had to submit to frisking, and one of these homemade knives was found on R. Okano. The reaction to this discovery was terrific and fast. The commandant was called immediately to the gate and he got into a towering rage. He took pistols out of the gun rack for each of his subordinates. Stark naked, Okano faced the muzzles of these seven pistols and he considered himself "a goner." Once he felt he might be shot he became fearless and collected. He was by no means very brave, but circumstances sometimes bring out the best in a man. He did not move and the captain was put in an awkward situation. He released the man, who would not be cowed, into the area, but immediately a whistle was blown three times. This signified an emergency muster and all the inmates were lined up in company formation. The entire garrison of military police came into the compound and a systematic search of each tent was made. The inmates were ordered to strip completely to their skin. They left their clothes in front on the ground. Three hundred of them, stark naked, stood in formation at 4:30 in the afternoon in order to allow the MP's to ransack their belongings. The sky was low with overhanging rain clouds and the moist wind blowing in from the ocean was cold and penetrating. The men were shivering from cold and fear. Every piece of garment on the ground was inspected. Many prohibited articles emerged in the search. Most of them were bits of paper with diary-like notations. Many metal tweezers and improvised pen-knives were discovered.

Seikichi Arata had no contraband on his person, but he was fearful of the possible development if someone had really contrived and possessed some important weapon: the whole camp would have had to suffer. The freezing ordeal lasted more than an hour. Seikichi was afraid that at such an emotional pitch any unhappy incident might happen. He hoped that everyone would behave himself and not cross the raging commandant. Fortunately it ended as an unforgettable experience and taught the people a lesson.

The Germans were also searched in connection with the Japanese trouble. "The Mixed Camp," as it was called, was made up of Germans, Italians, Austrians, Finns, and Norwegians. Most of these men were naturalized citizens. Some were refugee Jews who had recently entered the country and were not yet naturalized. They included a concert musician who had recently arrived from Japan, and a Norwegian artist and his wife. A petty officer, a member of the U.S. Navy for fifteen years, was also picked up. A third generation German-American was also picked up, and only black mark against him was that he had gone to Berlin for the Olympic games and had a distant cousin who was a U-boat officer.

These men occupied the same area but were partitioned off by an iron fence. They were not supposed to talk across the fence, but that regulation could hardly be enforced because the kitchen was the same, and people placed under the same restriction would naturally have sympathy for each other. In fact, the chief cook was, in civilian life, a chef at the Royal Hawaiian Hotel and all subordinate cooks and helpers were Japanese. There was another cook who had been in charge of the Young Hotel Restaurant. Thus it was impossible to keep the two groups apart, and what harm did it do to let them communicate?

In another adjoining area, construction of a two story wooden barrack was begun, and when completed the female internees were quartered. Since the number was small, all races were mixed, and the matron was said to be a very understanding and humane person.

Besides cutting down trees on the island, quite a few men were taken out to work on a vegetable garden. Since these had to work under the muzzle of a guard's gun, they refused to return to work one day, but seventy-two year old Rev. Kubokawa, a Buddhist priest who had recently arrived from Japan, volunteered to go out to work. He was always repeating the *Namu Amida Butsu*, ("I take refuge in Buddha"). In this sect, daily repetition of this phrase is encouraged, the more the better. At first there was a violent reaction to his "disturbing the quiet and peace." He conducted his routine way of life without giving heed to any complaint or sarcastic remarks. In time people began respecting him for what he was, and when this mild priest volunteered to go out to toil under the sun, younger men were shamed and followed him to the field. To the very end he persisted in this practice and his saintly way of life left a most profound impression among all men, irrespective of sect or religion.

Since the food was military rations, it was nutritious. The lack of green vegetables and fruits, however, was something all men complained about. To cooperate in the growing of vegetables was nothing more than a selfish measure. So it seemed until the greens were harvested. The produce graced the table of the guards and the camp kitchen continued to serve the usual rations of dried food and meat.

Since all food was conveyed from the mainland, it was natural that the commandant insisted that there should be no waste. A guard was posted at the waste can where each man cleaned his plate. Whenever there was remaining food, the man was admonished not to waste. Once the commandant himself was there to see that the edict was enforced. Mr. Ide who was arrested at his home without his glasses and dentures was unfortunate enough to come to the waste can at this particular moment.

"Clean up your plate. You have a piece of meat there. Don't you know that meat has to be convoyed from the mainland? Finish your plate."

Mr. Ide was bewildered. He could not speak English well. He opened his mouth and pointed to his toothless condition and shook his head.

The commandant was not in a mood to be cooperative. "My order is that you clean your plate." Mr. Ide understood this order by this time and he gulped down the chunk of tendon. He knew for sure he was going to have indigestion that night. In order not to be caught again, all men began wrapping hard cartilage and bones in pieces of paper to be disposed of later. What if the commandant should catch one with a small piece of bone on the plate? Could he distinguish a cartilage from a piece of tendon?

Rev. Goto who was discharged from the camp about Christmas time to work among the farmers and vegetable growers of the Kaneohe District, wrote the commandant that he was ready to send some bananas and papayas to supplement the meat-rich diet. The captain reported this to the camp and added that he refused this generous offer on the ridiculous pretext that, "You might be poisoned as you have many enemies on the outside."

The ordeal of tobacco-less days was an apalling experience. Luckily, Seikichi did not smoke and he was glad he was not a slave to this noxious habit. For two weeks there was no way of buying cigarettes. The guards felt sorry and they would light a cigarette, take a puff, drop it and kick it away toward a waiting inmate. The latter would pick it up, return to his tent and call his friends together. In a circle of men, this cigarette was passed around so that each could have the pleasure of a puff.

One day Dr. Takata was sent for. He was ordered to make a professional visit to some prisoners who were clearing the island of undergrowth and trees. These prisoners of different nationalities were housed in tents outside of the internment camp and a few of them caught cold. An armed sergeant conducted the doctor to the tent where a Chinese boy lay on a cot. While he was examining him, he caught sight of several cartons of cigarettes.

"Will you be good enough to let me have some packs of tobacco?"

"Oh, take all you want, doctor."

Dr. Takata pocketed four packages. "Oh, take some more," urged the sick boy who had broken the curfew law and was now imprisoned. The doctor thought fast but when he pictured the scene of the guard frisking his person at the gate he refrained from taking more. As it turned out there was no search and he regretted his caution. Seikichi distributed these cigarettes by the doctor's orders to as many groups as possible. The funny and curious thing about the whole matter was that though he had never wished to smoke in ordinary life and he was glad in such a crisis that he was a non-smoker, still when the acute famine was over, there arose in him a rather strong desire to start smoking a pipe.

It seemed that the camp life revolved around the latrine. It was a most well-tended latrine and kept spick and span by Mr. Ogata who forbade the use of the building until inspection was over at 9 every morning. At no time of the day was any mud found on the cement floor. Everyone had to take off his wooden clogs, wash his feet, and enter barefooted. Considerable dissatisfaction was felt and voiced among the people because of this ruling, but the detail in charge considered that building the most important place in the whole camp and took pride in maintaining its reputation of cleanliness. They were jealous of its immaculate state and were unduly vigilant and anxious for a commendation from the commandant.

It seemed that no matter in what type of work men were placed, the task apportioned to them became the most important thing in their lives and recognition of a well done job was looked forward to, like a child waiting for a pat on the back by the teacher. The men in this menial work detail did not expect any special favor from the commandant. However, for becoming a member of this latrine squad there was one compensation. Because of the soap issued for the scrubbing of the porcelain fixtures, one could do some laundering. Otherwise there was no soap available for the internees.

Because of the limited number of toilet bowls, Arata used to get up at 4:30 in the morning to perform his daily evacuation. There was no congestion then and nobody to bawl him out for mud or dirt. Many a time he had to feel his way in the room because there was no moonlight to guide his way. Nowhere else could the latrine become the spotless shrine that theirs was. Even in civilian homes an inspection of the lavatory may tell what kind of a housekeeper the mistress happens to be. It was repeatedly used as an example by the commandant to urge the "mixed camp" to keep their latrine cleaner.

During the period when the "tobacco famine" caused panic, the most aggravating daily ordeal was the tally of knives and spoons in the kitchen. Each man was handed fork, knife, and spoon at each meal. When the day was over, the number issued had to tally before the kitchen crew could retire to their tents and the lieutenant to his quarters. It was an ordeal for this young lieutenant. He was liked by all. Sometimes he was tested by the captain as to whether he made the correct report or not. It came to such a pass that the Japanese spokesman commented to the commandant: "This furor over a knife or a spoon missing is such a trifling matter to keep us on edge every evening. Why not issue chopsticks to us in lieu of the metal eating wares?"

The captain was not going to be dictated to from any source, especially a prisoner. "The army regulation calls for a knife, spoon, and fork. We have to abide by the regulations."

"All right, then. We'll use them, but why such a fuss over a spoon," countered the spokesman.

"You can use a spoon to dig yourself out of captivity."

"Dig myself under the Honolulu Harbor?"

"Yes, that's right!" the captain was obstinate. It was no wonder that he was considered the toughest officer in the Hawaiian army. He was disliked by most men, but in justice to him he was a very fair man. There was no racial discrimination in his handling of the different races. To him a job was to be well done and he was indefatigable in pursuance of it. He would have made an excellent combat officer but he was not qualified to "nurse-maid" prisoners, especially civilian prisoners.

After the first week, a certain degree of order emerged out of the chaos. The standing order to keep internees at hard labor continued until about Christmas time when an aide of the military governor came to the camp and announced the following edict. "We have made a mistake in putting you to work. Hereafter you shall only be required to do work sufficient to maintain your existence here and to police the ground on which you are allowed to roam about. Having done nothing criminal, you are not criminals. You are not war prisoners. You are only detained. Therefore you are not under military regulation. The only thing we ask of you is to be respectful when our flag is lowered at sunset each day."

This request was gladly followed. All stood at attention while the bugle played the beautiful piece each evening while the flag was lowered. If anyone should have been disrespectful, the men around him would not have stood for such behavior. After all, this country had given them their happiest years and had they been allowed to become naturalized, the majority would have become citizens long ago.

On about December 20th, General Emmons, who succeeded General Short, paid a visit to the camp and this order of the change of status from prisoner to detainee must have been the result of this inspection tour.

For two weeks there was no way of shaving and no change of clothes. Mr. Matsumura, the author, said, "If I ever should write about this experience I shall call it 'Life without a mirror.' We all look like ferocious bandits."

Razor blades were issued and there was a sudden uplift in morale as the two-week-old beards and mustaches came off. At noon, Sergeant Moran came back from shopping with post cards that he bought out of his own money so that "detainees" could communicate with their home for the first time since Pearl Harbor Day. It was a very real Christmas present and came from a sergeant!

On Christmas Day the regulations were somewhat relaxed and a fellow detainee, a professor of German extraction from the university, delivered a lecture to fit the occasion. The relaxation of work orders and change of status were instrumental in the appearance of smiles on the taut faces of the detainees because a post exchange was opened and cigarettes and daily necessities could be bought. The whereabouts of the concentration camp was made public and families were allowed to correspond with the detainees. Clothes were taken to the Immigration Station by families and these packages were brought over for distribution.

The New Year came and went and still there was no intimation of what awaited them. What would become of them? What would befall their families? Everything was darkness. The strain began to appear in the people's behavior. Those who were prone to be bombastic and talk big became very quiet and unobtrusive with the passage of days. Some who had commanded wealth and station in civilian life could not become reconciled to this revolutionary change and still tried to live in dream and fantasy of the past. In this crisis the intrinsic value of a man asserted itself. The goodness in a man came out. If anything good came from an act it was unadulterated gold because there was no promise of reward. Meanness or cowardly behavior was sometimes encountered in erstwhile respected men, both laymen and ministers, and this revelation brought nausea to others. On the other hand, nobility of character manifested itself in lowly fishermen and cooks, or in young men who had labored inconspicuously in normal times. These volunteered to do menial and unsung jobs without reward or adulation.

In January, digging of slit trenches along the fences about 2½ to 3 feet deep was ordered by the commandant. They were dug so that the inmates might take refuge in case of air raid. The trenches could not be any deeper because of subterranean water. Gas masks were also distributed for possible gas attack. Sergeant Moran who was then warden, taught them the art of putting on and taking off of these masks. The instruction was like going to primary school because it was pretty hard to teach old men new tricks. The part that was particularly difficult was a precautionary measure to stoop low, sniff the air and then take off the mask.

Even after a day of hard labor there was a lot of time and soon people began doing artistic things. Just as prehistoric people, when they were not pressed by the necessity of procuring of food and could enjoy some leisurely hours carving on the stony walls of caves, these men began collecting shells. With a little digging the ground disclosed many different kinds of beautiful shells and coral. It soon became a fad. Many began ornamenting the grounds immediately surrounding their tent.

The commandant admired the artistic accomplishment and encouraged this endeavor. From his viewpoint it was a means of keeping the detainees occupied, and from the latters' standpoint it was fun and competition in creative and artistic accomplishment. The design and motif were legion. The most common designs were calendars and flowers. One artist depicted the story of the hare and the tortoise while another was more ambitious and the dragon palace scene of the fairy tale of Urashima was portrayed. It gave the artist a chance to picture different fishes. One tent, Mr. Mikami's, showed a collection of oddly shaped coral. The contours of these coral assumed the most fantastic shape and resembled the different breeds of dogs. When about fifty of these were collected, "The Sand Island Kennel" came into being.

The "Mixed Camp" was chided by the captain for its laziness. The Europeans were chagrined and applied their energy to beautify their ground, but came out a very poor second. One product was very utilitarian and produced admiration from the Japanese detainees. It was a sundial. In two days the latter contrived the most accurate sundial, beautifully ornamented by coral and shells. This instrument worked so accurately that henceforth correct time could be told within ten minutes of the exact hour of the day. It was inconsistent again. No watch could be kept by the inmates, but such a device was applauded. It showed that the keepers were merely following written regulations and not the spirit of the orders.

On the fateful day and on the days that followed, arrests of Japanese persons were made on the slimmest pretext. Now hearings were taking place at Sand Island and many were released or paroled without restriction. Most of these had fallen afoul of the curfew law or had broken the regulation that was suddenly imposed only upon Japanese; such as the prohibition to approach the waterfront or within three hundred feet of any seashore. The shore patrol had picked up these men. Very few were released from the black-listed group. Among those few were the four elderly sick persons, Dr. I. Mori, Miyozuchi Komeya, Rev. Fujio, and Mr. Yamamoto who were continuously on their backs during the five weeks of their detention.

Rev. Chinpei Goto of Kaneohe was a very busy man. In addition to his work as company commander, he acted as an interpreter while the fishermen were processed at headquarters. At about Christmas time he was released and worked for the FBI, visiting as many detainees' families as possible to comfort and help them. He did admirable work in quieting distracted families. Many families were doing well, especially those that had grown children, but there were quite a few, especially of younger members, that were almost destitute. Not only were they looked upon by other nationalities as abhorrent and tainted because of the detainees, but many erstwhile Japanese friends kept themselves away from fear that they, too, might be suspected by the authorities by being too friendly to the families of the imprisoned men. Children were cautioned not to play with those from internees' families.

Perhaps there was some justification for this attitude because of the tremendous tension under which persons of Japanese descent had to live. Other nationalities and sometimes Japanese themselves, phoned the FBI that a certain Japanese was acting queerly or that there was a gathering of people that appeared suspicious. These clues the FBI was obliged to follow through, for such information could not be ignored. The hundreds of families that were interrogated naturally got very jittery and cautious. Once a person was thrown into the camp, fear and suspense were ended because of resignation and philosophising, but while he roamed "free" there was a natural tendency to cling onto his so-called liberty and freedom even if he had to live with the utmost trepidation. Thus, aside from a few staunch friends and immediate relatives, the internees' families were treated as though afflicted with leprosy.

One day the commandant came to the hospital tent and only Seikichi Arata was there helping the bed-ridden men. "Who is the best educated man in this camp?" he asked.

"What do you mean by best educated? There are many well educated priests and school teachers. What do you want to know?" queried Arata in return.

"I want to find out about a Japanese officer's action when he is a prisoner."

"Then maybe Dr. Takata can answer you. His brother is an admiral.

I'll go and fetch him. Please wait," and off went Arata in search of Dr. Takata who was playing *go* in a nearby tent.

When the doctor came, the question was put to him. "How will a captured officer want to die?"

Dr. Takata thought for a moment. "By the firing squad, if possible, with his uniform on. If he is allowed to commit suicide, he will do it by shooting through his brain, or *hara kiri* in the old *Bushido* manner."

"Well, this man will have no access to weapons, and so that is out. Will he wilfully create a condition to commit suicide?" He was rather ambiguous. Dr. Takata thought for several minutes.

"Do you mean by that statement will a Japanese officer try to climb a fence so that the guard will shoot him?" The commandant nodded. "No. On that point you may feel safe. He will not resort to such a method unless he is mentally deranged. He will not die like a fugitive. He will not commit suicide unless he is in uniform."

"That is all I want to know," and off he sauntered flipping his bunch of keys in his right hand.

Not long after that conversation, a small enclosure within the area was built near the gate. It was called the "bird cage," and housed the first prisoner of war, Kazuo Sakamaki, Lt. Junior Grade of the Japanese Navy, until his transfer to the mainland in February, 1942.

Before this special enclosure was built, he lived in a tent by himself, guarded twenty-four hours a day. During the early days when high school students did guard work, there was a Punahou School teenager. During mess time while he was in the dining hall with the detainees, away from the scrutiny of his superiors, he talked. "The lieutenant is our enemy. He failed and got captured because his small submarine could not be steered. He is an enemy but I cannot but admire him. He is a great guy. I am trying to teach him English. He was sent to get one of our carriers. He knew by sight the Saratoga which is out there now. His face is full of cigarette burns. He inflicted those the night before he was to be photographed. He did not want the people of Japan to recognize him. He branded himself so that he will be reminded that he is a captive, a coward that did not die. But I don't think he is a coward. He is a hero, in spite of his being our enemy."

The detainees were ordered not to speak to him and likewise he got the same orders, for he never did speak to anyone.

Almost every day there was unfounded wild talk that came under the category of KP news, a Sand Island creation, in contrast to AP and UP and other worldwide legitimate news-carrying organizations. Whenever there was news that bore the marks of KP origin, people came to the hospital tent for analysis and verification. Dr. Takata was trusted by all and his interpretation and analysis carried a lot of weight.

In mid-January it was evident that the people's morale had sunk very low because of the shortage of stimulating news and the prospect of their remaining in camp for a very long, long time became too apparent. There were many, especially among the young priests and international merchants, who had not sunk their roots in America, that wanted to return to Japan. Dr. Takata hit upon the idea of trying to boost this mental depression by a new approach. "Arata-san, go out and casually spread the news that there will be an exchange of civilian war prisoners."

"Doctor, is that true?"

"Never mind. Just go out and tell someone," smiled the doctor, composed in his usual manner. Within ten minutes, his tent was besieged by anxious faces.

"We heard the news of civilian exchange. Where did the news come from? Another KP news?"

"No, not KP news. Just Takata news." People were skeptical but willing to believe anything. Their faces glowed with anticipation. "What I am going to tell you is just historical fact. During the last world war there was an exchange of war prisoners who were maimed or otherwise reduced to a condition unfit to bear arms. These war prisoners were exchanged at a railroad station in Switzerland. A trainload of such German war prisoners pulled in from France and another bearing a like number of allied prisoners came in from the opposite direction. These two trains stopped on opposite sides of the same platform. Numbers were checked and accounted for under the supervision of neutral authorities conducting the exchange and when everything was satisfactory the trains proceeded to their destination. Now if such is historical precedent affecting war prisoners, then it is common sense that non-combatants can be similarly exchanged.

"If I know American psychology at all, before the summer is out there will be a tremendous public clamor assailing the Congress from the families of those who are interned in the Orient to speedily bring back the civilian internees. That this will happen is as clear as the sun rises in the East every morning. The American public will never tolerate

333

this unfortunate situation without trying to right it, and who will be the most logical ones for such an exchange but we? This is bound to take place. Watch and see." Thus the people were occupied with a thought, a hope, and a way out of this imprisonment, and for a week or more many appeared to be happy.

After Christmas day, when the status of the inmates of the camp became clarified, meetings for religious purpose were allowed about twice a week. There was no shortage in the number of speakers for there were many preachers of Buddhist, Christian, and Shinto religions. These took turns to talk on subjects that would help make the situation more bearable. There were many clandestine meetings on different subjects ranging from travelogues, experiences in the different wars, politics, literature, sociology, and science. Personal experiences of a few men in the war in China were very exciting and filled many hours.

Not all stories and lectures were of a high caliber and as is true in all congregations of men, the exchange of anecdotes, personal and hearsay, came down to the level of the human. Except for the prudish invididuals, such stories were welcomed because their naturalness and lack of malice made everybody laugh. And laughter was most needed by all. Before long, certain men became famous for being natural born raconteurs, especially of smutty stories. Away from the convention of established society the inhibition of revealing one's past gradually gave way and very exciting and interesting personal episodes were related by the most unexpected persons. The really good storytellers were asked to go from tent to tent after sunset to entertain, make other people envious of their past experience, and happy for an hour or so. A very popular subject was "My first love."

CHAPTER 22

Hearing Board

FROM THE BEGINNING OF JANUARY 1942, hearing boards were held at the Immigration Station for those that were detained at Sand Island. In groups of two or three dozen, they were taken over to the station and returned to the island when they completed their hearing.

Seikichi Arata's turn came about the middle of January. He was returned to the memorable large room, filled with three-tiered beds, in which two unforgettable nights had been passed in early December. "How is the hearing going on?"

"I think it is just for the record. We of the blue card are already condemned and no answer one way or another will sway the verdict," was the answer Seikichi got from almost everyone. Some of them were repeatedly investigated and grilled but the vast majority had only one session.

"What are the questions most commonly asked?"

"There are three boards. Each is made up of three members—two civilians and one military lawyer. My hearing did not take more than fifteen minutes and it seems I am behind this fence because I was once a *toritsugi-nin* for the Japanese consulate," volunteered Kyoichi Yamada from Waianae. A *toritsugi-nin* was an agent that was appointed by the consulate at different parts of the country so that legal papers that had to be sent to the consulate might be in acceptable form. To be deferred from army service, to report birth, marriage, or death to the Japanese village registry, etc., the forms were available from the *toritsugu-nin* and he performed this service gratis. It was doing a worthwhile public service job and a real convenience to the illiterate people who were quite numerous among the laborers.

Seikichi Arata had been in deep doubt—sometimes bordering on rejecting all yardsticks of morality, fair play, and loyalty—while awaiting the answer to a simple question, "Why was I interned?" Now he seemed to see the light, the reason for his incarceration. The honorable service he did for the foreign office of Tokyo during his younger days on Kauai years ago had him listed as an "agent" in the registry at the Consulate in Honolulu. Since his departure from Kauai he had done no such intermediary work for others.

"The function of the *toritsugi-nin* does not seem to be understood thoroughly by the American officials. They think we were spying for Tokyo. Collecting materials and figures for the Japanese government is what they suspect. Look at Yamasaki from Waianae who is a Nisei. He cannot even speak, let alone write, Japanese. Because his father did that sort of work at a store, the store was listed as a *toritsugi-nin* as a convenience for other persons in Waianae. Yamasaki is now the proprietor of the store since his father's death and he is here in Sand Island," continued Kyoichi Yamada.

"What other items do they consider as un-American or pro-Japanese?"

"The activity in the Shinto Shrines and the movement to send contributions and Red Cross supplies for the wounded in the China War also seem to go against the pleasure of the FBI. They have the contributors' list that appeared in the Japanese dailies. Do you remember the publicity that was given when certain groups contributed trucks and tanks for the armed forces fighting in China? The FBI considers that act in particular pro-Japan. Sure it is pro-Japan! But when we are denied naturalization and forever barred from becoming Americans we must remain Japanese. What is wrong in being pro-Japan! That should not be anti-American no matter how you try to interpret it. You can only be anti-China!"

Kyoichi Yamada was getting heated in his arguments. How many times this matter was discussed among detainees! Each time he touched upon this subject he could not help but become spiritedly engrossed; he felt a little better when a newcomer from Sand Island nodded approval to his expostulation.

On the day of his hearing, Arata was led to Board No. 3. There was a rectangular table around which sat Senator Akana, Attorney Sylva, and an army officer. "Good morning, Mr. Arata. Sit down. Smoke? No, then have some drops," Senator Akana, who presided, was very genial as he handed a box of lemon drops to the detainee who was naturally tense and ill at ease. His easy-going manner and attitude were a studied attempt to allay the fear and relax the tautness of the facial muscles. "Now, what is your full name and how long and where have you lived in Hawaii?"

"My name is Seikichi Arata. I came to Kauai in 1894 and now I live in Honolulu."

"Tell us about your family."

"My wife is living. I have three boys and two girls. All married. Twelve grandchildren. Biggest grandson is in the army at Schofield."

"What school did you finish in Japan. What school in Hawaii?" asked Senator Akana.

"Finished grammar school in Japan. No school in Hawaii."

"How many times did you return to Japan?" asked Mr. Sylva.

"Not one time."

"Did you buy any war bonds?" asked the lieutenant.

"Yes. Two thousand dollars."

"Why not more?"

"No money," smiled Arata.

"Were you a consular agent?" asked Mr. Sylva.

"What you mean, agent?"

"Same as *toritsugi-nin* for the consulate," explained Senator Akana.

"I was one when I lived on Kauai. I helped the people write out the form to send to the consulate in Honolulu. Free service to men who could not write."

"What do you think of the sneak attack on Pearl Harbor by the Japanese planes?"

"I am no soldier. I do not know whether it is right or wrong, good or poor war strategy. I am only sad that two friends should come to this sorry end and have to fight."

"Who you think will win?" asked Mr. Sylva.

"I don't know because I stayed away from Japan a long time. I know America is rich and can make strong warships and put many millions of men, well armed, on the field. But the Japanese can fight and if generals do not show better leadership, hard to say who will win." The three looked at each other and were a little surprised at this candid answer.

"Well, that is all Mr. Arata. You may return to your quarters," said

337

Senator Akana as he pressed a button to summon the waiting guard.

Seikichi Arata's hearing was ended and like the majority of such sessions, the procedure was a record for future reference. That he was to be detained for the duration was foreordained. Just then Rev. B. Miyamoto of Haleiwa returned from his hearing rather flushed and excited.

"I asked the hearing board for a character witness and designated Mr. Midkiff, the manager of Waialua Plantation. A reverse charge telephone was used yesterday to summon Mr. Midkiff. Because he is a very busy man I entertained little hope that he could make it. After all, in war time we detainees do not rate much. But he was there and spoke without hesitation, backing me up. Then he said, 'I brought the Reverend's wife and child with me and they are waiting in the hallway. If it does not go against regulations, please let them meet.' The army officer showed hesitancy toward this gesture and the meeting did not materialize. But think of it. A white American taking that much interest in behalf of an enemy alien. What a wonderful man! He is certainly an American through and through. An ideal that any man should strive for. I could have knelt at his feet." All who listened felt a lump in their throat. It was deeply moving and refreshing to even hear of a personality of such magnitude that transcended love and hate.

Dr. Takata was standing there leaning against the bunk and told his experience. "I was taken to Board No. 2. It was presided over by Attorney Thompson. After asking routine questions, Mr. Thompson said, 'We have a report here that you did very good work among all people in the treatment of cancer. You did that work free of charge as a consultant. I wish to thank you for that. Now unfortunately because of the war you are here at this hearing board. We have a report that you have a brother in the Imperial Navy.'

"Yes, sir, my younger brother is a rear admiral and is in command of the Fleet of the Home Waters. Then the questioner went on. 'Do you think the Japanese Navy was justified in attacking without warning?' To that I answered, I have one country and one flag. I cannot answer any more. The committee looked at each other and the lieutenant said 'A very good answer.'"

On the whole the hearings were routine. A few were questioned long and thoroughly but these were quite shaken and were close-mouthed when they were returned to the room. Some took as long as two weeks, but the majority were returned to Sand Island after one appearance at the hearing board. Some could not stand the strain. One attempted suicide by slashing his wrist with a razor blade. It ended in failure because the vessel cut was a small vein and pressure stopped the hemorrhage, but the small pool of blood scared the guards and they took away razor blades.

S. Sakamoto of Waianae was arrested in the middle of January and was thrown into a dark cell at the police station after grilling by the FBI. Everything was taken away from him, including his belt, and he was detained in darkness for four days and nights. He was then brought to the Immigration Station and thrown into a large room where he found a man in his early 40's, dishevelled, with a three day beard and set, staring eyes. He came up to the new arrival and said, "You are a newcomer here? You know they are trying to kill me? They have poisoned many and pretty soon I am going to die. I was forced to swallow some pills. Don't you ever drink the water from the faucet because it is poisoned."

Not knowing this man and having just arrived after a gruelling experience in dark solitary confinement, he was not sure of his fate himself. Like everybody else, he feared that the prospect of being shot was within the range of possibility. Now perhaps the time for his demise had arrived, judging from the babbling of this man. He was transferred from the police jail to be eliminated permanently by an easy, humane process using a potent poison. He was not too comfortable at the turn of events. Just then, the people who had been taken out for lunch returned to the room and then he found out the true state of affairs. Because this man was becoming psychotic, restless, and sleepless, Dr. Okimura had forcefully given him a sedative. This was mistaken for poison even though administered by his own countryman.

After returning to Sand Island this restless man acted queerly and could not sleep. He crawled under cots to hide himself and insisted that people were talking bad about him. He was effeminate in many ways and now insisted that he was a woman and pregnant. People were commenting about his "bulging abdomen." For two nights there were volunteer guards over him so that he would not stray out of the tent and walk within ten yards of the fence. Orders were that if anyone should approach the fence it would be interpreted as an attempt to escape and he might be shot.

On the third day Dr. Takata had the sergeant of the guards come to the tent. "Sergeant, this man is annoyed by other people. They suspect that he is pregnant. As a representative of the U.S. Army I wish you would examine him with me and if you agree with me that he is not pregnant will you please announce it to the camp and put a stop to this gossip and clear his good name?"

The sergeant solemnly swore, "That I shall gladly do. Nobody can speak falsehood against a decent person like you."

"That is right, sergeant. I want you to tell the camp what you see," said the patient and unbottoned his pants to exhibit his non-pregnant state. He finally was paroled and admitted to the Territorial Hospital for the mentally deranged.

On February 16th, there was an unexpected announcement that men whose names would be called were to pack their belongings and assemble in the mess hall. Furthermore, these men were not returning to Sand Island. First, twenty Germans and Italians were named. Then Japanese were called. But these seemed to include about everybody. One hundred eighty Japanese were to leave and only thirty remained uncalled.

Seikichi Arata was among the one hundred and eighty. Since he knew he was not returning he felt a lingering attachment to this place of two months' domicile, in spite of the hectic experience that could not be easily forgotten. This camp had been developed and made livable by their combined efforts. Now at the start to an unknown destination, even this not-too-pleasant spot held a nostalgic claim to many a heart. Those that remained behind had sad expressions on their faces. Some actually wept. Under these circumstances the ones that were going away were filled with a certain sense of expectant adventure and the break from the monotonous routine was a change that was stimulating, whereas those that were left behind to face the same doleful existence were made more desolate and empty by the sudden depletion of friends.

Across the harbor a barge conveyed the detainees, but this time there were no menacing muzzles trained on them. They were taken to the Immigration Station and quartered in one of the large dormitory rooms. On their way up the stairway they noticed a pile of carton boxes and suitcases and Seikichi Arata saw his name on one of them. This struck him as being queer because all his daily necessities and clothing had already been sent to him. He thought little of this discovery.

Then they were led into the interior court where former arrivals, in small groups, were waiting their summons from the officers. They were informed that photographing and fingerprinting were in progress. "What for?" was the spontaneous question, because under the circumstances they tried to interpret any procedure in a wishful manner and inwardly hoped that most of them were to be released. Being at war and having been under suspicion, it was natural for the authorities to keep such a scientific checkup on them, just as the police would subject suspects to such processes for future reference. From 4 P.M. to 4 A.M., they were destined to either sit or walk in the open air awaiting their turn.

When Arata's turn came, it was 4 A.M. It was the most humiliating experience to have these "convict pictures" taken: views from the front and side with an identification number across the chest. Fingerprinting was worse.

While waiting for this processing, Arata sat under the pavilion, but since there was no wall he had some difficulty in keeping himself warm. Dr. Takata and he walked back and forth accompanied by Mr. N. who had been in the German Army and was taken captive twice by the English in the First World War.

"I was a war prisoner in England for four long years. We were moved from place to place every three months doing farm work. This moving was done to prevent us from becoming intimate with guards and civilians. Since we helped them, the farmers were nice to us. The first two years are hard. After that a prisoner's life is not too bad," wryly smiled Mr. N.

"Four years! Long time, too long!" murmured Arata dejectedly.

"During the first two years, you get so restless, so hopeless, that many rebel. Many plan to escape. Some actually try. A few succeed. But after the first two years days go by very rapidly. Looks like we are going somewhere. The Americans, I am sure, will follow the English method of treating prisoners. If you find this prisoners' life hard to take, come to me. I can give you some advice and encouragement."

"We may have to get a morale boost some time and I'll remember you," smiled Dr. Takata. It was pleasant to talk to Mr. N. He was an educated, mild mannered individual and having a common travail to endure, they became almost brotherly in their solicitude of each other's

341

welfare despite their widely different backgrounds and nationalities.

At 7 o'clock they were aroused for breakfast whether they liked it or not. Some had not slept at all. They were marched into the inner court where under a drizzling rain they had to stand in line and eat. They could not take shelter from the rain, but criminal prisoners from the county jail who were doing work on the lawn had their meals under the overhanging balcony.

At 8:30 o'clock, Mr. M. Marumoto appeared and spoke in Japanese, "For the past ten days though you did not know, we, on the outside knew that you were to be moved to some colder place. Therefore, your families were instructed to buy warm clothing for you in preparation for this journey. According to international law you cannot be left in a warring zone and are, therefore, to be transported to the interior. The authorities had first intended to have you take leave of your families, but it was found that such a procedure would take too much time and would be inconvenient. We, the members of the Japanese Civic Association, have formed a committee of five who have made it a point to contact each family, dividing the work among ourselves. Thus, each family has been contacted and we have with us words from them and we wish to relay these to you. You in turn, will make your wishes known to these committee members and they will relay your messages. We shall call you in groups of five for this purpose." Mr. Marumoto retired and the door was locked.

Pandemonium ensued. The room was thrown into an uproar and heated discussion followed. Most of them were dumbfounded. The Japanese, following their upbringing, did not show outward emotions as the Germans and Italians who began cursing loudly. Just about this time those near the window looked out through the latticed windows and saw a throng of people. There were about five hundred. Members of their families had come to bid farewell, having heard that a last interview was to be accorded them. Apparently they were just told that such leave takings were not to be held, reversing the former announcement, for there was a loud clamor on the outside. A reverberating howl was taken up by the captives in the two rooms.

After fifteen minutes, men began reacting to the situation according to their respective temperament. There was a German who insisted on seeing his wife and children, whom he detected among the crowd. His insistence was such that the guards took him out, but in fifteen minutes he returned bawling. It was a pitiful sight to see a fifty year old, ruddy-faced man giving away to his emotions without reserve. In a way it was very effeminate for a man to act in such a way, and yet there was only sympathy from all because it was human and they all felt the same way. One of the Italians discovered his daughter and began to whistle a tune that perhaps had been a signal between the two in their happier, more peaceful days.

Seikichi Arata once saw a French movie concerning a criminal destined for Devil's Island. The scenes depicted the departure of the prison ship, transporting the dregs of Paris and "lifers" to the island off the coast of French Guiana in South America. What he remembered of this tempestuous scene was the unrestrained way in which the prisoners cursed the magistrates and everybody else. They threw out their fists against the officials who were exiling them to a hellish existence from which none returned. On the other hand, there were toughies who showed no outward signs of rebellion, but unable to camouflage the smoldering glint in their eyes, hid the violent emotions that seethed under their shirts by just spitting over the rails of the ship.

The human reaction to this "man's inhumanity to man" was so vividly portrayed he was forcefully reminded of it as he lay recumbent in his bunk trying to digest this crisis, rationalize it, become resigned to it, then project himself or his family into the future and try to discover if there were any bright left-overs, any ray of hope. For the moment, he saw nothing. This room contained a hundred men who were trying to concentrate on a similar problem, although the challenge, the measures to cope with it, and the probable solution differed in every case. Never in his life would he like to go through such miserable, tearful, depressing experiences again.

The room became quiet as the men got busy writing their letters of farewell. Not knowing any particulars of this exile from their beloved ones, they entertained scant hope that they would ever see their families alive again. They envisioned the worst, and their letters were like wills and last testaments. Because letters had to be written in English the few proficient ones did letter writing for others. As they wrote they wept. The translator also wept with the dictator because in composing the message the letter became the former's as well. Seikichi Arata wrote in his letter:

"My dear wife and children. I am to be sent to the mainland, as you

know, to a place the authorities are not willing to divulge. We do not know what will become of us, and what will happen on our journey. Perhaps I may never be able to see you again. Such is my feeling. It is best that I speak plainly on the premise that I may not return. I wish that all of you children will heed your mother's words and respect her being as personifying me also. Whatever she says will be the final word. She is to talk matters over with Sadao, but the final word is hers. When she is not able to carry on Sadao is to take over. But under all circumstances you must pool your energies together and work as a unit under this war time condition. If Hawaii should be attacked again act with this spirit of unity and try to survive. Good-bye and I wish you will all take the best care of yourself."

Toward evening Arata had his interview with Mr. Marumoto. There was nothing to say because his wife and son had acted from common sense and what had been done was what he would have asked them to do.

On the following day, army overcoats and denim duffel bags were issued. The baggage in carton boxes were received by the owners and put in the duffel bags. The good suitcases were to be sent directly to the ship and were to go to their destination with them, but this was not to be the case. The warm clothing bought and packed in suitcases arrived two months later in spring and were of no use until winter came around again.

Mr. Serikawa had been taken out under escort to see his chronically ill child who was destined not to live long. He reported that he met his daughter who had inside information that they were headed for Montana which turned out to be just a guess. Mainland detainees were kept at a camp in Montana.

After the letters were written there was no way of mailing them since nobody had a cent on his person. The officer in charge showed no human kindness and when approached with the dilemma he merely shrugged his shoulders, "No stamp, no go." He was an automaton. Many small persons invested with power assume such borish attitudes.

Finally Mr. Marumoto was contacted. He returned within an hour and announced, "I have brought stamps so that each of you may write to your family. Each family has deposited fifty dollars with the army for your use, but we cannot use it. These stamps are from the committee." The seven dollars worth of stamps sufficed and everyone, including twenty Europeans, was now able to send a note of farewell to his family.

The internees, for now their status again changed from detainees to civilian internees, were ready to be moved but did not go on board the ship until the 20th of February, 1942.

CHAPTER 23

Transfer to the Mainland

AFTER BREAKFAST, ORDERS FOR DEPARTURE
were given out and duffel bags were filled with belongings. Shouldering these bags, they were led down to the side of the Immigration Station facing Pier 2 and loaded onto trucks. Three soldiers with shotguns were on each truck, one on the driver's seat and two behind. All the soldiers wore steel helmets and were in battle array. Three armored cars with anti-aircraft guns formed a part of the procession and were stationed at the front, middle, and end. Non-commissioned officers and officers on motorcycles and sidecars paraded back and forth giving orders or just moving about. The atmosphere attending this departure was one definitely martial.

It made the internees feel rather important that so much ado was manifested in connection with their expulsion from the islands, but at the same time it seemed silly that so much fuss should attend it. They were mere civilians: law-abiding civilians for nearly half a century in the territory. What fear was there of their trying to escape or an attempt made to rescue them by outsiders? From Pier 2 the cavalcade proceeded to Pier 27 which was located about a mile away. Mercifully, the way did not pass through any congested area and just followed the waterfront. Since it occurred at an early hour, almost nobody was on this street. There was a European on Arata's truck who showed himself to be completely cowed and beaten. He squatted on the floor between the seats, took off his coat and covered his face and shoulders so as not to show his face to anyone on the street. He was constantly mumbling, "This is terrible! I do not want to be seen by my friends or have anyone recognize me!"

Japanese, at least Arata, did not feel that way. He realized that they were innocent victims of a war which was none of their doing. They

346

were now being forcefully removed from their legally established residences, more or less as scapegoats to make up for the blunder of the brass stationed in Hawaii. He feared that they might be paraded in the cities of the mainland as fifth columnists who had helped bring defeat to the American forces on December 7th. What a funny picture it would make, he thought, to be thus displayed as evidence No. 1: over forty men above the age of sixty! Still the vengeful American public would probably not miss a chance of throwing ripe tomatoes at them, for by this time the Japanese race as a whole would be anathema as far as the Americans were concerned. While such thoughts were coursing in his mind, the procession halted at a pier to which the U. S. Army Transport *General Grant* was moored.

Men of a labor battalion were busy loading freight cars on the pier. There was a Japanese-American soldier among them. Perhaps he had some one among these internees who was related to him, or perhaps it was merely his feeling of sorrow that friends of his family were being shipped away, disgraced. Anyway he left his co-workers and flung himself on the pile of sand with his face down.

Seikichi Arata turned his eyes to midship where the main gangplank was situated and saw ambulance after ambulance arrive and unload stretcher cases to be loaded for transfer to mainland hospitals. Actual victims of the war, maimed perhaps for life, were being transported home. They were injured in a war in which they themselves were not directly interested and perhaps these men were at heart pacificists and hated war. Who could tell? Most men, especially draftees, were as a whole against war. What a price to pay for the bungling of leaders, for there surely must be ways to settle disputes better than the wholesale slaughter and maiming of the flower of a nation: young manhood. His grandson, Edward, now on duty somewhere on Oahu might be sent anywhere now that the conflagration was world wide. He prayed inwardly that Edward might be spared the misfortune of a crippled life. He was Japanese enough to see the heroism of a soldier falling on the battlefield like a full-blown cherry blossom before the gust of wind, but did not wish a lingering death for his grandson.

Their names were checked by Lieutenant Spillner of Sand Island Internment Camp at the gangplank near the stern of the ship, and they went up the steps single file carrying their barrack bags on their shoulders. On the deck, Seikichi turned around and took a final look at his beloved Honolulu, under its mid-winter green, basking in the perennial sunshine. It lay peacefully indolent almost forgetting the holocaust of three months ago. The familiar outline of the hills and mountain range behind the city, the winding streak of road up Nuuanu Valley, the irregular outline of the range of razor-back like mountains to the right of the Pali that appeared like the battlement of a mediaeval castle, were clearly visible from the deck, and he was now bidding farewell to this scenery perhaps for eternity.

Across Alewa Heights, there was a single rainbow against the bank of rain clouds that covered the range to the left of Pali. There was no end to this sentimental indulgence and there was to be no holding the procession. He cast his eyes down into the interior of the ship. Carefully, he descended the almost vertical stairway into the depth of the hold, three flights below the main deck. About twenty bunks arranged in three tiers comprised a room.

The interior of this transport was very neat, and there was no odor peculiar to paint in close quarters usually associated with steerage compartments of commerical liners. There were no portholes as these rooms were probably below the water line. The ventilation system was excellent. A constant supply of fresh air was blown into the bowels of the ship and so life even in the depth below the water line was comfortable and enjoyable. After assignment to a room, the men found the door to each room under padlock. They discovered that the doors and the locks were newly installed and this area had been converted to prison quarters to transport war prisoners. The military police that had been on duty at the Immigration Station came on board and stood guard duty. Most of these men were arrogant, inhuman, and lazy. A Hawaiian-born lieutenant was among the guards, but he seemed to command no respect or have any authority over these soldiers. He should have understood these prisoners, but was callous or did not have any sympathy.

Dr. Takata found a man developing a large carbuncle on the inner side of his knee which was causing considerable pain. As in all infections of this nature, drainage was slow without adequate incision. "Lieutenant, this man has a carbuncle. He needs incision to make the pus escape. If this cannot be done, give us some gauze and some aspirin tablets."

"All right, I'll speak to the surgeon," blithely answered this officer, but nothing came from him. Finally handkerchiefs were used to bandage this area and the poor man had to endure the pain during the entire

348

trip until sloughing took place and nature saw to it that the diseased portion was replaced by slow reparative process.

About two men had chronic constipation and wanted to continue treatment with warm enemata. The medical officer was never notified and the men had to make the best of the situation by surreptitiously using cold salt water for instilling into their rectum for relief. A little kindness or human consideration on the part of the guards would have made the lot of these afflicted men much easier.

As soon as they were settled in their quarters, a spokesman for each room was elected. Dr. Takata was elected for this work in Arata's room as he was most proficient in English. Dr. Okimura was the over-all spokesman since he knew the officers that were escorting them to San Francisco. He had been kept at the Immigration Station the longest.

It soon became apparent that the greatest suffering was to be centered about the natural function of urination and defecation. Once in the morning and once in the afternoon they were let out for the purpose of emptying their bladders into two galvanized garbage cans placed at the foot of the stairway. For bowel evacuation, at a certain time of the day, usually in the evening, they were let out in twos and threes to perform this act. Elderly men with prostatic trouble or bladder infection suffered immeasurable pain and discomfort bordering on cruelty from this stupid regulation.

A single latrine was on the deck above, and the garbage cans had to be emptied into it about twice a day. When the sergeant came around, several of the younger men in Arata's room used to volunteer to empty these cans. It was a sort of work nobody really cared for, but in so doing at least twenty men in their room had a chance to urinate. Similar reasoning prompted other rooms to send volunteers and soon this unsavory job was considered at a premium and sought after.

Arata's room was fortunate in having Mr. Yamato. He was about four feet ten inches, on the plump side, and constantly puffing at a cigar. One of the soldiers took a special liking to him, because he was jovial and presented a comical sight puffing at a giant-sized cigar when he was so short. He was called "Pappy," and as a result Mr. Yamato was pushed forward to ask any favor from the guard. In order to have a chance to empty their bladders some were willing to miss food. Others went down on their knees and prayed to be let out. Some could not hold out any longer and defecated into the basin. Whoever thought that a group of men of different constitution and age could be regimented as to the time of urination and defecation? This torture was wholly unnecessary and if the commanding officer of the guards had any humane consideration at all he would not have subjected these people to such atrocious treatment.

The bigotry and narrowness of some small-calibered men were wont to come to the fore on some such occasion. Whoever it was that was responsible for the conduct of this crossing was indeed a small man, for ten days these men were subjected to this regimen. Those who crossed to San Francisco in subsequent contingents were even allowed thirty minutes or an hour on deck each day.

There was very good food on board. Rations were identical with those served the army personnel. Even the mess crew was not hostile. They could joke. About the second day out an officer came around to each room with Dr. Okimura as interpreter and he demonstrated the proper wearing of the life jacket. "From now on no matter where you go you will have to carry this life belt along with you. The string has to be tied in this certain way so that you will be able to untie it easily even when it gets wet and tight.

"If there should be an enemy attack and the ship gets torpedoed, you will be let out from your rooms but there shall be no crowding or jostling. You shall fall in line in single file. Anyone who starts a commotion will be shot. There will be no lifeboat for your accommodation. Therefore you must jump into the sea and await rescue."

Dr. Okimura went along and translated, but his translation was inadequate and the impression he conveyed was far from what had been said by the officer. Many men understood that the ship was going to be attacked that night. They failed to reason that nobody could foretell such an attack. Among the more timid ones the fear of impending death was germinated and a general depression seemed to have moved certain men to queer actions.

One man said, "I cannot die with this stubble of beard. I have to shave somehow," and began plucking his beard.

Another took it in a different manner, "My wife sent one new underwear. I'm going to change into everything new. At least I want to report to my ancestors in new clean clothes."

A well educated man with a timid heart said, "If we should get torpedoed, we have to think of food. There is no way of knowing how long it will take before we get rescued. I am going to swipe some bread from the mess hall and put it in my coat pocket."

A listener did not agree with this stratagem, "The moment you jump into the sea that bread will get soaked with salt water."

But in Arata's room, Dr. Takata clarified for the ones less proficient in English the procedure in case of disaster and everyone was calm, for the order was rational. They were thus ignorant of the emotional turmoil that swept some of the rooms. They could not grasp the real significance of the action of a man perched on the highest tier in the next room who could be clearly seen. He was flat on his back gazing at the pictures of his wife and children and wiping the tears that coursed down his cheeks. Rather notorious for being soft regarding his wife, they interpreted this scene as an outburst of his loneliness, but the next morning when they learned of his real concern they were not unsympathetic.

The possibility of attack and probability of a swim were no groundless fear. Soldiers told them that they were in a convoy of nine ships with the large *S.S. Lurline* in the center. The *General Grant* was at the front with a destroyer on each side. When the ships left Honolulu, Mr. Ihara who had been in the Japanese Navy told his friends that the sound of the screws was not altogether right and perhaps there might be propeller trouble. On about the fifth day out the engines stopped and the internees thought San Francisco Bay was entered because it was about the right number of days out of Honolulu. But after three hours the ship began moving again. They were later told that the ship had to get out of convoy for repairs for about ten hours cruised along.

Among the numerous lectures and story sessions at Sand Island, Rev. Kuchiba related shipwrecks he had experienced in the South China Seas on two occasions. "Whenever you get into a shipwreck there are certain things to remember. Wear as much clothing as you can on your person. Once you find yourself in the water the most important act is to grab for some object that will help keep you afloat. The third injunction is never swim. Every bit of energy must be conserved. Most death comes from freezing. Even in tropical seas prolonged immersion could chill the body through and through. To keep floating, hang on to any large object that floats and your strength will be conserved. If one keeps on effortlessly floating then the chances of rescue become better. I once hung on to a cabin table with two more men and the prevailing wind pushed us to the shores of South China. Not to swim falls in line with the second point, but is significant in that it is meant for the best swimmers as well. All available energy must be conserved for survival."

Seikichi Arata remembered every detail of this talk which seemed so apropos to the situation at hand. Remembering these admonitions, he kept his woolen underwear handy.

A loud speaker system announced from time to time different orders to the entire ship. Once or twice a day there would be, "All gunners, man your posts," and then there would be the "rat-tat-tat" of guns firing and occasionally cannon roars could be heard.

About three days out of Honolulu there was another order, "All soldiers, sailors, and noncommissioned officers, turn in your radios." Such orders kept the men jittery although probably all stemmed from security measures.

To while away time much singing, card playing, and story telling were in progress. A young man, Mr. Hashimoto, was desperately seasick in the beginning, but in the last few days he was able to eat and he finally related to his roommates in elaborate detail a most passionate love story. It made Arata recall stories of Boccaccio's *Decameron* he once read in translation and envied the vitality of youth that these men still enjoyed.

Mr. Matsuda, manager of the Yokohama Specie Bank, had a bunk next to Arata and they had intimate talks to while away the time. He had been in Honolulu only a year, but had been stationed in countries of Southeast Asia: Singapore, Java, Burma, and China. "You must have certain views on the Japanese problem in Hawaii and the United States since you lived most of your life in Hawaii."

"Yes, I have a positive one. Although we are not allowed naturalization I think that is a small point in the whole picture. We first generation will be gone in twenty years. Then all our descendants are by birthright American citizens. There will be no alien Japanese. All will be bonafide citizens. That apparently settles the question legally," mused Arata.

"You seem to have other ideas too," observed the bank manager.

"A few years ago, Gordon Chun-Hoon became a star football player at the U.S. Naval Academy. I was envious of the Chinese. They are accepted already in the most exclusive schools. The Chinese were the first to be excluded as a race from the United States, but now are admitted to the Naval Academy. No man who has Japanese blood in his veins has been given a job at Pearl Harbor. Even the Hawaiian National Guard will not accept more than ten percent Japanese on its roster. Our sons and grandsons are not trusted yet. This is a sad situation. This war has precipitated matters. How it will turn out for us Japanese on American soil, God only knows!"

"Maybe you can all return to Japan. If Japan wins or a negotiated peace is realized there will be unlimited opportunities for your children under the Japanese flag."

"No, that is not to be! The ideals and thoughts of our children and grandchildren are American. How can they get along in Japan? Even for me, Japan is not the place to live. I only hope the day will come that our grandchildren will be accepted at both Annapolis and West Point. Whether it will come while I am alive I do not know. But I know some day it will arrive and that day will mark the happiest turning point in the history of Japanese in America. So far it has been one sad event after another and this war marks the culmination."

On the second of March the convoy arrived at San Francisco Bay. About one-and-a-half hours later the internees climbed up the stairway to the main deck with their duffel bags and marched down the gangplank to the wharf. After being accounted for, they were transferred to the custody of the military police from Fort McDowell. Toward sunset they were ordered to get on a huge tugboat. The MP's were a lot more decent than the ones that had accompanied them from Honolulu. As the tugboat sped north, Oakland, Berkeley, and Richmond became resplendent with lights. There was a full moon. After three months of total blackout, the lights of the cities to the right were so beautiful that Arata without thinking turned to the engineer, "No blackout here?"

The pilot looked at him rather pointedly, "Who do you think we are? Afraid of you fellows?" and returned to his job of piloting.

The boat was moored to the wharf at Angel Island.

CHAPTER 24

To Wisconsin

THE HAWAIIAN CIVILIAN INTERNEES WERE housed in a large dormitory that used to receive the Oriental immigrants for three quarters of a century: first the Chinese laborers imported to work in the construction of the Southern Pacific Railroad that linked the west to the east, and later the Japanese immigrants to develop the agricultural wealth of California. They were ordered to leave their duffel bags and suitcases in a downstairs room. In groups of ten they were systematically processed in fingerprinting, photography, and physical examinations. Of all the examinations undergone, this place had the most efficient system. It was done thoroughly and slowly and it took from 9 o'clock to 6 in the morning. Seikichi Arata's turn did not come round until 4 A. M.

Charley Hashiba saw among the officers some of his old friends at Schofield Barracks near which cantonment he had run a bar. He was appointed to interpret. Arata was delegated to conduct the men from one place to another. There were half a dozen Mexicans among the soldiers whose duty it was to guard and order the internees to move in regular order without delaying the procession. One of the Mexican corporals gave Arata an apple. This simple act touched him deeply. Funny how humans react to trifling gestures under certain circumstances and he could recall very few acts toward which he felt so grateful.

After the fingerprinting and photographing, which were repetitions of those at Honolulu, they were each given two blankets and conducted upstairs. In one of the rooms they were told to spread one blanket on the floor and proceed to the next room stark naked. In this next room a medical officer made a cursory examination, looking primarily for infectious diseases. While this was being done, the non-coms went through their clothing. Arata thought this was a most efficient way of searching and examination. When done they were allowed to put their clothes on, led to a large room, and assigned beds. There was no time for sleep for at seven o'clock they had to stand in line for breakfast.

Then for six days there was a chance to do laundry, to stretch, to take showers, and to recuperate from the ten day ordeal in the prison ship. They sighed with relief when they saw rows of toilet bowls which they were at liberty to use at any time of the day. This privilege was such luxury!

California countryside in early March with its birds singing, cherry and acacia trees blooming, was a feast for their hungry eyes. Even the misty mornings that blanketed the bay region were invigorating to them who came from the tropics. They would not have complained even if they had to spend several months at this place, even in captivity.

It was soon noted that there was no order to the way the mess room was conducted. A suggestion was made to the lieutenant that the internees were willing to help in the kitchen. Volunteers were called. Mr. Masao Sakamoto took charge of the task and soon they were having rice boiled and prepared to their satisfaction. The mess hall became spick-and-span. The military cooks were pleased to have willing help to do the menial work and the Japanese were glad to get additional helpings, for the cool climate whetted their appetite.

About an hour after meals three times a day they were allowed to make use of the flat terraced ground above the dormitory. They walked back and forth to stretch their legs, played catch, or merely sat out in the sun gazing lazily at the ferry boats, the river boats, and the naval vessels and tankers that plied between Mare Island and San Francisco. Angel Island was called Fort McDowell. Their duffel bags were again examined for contraband. A Catholic father came in and talked to Italian prisoners in particular. He brought newspapers and old magazines and these were avidly read by the news-hungry men. The first intimation of the mass evacuation of Japanese from the West coast was gleaned through these newspapers.

These wooden dormitories were old and the beds were three-tiered. But the beds were so old that the springs were sagging. On the walls, there were elaborate carvings of Chinese characters that told the emotional life, frustration, and hopes of Chinese immigrants brought over to work on the Southern Pacific Railroad then under construction. Vociferous protests to the inhumanity of deportation, the elation of arriving at the port of the "Golden Mountain," for such was the name of San Francisco in Chinese, were composed in poetry of flamboyant language.

While at Sand Island, in order to maintain health, every morning at 10:30 physical exercise was made compulsory by the commandant. Only men excused by the doctors were permitted to stay out of these gymnastics. There was a young man among the Germans who had taken a course in physical culture in Vienna and he led his group in a most effective manner. Clad only in shorts they used to exercise and even roll on the sandy ground. There were ex-army men among the Japanese and Dr. Takata got permission to have Mr. Kabashima, an ex-artillery officer, talk to this German instructor about modifying his physical exercises to suit elderly persons.

The military authorities at Sand Island were pleased in a way to have them go through this drill, and apparently under the Geneva conference war prisoners are encouraged to conduct their own military drills for health reasons. Since the detainees were considered more or less in the same category these martial exercises were encouraged. Now at Angel Island someone suggested that they go through the same drill in this invigorating cool climate. Everybody willingly joined under the leadership of Mr. Kabashima. In one of the drills called *Ken tsuki taiso*, the flexed arms were held at the side of the chest with the hands clenched in fists. The legs were kept apart. With the first cry of *Yoyasa* the arms were shot upward, and with the second *Yoyasa* they were brought down to the original position at the side of the body. With the third yell, the arms were shot downward bending the knees at the same time and with the fourth the body and arms returned to the original position and station.

The entire group joined in enthusiastically with wild cries of *Yoyasa no yoyasa, yoyasa no yoyasa*, the body going up and down forcefully with these exhortations. In the still morning air of Angel Island this cry echoed and reechoed from the hills across the Bay to the slope behind them and as one of the Italians told Arata later, even the old men were putting everything they had in these exercises. From the barracks above this dormitory, hundreds of soldiers tumbled out to view this strange spectacle. It was later discovered that three good sized rocks had been hurled into the crowd and this was the end of mass physical drill.

On March 6th, orders to move arrived and the group boarded the same tugboat. It skirted around Treasure Island and tied up at one of the freight piers of Oakland. A train, the windows of which were lined with meshed screen, was in a siding and the internees boarded the old coaches. These were apparently used for transportation of criminals or Chinese immigrants landed at San Francisco but destined for Mexico. Forty members were sardined into each coach. For three days and three nights they had to sit in one position with only a blanket to keep them warm. The interior of the coaches was cold because both ends were open and the steam heat was inadequate because of this overventilation. Soldiers with shotguns were stationed at each end of the coach.

At large stations strict regulations to lower the shades and keep to one's seat were enforced. When the train was in motion they could move about in the coach, but this exercise was very limited and consisted mostly of going back and forth to the latrine, the door of which was absent. The user had to face the entire congregation of passengers. One of the guards who said he hailed from Lodi, California loaned Arata a pack of cards of which the men made good use. He also told them of the unfortunate discrimination against the Nisei soldiers in his outfit stationed near Santa Rosa. The Nisei soldiers inducted into the army prior to Pearl Harbor Day were discharged summarily because of their race, and he was bitter about the treatment accorded to his erstwhile buddies by the army.

The route eastward was on the Southern Pacific. The internees, astonished at the great expanse of unproductive desert land of Nevada, were like children when they crossed the Great Salt Lake. At Ogden, Utah, their train was routed over to the Denver-Rio Grande Railroad and traversed the most scenic route of the transcontinental railways. While passing through a tunnel in the Continental Divide they became blackened with soot which filled the interior of the coaches because both ends were open. After following the Arkansas River from its very beginning they saw on each side the snow-covered valley which was reputed to be beautiful in summer. Before they came to the Royal Gorge and Pueblo the train veered north through Denver and into the plains of Nebraska and Iowa. A small town in southwest Wisconsin, called Sparta, was their destination. Camp McCoy near this town was to be their temporary abode.

CHAPTER 25

At Camp McCoy

WHEN THE TRAIN STOPPED AT A SIDING there was an area covered with rows and rows of old black buildings enclosed by barbed wire fences. A welcoming committee was out near the railroad tracks. Alongside the officers, there were about thirty steel-helmeted soldiers armed with guns and fixed bayonets. The first group of men to clamber down from the train were those that occupied the last coach. Since this coach had no bars on the windows, only old men apparently too frail to escape had been grouped together. All of these men were either grey haired or bald. When they came down and lined up on the snowy ground, the soldiers must have felt silly. Evidently they expected fifth columnists from Hawaii: men pictured in the cartoons as having been responsible for the damage at Pearl Harbor. Soon the armed soldiers disappeared and they were found dispersed along the way between the barracks.

Coach after coach disgorged its occupants. It was a tragic sight. Men of different ages were wearing Panama and straw hats, white trousers, some even with tennis shoes. The only winter garment they had was the heavy army overcoat issued at the Immigration Station. The ground was covered with four inches of snow and icicles hung from the eaves of the barracks. The captain who conducted Arata's group of thirty told him that two weeks previously there had been a blizzard and the mercury had been fifteen below zero.

There were eight Japanese men who had preceded them by three days and they had come from Fort Lincoln, Bismarck, North Dakota. These men were interned at Seattle and were international merchants: officials of the Yokohama Specie Bank, Japan Mail S.S. Co., Yamashita S.S. Co., and the Sumitomo Bank. They were at the gate to greet the new arrivals. They had the boiler going for a hot shower, and the barracks were heated with central stoves.

In greeting, Mr. Arai of the Specie Bank said, "When we arrived from the north the colonel came to us and disclosed the news that one hundred eighty Japanese were coming in a few days. He feared that there would be a lot of roughnecks and wanted to find out the best way to handle these arrivals. I assured the colonel that Japanese were different from other races and I was certain no trouble need be anticipated. The eight of us could be entrusted with the entire preparation and everything would run smoothly. The colonel complied with this suggestion and I think he is well satisfied now."

"We are so glad you are here. For one thing these stoves are devices very foreign to us. You must teach us how to keep the fire going all night long."

The landscape of Southwest Wisconsin was made up of rolling hills with an abundance of oak and pine trees. As far as could be seen from the enclosure, the farmers were engaged in dairy industry as barns and silos dotted the valley. In addition to the one hundred eighty-eight Japanese, there were about a hundred mixed European nationals. Most of these were from mainland cities and among them were the leaders of the Deutsche-Amerikanische Bund. Catholic priests, engineers, and professors of language were among them. From the one or two editions of camp paper humorously called "The Latrine," it could be discerned that there were many well-educated, literary-minded men among them.

The men were quartered in barracks constructed in the days of the CCC. In the early 1930's when there was worldwide depression, America was severely affected economically. President Roosevelt organized the Civilian Conservation Corps, recruiting the idle youths of the cities to do public work and reforest extensive tracts of non-productive land under quasi-military discipline. Some boys of this corps were quartered in this camp. The total capacity was one thousand. The Japanese internees were to remain here for seventy days, from March 9th to May 29th.

After the unpleasant experience at Sand Island, the gruelling experience across the ocean, and the train, this period of respite was a complete mental relaxation. They agreed that a great deal of this happy state was due to the unusual personality of one man, Lieutenant Colonel Horace Ivan Rogers, a Detroit lawyer in civilian life who happened to be in charge of this internment camp. He was a man of superb quality, with deep understanding of human nature. He was a rare individual in that he could be a strict disciplinarian as an officer of the United States Army, but he could also, without hesitation, show signs of human kindness when an elastic interpretation of regulations did not infringe with discipline and maintenance of order. He took command several days after the arrival of the Hawaiian contingent.

There were two official roll calls a day: one before breakfast and another at 4 P.M. Colonel Rogers made a practice of personally checking the number at 9 P.M. Leaving two guards of enlisted men outside, he came alone into each barrack. As he walked into the center aisle counting on his hand computer, he nodded a "good night" to everyone.

At first this democratic procedure of the commander was considered as being careless by the internees. They were educated to respect rank, and for a colonel to do this appeared below his dignity. But soon everyone began to admire this particular trait in the man. He was fearless and at the same time courteous. His last words were a "good night," and in a short time most of the men sat up on the bed Japanese fashion with buttocks resting on the soles of their feet, a position usually accorded a superior, bowed to him and returned the smile and "good night" salutation. Not all did, but those who did, and these were in the great majority, performed this obeisance from the bottom of their hearts. Whatever complaints they had, they could speak directly to him on these occasions and he showed no outward annoyance at this direct approach.

One night as the colonel made his rounds, he announced in the last barrack. "There is now in the northern sky nature's wonder that you from Hawaii have not yet seen. From this latitude we sometimes can see it rather plainly and clearly. Tonight there is a typical play of these lights over the North Pole. I'll give you permission to remain outside for an hour to see and enjoy these Northern Lights. You may not have another chance."

Toward the north, half way up the dome of the sky, above the banks of white clouds a long shelf of silvery, boiling lights that extended quite a distance was seen. Since there was no color, the uninitiated might have missed it altogether. The aurora borealis was usually pictured in rainbow colors, but from this latitude it was silvery and not very spectacular. The nearest comparison was a movie taken at night on a black and white film of the overflow of lava from a volcano coursing down the side of a mountain.

Dr. Okimura was elected coordinator of the Japanese group and one day he told the colonel, "As you probably know we went through some very unfortunate experiences during our incarceration. The treatment we received at Sand Island was such as to make us lose our respect for the traditional fair treatment of the American way. The way we were treated on the army transport coming over was really callous inhumanity. Now without any ulterior motive I can say for the group that your treatment of us has more or less taken the sting out of our enforced captivity. Everyone in our group is really thankful and fortunate to be in your custody."

"Well, I look at the whole thing this way. The fact that you are prisoners here is a result of politics. You are the unfortunate victims of international politics. In the last war you were our allies. In the next war you may again be on our side. Therefore, as long as military discipline is observed, there is no sense in making your life any worse than it actually is. Besides, looking over your men, the majority are gentlemen. I have come to realize that I shall have no trouble with you people. As far as you are concerned, I think these fences are not necessary. This is the most interesting episode of my army experience. Yet I am a line officer and have put in my application for combat duty. How long I can be with you I am not certain, but as long as I am here I shall treat you all with human consideration."

Two weeks later an incident took place outside of the camp among young men working on the road leading to the gate of the camp. It seemed that a guard prodded the men with his gun and the workers dropped their shovels and returned to camp.

"Dr. Okimura, your men refused to work and returned to camp today, but that work is necessary for the maintenance of the camp and according to international law you should repair it and keep it in working condition," Col. Rogers opened the conference mildly.

Dr. Okimura countered, "Today's affair was unfortunate in that the soldier used his weapon to direct the workers. That is only a minor point in this question of work or no work. My men contend that they will willingly work to police the grounds they use and do whatever is necessary for their own well-being and health. This magazine here reports on the war prisoners at Zentsuji, Japan. Although Japan is not a signatory to the Geneva Conference on the treatment of war prisoners, she is abiding by the protocols of this international agreement. We want to follow that too. If there were any work to be done the internees should be compensated. Since we are not looking for compensation we shall not work."

"A distance of ten feet outside of the fence must be cleared of grass," insisted the colonel.

"But colonel, that part is outside the fence and we cannot use it in our walks. Therefore the men refuse to clean it."

"It is meant to keep outsiders from getting near the enclosure."

"Then, doesn't it follow that it is your concern as captors more than ours within the enclosure?"

"But the road is different. Trucks use the road to transport your supplies and food. Therefore it is concerned with the maintenance of your subsistence."

"If that idea is to hold water the road leading to the Pacific Ocean can also be construed to contribute to our welfare," laughingly retorted Dr. Okimura. The colonel smiled too, and he showed the coordinator the instructions from Washington concerning this aspect of war prisoner handling. But the colonel was fair enough not to push this point although he could have.

At one time it was reported that about nine knives were missing from the kitchen. All of a sudden the MP's invaded the compound and made a house to house search of the European section. But when they came to the five barracks occupied by the Japanese, the coordinator was summoned.

"Dr. Okimura, go to your men and ask them to produce any article that was 'mistakenly' taken to the barracks." Such an understanding of human nature was a revelation. Needless to say there was voluntary return of anything that was not theirs by the internees.

Mr. Sakamoto was the chef and one day, early in April, he spoke up to the colonel who came to inspect the kitchen. "Colonel, Japanese Christmas is coming pretty soon. Can you, maybe, permit us to hold special services?"

"What do you mean by Japanese Christmas?"

"Most of us are Buddhists. Buddhism was founded by Prince Siddharta of India and he was born on April 8th. It is a special day of observation by us," explained the chef.

"Why, yes. By all means. If you'll let me attend the service, and if that does not interfere with the program, I shall be highly honored."

The colonel was intrigued. "You shall have extra food to celebrate that day too," he added with a smile.

This news was received with joy by the majority of the men and immediate action to prepare for the occasion took place. Rev. Oda was an expert in the art of artificial flower making and was master in the classical art of floral arrangement. He got hold of a large leafless oak branch and transformed it into a flowering cherry tree. He cut toilet tissue paper into hundreds of cherry flowers and dyed the petals with beet juice. Rev. Takahashi fashioned out of a large carrot a nude, newly born prince. Tradition said that as soon as Prince Siddharta was born he took three steps, and pointing to heaven and earth exclaimed, "Between heaven and earth, I alone am holy."

Every man came resplendent in his Sunday best. There were about thirty priests of every denomination and there ensued a very solemn ceremony that was observed by all sects of Buddhism. Rev. Nago with his venerable flowing beard was the chairman and when he alluded to the annual interdenominational flower festival at Waikiki his voice quavered as he reminisced and described the service with deep feeling. Dr. Okimura sat next to the colonel and a major that came along. He explained and interpreted as best as he could about the significance of the ritual.

When it was over, Col. Rogers asked leave to say a few words of thanks for the privilege of being present. He began his speech with "Gentlemen." This simple word was strange to the ears of all. For six months, they had been addressed to as "you guys," and "you so and so," and at best "you men." Even those who did not understand English well knew what the first word the colonel uttered meant. The fact that they were able to hold this religious service was in itself an unexpected good fortune and for the commandant to address them courteously was pleasantly disarming considering the high-strung, taut nerves of the internees. His address brought smiles to many faces that had been habitually brooding and solemn.

As soon as they became adjusted to this wintry climate some men began a strange activity. The roads were covered with hard pebbles brought over from some lake-bed or river to reenforce the sandy ground on which the camp was built. Men were seen crouched on the road for hours. It turned out that they were gathering black and white pea-sized pebbles of uniform flat shape and within a week there were games of

363

go being played in every barrack. Just about this time, *Life* magazine had an issue explaining the game of *go*. From the days of feudal systems this game was very popular among the warrior class as it was based on strategy of surrounding, attempts to escape, counter-maneuver, and a struggle to acquire as much territory as possible. Whereas *shogi*, comparable to the Western chess, was popular among merchants and artisans, *go* belonged to the elite and the military. In an attempt to unravel the mind of the Japanese military, the *Life* staff must have made a study of this game. Inspired by this article, American officers came into camp to watch these games when word spread that the internees were indulging in this pastime. The collection of pebbles did not stop and almost everyone began looking for the beautiful and bizarre.

"Dr. Okimura, what do you think is the motivation behind this trait among the Japanese?" asked Col. Rogers.

Dr. Okimura thought for a little while. "There seems to be an innate characteristic of the Japanese to play with pebbles and rocks, even among grown-ups. This was evidenced at Sand Island when they collected corals and shells. During their childhood there is a period in which boys and girls play with pebbles and mud. Lafcadio Hearn, the author who introduced Japan to the world, marvelled at this pastime among the children and in his inimitable way explained this phenomenon as a racial reminiscence of the legends of the *Sai-no-kawara*. According to this folklore, children in Buddhist purgatory would be piling up stones and pebbles chanting a prayer with each stone for the well-being of parents still in earthly existence. A mean devil would come along and knock down the pile of pebbles with a rake. In this manner the perpetual game of piling up and destruction goes on. Hearn sentimentally saw a connection between this childhood occupation and popular belief."

"That is very interesting. What are the men especially looking for among the stones? Any gem or some such find of monetary value?"

"No, I don't think so. We have no stone of any such hardness in Hawaii and so I doubt if any is aware of the existence of such a stone. They are merely anxious to find something beautiful. And you will be surprised to see some really beautiful hard pieces."

"In that case, I'll send a few truckloads into the area so the old men can divert themselves." And true to his promise three truckloads of lake bottom pebbles were brought in for the specific purpose of giving the men something to occupy their time and have some fun.

Dr. Kohatsu, in charge of the hospital, saw that the pressing problem was to prevent mental deterioration to which many were beginning to succumb. One of the symptoms were the bitter quarrels that used to take place, especially among the older ones in Barrack No. 2. He saw that something had to be done to stimulate them, and he asked for a news broadcasting committee to be formed. It was something vitally needed and his request was immediately taken up.

Every evening, including Sundays and holidays, a daily resume of newspaper and magazine articles and news of Hawaii as gleaned from personal letters were broadcast by three members, headed by Mr. Shiochi Asami, the editor of the Nippu Jiji of Honolulu. Each of the three speakers had to spend from two to four hours of daily preparation to deliver the forty minute report, but it was pleasant duty as the audience was appreciative. Many even took notes at this session, particularly of the editorial trend of the leading newspapers of Chicago and New York.

Someone suggested mass singing before these daily meetings. Many ex-school teachers qualified. An old piano had been brought into the recreation room by Col. Rogers and this served a most useful purpose in maintaining the morale of the group. As days went by the mental state of resignation, to which all had to end up in such a life, overtook them. The people, even the most morose, had to accept the fact that no matter how they fretted they were destined to be interned for the duration of the war. The will to live and the struggle to survive under the worst circumstances asserted themselves and in due course everyone became cheerful. This mass singing had a part in the morale-building, for flushed cheeks and even sparkling eyes were noted at the end of the news broadcast.

As a further step in maintaining and promoting morale at the camp, athletics were encouraged and baseball games were started. The colonel brought in old gloves, bats, and balls. Mr. Uyeda who hailed from St. Louis and who had been a pitcher in the minor leagues during his youth took charge of the league. A grand opening of the inter-barrack series was celebrated when two colonels performed the ritual of pitching and batting the first ball. Almost every day these ball games were played and since men in their fifties took part, one might conclude that the competition was dull. Actually they were hotly contested. Most of these men had played in the "old man's softball league" among the business firms of Honolulu. The championship, however, was not decided. Before that day came the group was transferred to a new home in Tennessee.

When life is strictly curtailed and regimented and when there is uncertainty as to how long the confinement is going to last, the mind works in a peculiar manner. Even those who are not attracted to clairvoyance and fortunetelling would at least become intrigued by predictions made by such men, enough so as to remember and cogitate on the possibility of the outcome when a prophecy was made.

There was a soothsayer among them, Minetaro Hori. He was sixty-eight years old, four feet eleven inches tall, solidly built, and immensely strong. His hair was jet black and slightly curly, although slightly thinning at the vertex. He wore a pair of horn-rimmed glasses and his hearing was extremely poor. One had to shout into his ears to make him understand and he was, therefore, oblivious to gossip and was not particulary interested in the news and events of the world. For this reason, he even appeared dumb. But he had to be specially treated because of his terrific snoring. Nobody wanted to share tents with him. At Sand Island, the "admiral" got the snorers, the teeth grinders, and those that talked in their sleep in one tent. Hori was a member in this special tent.

This man became a popular figure in the contingent. It soon became known that he was a wizard in foretelling dates. Sometime about the middle of January, 1942 he had foretold to those near him that on the 17th day of February the group was leaving Sand Island. At that time there was no intimation whatsoever of any movement, but this old man, by picking up a coral and studying its contour by a method only known to himself, deduced in a mysterious way a concrete fact. It came to pass that on the very day predicted, like a thunderbolt out of a clear sky, they were ordered to pack and were taken to the Immigration Station. At the Immigration Station he correctly foretold the date of sailing.

At Camp McCoy, Hori was treated with a certain amount of respect. Seikichi Arata took special interest in him and supplied him with his allotment of cigarettes because Hori was an insatiable smoker. He told Arata that he had locked himself up in the sacred mountain of Minobu in Japan and had gone through the rough purifying ordeals, much like the fakirs of India, in order to attain a state of mental void or selflessness in which one was privileged to communicate with the mystical and supernatural. He was looking forward to his return to Japan so that he might spend some weeks again in the mountains to further perfect himself in the ways of the gods. He was constantly chewing green pine needles and he claimed that he derived immense benefit from its juice in keeping up his stamina. He was a man of remarkable virility. He cared little about what was happening in the camp.

About the middle of March he announced that on the 18th of April, there would be "startling news coming from one corner of heaven." In Japanese he said, *Ten no ikkaku yori kwai ho kitaru.* He told Arata that this was sure to come true because he had tested this prediction by three methods and all agreed. When such agreement was obtained, one of which came in his dream, then the incident was sure to take place. Such an augury was *shin taku,* or "god's words." His roommates noticed that Hori sometimes had turbulent nights during which he seemed to undergo terrific punishment in his dreams. Even the Germans and Italians looked forward to the 18th of April.

But the startling news coming from one corner of heaven turned out to be the terrific news of the bombing of Tokyo by General Doolittle's raiders. The internees were stunned by the audacity of the fliers, and they had to acknowledge that there was in Hori's soothsaying something that could not be wholly explained by modern science. The "startling news" was a demoniacal one not to the liking of the internees, but Hori was accurate in prophesying the 18th of April as a unique day.

With the passage of months and improvement of morale everyone became resigned to his fate of remaining in this internment camp for the duration. The daily games and activities blunted the edge of the highly strung nerves of the men and reduced them to more or less happy, carefree school children. In contrast, the German and Italian camp was full of bickering and fighting. A distrust of each other was the general rule. No one was sure of the exact status and attitude of the next-bed occupant. Spies in such a camp working for the captors were no rarity. To gain a selfish end, nothing stopped or restrained some people's nefarious actions. Europeans who had come from Hawaii used to come around and watch the baseball games and asked to be allowed to join the teams. They really envied the cheerfulness and the poised attitude of resignation of the Japanese captives. There were two Germans who ran amok, struck the guards, and were placed in solitary confinement.

There was a canteen for the internees and daily necessities could be purchased. Even beer was available and coupons were distributed so that everyone had an equal chance to buy. Germans had a grand time and there was a fellow who drank thirty bottles. Soon the canteen was roaring with German songs. *Wir fahren nach England* topped the many barrack and marching songs, but soon beer was no longer available. A warden does not wish to have boisterous prisoners on his hands.

Cash was allowed, but Hawaiian internees had nothing to spend. When they left the islands they were penniless. All money had been taken away when they were arrested. Each family deposited fifty dollars with the army authorities but nobody knew where that money was. They were not able to buy even a three cent stamp to let the family know that they had arrived safely. Not only this, but all the baggage with warm winter clothes stored in the hold of the *General Grant* did not arrive until May when the weather became moderate and summer arrived even in Wisconsin. At this critical period the eight men from Seattle did a lot for the Hawaiians, buying cigarettes and stamps for them. Many wired home "collect" and got some money, and this amount was shared among friends.

Rev. Oi wanted to start a flower garden and requested some top soil. He asked the colonel in one of his rounds at night for this favor. The request was granted. A truck was to be sent out for this rich soil and Seikichi Arata volunteered to go out as shovel man. He wanted to get out of the enclosure to breathe the air that seemed sweeter. Was there any difference? There was a soldier on the truck beside the driver but so trusted were the Japanese that his presence was a mere formality. The truck sped along a paved highway in the extensive pine covered domain which was a part of the twenty thousand acre Camp McCoy training grounds. On the way, there was a company of infantrymen maneuvering with tanks and war dogs.

As Arata watched the pine tree tops pass by, he tried to visualize the day when he would be on his way back home, free from the chain that tied him down to a miserable existence in such a concentration camp. He imagined he was on a train heading west; he closed his eyes and the jostling of the truck gave him a delusion of freedom and travel. But this beautiful dream was shattered when the truck stopped near a creek and the men got down to shovel soil into the truck.

As far as beautification of ground was concerned, the Germans were superior. Not only did they plant trees around their barracks, but grass and flower beds were prepared. Apparently there was a landscape architect, for a beautiful rock garden was built on the sandy dune that occupied one corner of the enclosure. The oak trees were just beginning to put on their spring garment of young leaves and this sight was very strange and beautiful to the Hawaiian internees. They saw beauty in the spring verdure aside from the more commonplace flowers that usually are associated with spring.

Toward the middle of May the colonel announced that one-half of the group was to move to some southern camp. The other half was to remain at Camp McCoy which was to become a reception center for mainland Japanese internees who were in the two northern camps; namely, Fort Lincoln, North Dakota and Missoula, Montana. Both of these centers were under the Immigration Service and those interned were to be shipped south to Camp McCoy before they were assigned to permanent internment camps under the War Department.

On the 29th of May, orders were changed and the entire group of civilian internees were shipped south. The reason this last minute change was made became apparent later. The 100th Infantry Battalion from Hawaii was to arrive soon after their departure. It was deemed unwise to keep the two groups in the same locality. After all, many sons, grandsons, brothers, and relatives of the internees were serving in this unique combat unit which was destined to win fame on the battlefields of Italy and France. The internees did not know anything about it at that time. On the day prior to departure they chopped about two cords of wood to be used for the cooking stove on the train.

Coaches similar to the ones they came in from San Francisco were used, but the food was worse as they had to do their own cooking. This trip was to last only twenty-four hours and the destination was a military secret. After leaving Sparta, the part of Wisconsin they passed through was beautiful. It was mostly dairy country. Lilac was in bloom, and the landscape was green. Since Rev. Kanow of Nebraska, a graduate in agriculture, was in the same coach, the trip was very instructive. He pointed out the various flowering trees and rock formations on the wayside, indicating glacial markings on the surface of huge boulders that dotted the flat wheat fields. These marks were made by the glacial tongues of the icy mountains as they advanced southward when the earth became suddenly much colder in the icy age. Thousands of years later when the earth became warmer, the ice melted and left a flat, fertile plain in its wake.

The train passed through Milwaukee and Chicago and arrived at Memphis in the morning. From Memphis it headed eastward and began climbing onto higher ground. These people from Hawaii were astounded to see poor white people living in ramshackle houses among the hills. This was the hill-billy section of the Appalachian Mountains. To find such poverty in the richest country in the world was hard to believe.

They were accustomed to think that white people were all well-to-do, for that was the case in Hawaii. No matter how incapable and inefficient, a white skin assured that person a lucrative job and the "Big Five" of the islands saw to it that this number was kept small. White man's prestige was maintained even at the cost of retarding caucasianization of the Hawaiian Islands. Now to see the poor whites in their home ground was a discovery indeed. The train climbed to 2,000 feet to a plateau of many huge oak trees. A large airfield and a town called Tellahoma came into view. Their destination turned out to be a little beyond this town and at a siding trucks were awaiting them.

CHAPTER 26

In the South

CAMP FORREST WAS ABOUT TWO MILES from Tellahoma, population 20,000. It was situated in a southeast corner of the state of Tennessee, bordering the states of Georgia and Alabama. This plateau extended east up to the Cumberland Mountains and an intervening woodland could be seen for about fifty miles toward the east. Many varieties of aged oak trees appeared indigenous to this locality and there were furniture factories along the railroad. The drainage of this plateau seemed incomplete and the camp site was near marshy ground. The internees soon discovered that the chorus of frogs kept them awake half the summer nights. The camp was for about 40,000 troops, both white and colored. A portion of the military camp was enclosed by high barbed wire fences with high watchtowers at the corners and to this area the trucks conveyed them.

Lt. Col. Rogers who had accompanied the internees from Camp McCoy, must have put in a good word for the Japanese because the treatment was good from the beginning. When a member overheard nasty remarks by some of the soldiers who were processing them, he reported this immediately to the officer in charge. The latter immediately relieved these soldiers of their duties. After another baggage inspection the men were conducted to the enclosure. The one hundred and ninety men were divided into two companies. For one month while they sojourned at this camp there was no coordinator.

Lt. Col. Rogers came to see Dr. Takata. "I am about to leave you now. There will be no coordinator at this camp. Each company will act independently under direct supervision of the army. I wish you all luck. You all were fine and acted as gentlemen while in my custody, and I have spoken to the commander, Major Laemmle, to that effect. I am

371

sure you will receive fair treatment from him. I hope all of you will enjoy good health until the war ends."

The men were immediately gathered. "Colonel, we shall never forget you. You have personified the best that we expected of an American gentleman and officer. After the war may we meet again under better circumstances. Now men, let us give three *banzai* for the colonel," and there resounded loud cheers from the assembled men. Perhaps this was the only *banzai* heard during the war in an American army camp for an American officer.

Seikichi Arata stuck with Dr. Takata who became the captain of one of the two companies. He was asked to head the labor battalion, the work of which was merely policing one-half of the enclosure. Mr. Kawasaki was appointed secretary and he did a lot of letter writing for the men, because correspondence was permitted only in English.

The company was under the guidance of a young second lieutenant who was a recent arrival from the Georgia National Guard. In civilian life was an owner and operator of a small telephone company in rural Georgia. Master Sergeant Divine was very capable and was an expert in the handling of men. He went as far as to do little odds and ends for the men, such as buying coats and other necessities whenever he went to town. Instead of his taking roll call and checking the men each day as was done in the other camp, he left this routine to Dr. Takata and his staff. The counting was done at mess time so that men would not be bothered to stand in formation. In the distribution of raincoats and shoes which was later done, he saw to it that his company got new ones. For such little considerations on his part, he won the hearty cooperation of the men and he was free from any trouble or annoyance. He delegated most of the work to the very industrious and obliging Kawasaki. He even gave Dr. Takata a police whistle to be used in signalling to the men in the company.

Major Laemmle was a retired cavalry officer and a good Catholic. He was fair and tried to do his best to make the life of the internees bearable as long as discipline was observed. Araki, who was one of the few Japanese Catholics in the group, worked at the canteen and did much to get favorable attention from the major. A colonel who was in actual command was a wiry, small sour puss who came around once or twice. It was said that his sister was a captive in Manila, and so he was not well disposed toward the Japanese.

Due to the Southern latitude the days were extremely hot, but thanks to the elevation the nights were cool. Almost once in three days terrific electrical storms with pouring rain visited this region. On other days there would be a swift change in the atmosphere resulting in a tornado-like sandstorm followed by a cloudburst so swiftly that many times the men did not have the chance to batten down the storm shutters. Since the water could not seep into the clay soil, it flowed in streams into the stockade from adjacent areas. In order to rectify this situation it was evident that ditches should be dug outside of the compound to carry off the water, but the internees refused to work outside of the area as they did at Camp McCoy. Major Laemmle did not press this point too far and let it go at that.

This camp was built in a peculiar manner. Each hut was on a cement floor and was large enough to accommodate five beds arranged along the walls on three sides. There was a lumber wall about four feet above the floor and wirescreen netting took the place of the solid wall above this level. Boards that opened outward and upward acted as storm shutters; in other words they were like temporary, inexpensive beach huts. To take care of the winter cold there was a small cone-shaped stove in the middle of the room. From this cone a cylindrical tube shot straight up to carry off the smoke.

Ten of these houses were built facing another ten, and in the middle there was a long gravel-filled walk which led to a shower and bathroom with the latrine beyond that. The latter offered very little privacy and passersby on the outside could peep in and see what was taking place. At the opposite end of this walk stood the kitchen. The long middle walk was strewn with sharp, crushed rocks and made walking precarious if not dangerous. Beyond the kitchen and on elevated ground there was a grove of oak trees and beneath these, in the shade, benches were placed where the men could get some respite and relief from the fierce afternoon sun.

The Italians constructed a bowling court a little beyond the oak grove. It was an enclosed area smoothed out to play their peculiar brand of outdoor bowling. Soon there were outdoor motion pictures in this grove of trees.

There was one alert exercise when the entire Gulf area went into a complete blackout under simulated air attack. The only thing the internees had to do was to fall into formation in the oak grove and be accounted for.

Wartime conditions sometimes produce strange encounters which are amusing if taken philosophically. While en route from Wisconsin there were two Italians in a coach. One of them was a former captain in the Italian army. A soldier guard with a shotgun on his lap faced the prisoners and this Italian captain recognized the young soldier as having been an office boy in a St. Louis concern where they were both employed. They grinned at each other. While at Camp McCoy there were two Japanese-American soldiers who perhaps acted as censors of the mail. Of course they never entered the compound, but one night they accompanied Colonel Rogers in his nightly rounds. To his surprise, Mr. Takahashi of the Japan Mail S.S. Seattle office recognized one of these soldiers as having worked at his office prior to the war.

Seikichi Arata mixed with the Germans. He was curious to find out where they came from and what sort of ordeal they had undergone. At this camp the races were free to mingle within the area. The Germans had been evacuated from Panama.

"I am an Austrian and a civil engineer. When the war started, we were all rounded up, I think like you men, and thrown into camp. For two months—and it was the rainy season in Panama when everywhere was muddy— we had to work at the point of guns. During these two months food was so bad I ate only one piece of thin beef," began this intelligent looking man in his early forties.

Arata answered, "In Hawaii the food was excellent. We ate what the soldiers ate. The only thing we wanted was more vegetables."

"Then you were lucky. At last we were to be transferred from Panama to the Gulf States. The steamer was a freighter. Only women were allowed to stay above and we men were ordered to the hold of the ship. The stagnant air in the bottom of the ship was so bad that before the ship began moving several men were about to faint. Harsh words were exchanged between us and the soldiers. The soldiers began to lock the door. Then a German physician placed himself between the door and room and refused to budge. He preferred to be shot rather than die from suffocation. The captain of the guards came because of the rumpus. His sense of humanity was appealed to. He saw the reasonableness of our complaints, and allowed us men to go on deck, too, for fresh air."

"We were also placed deep in the ship and could not go up on deck but ventilation was good," added Seikichi Arata.

"Oh yes, there is an Italian who has with him a note some Japanese gave him in Texas. I'll go and call him," the Austrian left in a hurry and returned with a stout, short, dark man. "Joe, this Japanese man understands English. I think you can give him that note," said the Austrian. "When I was in a Texas camp there was a group of Japanese who came from Hawaii. When we left that place he gave me this note to hand it to any Japanese I might come across. Here it is." It was a note that was rolled up and placed in a Colgate cream tube. Arata opened the note and read the following in Japanese.

To Whom It May Concern:

"We are the third contingent from Hawaii and now domiciled in Houston, Texas. One hundred and nine of us from Hawaii are all well. In this camp there are Japanese from Alaska and California with us. These European internees will be leaving this place for some unknown destination. Maybe this note will fall into the hands of some of our old friends and with that hope we are entrusting it with this friend. It is like putting a note in a bottle and dropping it into the wide ocean but sometimes the wind, current, and tide will carry it to some haven where it may receive welcome.

Y. Kusao
June 1942.

That night at the news broadcast the contents of this note was published. Since no news of such movements was passed by the censors, what became of those left behind at Sand Island was a complete mystery. This was news indeed and it meant that scattered over the different army camps many thousands of Japanese were interned.

While the group remained here Mr. Uyeda of St. Louis and Rev. Kuchiba of Honolulu were taken sick and they were transferred to the base hospital. They received the best medical attention and were grateful for the care. The priest underwent an abdominal operation and because of his scant knowledge of English, two Japanese-American orderlies were detailed to look after him and made his stay anything but lonely. It was later found out that one of them was an X-ray technician, a college graduate, but was specially assigned as an orderly to make Rev. Kuchiba feel at home.

Kazuo Sakamaki, Lieutenant Junior Grade, Imperial Japanese Navy, was in solitary quarters at Sand Island for three months and during this time he had nobody to talk to. A general order was that if any civilian internee was caught talking to him, he would be thrown into solitary. The lieutenant apparently knew about this order and so made no attempt at talking to anyone. The officers and non-commissioned officers used to go to him and exchange a few words. Both sides showed courtesy, saluting each other as befitted officers although belonging to opposing countries. Apparently Lieutenant Sakamaki was not unhappy. The three meals were carried to him by the warden of the camp, a sergeant. He was in the group of the first contingent of Hawaiian cilivian internees that sailed on the *General Grant* and arrived at Fort McDowell on Angel Island.

At Angel Island while the civilian internees were getting their second typhoid and para-typhoid inoculations a sergeant came in to report. Dr. Takata was then helping in the injections as the sergeants prepared the syringes.

"Sir, the captive naval officer does not want to be examined nor to be injected."

"Why doesn't he want to?"

"I do not know. He seems to understand English all right."

"Well, I'll make him take it," and the major stalked out of the room. Evidently he failed for the medical records were not complete until the contingent was ready to leave Camp McCoy for Tennessee.

When the Hawaiian civilian internees arrived at Camp McCoy there was no provision to accommodate any war prisoner and the captain in charge of housing brought the captive lieutenant to the barrack in which Dr. Takata was quartered. He was trying to have the lieutenant remain there for a few nights but was evidently encountering difficulty. Perhaps the interpreter's efforts were not convincing and so the doctor volunteered to smooth things out and joined the conversation. The interpreter conveyed the request, but the war prisoner paid no attention and in his broken, inadequate English was trying to say something directly to the American captain.

"Captain, may I help you in this quandary? Perhaps I can make him understand," offered the doctor.

"Please, go ahead," the captain welcomed the help.

To the lieutenant Dr. Takata spoke in Japanese: "Please do not misunderstand. What the American captain is trying to say is that you are to stay with us civilians for a few days while your quarters are being made ready. While we were at Sand Island, strict orders were issued not to talk to each other, but we are now under a different command. Apparently you are afraid that by your talking to us or mingling with us you will cause us trouble. You may feel assured that we, one hundred and eighty who came on the same boat, are not only glad to have you with us but are really proud of you. If your hesitation is based on sensitiveness due to your present status please dispel that idea instantly. After all, we are all prisoners and we feel no dishonor in remaining in this role. Again I repeat, we have nothing but the highest respect and gratitude for your exploits. Please come in with us, for we shall be only too honored by your presence."

The lieutenant looked at him, digesting what was said for a minute or so, bowed from his hips and said *Onegai shi masu*. (Thank you and I'll leave it up to you.)

For three days and three nights he mingled with the civilians. His features became relaxed. He smiled and listened avidly to the talk that went around but he was not communicative. A few thoughtless men who ought to have known better began pestering him with questions which were embarrassing. He handed a note to the men, the gist of which was to the effect that being in his position it was neither decorous nor right to say anything. Would they please not ask him questions. Yet perhaps it was human nature for the elderly people to be inquisitive as to how this naval officer survived the attack in his midget submarine. Rumor was that each of these subs were manned by two. What became of the other man?

He was segregated after a few days in an adjacent compound and lived in a barrack that could hold forty men. Here he was guarded day and night by a relay of soldiers armed with clubs. The guard was near his person all the time. He had to attend to the furnace himself and while he took a stroll within his compound his guard dogged his trail. It was evident even from a distance that he was becoming a different man. His features assumed a certain harshness and the brooding brow and unsmiling expression betrayed the inner turmoil that was constant. To become a captive was tantamount to joining the legion of the dead. At least that was the philosophy of a Japanese officer. For that reason he refused to submit to physical examination by an enemy doctor, and refused tobacco. He smoked the cigarettes that were on the tray offered by the civilian internee cooks but did not want anything directly from the army. He became stubborn and unreasonable. The colonel offered to tailor a uniform of the Japanese Navy if he would but describe the type, but he steadfastly refused saying that the fatigue uniform of the U.S. Army enlisted men was sufficient and he did not need any better.

There was an occasional visit by a general who was said to be in civilian life a warden of some large penal institution near Chicago. His trained eyes were critical and effective. Following each inspection tour rules became more stringent. New barbed wire fences were constructed between each row of barracks. The implication was clear. His experience had taught him that if a riot should take place among the internees, a measure to contain each segment in smaller groups was the best method and he was ready for such mob action. Chicago gangsters were handled most effectively in this manner! Apparently, to the general's views, the human factor did not count too much, and Lieutenant Sakamaki continued to be under guard twenty-four hours of the day in spite of being within a small barbed wire fence.

Dr. Takata was told by the Jewish medical officer at the dispensary how stubbornly the captive lieutenant was behaving. One day he told the army officer, "Doctor, you have been very good to us. Whenever we needed help you were always ready to provide us with anything that was available. I wish to do something for you. Some time ago you told me you were having difficulty in having Lieutenant Sakamaki submit to a physical examination. I think I can help you in that task."

The army doctor thanked him for the offer and a few days later reported, "I transmitted your offer to the commandant. He said that we might have to ask you to do it. In the meantime if you want to see the lieutenant or talk to him you may do so any time."

Dr. Takata was surprised but did not want to abuse or take advantage of the gesture of the colonel and so the condition remained in status quo. But when the exodus from Camp McCoy became imminent, he was asked to examine the lieutenant. "Lieutenant Sakamaki, it seems we are all leaving together for some destination not yet disclosed and you are going with us. The army has to keep a physical record of all men under custody. We have had our physical examination. It is just a formality. We know you are physically fit because otherwise you would not be what you are. Will you please let me examine you?"

He had specifically asked the sergeant to remain while he made his examination so that there would be no questions asked afterward. Lieutenant Sakamaki, without saying anything, took off his shirt, submitted to everything asked, and cooperated well. Thus ended the stubborn non-cooperation that began from Angel Island and lasted three months.

At Camp McCoy a German doctor who had been in the Austrian army for four years was vehement and used to get into hot arguments with the American officers. "In European countries, an officer is an officer even if he is a captive, and an orderly serves him. Why that officer is lugging his own coal for the furnace escorted by a guard with a club! How would you feel if you were treated like that Japanese officer, should you be unfortunate enough to become a captive, for it can happen you know!"

"It is not that we do not feel like you do. The whole thing comes from higher-ups and we are only obeying orders," answered the medical officer rather apologetically.

At Camp Forrest, although the lieutenant was placed in the same area as the civilian internees, he occupied a separate hut. Again, a guard with a club was in the hut every hour of the day. He was followed to the latrine, on his walks, and even while he was asleep there was a guard within the room. Two medical officers, one a lieutenant colonel and the other a captain, who came to the compound on official duty once remarked, "That war prisoner will some day go nutty. Who can endure being watched that closely twenty-four hours of the day." The comment came from them without Dr. Takata asking them for any opinion.

A week after their arrival at Camp Forrest, Mr. King from the International YMCA of New York came to visit the camp. Leaders of the camp particularly interested in education and recreation were assembled, and in the presence of Major Laemmle had an interview with this social worker. "The International YMCA is trying to do educational work among war prisoners and civilian internees, both among the Axis and Allied Nations. Because hundreds of thousands of men and women are compelled to remain in camps at the prime of their lives, we feel that the idle hours should be devoted to pursuit of learning that would better them culturally and prepare and improve them for something better when the war ends. You have heard of Dr. Schweitzer, a medical missionary to Africa? Well, because of his German nationality he was interned during World War I. He did not pass the time idly. He studied and wrote volumes on religion and music during his captivity. He is a good example of one that utilized this period of inactivity to produce work that could not otherwise have been accomplished as a busy medical practitioner among the African aborigines in the Belgian Congo.

"The YMCA is conducting this program on both sides. The program aims to promote recreation and also to encourage and assist in the formation of educational classes. Any subject can be taught from grammar school up to University subjects. The only exception is chemistry. The only condition we stipulate is that prisoners or internees must furnish their own instructors. We furnish the rest including books and materials."

Then they went into discussion and itemized what articles were desirable. These consisted mostly of books, playing cards, Japanese chess, and even *hanafuda* or flower cards to play games, and after several weeks they arrived at the camp as promised. When this talk was about to end, Dr. Takata decided on the spur of the moment to introduce the plight of the captive lieutenant.

"Major Laemmle, can I talk about Lieutenant Sakamaki? He is not in our group, but we all are vitally interested in him."

"I don't see why not. Go ahead," answered the genial major.

"Mr. King, you said at the beginning of this talk that you were also interested in the welfare and education of war prisoners."

"That is right. In fact that constitutes the greatest part of our work."

"We have a war prisoner with us. He is an officer of the Japanese Navy and we are not at all satisfied or pleased with the way he is treated. He is treated well as far as bodily needs are concerned. But as a medical man I can say that the treatment that was accorded in the last three months is a life no man can endure very long. There will come a time when his nerves will snap and he will be a mental patient. He is constantly under guard, trailed, every one of the twenty-four hours. Knowing that there is no way of escape, why should he be subjected to this infernal irritation. It is punishment of the worst sort. If the army is afraid that he will commit suicide then we can assure you that in his right mind a Japanese officer will not take his life unless he is resplendent in his uniform, for a uniform will make him an officer. But if the present treatment continues then a catastrophe may result because his sanity may be lost," he stopped as he was getting heated in his expostulation.

Mr. King was looking intently at the doctor, "That is a very interesting fact: a Japanese officer will not commit suicide without a uniform. Go on."

"You may feel that I am partial in my views in this regard due to my being Japanese. You can ask and consult your medical officers of this camp for they hold the same opinion and concern. In fact they voluntarily expressed their fear just the other day. I should think that he could be left alone as he was at Sand Island where he led a solitary life but was not hounded day and night."

Major Laemmle interjected, "I have felt the same way and been pondering as to what could be done to better the situation. Perhaps he can be put in a different area and only when he goes out to take a stroll a guard might be detailed to follow him. I am perhaps not divulging military information when I say that Washington considers him 'hot stuff.'" By his attitude one could perceive how humane and gentlemanly the major was.

About a week later, whether this talk had anything to do with the matter or not, Lieutenant Sakamaki was free to attend different classes and meetings, although followed by a guard. The internees could even talk to him and it was evident that the chronic tension of his facial muscles gradually relaxed and he seemed to be a happier man and talked freely about trivial matters. Not a word was uttered about the war or his participation in it. He was still ashamed not to have died. When a movie, *The Union Pacific*, was shown for the first time in the oak grove, the major summoned Lt. Sakamaki and had him sit next to him.

The treatment was to continue in this manner from Camp Forrest to Camp Livingston, the next camp, and he attended as many classes as he could until new prisoners arrived from the South Seas at the Louisiana Prison Camp. He then became teacher and morale officer among the sailors and continued to do so until the end of the war and his return to Japan.

In Wisconsin, warm woolen trousers of the army plus mackinaw coats originally used by the youngsters of the civilian conservation corps were issued to the men. In Tennessee, these were taken away and green shirts and green pants were distributed. To the internees' astonishment, these fitted them perfectly. They wondered about this coincidence, but had to smile when they found out that these green uniforms had been destined for the Philippine scouts for jungle fighting, but with the fall of that archipelago these uniforms were no longer needed and were turned over to captives. Whenever they had to leave the camp for any work outside, such as fetching food stuff or coal, or reporting to the dispensary, this green uniform had to be worn. But the dye was of such quality that after several washings the original khaki color emerged in blotches.

This plateau must have been subterranean in the geological ages for the grounds abounded in fossils of insects and the worm family. The shape of worms was maintained in a harder-than-quartz substance. Just as shells occupied the hours of the men in Sand Island, pebbles at McCoy, Tennessee offered these fossils. Drilling these to make watch fobs became a rage, but without tools it was a very laborious process. Old nails picked up from the ground were used to bore a central hole. A carpenter of the old school devised a simple mechanical rotation gear by the use of a wound string, causing the boring metal to make a turn one way and then another by merely pulling the string and letting it go.

About ten days after their arrival at Camp Forrest, the list of men assigned on the first exchange ship was published. It included thirteen members, ten treaty merchants and three former residents of Hawaii. In connection with this list from which so many were excluded, people began ridiculing Minetaro Hori, the Inari shrine priest and camp soothsayer, concerning his undependable fortune telling because they were not on the list. This was a selfish, cruel thing to say. By this time it was pretty evident that Hori's predictions had an uncanny accuracy regarding dates, but was unreliable as to events, circumstances, and the number involved. The old man was hurt by the fickleness of his friends and became despondent.

Seikichi Arata sought him out. "Don't feel bad about the *Gripsholm* Exchange of Prisoners. I know you promised many that they could have a free passage to Japan. You yourself believed you could go. Don't pay any attention to the malicious tongues. I bet they will come crawling back for some service later on. Your predictions came true for the thirteen fellows. Your August 23 prediction will be a happy day for the passengers of the *Gripsholm* because about that day they will set foot on Japanese soil. Therefore I don't think you have failed."

He seemed to appreciate this interpretation and after that whatever prediction of the future he made, he revealed it to a picked few, among them Arata. Early in June he said that at least one person was returning to Hawaii. This prophecy came true, but it was eighteen, all of them citizens who had been mistakenly taken out of Hawaii. Under martial law in Hawaii, citizens of the United States were held in camp, but it was illegal to keep citizens behind barbed wire in the Continental United States even in war time.

On the day when the thirteen picked to board the *Gripsholm* were about to leave camp, all the camp inmates gathered around the gate. Each member was checked against the photograph that had been taken at Angel Island. As they lined up ready to go, the congregation sang *Aikoku Koshinkyoku* a patriotic song then in vogue. Those who sang felt their voices quiver; those leaving felt tears unashamedly running down their cheeks. Months of camp life had bound them like brothers. Whatever differences of opinion might have arisen in camp were forgotten in this scene of leave-taking, and the best trait in them came forward and they wished the departees "Bon Voyage."

It was rumored that Camp Forrest was set apart as a camp for Japanese Internees and capable of accommodating 3,000 inmates, but eventually Italians were to remain here and the Hawaiian contingent was to move again. Their sojourn here was only one month. The next travel was again twenty-four hours.

After an uneventful boarding of the train, the course retraced itself to Memphis, crossed the Mississippi River, and entered the swamplands of the delta district of Arkansas. It was interesting in that they had seen the very beginning of the Arkansas River in Southern Colorado in the Rockies when they were brought east over the Denver, Rio Grande Railway. They had seen the frozen Arkansas River at the stage when it was no wider than a brook and in their wanderings they were crossing the wide, swollen Arkansas River just as it joined the mighty Mississippi River. To the Hawaiian internees the great expanse of this swampy region was a revelation of how great, undeveloped areas still awaited the industrious. The unusual nocturnal beauty of the swamplands, suddenly lit up by myriads of fireflies that were stirred from their resting places among the tall reeds and underbrush by the roaring onrush of the train, was to be long remembered.

The following morning the train arrived at Camp Livingston which was situated on elevated ground in the flat delta country of Louisiana.

Rev. Kanow of Scotts Bluff, Nebraska, was an agriculturist as well as a minister of the gospel. He utilized this opportunity to educate his fellow internees in things American, material, and cultural. He believed in America and did not feel ashamed of being interned for security reasons if the FBI thought it was the only way. He told the Hawaiian contingent that the state of Louisiana was not much above sea level and the highest ground was scarcely over 500 ft. Camp Livingston must have been on the plateau section for it was sandy, covered by groves of Georgia pine, and delightfully like Japan. From the standpoint of agriculture it was unproductive but ideal for soldiers going on maneuvers. It was about ten miles from the city of Alexandria. The train proceeded into a branch line that entered the military cantonment and to the left an enclosed area with towers was seen. Everyone guessed that that was their destination, but it turned out to be a military prison camp for American soldiers.

When the internees alighted they were told to leave the larger baggage at the depot and to carry only the smaller suitcases. The more suspicious ones held on to their belongings because they were not told that a three mile hike awaited them. They must have presented a very entertaining spectacle as they marched along on the paved highway with suitcases in each hand or slung over their backs, marching two abreast with armed guards on four sides. They sweated in the afternoon heat. Frequent rests in the shade of pine trees had to be taken.

Nurses of the hospitals and soldiers idling in camp came out to view this strange procession. Several soldiers tried to snap pictures, but these were stopped by the escorting military police and one camera was confiscated by the captain of the guard.

In front of Seikichi Arata was a Mr. Matoda who was loaded with two suitcases. He was a notorious, chronic "belly-acher" since Sand Island days. For him Arata had no liking. Perhaps when this man, who should be mellow by now at his ripe age of sixty, showed an antagonistic attitude on every subject big or small it was just for the sake of differing. Whenever one advocated "East," he would insist on "West." His pugnacity was notorious in Honolulu politics, and internment did not soften him. But now under the Louisiana sun when Arata offered to relieve him of one of the suitcases, he did not demur. This was about the only time that he acquiesced to any proposition without voicing a protest. It was funny and there was impishness in Arata when he took over the excess baggage.

The destination was the familiar enclosed area: the double fence with watch towers interspersed outside. When they entered the gates there were huge characters *Kwangei* or "Welcome" written on wrapping paper and there came a tremendous outburst of shouts in unison, *Banzai*. It made them feel good to be royally welcomed. The one hundred eighty men were divided into two groups in alphabetical order and Arata was placed in the J area. The other half were quartered in the K area.

Seven hundred Japanese internees had preceded them to this place from Fort Sill, Oklahoma. Among these were 400 West Coast men, 160 from Panama and Costa Rica, and 150 from the Hawaiian Islands. These Hawaiians were the second contingent composed mainly of men arrested on the islands other than Oahu.

The J area was peopled by Panamanians and the Hawaiians, whereas the K area was occupied by the Stateside Japanese. The barracks in this camp were more spacious than at Tennessee and cleaner and newer than at Wisconsin. They were about three feet above ground built in rows along a gradual slope of a pine grove. Ten beds could be accommodated in each barrack. Mosquito screening and storm shutters were built in along the same pattern as the huts in Tennessee.

About 500 men were to be quartered in each section and these were divided into two companies because two mess halls served each area. Japanese internees occupied only two of these, but the entire internment camp enclosure was enough to accommodate 5,000 prisoners. The new arrivals from Tennessee had swollen the population to about 900 and one war prisoner.

Newcomers to an established society are always at a disadvantage. For various reasons, the leaders of the Tennessee group decided to become assimilated and to cooperate harmoniously with the then-established governing body. This spirit was especially necessary in the J area which was dominated by the second contingent Hawaiian group which was made up of men from other islands. Any hint or tone of criticism from the new arrivals was certainly to be construed in an ill way by the men running the company and this reaction all wanted to avoid. There was a small faction among the new arrivals that was not satisfied with the status quo and clamored, although not too loudly, for a separate company of Honolulu men, but the majority were glad to just melt into the existing body and enjoy the leisure and carefreeness without sharing in the headache and responsibility of running this conglomeration of individualists. It was funny and revealing of human nature that there was a play and desire for power regardless of the station in life or the question of profit.

The people from Panama were in a different category. Most of these people had been barbers in the republic of the isthmus. Barbershop operation was cash business and the initial investment was comparatively small. After several years at this trade a small amount of accumulated cash enabled the barbers to branch out into other mercantile pursuits of respectability and gentility. As the Jews in the United States could get a good start by peddling, so the Japanese got a start by cutting Panamanians' hair, but before the war they lost their shops by stringent anti-Japanese laws. Having lost their means of earning a livelihood, they became destitute and appealed to the Japanese government for help. The last Japanese commerical liner speeding to the Pacific coast, but which had to return to Japan because of the Pearl Harbor attack, was to have picked them up to transport them home. These people spoke no English. Their talk was Japanese and Spanish. When they arrived in Oklahoma from Central America, they were treated cooly by the mainlanders. They met with more brotherly feeling from the Hawaiians. That was the reason why they elected to be in the J area with the Hawaiian contingent when they were removed to Louisiana.

The leader of this group was Mr. Amano who was a graduate of an engineering college in Japan, and had become successful in diversified fields of activity. He conducted a large department store in Panama City, leased many thousand acres of forest lands in Chile, owned fishing boats that fished along the coastal waters of Central America with bases in Costa Rica, and was interested in growing medicinal plants in the mountainous region of Peru where the cinchona plants for quinine were indigenous. He had married a girl of Japanese-Peruvian mixture and laid his roots deeply into South American soil. He had left for Japan on the *Gripsholm* at the first exchange of civilian prisoners, but his trusted aide was spokesman for the one hundred sixty men from Central America. Several of these had Panamanian wives whom they were planning to take home to Japan, but these women were in another camp in Texas.

The Louisiana scenery reminded the Hawaiian Japanese of their mother country. Pine trees are not found in Hawaii and to live among these trees, listening to the whirring sound of the leaves, made them feel that indeed they were away from their adopted country. The high humidity was similar to Japanese summer months. But the presence of deadly snakes sent a chill up their spine.

Dr. Ohata of Maui brought out a jar with a beautiful snake preserved in formalin. "This snake is called the coral snake. It is beautiful, is it not? Red, yellow, and black mottlings on its short body. I heard that this is the most deadly snake of the North American continent."

"How did you catch it?" asked a curious young man who was spellbound by the beauty of the reptile's skin.

"Oh, I did not catch it. When we first arrived there were quite a few roaming around because this section was not occupied. All together six were killed in this J area alone. It was so beautiful someone tried to capture it to make a pet. Luckily he was not bitten. It is said that within a few short minutes the victim will become paralyzed by the poison. It is related to the cobra of India, and *habu* of Okinawa. I heard from the medical officer that there is no anti-serum. So be careful at night. It may lurk in the grass or hang from a pine branch."

The people were impressed. Coming from a snakeless country, reptiles were interesting and fearsome. "What kind of poisonous reptiles are found in this country? I heard of the—rattlesnake."

Dr. Ohata was apparently interested in snakes. That he kept a specimen was enough to class him as a naturalist. "There are four varieties. The rattlesnake, the water moccasin, the copperhead, and this coral snake. A strong medicine is being manufactured to neutralize this poison when one is bitten. Immediate injection of this anti-serum will make the snake poison ineffective. This anti-serum is effective against the first three snakes. The coral snake, like the Indian cobra, has a poison that hemolyzes blood. It melts the blood corpuscles down to liquid. Therefore, it is 100% fatal."

The heat was very intense during the day and soon men learned to dig into the sandy soil under the houses. Fortunately the floor of the houses were at least three feet high and it was not much of a job to dig a nice hole to escape the heat of the day. Sloping ground made these excavations easy. It was a funny sight and reminded an onlooker of a chicken resorting to similar tactics during summertime on a farm.

Most of the men from the West coast and Hawaii were in the fifth or sixth decade of life, but those from Panama were younger. These men decided to have wrestling matches. An earthen outdoor ring was constructed according the regular Japanese *dohyo* or wrestling arena on the slope of a small gully between the two adjoining enclosures. When this arena was built and ready for use, Rev. Miyao of the Izumo Taisha Shrine of Honolulu conducted the purification ceremonies. Rev. Tatsuguchi used to be one of the best collegiate wrestlers in the Kansai district of Japan. He became the coach and every evening for one-and-a-half hours there was a great throng to enjoy the rough and tumble of this very fast competitive game which is perhaps the cleanest of all sports. It is a contest in the measure of superiority in the art of bodily combat without weapons or tricky holds. The factor of weight difference is also negligible, and skill and wiriness play a deciding role in the outcome.

The army provided a barrack with mattresses to cover the floor. Judo classes were started and there was ample opportunity to improve in this art as there were many third, fourth, and fifth class men who were entitled to wear the black belt, to act as teachers.

An array of equally accomplished fencers was among the group. Two *renshi* class swordsmen were among the Hawaiian contingent. This rank is about the highest award granted instructors of this art. Japanese swordsmanship, much like the German use of the broadsword, was perfected during the feudal days when men depended on the use of the sword to prove their utility to the reigning war lords. Adherents of this sport encouraged it even in the days of firearms, from the standpoint of character building. These men fashioned wooden swords with which they began mass practice in the fundamental forms and movements, accompanied by a yell (*kakegoye*) to keep rhythm and add zest to the exercise.

The commandant countenanced and even encouraged different sports, but could not tolerate this display of martial exercise. These wooden swords in capable hands could be just as destructive in hand to hand combat as the steel of the *samurai* swords. This ban on the sport of *kendo*, or swordsmanship, was not resented. The reason for its disfavor was reasonable when one placed himself in the position of a commandant entrusted with the orderly conduct of a thousand or more "potentially dangerous" individuals. The inmates accepted the prohibition in good grace. A nine hole golf course was constructed in an empty area and enthusiasts began practicing daily with capable instructors like Mr. Uyeda from St. Louis who was a semi-professional.

"Arata-san, we of the outer islands had it easier after Pearl Harbor than you on Oahu. On Kauai and Maui we were even allowed to see our families and home cooking was brought in to supplement the prison fare. We were detained in the county jail and the wardens were local people. But on the Island of Hawaii people were detained at the Kilauea Military Recreation Camp and being under the military, treatment seemed to have been rigid. Above all, at 4,000 ft. elevation, they suffered from cold," a merchant of Lihue reminisced as he called upon Seikichi one day. It was good to talk about sundry matters concerning Kauai and recall the "good old days" on the Garden Island. Both of them had spent most of their youth and the prime of life there.

"Not only that, you people were luckier than us on the passage to San Francisco. It was a virtual hell for us in regards to natural elimination," said Arata.

"Yes, we heard about your plight. But perhaps you will be interested to learn of the barber who was shot at the Oklahoma camp. I know because I witnessed the shooting. I was involved as a material witness. I got a copy of the account prepared by a committee to be filed with the Spanish Embassy for future reference. Maybe you want to read it. I'll leave it with you."

Seikichi Arata took the copy to Dr. Takata who read the detailed report and told him about the content, the essence of which was the following. "This man was found to be acting rather queerly but was not hospitalized nor examined by medical men. One morning after breakfast, two men who were taking a stroll along the fence saw, to their amazement, this quiet man running parallel to and very near the inner fence. On the other side of the fence a soldier was running with his hands on his pistol holster. This meant only one thing. The inmate on the inside was being trailed by a guard who sensed a get-away. When the inmate came to the gate he climbed over the lower portion of the inner fence without much difficulty and then tried for the outer gate. His success was due to the fact that at the gate there was no inwardly protruding extension of barbed wire. By this time the two spectators ran after the Japanese who apparently was intent on escape. They yelled at the top of their voices, 'Soldier don't shoot. He's crazy.' But the shadowing soldier by this time drew his revolver and when the internee was climbing the outer fence he began taking aim. The guard who was on a nearby tower also yelled to his comrade on the ground, 'Don't shoot,' but without avail. Three shots resounded in the quiet morning air and the man fell dead. Dr. Sekiyama was instantly summoned and he pronounced the man dead. A few weeks later, Dr. Sekiyama, the two witnesses, and two representatives of the internees were asked to testify before the court-martial, but they were not even given a chance to tell their side of the event. They merely warmed the bench for two hours in the ante room. The soldier was acquitted."

"Dr. Takata, is there any question as to the unbalanced state of mind of this man who in broad daylight climbed the fence?" inquired Seikichi.

"None whatsoever. He was insane," answered the doctor in deep thought.

"Then under civilized practice, is it condonable to acquit this soldier? Even his fellow soldier admonished him not to shoot! That soldier must have had a very itchy trigger-finger. He must have waited for an opportunity like this to vent his hatred on us."

"That is one way to interpret the incident, and is chiefly our way of judging it. But the other side must also be judged fairly. That the witnesses were not even questioned must have been due to the reason that the soldier was doing his duty as ordered. He must have been cleared because he was following his superiors' instructions like a good soldier."

"I do not understand. Why should a soldier be acquitted and condoned for an act that is so brutal?" Arata was unconvinced.

Dr. Takata was now smiling. "In all military organizations unquestioned obedience is the first requisite. No matter how absurd the order, commands must be carried out without question. The success of military operations is based on this unswerving, uncompromising concept. If every soldier or officer were to interpret a situation according to his own capability, coordination is impossible. To let you understand it more easily, I once saw a cartoon of a German soldier using a hose to water the lawn in a pouring rain. The caption of this cartoon was 'a perfect soldier.' His order was to water the lawn, and he continued to do so in spite of the rain. The strength of the German army is this obedience."

"But this incident revolves about a man being shot. Nothing like working a hose."

"Yes, that is true. But this soldier was apparently instructed to shoot anyone climbing the fence. He was not to use his discretion. When a soldier can prove that he acted according to orders the entire army must stand behind him. This is the United States Army's stand, I am sure, and I think the Imperial Japanese Army would do likewise," Dr. Takata patted Arata on the shoulder. "There are always two sides to any question. To change the subject, how is your grandson making out?"

Arata was jolted back to a subject more real and near to him. "I was just informed that he is with the 100th Infantry and of all places, training at Camp McCoy. Apparently that regiment moved in right after we left there for Tennessee."

CHAPTER 27

A Soldier Visits His Grandfather

EDWIN ARATA WAS ON A SOUTH-BOUND train. Many things had happened in the years' time since Pearl Harbor Day. That weekend he was at home, but called back to Schofield Barracks by radio announcement. He went down to the Army and Navy YMCA hoping to get on a bus, but none was available. At the corner of Fort and Beretiana Streets he was picked up by a soldier and returned to camp and put to digging trenches. Then came the humiliating experience of having their guns taken away. Only soldiers bearing Japanese names were singled out. Although he himself had only half Japanese blood, his name classed him as Japanese. In a few days the rifles were restored with apologies, but the feeling was not the same. They felt they were not trusted.

A humorous but poignant talk at camp then was of a comrade that turned to his friend of Japanese extraction and said, "If the Japs land, who I shoot? You or the Japs."

The patrolling of beaches came next, as the draftees who were in basic training were incorporated in the 299th Infantry of the Hawaiian National Guard. Finally the formation of the 100th Battalion took place and all men with Japanese blood were transferred to this unit. Quite a few full-blooded native Hawaiians, reluctant to become separated from their buddies, falsified their ancestry and joined this outfit. It made the boys feel very happy.

The officers were picked men too. Col. Turner was Hawaiian born, and all others had resided in the territory for a number of years and understood the boys' ways. Japanese officers in this combat unit were all lieutenants. It seemed to be a rule of the War Department that no captaincy was to be given officers of Japanese extraction, although there was a Captain Kawasaki in the medical division.

When they arrived in Wisconsin there were brawls with civilians at first and then with the Texas Second Division boys. Colonel Turner went to bat for his boys in all cases and came back with fire in his eyes.

"When you go into town, don't go singly. Behave yourself and don't get into trouble if you possibly can. But sometimes you cannot back out. When you go into a bar and have a just cause to resort to fists, first look around and size up the situation. If you think the odds are against you retreat gracefully. But if you think you can beat them, go ahead and give them hell. I'll be behind you."

Edwin Arata saw tears well up in his lieutenant's eyes. Lieutenant Fujita used to say, "We are being watched by the entire nation. Let us give all we've got. Show the whites, that we, though small in stature, can out-match and out-fight them. Let us fight for our parents, brothers, and sisters living in Haiku Maui, Hakalau Hawaii, Lihue Kauai, and Honolulu, who are permitted to remain in their homes. We have to return this consideration of the army by letting our blood flow freely wherever we are sent." As a consequence, training was very intense and hard. But *esprit de corps* was high. Everyone knew what was expected of him.

The people of Sparta, Wisconsin, were very nice to the boys after they got to know each other. Invited to homes, the boys reciprocated in Japanese fashion by bringing gifts to all and especially to the older folks of the family. Courtesy is appreciated the world over. To be a little different sometimes adds spice to an act. Edwin particularly remembered the afternoon he spent at a home with a few buddies when the guests did all the dishes to the amazement and delight of the women folks. Hawaiian articles began to arrive as tokens of appreciation for the kind Wisconsin people. It was a beautiful fraternization.

Now Edwin was going to meet his grandfather in a Louisiana camp. Naturally it was an extremely abnormal situation fraught with damaging factors that could destroy the morale of a soldier who could with justifiable reason react violently to the incongruity of the situation. What was he fighting for? Col. Turner allowed him to visit an internment camp because his father in Honolulu urgently wrote the colonel for this permission. Of course the colonel was afraid of the possible effect on the young, pliable minds of the soldiers when they would see their kin incarcerated behind barbed wire. Edwin Arata was to be a test case. Whether his mixed blood was going to be a leavening factor to modify the impact and effect a favorable turn of events it was hard to say, but it was a likely reason that Col. Turner finally decided to grant this permission.

When the 100th Battalion went to Wisconsin it was early summer in June. The boys lived in tents. Training was vigorous but they could endure it. Then came winter and the first snow to the majority of them. They moved into regular barracks. Training was pushed under wintry conditions just as vigorously and it enhanced the morale of the boys. Soon they were transferred to Camp Shelby in Mississippi. The people of nearby towns were not as friendly and the existence of color-consciousness among the Southern people was brought to the attention of the 100th boys. They were told to avoid getting into trouble for their main objective was to get ready for the campaign in Europe.

Now on this train south the coaches were packed with traveling people. His presence excited no curiosity among them. He was self-conscious at first, but forgot it in the crowd. He had gone to visit the metropolis of Chicago, but then it was as a member of a crowd. Now he was alone and his destination was an internment camp. What would these people think and how would they react if they were to know that his grandfather was classified as an enemy alien and kept behind barbed wire? But they would not know that he was a model citizen who never ran afoul of the law, was a backer of all things American although he was never allowed the right to become naturalized because of his race. The only fact they would consider was that "he was interned and there must be a good reason." It made him sick at heart to think about this ironical situation. Perhaps many of the boys had this indignation to subconsciously vow "I'll show you!"

He was asked to wait in a room when he arrived at Camp Livingston. This office was just within the barbed wire enclosure. There were two groups of visitors besides himself. Both of them consisted of women who had come to see their husbands and fathers. They were mainland people and had driven from Colorado where they were permitted to carry on their work as usual. He looked out of the window and noticed that the compound had a row of double wire fences. This building was within the outer fence. A wide gravel road made a complete circuit of prison-designated areas containing drab tar-papered barracks. Buildings that housed the dental and medical dispensaries and the hospitals were within the outer enclosure.

His grandfather came into the room, incredulity on his face. He was told there was a visitor, but who could there be that he knew in Louisiana? Edwin in uniform was waiting for him. He was choked with emotion and could not say anything. Just a tight hug from his tall grandson, and a return embrace were all that passed between them.

Silence was eloquent. There was no need for words. Many a time when Edwin was small he was his playmate. As the first grandson, Edwin had received special attention in childhood and grandparents were wont to spoil him.

"Well, well, this is an unexpected surprise. Whoever was responsible for this visit certainly deserves my deepest gratitude. Some mainland fellows were visited by their families, but no Hawaii man has yet received any visitor."

"I think Dad wrote to Colonel Turner. You know we are in Mississippi now and are training hard. Maybe before long we'll be shipped overseas."

"Well, as long as you are a soldier you are liable to be sent where it will do the most good. How are the boys doing at Camp Shelby? That's the camp's name, isn't it?"

"Oh, we are OK I guess. We are all ready to do our best. But just because soldiers in the Japanese army march thirty miles a day, they expect us to do the same. An officer who read a report of an American officer attached to that army before the war figured that we Nisei could do likewise. Maybe we need more rice. Potatoes, potatoes, and potatoes. In this rice-raising southland they should get more rice for us."

"Ha, ha, ha, that's the spirit. Gripe all you can. But do your best and march that thirty miles!"

"Yes, that is what we are doing. And in snake-filled fields and bushes too. Chiggers are our worst enemies."

"What's chiggers?" asked the grandfather.

"Little insects that burrow into your skin. I tell you, this southland has all sorts of insects and reptiles to waylay you. But we are so tired we don't care what's on the ground. Now let me ask you, grandpa. How are they treating you here in camp?" Edwin was now inquisitive. He knew there were going to be a lot of questions that he had to answer back at Camp Shelby. Many fathers, uncles, and teachers were in detention. The leaders of the Japanese community in all the islands were gathered here at Camp Livingston and other camps.

Seikichi Arata smiled at his grandson, and patted his arm. "We are well cared for. In fact we get goldiers' housing and food. The only difference between you and us is that we are not allowed to roam around the country as free citizens. But we manage to find amusement and have classes to attend. Idle hours are profitably used to learn something that we could not do while we were busy working for our living before the war. There are all sorts of lectures on religions, travel, art, philosophy, and politics. Among two thousand people there are many learned men. When you return to camp tell the men of the 100th Infantry that we from Hawaii are well adjusted to this life and are merely waiting for the war to end. We are not bitter about our lot and are waiting for you to show to the American public what your heritage is.

"Tell the boys not to blame the United States government for detaining their elders in camp. The Americans do not understand the sense of loyalty that is a part of the Japanese character. Perhaps they are afraid of us. I don't blame them. I heard that Germans were treated the same way in 1917. But in this war they are not so harshly treated. Perhaps we can prove that we, too, can be trusted. You who are in uniform can do the most to prove this point and I am extremely proud that I have you, my grandson, among those that will spearhead this fight for recognition."

Edward knew his grandfather was of the old school; full of the sense of loyalty to country, to family, and friends, but it was the first time he heard him propound this sentiment which they, the young ones, were more or less obliged to philosophize and rationalize if they were to remain sane. To have to fight for freedom when your own kin was kept behind iron bars just from suspicion? "Do you all feel that way about this internment? You may be an exception in this large camp."

Seikichi smiled. "Of course, there are many with different ideas. There are many who are returning to Japan on the first available ex-exchange steamer. But most of us who have lived in the mainland or Hawaii and have raised their citizen children will elect to remain. This is their land, their country. Parents will stick with them."

Edward looked intently at his grandfather as if he were looking at him for the first time. "Is there no bitterness in you? Aren't you mad inside at the treatment you received?"

"Perhaps in the beginning. It was so sudden. It seemed we were betrayed and double-crossed. Not to be trusted hurt above everything.

But now we can see why we are detained. At a time like this a thorough sifting of the wheat from the chaff cannot be done. The innocent must suffer with the dangerous. It is for the security of the nation."

"But you have always prided yourself on being of Japanese blood. You are not a citizen of the United States. Moreover you cannot ever become naturalized no matter how you try."

"That is right. I am an alien. I am a Japanese national because I was born in Japan. But which country gave me most? I spent the first twenty years there, but the next forty mature years were in Hawaii. Citizen or no, I love Hawaii and that is my country and I'll be happy to be buried there. I am no longer swayed by flag-waving patriotic songs or frenzied by the harangues of demagogues. I do my own picking."

"I am glad I came here and had this talk with you. I realize what I'll be fighting for."

CHAPTER 28

A Free Man Again

ONE APRIL DAY IN THE YEAR 1944, ON AN eastbound train from Santa Fe, New Mexico, Seikichi Arata and three fellow-internees were heading for Denson, Arkansas where the Jerome Relocation Center was situated. After two-and-a-half years behind barbed wire, these men were free to travel anywhere in the continental United States, except to the Pacific coast. It was an exhilarating feeling to be able to move about without the constant presence of shotgun-wielding guards.

At first they felt self-conscious and could not help but become flushed. They assumed a tense, upright sitting posture, and unconsiously looked straight ahead and then out of the window. But as the train moved out of the station and sped into the vast expanse of the desert a timid glance at fellow-passengers assured them that nobody was paying any particular attention to them. Their Japanese physiognomy excited no resentment, not even curiosity. They might as well relax and enjoy their first hours of freedom. Perhaps the easiest way was to close one's eyes and review the past twenty-four hours of leave-taking at Santa Fe Internment Camp. For some time people were being paroled out of camp to their families in Midwestern and Eastern seaboard cities. Most of these were fathers of soldiers and the process was apparently limited to Stateside people. Those that had families residing in the relocation centers proceeded there to lead a more normal life, but continued being wards of the government. Seikichi Arata was among the first Hawaiian parolees and, since he had no relatives, he chose this Arkansas center because there were hundreds of Hawaiian evacuees there.

In June, 1943 all civilians in the several army internment camps were transferred to the jurisdiction of the Justice Department and the Japanese were concentrated at Sante Fe, New Mexico. This city was founded in 1540 by Francisco Coronado who had advanced northward from Mexico with three hundred soldiers in search of gold. It was the oldest city in the United States and was a health resort town: cool in the summer. Elevation was seven thousand feet. Until acclimated, the transferees from the Louisiana camp experienced some difficulty in breathing. Barracks were old and there was only one mess hall to feed two thousand people. While in former camps the internees were given papers to the effect that they were interned for the duration. Now after transfer to the Justice Department, they were processed again and those that qualified were paroled to the outside. Therefore, there was a constant sense of longing, wishful thinking, envy, and writing outside for help, and an appeal to the Justice Department for a review of individual cases.

Seikichi Arata had received the sad news that his grandson, Edward, who was with the 100th Infantry Battalion and had come to visit him at Camp Livingston, was killed in action after crossing the Volturno River in the hard-fought campaign to oust the Germans from the Italian Peninsula. In a few hours the entire Hawaiian contingent heard of the news and a religious service was held by the priests. They all knew of Edward because his visit to his grandfather at Camp Livingston had created a sensation at that time. They all felt that Edward was a symbol of Hawaiian boys, because almost every one had a son, a grandson, nephew, or pupil in the 100th and in the newly organized 442nd Regimental Combat Team, made up of Hawaiian and mainland boys. The latter was being sent overseas to join the hard-fighting All-Hawaiian outfit, which had demonstrated to the War Department beyond any doubt the loyalty of the Nisei.

That there should be men killed or maimed in battle was understood in the abstract, but to have it occur so near oneself was another matter. After the recitation of the Buddhist sutras, not only the priests but laymen got up and made speeches of condolence that came from the bottom of their hearts. Seikichi was deeply moved.

In the many long nights to follow when he could not fall asleep easily, scenes of sunny Hawaii appeared in his mental retina, but more than anything else he recalled the happy days of Edward's childhood, his growing up, his escapades, his chastisement, his contagious laughter, and his periods of wild jubilation, typical of an extrovert teenager. How grown-up and thoughtful he had become when he came to Louisiana on that visit which turned out to be the last meeting! He died young, without tasting the joys of life, but perhaps it was just as well. In the transmigration of the soul and being, he would certainly be born to a better world and life in the next birth. So reasoned, Seikichi felt peace in his mind.

At Santa Fe he got to know many Stateside Japanese. The leaders of Japanese communities in different cities and towns were there, but the influence of environment on personalities of people was never more eloquently shown as when Hawaiian people were compared to their Stateside counterpart. Mainland people had developed a pure business approach to most things in life. They were very egotistic and cold. After all, the islanders might be provincial, but they retained the warmth, neighborliness, and solicitude for their fellow man that characterize small town people. They embodied without realizing the "Spirit of Aloha," and in such an abnormal community it was no wonder that they sought each other's company. Any news from the islands was shared by all. Censorship of mail was maddening. An airmail letter at times took two to three months to arrive from Hawaii because it was censored at Honolulu, New York, and then at Santa Fe. Not knowing this fact, families continued to spend eighty cents per letter hoping that money would buy speed.

But now all such restriction was over. Arata just had to sit out the war at a relocation camp. At Jerome Relocation Center there were hundreds of island people who had been sent over because they were not essential to the war effort. Perhaps he could find someone that he knew on Kauai or in Honolulu. After transferring at Kansas City he took a south-bound train which passed through Little Rock and he was told by the conductor to get off the train at a small station called Denson, in the state of Arkansas.

He was led to a processing station and there Nisei girls interviewed him. It was the first time in two and a half years that he came near to a female of any race. How young, vivacious, and attractive they looked. All the paper work was attended to and he was assigned to Block 39 when they learned that he came from Hawaii. A truck from the Housing Department was summoned and the four were taken to Block 39 with their luggage.

This flat delta district was beautiful. The surrounding country was a forest and the center itself was green with vegetation. It was already spring in Arkansas, whereas at Santa Fe it was still cold at night and remnant of wintry snow was in low hollows. The change was such a contrast, but the change within their heart was a great deal more. The sense of freedom was tremendous. Among their own kind the four men could look everyone in the eye. There was no feeling of guilt, because theirs was not an incarceration for any criminal act; rather than shame it was an exuberant feeling of pride that assailed them.

The people of Hawaii in the center looked up to them with a certain sense of respect and sought information from them as to the condition and prospect of release of their beloved that were still at Santa Fe. Since Arata was among the first parolees from Santa Fe of Hawaiian internees, because of his grandson's service in the army, families that had sons in the service got a great boost in morale. Their father or husband would soon be released. And even among those without such army connections, since Santa Fe was under the Justice Department, the policy was now the same as that of the War Relocation Authority.

People were encouraged to leave the centers, except those with records that precluded them from leaving, to find employment in the vast Middle West and once more become gainful citizens of the nation. But many were afraid to face the hostility of people "on the outside" and elected to remain and loaf in the enclosure until the end of the war. The fences at these centers were not high and consisted of four strands of wire, not any more than what one would find around a cow pasture. The people did go in and out into the forests freely and went on a shopping tour to the nearby Lake Village.

BOOK V

Homeward Bound

Prologue

IN ACCORDANCE WITH THE RITES OF
Japanese Buddhism, the relatives of Seikichi Arata went into mourning
for seven days. At the end of this period there was a small party to which
a priest and those close to the deceased were gathered. This constituted the
lifting of the mourning period. A feast including fish and meat was prepared.
These articles had not been touched by those in mourning during this period
of sadness. This abstention in their diet reminded them of their recent
bereavement and they were, for a short period, practicing the austere and
strict discipline of the monastery monks of the East.

When the reading of the sutra began, a tray bearing burning incense
was passed around and each took a pinchful of the powdered form and
added it to the smoldering fire. Symbolically, this practice signified accepting the essence of the Laws of Karma that governed the life of a mortal
being: that life was but a transient existence on this planet and a mere
moment in the endless space of time. Sooner or later the living would have
to join the multitude that had preceded them in the world beyond. When
the sutra was read the priest faced the people and in a very friendly intimate
way began:

"We are gathered here tonight just one week after the passing of your
beloved Seikichi Arata. I knew him well at the internment camps and the
relocation center in Arkansas during the war. He exemplified the Hawaiian
pioneer. He labored in the plantation to help build the economy of Hawaii
during the days of the monarchy, fathered children to enrich the territory,
and saw grandchildren don uniforms and go to the call of the nation. He loved
Hawaii. I know this because we had many long hours of discussion. It was

405

fortunate that he lived long enough to learn that The Hawaiian Statehood Bill passed Congress. I know that to him this news was a crowning glory to all that he wished to see come true. May he rest in peace.

"In the Shinshu Sect of Buddhism there is no guarantee that prayer will affect the dead. His course had been fixed by the Laws of Karma, the laws of Cause and Effect during his lifetime. He reaps what he sowed. But Amida Butsu, the savior, had perceived the frailty and weakness of the majority of mankind and from his boundless and infinite love for the world and its teeming millions, vowed that He would not rest in peace until everyone in the universe entered the perfect existence in Nirvana. We are here not to pray for the soul of Seikichi Arata, but have come together tonight because of our common memory of his goodness in life. Through his instrumentation or medium we may think about our savior—about the meaning of our existence in this world—and strive to become better men and women. The deceased father of this household is with you in spirit and is hoping that you will not forget the real significance of your being born."

Minoru was listening to the priest talk about the law that governed the universe: the Karma, the law of Cause and Effect. Nothing occurs as an accident. There always is a cause. Why and how did he return to Hawaii after he had decided to plant his feet on stateside soil? It was the advice and urging of this man who had just passed to the great beyond. Why had his family become so intimate with this man? There was the friendship and association with his son at school in 1921 when they studied in Honolulu and the great evacuation and relocation of the Japanese population of the Pacific Coast States to the interior where he met the deceased. In retrospect the entire fabric of life seemed to have been prewoven, but evidently it could be explained by the all-embracing Law of Karma.

CHAPTER 29

Tule Lake Relocation Center

"WHAT A PLACE! WHY, THERE IS NOTHING in the room but iron beds, mattresses and old blankets," dejectedly said Robert as he sat down on the iron cot as soon as he entered the assigned apartment in Block 6. The other members of the family looked about the bare walls of the twenty by twenty-five foot room. The floor was littered with lumber and shavings. Everywhere a layer of fine dust and sand covered the surface. There was a large pig iron stove in the center of the room with a chimney straight up through the roof. This heating device reminded them that in the winter the temperature was going to descend much more than at Sacramento.

Minoru Murayama looked out of the window which was six-paned and slid lateralwise to shut out the cold and sand. The construction of this center had been rushed day and night to meet a deadline and there was neither time nor manpower to tidy up the area. The rear of the barrack that confronted him was littered with odds and ends of lumber and tar paper that were used to cover the walls and roof. He had just arrived with his family among a group of vanguard workers from the Sacramento area to prepare this small city to receive the thousands of evacuees from Northern California, Oregon, and Washington that were to follow in a few weeks. A similar group of workers had arrived from the State of Washington about a week earlier and they had already begun organization work.

When the Sacramento train pulled into the railroad siding, trucks operated by the Washington men transported the new arrivals to a large warehouse in which desks and chairs were installed and young women from the north processed the families from California. The family was the unit, designated by a number. Each member was photographed, like criminals for the rogues' gallery, and fingerprinted.

In war time and for an emergency undertaking, such humiliating treatment could perhaps be condoned, but just the same there was a turbulent resentment in everyone's heart. To be uprooted on short notice, labeled as a security risk just because of racial extraction, and now herded together in this bleak camp for the duration of the war, irrespective of how loyal a citizen may be to the country of his birth, was a fact not altogether easy to swallow. It might have been more gracefully accepted had other Americans of German and Italian descent been similarly treated as a war measure.

Evacuation from coastal areas of the Pacific slope for a distance of one hundred miles was imposed only on Japanese, irrespective of citizenship. The galling content of this edict lay in the realization that the governing body had no trust in Japanese-American citizens who were far more Americanized than was realized by the policy makers of the nation who were sorrowfully deficient in the knowledge of what Americanization had accomplished, not only among the native born group, but even among the aliens that had found the American way of life preferable to the age-long habits handed down from their ancestors from time immemorial. "Once a Jap, always a Jap," so had General De Witt stigmatized the persons of Japanese ancestry and put into motion an unprecedented mass evacuation of a race.

This movement could be compared to the displacement of the farmers of the Ukraine or Caucasus to the communes of Siberia by Soviet Russia. One less bitterly critical could find solace in discovering a counterpart in the romantic account of Longfellow's *Evangeline:* the tragic forced emigration of the French settlers of Arcadia in Canada to Louisiana Territory. The former was condemned as brutality that could only be carried out by inhuman communist dictators, and the latter an inhumanity against fellow minorities prepared in the garb of sentimentality and romance to induce copious sympathetic tears of the adolescent, but the only difference was of scope and magnitude.

How historians would interpret this emergency measure and hysterical outburst against a helpless minority Minoru speculated, for eventually it had to be evaluated by more balanced and trained individuals in a more stabilized era, for such critical analysis constituted the backbone of American democracy. Like any society of peoples, America was full of crooked politicians and unscrvpulous rascals in government places, but democracy was courageous enough to clear house in sober moments.

Be that as it may, Minoru was now mentally re-enacting the scene at the Sacramento Station when family after family was transported on military trucks, disgorged onto the platform with just handbags of clothing and boxes of minimum daily necessities. Forlornly waiting for the arrival of the remainder of the contingent that were to make up this vanguard unit, they presented a sorry spectacle. There were the aged and the sick and the maimed. The military was merciful in that it adhered to the rule: keep family members together as a unit. They sat on their luggage and boxes while the young and restless paced the platform.

Expressions of resentment were conspicuously absent; days of anger were past. Now there was complete resignation and they acted as automatons, like sheep driven to the market for slaughter. Where they were destined to be transported nobody knew. It was a "military secret."

The non-commissioned officers and enlisted men of the military police were kind and helpful, assisting the women and the aged in alighting from the high trucks. Nevertheless, they were armed. With military punctuality the evacuees were brought to the station, counted, and loaded into the coaches. At the signal of a whistle, without fanfare and without anyone seeing them off, they left their homes behind.

The train headed north through the flat fertile farmland, crossing rivers, wheatland, and orchards. It wound and climbed its way among giant sequoias and pine trees to the plateau of the Oregon border. It traversed grazing land and finally crossed a lava-strewn district and came to their destination. The bare mountain to the left was no higher than a hill; only the proximity made it appear imposing. To the right in a vast compact area was an unmistakable town. There were rows and rows of black barracks in a bleak setting of desert land and in the distance, on a higher elevation, a solitary mountain shaped like an abalone stood like a landmark. There were high fences around the area with watch towers. The name of this camp was Tule Lake Center.

June the Second in Sacramento was already full summer and it was hot, but at this elevation of five thousand feet the evening was comfortably chilly. From a nearby hall metallic clanging resounded and without being told everyone knew that it was a summons to supper. Having nothing else to do the Murayama family of seven stood up to go to the mess hall.

In the course of twelve years, after completion of internship at Omaha, Minoru had married a girl born and raised in Sacramento and they had three children: Mary, Robert, and Russel. Both of his parents were still healthy. No longer did they toil on the delta farm, but lived with their eldest son. The other children had left home to begin their life in the vicinity of the capital of California.

The dining hall was a huge place and built to accommodate two hundred and fifty people, roughly the number that were to reside in each block. Cafeteria style serving was done and each had his tray loaded with sausage, sauerkraut, potatoes, bread pudding, and bread with oleomargarine. It was appetizing and each found that he was hungry after the long hours of jolting in the springless railway coach. When the early diners were finished an intelligent looking young man appeared and spoke to the assembly.

"My name is Kubo. I'm from the Puyallup Center and formerly from Seattle, Washington. Welcome to the Tule Lake War Relocation Center. We have been here a week trying to get this center organized. As you have seen since your arrival, everything has to be done from scratch. You from Northern California and Oregon will have to help us get this place organized to receive the bulk of the evacuees who will follow in two weeks. About five hundred of you have arrived today and you will choose or be channelled into the type of work you are trained for or want to get a crack at. Being a community of people, the usual kind of work necessary in the daily lives of any society will be found here. You will be assigned to any type of work, but it will not be free enterprise like on the outside. The WRA will pay twelve, sixteen, and nineteen dollars a month plus clothing allowance . . . about three dollars per person.

"The project director is a man of understanding. You will like him. He sympathizes with us in this catastrophe that has hit us and is trying his best to make our lot easier. There is so much work to be done. You will be allowed about a week to get settled. Only bare walls and beds will greet you tonight. Your luggage will get to you as soon as the boys can haul it. There is a pile of scrap lumber which can be used to make your apartments more livable. Help yourselves to it.

"Other jobs can wait, but we need cooks and kitchen workers, and boilermen for the shower room. Tomorrow, you will have to elect a block manager to represent you in a hundred and one things to get the members settled, to straighten out and help our bewildered fellow men, and to confer with the administrative personnel. We have these questionnaires here and I wish you to signify your choice of work. Nobody can force you to work, but to make this life tolerable there must be cooperation."

Kubo was an aggressive second generation businessman. He was able to present his points well and people listened to him. Many remained to scrutinize and fill out the papers. Minoru left with his family because he came to this center as a physician and that was the function he was expected to perform. He was assigned two adjoining apartments because of his parents. How could these rooms be used to the best advantage? What to make: chairs, tables, shelves, and closets had to be constructed.

Minoru reported to the hospital the day following arrival to inspect for himself what equipment was available and what personnel he had to work with. The medical director was an elderly Caucasian practitioner who seemed outwardly amiable. What was behind the affable exterior only time would disclose.

In these hectic days when war fever was at its height and racial feeling accentuated, men working at the relocation centers could be put into several categories. There was the really humanitarian, idealistic type and of these there were quite a few. These braved the criticism of "Jap lovers" from their friends, but they lived staunchly by their principle. Some had spent their lives in Japan as teachers and missionaries and sought this opportunity to help and counsel these bewildered unfortunates. There was a Catholic priest who was a friend to all. He had spent his early years in Korea and Japan and now did errands for housewives. Bobby pins and little knick' knacks that could not be obtained easily he would get for them. Then there was a grey-haired lady missionary who had spent her life in Northeast Japan and now worked in the personnel department. She counselled the people in their own language and conveyed the impression immediately that she was a real friend.

When war finally ended and a Nisei fellow-worker exclaimed, "Oh, I am glad the war is ended. I am glad that Japan lost!" she changed her expression and reprimanded the young Nisei.

"Never say such a thing even if at heart you think so. What would the old Japanese feel to hear such remarks. They may be glad the war is over. But they are, I am sure, not pleased for Japan, their country, to have lost. Yet they may not want the United States to lose. It is a funny psychology and hard to explain. I can sympathize with that sentiment, because Japan is my second home. You must spare the feelings of your elders!"

Ultimately, when the camp was abandoned and nobody remained, she collected carloads of pots and pans from the junk heap and prevailed upon the army to transship these boxes to war-stricken Japan where these discarded articles were welcomed by refugees.

In the second category were many Caucasians who had known the Japanese on the west coast prior to the war, had been able to see them as individuals with good and bad among them, and resolved to do something for them when the powers-that-be embarked upon this unprecedented un-American evacuation and imprisonment purely on ethnological grounds. They were idealists and men with conviction and principle. On the other hand, the third group were misfits who could not fit into the war-effort of the nation and were attracted to lucrative jobs to lord over the inmates of a concentration camp.

A dozen young men and women were working under white personnel directors. The hospital was patterned after an army base hospital: a central administration department which was connected by corridors to five wings, each containing a large ward with about thirty beds. There was another wing that served as an out-patient department. Workers were busily putting in beds and opening boxes of supplies that came from the San Francisco Army Medical Depot.

Since all the evacuees already arrived were physically healthy there was not much work, but by the time mid-June arrived and ten thousand or more poured into the center, the hospital would be humming with activity. Until then, there would be a respite for the doctors and nurses. Two ambulances were on duty and a doctor could be fetched whenever there was an emergency. Dr. Murayama went home to Block 7. Block 7 was nearest to the hospital and only about a thousand yards away. The hospital and dispensary were in the area reserved for Caucasian administrative personnel, apartments, and military barracks. Military Police were stationed in this area. Although free to leave the center, the Caucasian employees also lived within the enclosure and passes had to be shown whenever they passed the gates.

Tule Lake Center was situated in Northern California near the Oregon and Nevada borders. It was on a dried-up lake bottom which included 32,000 acres of land, but as far as the evacuees were concerned, they were confined within an area of about one and a quarter square miles. The area was encircled by a barbed-wire fence and guarded by Military Police in watchtowers placed at regular intervals outside the fence. To the north of the enclosure and on the other side of the railroad track there towered a precipitous small mountain that resembled the outline of Diamond Head of Honolulu from a certain angle and was called Castle Rock. To the east of Castle Rock the "farm" was located. The land was fertile and potatoes were cultivated by neighboring farmers. Due to the elevation, summer was short and the growing season did not exceed more than four months.

The project was roughly divided into four areas: the administrative section, the warehouse and factory section, the hospital section, and the residence area for the Japanese evacuees. All these buildings were inside the fence. Immediately inside the gateway was the Provost Marshal's office where all incoming and outgoing traffic were examined. The evacuee section was separated from the rest by a wide firebreak and in geometrical pattern the sixty-four blocks of primitive living quarters were built.

Each block, composed of fourteen barracks, was the basic unit. Nine blocks were grouped together to form a ward, and the wards were separated by firebreaks of two hundred feet width. Each block was designed to house 250 evacuees. Barracks were divided into individual apartments, intended primarily for sleeping quarters. There was no vegetation in the project except for a stubble of desert grass, and with the slightest wind clouds of dust and sand would seep into the apartments through minute cracks. Sand storms and whirlwinds were not infrequent. Much had to be done in order to add color to the scenery both outside and inside the living quarters.

The night of arrival the Murayamas slept in what they were clad, for the baggage could not be distributed as the contents had to be examined by the Military Police for contraband such as weapons, cameras, and short wave radios. Dr. Minoru Murayama sent his wife and children to attend to this matter because he felt he had to report to the hospital.

Meanwhile, the elderly member in the person of Torao Murayama now in his mid-sixties, examined the room to see what improvement could or ought to be made to make this temporary abode more livable.

Their apartments were of the larger size, twenty by twenty five feet. The exterior walls and roof were covered with shiplap and tar paper. To keep the cold out the inner surface of the walls was reinforced by fireboard ceilings and sheet rock walls. A crude floor was constructed of shiplap and it was destined to dry soon and buckle because of its green state, leaving wide gaps in the floor. There were three windows, two in the back and one window and a door in the front. The other two walls were partitions or the ends of the long barrack.

Torao was reminded of the camp life at the Waipunalei plantation forty years ago when he, as a young man, landed in Hawaii. It somehow did not appear strange or distasteful to wade into this chaotic mess and construct something decent. The challenge seemed to rejuvenate him and he felt that his family now depended on him to show the way, for he alone had experienced such a life. He looked around for sites for shelves, closets to hang clothes, and screens to separate the beds from the "living room." Chairs and tables were necessities; clothes lines to hang the laundry would soon have to be erected behind the apartment. A box to keep coal for the stove had to be fashioned and kept near the door.

He remembered what Mr. Kubo from Seattle had alluded to the night before and he made several trips to the lumber pile and transported several loads of scrap lumber with the aid of his grandsons. It was a matter of survival; first come, first served, and let the late-comers shift for themselves, for obviously there was not sufficient lumber in the scrap pile for ten thousand people. There were no tools to work with, but he stacked up the lumber in front of the apartment for future use.

At the block manager's office he inquired if there were any carpentry tools to be borrowed. "The best way for you is to order what you need from Montgomery Ward or Sears & Roebuck. Here are the catalogs. From the Oakland stores you will receive the goods in a week or so."

Torao went home with the catalog and with the suggestions of the women folk a list of cloth for curtains, carpentry tools, and sundry items were ordered. For a long time, until the post exchange store was established on a cooperative basis, the mail order houses were to do a thriving business for suddenly 100,000 people became their customers.

With the middle of June trainloads of evacuees began to arrive daily, at the rate of about five hundred persons, from the assembly centers of the three Pacific coast states. Altogether, 16,000 people were to make up the population of this overnight city. What Minoru and his vanguard group had to undergo these subsequent arrivals went through: registration, fingerprinting, assignment to apartments by the housing department, and job finding.

As a physician he went with one of the Caucasian doctors to meet the train, and walk through the coaches to inquire if every one was in good physical condition. He looked over the people who had come from the county hospitals or those who had been removed from their sick beds and made arrangements to transport them in waiting ambulances to the hospital wards upon arrival. The processing of these sick people could be done later by the Nisei clerks at their convenience.

The tide of evacuees swelled the "Colony," the hospital inmates increased and the number of physicians also multiplied rapidly. Properly trained personnel in laboratory work, pharmacy, nursing, and dentistry appeared to lend a hand in sharing the work load. In due time a working unit was organized. The number of nurses was inadequate and a program of training nurses' aides and male orderlies was begun. Recent high school graduates were given practical training and these youngsters were made of the right mettle and imbued with spirit of service for they knew what was expected of them when they applied for work in the hospital. They were instructed by Caucasian and Japanese registered nurses.

Naturally, some could not stand the bed pans and direct contact with the emaciated and near-dying. But those that survived this training and continued to work became enriched spiritually by this life of service, and not a few resolved and went through nursing school on the "outside" when these institutions flung their doors open to Japanese-Americans once again. Some girls were particularly capable, efficient, and poised. They were taken into the operating room, first as scrub nurses but later, when it became necessary because of resettlement of doctors and registered nurses, these girls became first and second assistants even in complicated abdominal operations. Many were taught the rudiments of midwifery while they assisted and later, when occasion arose, they carried to completion normal deliveries in the absence of the doctor on duty who might be occupied in another emergency or another delivery. And to their credit, they became first rate midwives.

There was a knock. "Is Dr. Murayama in?" Minoru went to the door and opened it.

"Well, well, come right in Bill. This a pleasant surprise. Did you come by yourself? Where's the Mrs?"

"She is busy like all newcomers getting settled. I just stepped in to say hello since I heard you were located in this block. We are in Block 30 with some of the Sacramento group." Bill Yano was from the Sacramento delta district and a grower of asparagus on Holland tract. Murayama had begun his medical practice in the center of this farming district at Courtland and had known Bill for over ten years as a friend and patient.

"How are all my patients doing? Let's see, you came in four days ago didn't you?"

"That's right. From the Assembly Center we packed up and were loaded in those rickety coaches. Didn't know where we were headed for but anyway we felt we would join our friends. After the Assembly Center this place is not too bad. Maybe we'll like it. I like the coolness in the morning and evening," smiled Bill. There was no bitterness in him: a farmer who had to abandon a hundred acres of asparagus land at the height of harvesting. Dr. Murayama looked at this sturdy farmer who was born in Japan, but educated in California and more American than Japanese in his thoughts and actions.

"What are you going to do? Have you been assigned to some kind of work?"

"My friends elected me block manager."

"I am glad that you accepted it. We need good men to become leaders and I know your friends have thought about it when they elected you. How about the job situation?"

"That is where the headache lies. Quite a bit of hard feelings have arisen between the early arrivals and us late-comers. Most of the good jobs were filled by them. Even the key kitchen workers of my own block are men from Washington and Oregon. We supply the dish washers and waitresses. But I was at the personnel office today and I think we California men can work on the farm. The area east of the Castle Rock used to be productive potato land. We are going to raise vegetables for this and other WRA centers. Hog and chicken farmers will be used in these enterprises and California men are certainly qualified."

"I hope all can get some sort of work. There is nothing like idleness to sicken a man's mind. Sixteen dollars a month is ridiculous, but is better than nothing. Not all people have had money as ready cash. Most of you had money as investment in crops, I know. Pretty soon many of us will not have anything except what is doled out to us as wages and clothing allowance. Has the block managers' council discussed it yet?" curiously asked Minoru for he could almost visualize what the next year would witness regarding the plight of the people.

"There seems to be a plan to allow young men to go out as seasonal workers to the beet fields of Idaho and Montana when the harvest begins there. Another plan is to send out young men, cleared by the FBI, to work on the railroads as section hands. But these are in the planning stage yet."

Dr. Murayama was deep in thought. He knew the temper of the first generation people who had spent all their lives in America on the farm and were Japanese to the core. Now when they were put behind barbed wire fences, guarded by Military Police with shotguns, their bitterness was crystallized into a resolution: "If I am treated as a Japanese to such a degree, so will I become one in fact." Even the urban population that had been more Americanized gradually acquired this philosophy as months went by without much to do, time to brood, and association with frustrated compatriots.

"Doc, I am afraid there will be a considerable fight for power among the different factions. First, there are the regional differences, people from each state are slightly different in outlook and thought from the others. People from Washington and Oregon are more Americanized. Then there is quite a deep gap between the Issei and Nisei. Young as they are, the Nisei are aggressive and they are in the favor of the Caucasian WRA directors. They are placed in more responsible positions and have ready access to the administrative offices. The Issei are more experienced and worldly and will not, I am afraid, take second place to the young up-starts. There will be bad feeling and nasty name-calling. Already I have heard accusations of *inu* (informers) hurled at the ones that are working at the central office of the administration."

"I do not understand why people should become so hepped up about politics in a place like this. I really don't. What is your opinion?" inquired Minoru.

Bill Yano thought a while. "There may be two sides to the question. The dominant force behind this drive for power by some is something inherent in man. He wants to get on top. I heard that even in prison cells there would eventually emerge a chief to rule the inmates. This

417

may be a prison camp, but it can also be interpreted as a small crowded community along communistic lines because there is no profit motive in the usual sense. Some people try hard to get on top even without any profit coming out of the position. The other is a baser one. Certain jobs are lucrative. I heard that certain chefs are making home brew out of rice and sugar. Where would rice and sugar come from except by their chiselling on the supply that is allotted to the block kitchen."

"That is a possibility. I realize how easy it is to accumulate a stockpile of rice. But sugar is different. As I understand, two teaspoonfuls of sugar per day is allotted each evacuee. How can the kitchen chef chisel on this small amount?" asked Minoru incredulously.

Bill Yano merely smiled. "But it is being done. Because the two teaspoonfuls to 250 people is not so small, a rake-off every day even in very small amounts may add up to quite a bit in the course of a week or two. Did you hear about the latest happening when a Caucasian employee of the warehouse got into a traffic accident between this center and Klamath Falls? The station wagon he was driving collided with a train at a crossing. His car was smashed up badly, but he survived because the train was going very slowly in this country siding. People were surprised to find the highway strewn with Grade A meat. You know meat is rationed on the outside. He was transporting meat meant for us to be blackmarketed in Klamath Falls. There seems to be quite a bit of such finagling taking place in the warehouse division."

"Maybe so," Dr. Murayama recalled the story he heard from patients from Santa Anita Assembly Center several days ago. "I heard that Santa Anita people were fed spaghetti every day for 10 days without much trimmings. When you rake off fifteen or twenty cents a day from each of 16,000 people, you can figure out what a fat income the mess department groups must have enjoyed. The strike at that Assembly Center that culminated in the use of tanks by the MPs' brought this grievance to light."

Lillian Murayama was California born and educated in the schools of the delta district of Sacramento River, Sacramento City, and the University of California. She spoke very little Japanese. Her parents operated a pear orchard on Grand Island and only at home was she compelled to speak the language. The Language School at Courtland

418

was of grammar school level only, and after that she had no chance to learn any decent mode of speech, for the language was very intricate and hard. Rather than use it incorrectly and offend others or be laughed at, it was wiser not using it at all among strangers. In time she used it only among intimates. Among other people she pretended she could not speak. Within her family only English was spoken to the children, but to her in-laws she was forced to use Japanese. Also among old friends of the family from the delta district she was at home and reverted to her childhood vernacular without hesitation, heedless of the infraction of honorifics and grammar.

Mrs. Nosaka had dropped in. "Lillian. We have been here in Tule Lake three months already. We like the people and are making many friends among them. We have people from Washington and Oregon and Southern California. More like a vacation for us women."

"That is so. No cooking, no dish washing, and no work in the fields," laughingly chimed in rotund Mrs. Araki.

"That is good," answered Lillian. "You two came from Japan directly to Sacramento Delta as picture brides and must have spent all those years there, worked hard on the ranch, and raised your family. I know because I used to help Mom too." The creases and wrinkles in their faces told the history of these women who labored in the celery and onion fields. Middle age obesity was now catching up. They came of good peasant stock and were strong, docile, and patient.

"But now we are women of leisure. After three months of doing nothing I am getting restless and have joined a class of *ikebana*: learning to arrange flowers and shrubs. It is something I wanted to learn all these years. In Japan we were too poor and in America too busy raising a family. But now I can indulge in that art and I feel like a lady. Ha, ha, ha. Araki-san, I heard you started something too."

"That is right. I started to knit not long after we arrived here in June. There is a lady who knows many different designs. Then I joined a class of *Shigin*. There is a teacher from Los Angeles who conducts classes of modern *shigin* singing. This school is not the rough masculine type of singing that young men used to bellow in the Meiji era when we were young. Even women can sing this modern version without appearing immodest."

Lillian nodded and added, "We have pupils in this block too. I heard there are hundreds now learning this *shigin*."

Mrs. Nosaka pondered for a while. "Did you hear that at the other end of the camp people began making beautiful objects of art by using shells?"

Lillian was incredulous. "And where can you get shells? This is a plateau country, elevation 5,000 feet."

"Anyway, I heard this was a lake. Tule Lake has become smaller and where we are located now was once lake bottom. Fresh water shells must have been plentiful for if the sandy soil is dug shells come out in sackfulls. If you go out near the fence where the sewage disposal plant is located you will see people digging away. Most ingenious objects and beautiful things have been prepared. Maybe someday there will be a souvenir shop to sell these trinkets."

"I wouldn't be surprised. People are trying to turn everything into money."

"Talking about money, have you been to the canteen lately? I don't know where the people hide their cash but they certainly are buying things. The other day fresh tuna arrived from San Diego and in no time the fish was sold and cut into small pieces suitable for *sashimi*."

Lillian smiled. "For the children's sake we have our meals in this apartment rather than go out to the mess hall. My husband and I feel that in such a life, to preserve the privacy of a family, we should take our meals here and we added that tuna *sashimi*. It was fresh and good. There is a man in Block 13 who came from Washington. He is from Kumamoto Ken in the old country and discovered that my father-in-law came from the next village. Now we occasionally get a present of *sashimi* and also a bottle of home-brewed *saké*. Ha ha, and it is good too. I tasted it myself."

It was a phenomenon common to all relocation centers to see people become engrossed in the creation of beautiful things out of pebbles, rocks, shells, and twisted branches and roots that were locally available. Classes in various cultural endeavors were opened; painting in oil, black and white ink painting of the Japanese school, calligraphy, music in all forms, floral arrangement, tea ceremony, knitting, embroidery, sewing, and other handicraft were taught by evacuee teachers. English classes for adults were held besides the regular classes for youngsters. Older men gathered in the strategically situated recreation

420

barracks of the different wards and spent many hours in playing *go*, *shogi*, and *hana fuda*. Recounting old stories pertaining to the pioneering of the West was a pastime in itself. They never got tired of telling and retelling the same stories and did not lack a sympathetic audience. It was a shame that the rising generation did not show more interest in what their fathers had gone through in the early rough and tumble days.

There was unlimited social activity for the teenagers and young people. Baseball and dancing flourished. Many of these young people were born and raised in isolated regions and for the first time they were thrown together with many young people who were exclusively of their own kind. A new sense of liberty was experienced and many ran wild.

To Lillian and Minoru Murayama the activity of the children was of prime concern. They were thankful that Mary was pre-adolescent. Eating at their own apartment rather than at the mess hall was a cautious practice by many families in order to control the younger boys. In the mess hall the children ran about playing hide and seek while people sat at the table. Parents could not restrain them. It fell to Mary's lot to fetch the family tray to and from the mess hall, but she was a good girl and did not mind. There were several other families that did likewise and it was a game for her to be entrusted with a responsibility even at eleven. It made her feel that she was a grownup.

The primitive condition at this center was bleak and inconvenient, but since thousands were in the same plight, Mary became adjusted easily and could see beauty, adventure, and experience satisfaction. Getting up at five o'clock to help her mother do the family washing before others cluttered up the laundry room was fun. To feed the seagulls that flew low to catch the morsels of food thrown into the air in the morning was a beautiful and exhilarating sight. Pancakes four times a week for breakfast was a little too monotonous and they ended in a feast for the ever-present seagulls that had their roost in nearby lakes. They had become attracted to this place that offered better hunting than the shrunken Tule Lake which was their natural home and feeding grounds.

Winter came to this highland rather early and the stoves in the living quarters had to be kept burning day and night. Coal trucks dumped their load near the boiler room in the center of the block. It was fortunate that the camp did not want for coal even in wartime conditions.

The WRA should be commended for this constant vigil. But in order to get large pieces, one had to go early, get hold of the only wheelbarrow, and cart away the choice ones. Thus, even at midnight Minoru attended to this chore. Soon snow delighted the center children and the Military Police were good enough to allow them to play on the slopes of Castle Rock outside of the fence. Sleds were improvised and as a result several broken bones had to be treated by the staff at the hospital.

Since no house calls were made, the ambulances were kept busy transporting patients back and forth to the dispensary. All the ambulance drivers were young men and were an interesting group. Jimmy was from Placer County, Hank was from Central California, and Fred was a *Kibei* (American born; educated in Japan past the period of adolescence). Dr. Murayama found the nights of 'on duty' which he had to fill at least once a week, sometimes boresome. He spent hours talking with these young people. It was early February, 1943.

Jim was a typical country Nisei. "I was drafted into the army and stationed near Monterey when the war broke out. Immediately the Nisei were removed from combat training and our work consisted of mowing lawns and trimming hedges. They should have discharged us then if we were not wanted, but no, we were just kept doing menial work. At one time President Roosevelt visited the camp, and you know what they did to us? All us Nisei were locked up in a barrack room with armed guards posted at the doors. When the review was over and the President gone we were let out."

"But you were discharged," inquired Hank "otherwise you would not be here now."

"That's right. They let us out, and I am glad to be out. At least I can look after my parents now."

Dr. Murayama asked with a twinkling in his eyes, "Jim, will you volunteer and join the army again. I read in the newspapers that an all Nisei outfit is being formed. The 100th Infantry Battalion from Hawaii is apparently showing its fighting prowess on the Italian front."

"Not me. Let others do the volunteering. Not after what I went through. And I don't like the idea of a segregated unit made up only of Japanese. Why not treat us equally as other Americans. Why an all Japanese unit? To put us where casualties are highest? No, not for me," spat Jim disgustedly.

Hank was less belligerent. "I think it may be a wise thing for us to do some fighting rather than rot in this concentration camp. I know many will say, 'Join the army and die after what the government has done to us?' Still I am not so sure if it is right for us to sulk and take a negative attitude. Yes, we are all mad about this stinking treatment we received, but are we right in sitting back when our country needs us?" his face was flushed now. Evidently he had been thinking about this problem and now given an opportunity was almost thinking aloud.

Dr. Murayama was studying this farmer's son who was doing his own thinking, and he could see that decision was far from being reached. Sentiment in the camp was not conducive to clear thinking. The pressure of the Issei was strong now that everybody was forced to decide one way or another regarding a loyalty oath, and his mind went through the experience of the previous night.

In February 1943, every Japanese person seventeen years of age and over was required to fill out questionnaires that were complicated and long, including some thirty questions. Most questions dealt with his past history and activities, but also delved into facts as to whether close relatives resided in Japan, details of foreign travel and foreign investments, membership in and contributions to societies and clubs, magazines and newpapers customarily read, possession of dual citizenship, etc. The crucial questions that turned all centers into seething cauldrons of bitterness and discontent were numbers 27 and 28. On the form for male citizens these read:

Question 27.—Are you willing to serve in the armed forces of the United States on combat duty, wherever ordered?

Question 28.—Will you swear unqualified allegiance to the United States of America and faithfully defend the United States from any or all attack by foreign or domestic forces, and foreswear any form of allegiance or obedience to the Japanese Emperor, or any other foreign government, power, or organization?

On the form for the female citizens and aliens of both sexes, the questions were formulated as follows:

Question 27.—If the opportunity presents itself and you are found qualified, would you be willing to volunteer for the Army Nurse Corps or the WAAC?

Question 28.—Will you swear unqualified allegiance to the United States of America and foreswear any form of allegiance or obedience to the Japanese Emperor, or any other foreign government, power, or organization?

Dr. Murayama saw nothing wrong with the questions asked of males and he felt all answers should be in the affirmative. A mass meeting was held in every ward and he was at one. The meeting was conducted in the Japanese language as the Issei were most directly concerned. To a lesser extent *Kibei* (citizens who had been brought up in Japan) were stirred because they were at draft age and their emotions were worked up more keenly than other young men.

One merchant Issei in his late forties had the floor. "Ladies and gentlemen. You have read the all important questions, numbers 27 and 28. We who are Japanese nationals are Japanese until we die. We are not allowed to become naturalized by the United States. How can we forswear allegiance to our emperor? If we did so, we should become men without a country. It is a very foolish question to ask anybody in our category. There is no way but either to refuse to answer or answer 'no' to both questions."

A bald-headed farmer stood up. "Our farms and homes were snatched away from us. Half a century of blood and sweat have come to naught. Now the U.S. Government is trying to send our sons, after all the inhumanity done to us all, to the battlefield as cannon fodder. I believe we should all answer 'no' to both questions."

Minoru Murayama could not contain himself any longer; at least he had to say something even just to satisfy his own self respect. Luckily, he was able to speak sufficiently good Japanese, thanks to his schooling in Honolulu. California Nisei were too young to cope with and buck their elders. Also, since he was a physician the people would at least listen to his propounded views. Their temper was ugly; perhaps they would brand him as *inu* and "pro-administration." But of all the trades and jobs in the center, doctors were least expendable. He could have his say and perhaps get by. He stood up.

"These two questions are posted by the Federal Government. Like Federal Income Tax you cannot evade the questionnaires. You must answer them. I agree with the first speaker, the questionnaire asked of the aliens is foolish. I think you Issei have a perfect right to answer 'no' and I think American public opinion will sustain you, once the whole thing is clarified to them. But I see no reason why any American

424

citizen should side step the first set of questions. It is as plain as $1 + 1 = 2$. We have been treated meanly. No minority race has been so man-handled in the history of the United States. But we should not mix up two clearly defined issues. When we fight, we fight for the ideals of that government. General De Witt and his gang drove us out of California to be sure. But they are individuals, functionaries of the government who had the upper hand in policy-making. Many thinking leaders of California openly opposed this mass evacuation although they could not prevent the popular movement. You all know that. We have friends on the outside. No matter what anti-Japanese rascals have done to us, the American Government and its ideals remain the same. Your sons and brothers have been bred and nurtured in that ideal. It is not right for you, parents, to adversely influence your sons' decisions." Minoru still stood and he was flushed, carried away by his own enthusiasm.

The bald-headed farmer stood up without waiting for permission from the M.C. "Doctor, no matter what your arguments are, I cannot bear to see my son go out and die for those that treated us like this."

"All right. That is your feeling. What is the reaction and conviction of your son? After all it is his life and future. You won't be living thirty years from now, but your son will be here for half a century. Your grandsons and their progeny will continue to call this country their own. You cannot decide what is good for him for he will have his own decision to make and for all you know he has already made up his mind."

A young man stood up and from his proficiency of the language, it was evident that he was a returnee from Japan. He said: "I feel like the old gentlemen. We should not answer these questionnaires because this is a prison camp and there is no freedom. We are not free citizens and therefore not obligated to carry a gun."

"From the American way of life you are perfectly free to have your own opinion. But not to answer is to me cowardly. Why not answer 'no' like a man. The administration is trying to get us to fill out the questionnaires; they are not trying to make us answer 'yes'."

The above episode was vivid in his mind as the discussion went on at the dispensary. Fred had said nothing. "Fred, what are people in your ward doing about this matter of registration?" asked Dr. Mura-yama.

"Not only in my block and ward, but as I come in contact with many people transporting them back and forth in the ambulance and talk among my friends I gather that the sentiment of the colony is swinging toward one of non-cooperation and refusal to fill out the questionnaires. The representatives of the army, one officer, two white sergeants, and one Nisei interpreter technical sergeant, are getting very few volunteers for the new all Japanese combat regiment."

"If you don't answer, then there will be no clearance from the FBI."

"That is right. Most of them intend to sit out the war at this camp rather than go out and face a hostile world. The reason that dominates the thinking of people who hesitate to answer the questionnaire is the fear that the family will be broken up. They figure that answering affirmatively would give the WRA the power to evict anyone to relocate outside. Pretty bad news is filtering in concerning girls that have gone outside and were eventually seduced by low elements of large cities. They may all be baseless, but this news does not help the camp morale. Parents are influencing the young people to remain and sit out the war."

"We'll then become wards of the government, just like the Indians," said Hank.

"That is right. Soon we'll lose all initiative, but I hardly think there is oil in this sandy lake bottom," Dr. Murayama said wryly as he heard footsteps and an orderly appeared at the door.

"Doctor, there is a Mrs. Kudo in Ward X and the medical director has asked you to examine her. She may be a case for commitment," was the first intimation Dr. Murayama heard that there was a mental case in the house. He went along with the orderly with a heavy heart. Such interviews were always unpleasant and depressing. Even under normal conditions cases of deranged minds were the height of human tragedy for all concerned. The patients themselves were the only ones not to feel the impact of this change, because beyond the initial stage they usually felt that nothing was wrong with them and were annoyed to be made the center of so much fuss, but the immediate families' agony was terrible and tragic. On the other hand, if the feeling of the families was one of a philosophical resignation to facts, then the examiner was the one to suffer with his analytical mind attempting to probe deeper into the wherefore of this mental derangement and the natural deduction would be that it was the result of this unprecedented mass corralling and the consequent offsetting of mental equilibrium for her who could not stand the strain. Such persons might have succumbed to the same mental ailment under normal conditions anyway, but the very fact that they were forced to lead such an abnormal life gave them an excuse to blame all such tragedies on the present abnormal community life.

He interviewed her the next morning. "Mrs. Kudo, how are you this morning? Did you sleep well last night?" There was no answer to this solicitous inquiry; just a silent stare transfixed to the corner of the floor and a continuous rolling and pulling at the hem of her dress. The food had not been touched; the bowl of cereal and plate of scrambled eggs were on the tray undisturbed. Nurses were not successful in having her change into a hospital gown the previous night. She was admitted on the complaint that she had suicidal tendencies and she was detained in a room with rough wire mesh on the windows for her own protection. The cotton dress was wrinkled, her hair was dishevelled, and her rather dark face was without a trace of make-up. Her shabby shoes were the usual out-of-shape pair that all women wore in this dusty, sandy center. There was no sense in wearing anything other than a sturdy tough variety and keeping luster on shoehide was next to impossible. The blank expression on her face registered no emotion and the facial muscles did not move.

"Mrs. Kubo, I am here to aid you if I can and so you must help me by answering and by doing things that I tell you. Can you tell me what happened last night, or what you did at home?" The middle-aged woman's gaze was fixed low at the corner to the room and did not swerve for a moment. She seemed oblivious to her surroundings and whether or not she heard his question was doubtful. Evidentally, there was no use in further questioning. She was in a depressed state of mind and no amount of coaxing would bring her out of her shell. She had firmly retreated into this protective haven and until the proper time arrived she would not emerge to face reality.

To the husband who waited in the adjoining room the doctor turned for elucidation of the cause and history of the case and to do so he locked the door so that they could discuss the matter alone. "This is a really sad state of affairs and my sympathy goes out to you. We must try to go to the bottom of the matter and find out the probable cause. You must be honest with me. Can you tell me in sequence the events that took place? Please begin with her girlhood if you know about it and what happened since your marriage. Add events that you think significant in the light of this present condition. These facts are necessary in the analysis of the case and in deciding of the kind of treatment most suitable for her." The doctor began his conversation gently in order to gain the confidence of the man.

"For many years I lived in San Francisco and having made a little money I returned to my native country and there was introduced to a girl born in California, but taken to the Orient by her parents in her infancy and educated in the ways of Japan. She was ideal for my wife as far as the legal aspect was concerned because, being American-born, she could accompany me back to the United States. We were soon married with hardly any period of courtship as is the custom in the old country. Her parents thought it was a fortunate match as she could return to bountiful America, her birthplace. She herself was filled with nostalgic dreams. After our return to San Francisco we both worked hard in restaurants and groceries and finally saved enough to become independent. We bought a dry cleaning establishment." The man in his late thirties seemed a very nervous sort; a very irritable and sour expression was on his face. He was not a very pleasant type to talk to and the information he was imparting to the doctor seemed rather reluctantly given, but as it came to light later, he was a high school graduate in Japan and so realized the significance of his telling everything he knew concerning her case.

"I am not bragging when I tell you that we made money for our business prospered. The Caucasian clientele trusted us in the quality of work and our promptness in delivering goods. In order to acquire that reputation we literally slaved at our trade. She worked from dawn far into the night. Money was the only thing that mattered. We denied ourselves every form of luxury and recreation. Not only did we not go to the cheap movies of American production because she did not understand them, but she refrained from attending the occasional Japanese entertainments that came to town. We were just about getting on easy street when along came the war and the mass evacuation. We were sent to Tanforan Assembly Center and then transferred to Tule Lake."

"Was she entirely happy? Did she not want something more from life?"

"Well she came from a family which had saved some money in their toil in the strawberry farms near San Jose, but after the family went to Japan the little nest egg soon dwindled to almost nothing and they would have gladly returned to California. But by that time the period of two years allowed by the consulate in Kobe for a reentry into the United States, had expired. The parents could not come and the children had to make the best of the employment opportunities in the neighboring textile mills as soon as they were graduated from the village school. Therefore, she knew the taste of bitter poverty and the dread of insecurity. And so it was no urging on my part that made her so industrious. Like for all other women, life in this center in the physical sense is almost a utopia for her. Really, women have nothing to do for the most part, provided they do not work regularly at some job and get on the WRA payroll.

"My wife has had no regular employment and so after cleaning and mopping our apartment and doing the family washing, there is nothing to do but to sit around and gossip with other women. But she is not a sociable type and has made few friends. She seems to have relaxed in this center for the first time since her arrival in America. I am glad of it for she really deserves a vacation. But like everybody else this vacation with its indefiniteness as to duration has been getting on our nerves and we are hoping for an early peace."

"That is a pretty good background that you have painted for me. Now coming down to the present illness, can you tell me how this all came about?"

"I think you have in your record that she made about two visits to the dispensary for headaches and various aches over her shoulders and back."

"Yes, there are two entries about one month ago. The examining physician did not think there was very much wrong with her and she was sent home with some simple remedy."

"That is true and she felt well for a few days, but when one day she mentioned her symptoms to Mrs. Abe, our next door neighbor, she was told of the miraculous healing powers of Mrs. Takahara, the 'Odaishi priestess' and by all means she should go there."

Apparently Mr. Kudo himself did not believe and when the narrative came to this point his attitude became one of sheepishness and hesitation. "You know how women are and a domineering type like Mrs. Abe was soon leading my wife to the altar at Mrs. Takahara's apartment in Block 23. After the first visit she seemed very happy and was full of smiles. I was glad for her and thought perhaps there was something in this priestess's pretensions, but after the second visit there appeared

429

an indescribable gloominess and unhappiness in my wife's expression. She began to sit by herself in deep meditation and although never very jolly in her former self, still she was not too moody. That night she asked me if I would accompany her to the church the following day. When asked the reason, she would not answer. She just wanted me to go. I am not religious and in fact never entered a temple or church, but seeing she was so anxious for me to go, I consented to keep her company the next day."

"What sort of a person is this priestess and what did she say to you?" The doctor was getting interested. In fact, he was not aware of the presence of such a cult in the center.

"The apartment was no different from ordinary ones except that there was a very pretentious altar with gaudy decorations like those you see in ordinary temples on the outside. Several chairs and benches were in the room and by some way or another the WRA had authorized an extra room for religious worship. Mrs. Takahara is in her late forties and to me is no different from any other women. I doubt if she is even halfway educated.

"After reading the sutra she faced me and said, 'You are Mr. Kudo, I presume. Your poor wife is now being troubled with this sickness which is the result of a certain neglect on your part and also due to certain sins she committed in her past. In order to get well she should expiate for these sins and become a real believer in Buddha. Your entire family should come to the service and lead a life in the service of religion. What your shortcomings are, I related to your wife yesterday and so get the information from her since it is perhaps easier for you to be told by her.' I was dumbfounded and too indignant to say anything. What could I say to a stranger? So, after we returned home I confronted my wife and made her tell what our neglect and her sins were."

His manner of conversation became more difficult and so Dr. Murayama offered him a cigarette. He said slowly, "You know when she said that the priestess had frowned upon our neglect to keep up the memorial services to our deceased ancestors and to perform the religious services when their name days and anniversaries arrived, I had no answer or apology for that was true. But I am asking you, who in this day and age of hectic business competition can be thinking of these apparently trifling observances? People doing nothing may remember such practices.

"When she reminded me of the two induced abortions we had performed during our days of trial and tribulation after we had bought the dry-cleaning shop—we were so deeply engaged in the task of making 'a go' of the business and considered the two children we already had were sufficient for the time being—I was shocked out of my wits. She had put the question point-blank to my wife and declared, 'You are being punished for the criminal disposal of the unborn children you were callous enough to destroy. These unfortunate souls are now in hell and awaiting to be saved from hell fire. I can see the poor infants squirming from the tongues of flame that threaten to engulf and scorch them. They are crying out to be saved.' Naturally, this accusation cut deeply into my wife's conscience and to her inquiry as to how she might succor the infants, the answer was that our family was found short in religious fervor and that the entire family should become converted to the faith.

"From that day on I was pestered by my wife to accompany her to Block 23 daily and naturally we could not go empty handed. Attendance at the service in the apartment was not enough, and we were persuaded to go to the empty lot near the sewage disposal plant and attend nightly prayers in the cold night wind. There were many there and my wife was one of the many that seemed to be deeply involved and in the clutches of this pseudo-priestess. I later found out that she is no bona-fide religious preacher. As to my wife, she is now hearing the wailings of her unborn children, mumbling about neighbors and passersby staring and talking about her. She asks me to walk about with my eyes fixed on the ground. I should not look people straight in the face because of what we had done. Last night she tried to hang herself." After this lengthy recital the man showed a certain degree of relief, for it must have been hard to divulge family secrets even to a physician.

"That makes the case pretty clear. Now, can you tell me if there was any incident in her past that was out of the ordinary either in her talk or actions?"

After pondering for a while, Mr. Kudo resumed his talk. "Yes, there was a time while we were living in San Francisco when she had a spell of talking queerly and it lasted for about two months. She seemed to be extra-retiring and tried very much to avoid meeting people, even neighbors. She suspected that they were talking about her and staring at her when she went to do her shopping. This lasted for about two months. She got completely well and we thought nothing of the experience."

"Is there anyone in her family who was afflicted with nervous disorders such as insanity or epilepsy? And how are your marriage relations?"

"You know how careful we are in Japan regarding that sort of thing. Before marriage was contracted an investigation was conducted and I am pretty sure there was no such trait in the family. Of course there might have been a slip somewhere, because a *nakaudo* (go-between) marriage is notoriously defective sometimes. After we got married there was no real quarrel that I can think of. She was obedient and even if I were at times domineering she was not the type to fight back. So, as a whole our family life was without the usual squabbles that I know exist in other families. After the birth of the two children her attention became centered on them and there seemed to be more contentment for her from that quarter than could be imagined possible."

It was a plain case of mental derangement and during the period of observation in the hospital she continued to behave in the same quiet, depressed, and resigned manner. Routine examinations regarding her physical state being normal, she was to be committed to the state institution as there was no provision in the WRA setup. All such cases had to be taken to the county seat, Alturas of Modoc County, about sixty miles to the southeast. During peace time, such patients had to be kept under observation by a county physician for several days and then taken through a court procedure in which two physicians had to swear to the advisability of the commitment. But under war time conditions the observation period was dispensed with and only the testimony of two doctors was required.

As these cases occurred mostly among evacuees that could not speak English fluently, and history-taking required a thorough knowledge not only of the language but of the customs, traditions, superstitions, and all likes and dislikes common to any race, evacuee doctors were necessarily assigned to such work. To such a trial an evacuee doctor had to go along for testimony in company of an appointed Caucasian doctor. It was one of the most disagreeable kinds of work an evacuee doctor had to perform.

The people that made the party to Alturas consisted of the two doctors, an internal security man to act as a driver for the trip from Alturas to the state mental institution, a nurse to accompany the patient to the institution, and the husband. A Ford station wagon was driven by the security officer and Minoru was in Dr. Marks' Buick. At eight o'clock in the morning they were to assemble at the hospital. There had been no rain or snow for a week. Still, the weather might change at any time. Considerable red tape had to be gone through, in spite of the preliminary arrangement made by the medical superintendent with the Provost Marshal the previous day. Internal security passes for the evacuees going out of the center, the WRA allowance for the meals to be taken outside, the military pass for the evacuees, etc., consumed at least three quarters of an hour.

From then on it was a speedy run of one hour and a half to the county seat. A non-commissioned officer of the Military Police was assigned to guard the Japanese to forestall an escape; a laughable precaution on the part of the military, but a very unpleasant ruling from the evacuees' standpoint. They felt degraded being followed by this soldier who carried side arms all the time. This sergeant was not a bad fellow. He had returned from Italy and had seen the 100th Infantry Battalion in action and knew two of the wounded boys that came back to the States with him.

Just south of the camp there was a wheat field that looked white. On close scrutiny it was covered with thousands of wild geese. This region was a virtual paradise for hunters during the winter months. Minoru had only seen these myriads of geese flying in formation over the camp, especially in the mornings and evenings, and occasionally came across mortally wounded birds that fell within the center. They seemed little disturbed by the passing cars.

The cars soon entered the Modoc National Forest. There was a large wasteland of lava that resembled the lava fields of Hawaii except for the occasional trees of northern habitat that broke through the crusty surface and were thriving without competition. Spruce, cedar, and holly seemed to abound. Dr. Marks told Minoru that many deer were at times visible, but unfortunately there were none that day. They met no car enroute; traffic was certainly light in this section on account of the restriction of gasoline.

They were steadily climbing and finally entered a magnificent forest of tall pines through which the road extended as far as eyes could reach in a straight stretch of asphalt. The trees were never cut and grew to the lofty height of seventy or eighty feet. In this pine forest there was a wayside cottage, in front of which was a signpost that commanded every car to stop. It was a station of the California Department of Agriculture to prevent any out-of-state fruit from coming within its boundary. It was curious to find this station here, at least thirty miles inside the boundary line. Of course this section would be a good natural barrier for this sort of regulation, but then a great district of geographical California was treated as part of Oregon.

Past this forest reserve there was a sort of plateau and the road meandered down into grassy land of the valley. In the distance there was a towering mountain range. Into this valley they traveled for about twenty miles to the town of Alturas. It was a typical California County seat with a branch railroad passing through the edge of the town. A great white elephant in the form of an imposing mission-styled concrete building with a belfry stood about fifty feet from the railroad. It was explained that although this was built for the railroad it never had been used.

The other car bearing the patient and husband with Miss Perkins, the nurse, arrived. The doctors proceeded up the main stairway of the courthouse whereas the second car went to the rear. The essential details of the case had been telephoned ahead to the district attorney and his secretary produced the necessary papers in triplicate for them to sign. As there was a criminal case being tried before theirs came under consideration, Dr. Murayama sauntered into the courtroom from the rear. The case being tried was a recent affair that happened at Tule Lake. There was a drunken party in the course of which one member stabbed another. The whole affair seemed hinged on some gambling altercation. The accused was alone and what the district attorney was trying to put across was not very clear to the defendant. The district attorney caught sight of the doctor in the rear of the courtroom and asked him if he would not interpret. He was just and fair and wanted the defendant to have legal counsel if he so wished. It turned out that the Japanese had no money and the court was going to appoint one to help him in puting up a semblance of defense.

After waiting some time, an old man about seventy who resembled an unkempt hobo came into the courtroom, definitely under the influence of whiskey, although not to a degree of betraying his condition in his gait. Evidently he was within beckoning distance of the court and whenever such a hand-out was possible by the judge, he was there to profit by the occasion.

"Mr. Henderson, we have here a man accused of attacking another man with a deadly weapon at Newell, California. He is accused of having inflicted on this other person an injury that necessitated seven stitches. He has no money and the court is asking you to take the case and prepare a proper defense for him. Will time until Saturday morning be sufficient for the preparation of the defense? That will give you three days in which to prepare your defense."

"Your honor," shouted the old man leaning across the table. With an apparent demeanor of deference and humility derived from life-long habit and looking up into the benevolent face of the judge, he continued, "I shall take the case, but not this Saturday. This is one of the days I simply cannot work. You see, back in 1897 when I was in active practice and your father, bless his soul, was sitting on that bench that you now occupy, it was that Saturday when we organized and met for the first time in Modoc County as an organized Democratic Party. It was a gala day with parades and free barbecue dinner and to this day on that anniversary I am not in a mood to work. Therefore, if it pleases your honor, I should like to ask for a further postponement." The judge must have had similar experiences with this old-timer before, but in all seriousness referred to his calendar and said "All right, Mr. Henderson. The court will take up your case on Wednesday of next week."

"Your honor. Another thing. The accused does not seem to speak the English language very well. To make a proper defense there should be an interpreter to facilitate understanding between counsel and defendant."

"The accused can speak some English and with enough time you will certainly not find it difficult to understand him. It is understood that the case will be ready for presentation on Wednesday next week."

It was an effort to stifle the laughter that welled up in one's throat and Dr. Murayama went out into the hall and back into the district attorney's office where the patient, husband, and nurse were waiting.

The waiting room was rather small. The very efficient and pleasant secretary was an attractive feature in an otherwise oppressive atmosphere. She made the people feel easier. The picture on the wall of the "Old Glory" waving against the background of fleecy clouds gave a dignity to the room in its simplicity of decoration.

Mrs. Kudo was in a strait jacket because she had put up resistance to her removal from the hospital. She must have sensed in the move a separation from her children. She was huddled up in her overcoat and canvas restrainer and looked very little, subdued, and beaten. Fear was apparent in her figure and she kept her gaze concentrated on the floor, never once venturing her eyes upward. To her husband sitting next to her she kept saying in undertones, "You must not look upward or straight at other people. It is wrong and you must keep your eyes down or else you will be punished." This seemed to be the only concern for the occasion and she kept repeating the phrase over and over again to him.

Suddenly she raised her voice. "Oh, Japanese gentleman, are you there? Will you please tell them that I am all right mentally and physically and that there is nothing wrong with me? I want to go back to my children. Don't let them take me anywhere. I must return to the center. I simply must, and they must not take me anywhere else!"

Dr. Murayama felt like a heel. Knowing fully well that she was being taken to a place where the best treatment could be given her by experienced personnel, that her plea arising from a deranged mind should not influence him even for a moment, he could not surmount the feeling of compassion for this helpless woman. That this should have occurred to anyone among his own kind in a concentration camp made the fact of double significance in its tragic meaning. He could not stand it any longer and walked away without attempting to answer her.

The court went into session over this case. It was mere formality as the case was so clear and the person committing the patient was her husband, but the legal aspect had to be above board according to the legal code of the State of California. The judge was to sit on a raised dais. To his right on a lower platform was a chair where the witness was to be seated. At the same level and toward the center and left there were two tables where the secretaries of the court had their station. Perhaps due to a dearth of young and attractive secretaries, there were two unkempt women in their fifties mechanically taking down in shorthand the proceedings of the court while they kept chewing gum incessantly.

On the main floor to the left were chairs in which the patient or person under trial was seated. In the center of the room just in front of the railing there was a long desk where the district attorney and the doctors, expert witnesses, had their seats. Behind the railing an audience of about a hundred could sit on benches arranged like pews in a church. When all were seated, the judge came in and on his entry the entire audience rose to their feet.

The judge looked like a gentleman, through and through. He was in his fifties or early sixties; unhurried, kind voice, and the grey hair imparted to him an aura of dignity, wisdom, and fairness. "Setsuko Kudo, you are brought before this court with the complaint of having illusions and delusions, that you tried to hang yourself and are suffering from a condition called schizophrenia. For the treatment and protection of yourself from harm, it is hereby petitioned to send you to a state institution. Do you want to have legal counsel to aid you in deciding whether you should be sent there?" The judge was addressing the patient but the woman did not understand. The district attorney, Mr. Lederer, was on his feet.

"Your honor, the husband of the patient is here and waives all legal counsel and agrees to send her to a state institution for treatment. The patient herself is noncommunicative."

"In that case we shall dispense with the legal counsel and proceed with the medical testimony. Dr. Marks, will you take the stand. Please be sworn in."

Dr. Marks took the stand and was sworn in by one of the unkempt old women. The judge continued. "What is your name?"

"Harry K. Marks."

"Are you a duly licensed physician?"

"Yes, sir."

"Do you take care of the sick and are you regularly employed by the War Relocation Authority at Newell, California?"

"Yes, sir."

"In the course of the care and treatment of this patient, Mrs. Setsuko Kudo, have you come to the conclusion that this patient is suffering from schizophrenia and that she requires institutional care?"

"Yes, sir."

"Why can you not care for her at the center hospital?"

"Because there is neither the personnel nor the facility for the adequate treatment for this type of patient."

"In case the patient does not have any funds to pay for her hospitalization, is the cost to be defrayed by the War Relocation Authority?"

"Yes, sir."

"Mr. Lederer, do you have any questions you would like to put to the witness?"

The district attorney got to his feet and facing the doctor in the witness chair, asked "How long have you known the patient?"

"About one month."

"According to the report from our social service worker, neither the patient nor husband seem to have any money."

"That is true, your honor."

Dr. Marks descended from the platform. Dr. Murayama had to go through the same formalities, and in addition the judge asked to which institution he preferred to send her. According to prearranged consultation with his colleague, he suggested Stockton.

The judge then pronounced, "It is then agreed that the patient, Mrs. Setsuko Kudo, is to be committed to the State Hospital at Stockton for treatment, the expense of which will be borne and defrayed by the War Relocation Authority. The travel to the said hospital at Stockton will be under the custody of the internal security officer of the Relocation Authority at Newell, California."

This concluded the formal part of the hearing and the rest consisted in the signing of papers requested by the judge. Miss Perkins, the nurse, led the weeping woman out the rear of the building and the parting of the man and wife was not a pleasant sight. She was not unaware of the impending departure and separation, but there was no loud wailing. Inured to poverty, accustomed to being at the receiving end of raw deals in life, she already was evidently readjusting her thinking to the inevitable acquiescence she had to make. If her mental reasoning was not sane and normal, she at least felt that something was radically wrong and she was made powerless to assert her wishes. The canvas restrainer that immobilized her to such an extent as to prevent her even to scratch her nose was evidence enough.

The Ford station wagon was started and amidst pleasant raillery between the Caucasians, the car sped forward. There was profound silence among the three Japanese.

Tule Lake War Relocation Center was one of the larger centers, accommodating 16,000 or more people. The two centers at Gila and

Poston in the deserts of Arizona were about of equal size, while seven centers at Minnedoka, Idaho, Topaz, Utah, Heart Mountain, Wyoming, Granada, Colorado, Jerome and Rohwer in Arkansas, were about one half the size of Tule and contained 8,000 people. Because the population at Tule Lake was made up of people from the three Pacific coast states, there was a certain degree of dilution in the rivalry, feuds, and vice of organized society in the various cities, but it so happened that the worst elements of Sacramento were bodily transferred here. The gambling syndicate of that city continued its activity in this center and exerted a disturbing influence in camp politics. The chief of police was a gambler from Sacramento and so the general trend could be roughly guessed. These "Tokyo Club" gamblers were not vicious and not the prototypes of the Mafia and other organized criminal gangs of the other minority racial groups. All were small-time gamblers. Nevertheless, it was a nauseating aspect to the majority of decent people that such a situation should prevail when everyone was reduced to this condition of misery and poverty. Why poach on the men whose bank account was low and with no prospect of additional income in the foreseeable future? Why continue an outside feud, or play power politics in a place where brotherly love should be the guiding force?

The teenagers had no restraint and ran wild. Social dances and organized athletics could only reach a few, and idle time lay heavily on their hands. The grown-ups indulged in camp politics and gossip mongering, because not all could be given jobs to occupy their time. Numerous fracases took place. The culmination was murder, but the truth was never brought to light, although suspicion of the gamblers having a hand in the act was strongly entertained by most of the people.

The same rivalry could be discerned among the medical practitioners from Sacramento. Dr. Murayama was glad that he was not from that city. It became so obviously bad and detrimental to the smooth function of the hospital that some had to be dispersed to other centers and Dr. Emura of Southern California had to be installed as the chief surgeon. This remarkable man steered the course of medical work, cooperating fully with the medical director so that the people in the center would get the best possible medical care. How well and peaceful a center was conducted depended in a great degree to the personal diplomacy of the project director. When there was kindness and diplomacy as in Amachi, Colorado or Rohwer, Arkansas, peace prevailed and a strike was unheard of. Tule Lake was ridden with such incidents, and it did not speak too well for those that ran the project.

The Japanese people are like the Latin people. Reared in the land of volcanoes, they are wary and emotional, quick tempered, and reckless. But visited by annual typhoons and numerous earthquakes in the course of centuries, the inhabitants developed a philosophy of resignation. Centuries of feudalism had ingrained in them a discipline that was excellent in time of peace, for they made good law-abiding citizens. In time of stress, they became docile and putty in the hands of any leader. Now they looked to the project director as a provider of food and shelter, but the Caucasian personnel were a class apart, beyond the fence. And the petty small people invested with power lorded over these docile people who became increasingly servile as months went by.

The WRA said categorically that any medical care could be given as long as the drug was available or any surgical operation could be done if the surgeon with the technical skill could be found among the evacuee doctors. However, as it worked out, the Caucasian medical superintendents balked at operations scheduled as being non-emergency and unnecessary. A hemorrhoid could be disabling and render life miserable, but was not an emergency condition in the sense that life was endangered. Only a clinician could evaluate the real urgency of an operation and he had to be a good salesman to get permission to operate from his superior who merely sat in his office and passed judgment. Dr. Emura was a persistent man and as a spokesman for the doctors obtained permission for more operations in this center than anywhere else. He got on the good side of the superintendent, so that more latitude was obtained for freedom of operations. "You've got to polish the apple sometimes," he would comment wryly and the old people got their hernias repaired. There always is an Achilles' heel to train an arrow at.

One day Dr. Murayama was busily circulating among the curtained booths in the out-patient department when a man with a peculiar hand injury was brought in. He was a small, skinny man in his late fifties. He wore a khaki shirt and dungarees and was not a very clean individual. An indescribably disagreeable stench was about him.

"How did you get hurt?"

"I was walking along the barbed wire fence when I scraped my hand against the sharp barbs of the fence."

Minoru could not reconcile the arrangement of the marks on the skin and the swelling that had already become visible. "Mr. Kaneshiro, you must tell us the truth. These marks are not what you tell us. You must have been bitten by some animal perhaps?"

"No. It is as I have told you. Barbed wire."

"All right, I'll take your word for it. But if this is a bite from a dog or any other animal there must be special medicine to fight off the poison. If you are concealing something you are the loser for you may yet die."

The old man's face assumed an expression of fear and he blurted out. "Then I'll confess. Near the fence I was catching snakes, rattlesnakes. I was bitten then."

Minoru had never treated a rattlesnake bite. The swelling about the fang marks was increasing. It was pinkish, hot, and painful. He applied a tourniquet right away and sent a request to the pharmacy for "antitoxin." Fortunately there was one vial in stock. He injected the serum around the fang marks to act locally and the remainder of the precious medicine he injected on the inner side of the tourniquet to combat the poison that had already spread throughout the body. The patient was then hospitalized.

In his rounds of the ward the next morning he examined the hand. To his amazement the swelling had decreased, the redness subsided, and Mr. Kaneshiro was in smiles.

"Now don't you think that this serum is remarkable? You know you may have died last night from that rattlesnake bite. Now tell me. Why did you make up stories like that and lie to us?" inquired Minoru not unkindly. There was neither recrimination in his manner nor in his speech. There was kindness that came from the satisfaction of work well done.

The man was evidently embarrassed. "I am a professional snake catcher. In Okinawa there are many poisonous snakes and I was good at capturing them."

"Snakes for what purpose?"

His confidence was returning. Pitying the ignorance of this doctor, he declared, "To make medicine. All these poisonous snakes are valuable and make good medicine."

Now Dr. Murayama remembered this man. He had not met him, but at the beginning of the center there was an application from one

441

S. Kaneshiro to be permitted to work on hospital patients. His qualification to make use of the hospital was non-existent, but he wanted to help those that were sick in his own way by "Oriental medicine." Naturally, non-orthodox medical practice was not permitted by the WRA.

"How do you make the medicine and for what disease would you give them?" inquired the doctor.

Spurred on by these questions Mr. Kaneshiro could not miss this chance of advertising his wares and qualifications. "The snakes are skinned and smoked until charred. The charred powder keeps for years and is used for many and all conditions that human bodies succumb to. It is a powerful medicine for lost manhood. Whevever you feel weak, a daily use of a small amount will restore health…. It makes the liver work better. It is an all-around medicine. Only you cannot take too much. Too powerful!"

"How do you catch the snakes?" Minoru was enjoying this session. Patients in nearby beds were sitting up and listening to this dialogue.

"In Okinawa there is a castle in Shuri. This was the castle where the king lived before annexation to Japan. There was a wall made of loose rocks piled one on top of another and in among the cracks and crevices the dreaded *habu* lived and multiplied. These poisonous snakes were not large, but very wiry and active. They jumped several feet and when one was bitten there was not much hope. I used to catch them first for fun, then as a profession."

Dr. Murayama was impressed. He knew that the *habu* was like the coral snake of the Americas and the cobra of India. There was no antitoxin for these snakes because the poison from the fangs had the property to break down the red blood corpuscles rapidly and the victim died in a matter of minutes.

"I have two sticks. The long one three feet long is in my left hand, a shorter piece one foot long in my right hand. I sneak up to a sleeping or unwary snake and with the long stick pin the reptile down to earth at any part of his long body. Then the right stick is used to immobilize the head or neck. The left stick is placed in my pocket. I use the three fingers of my left hand to grasp the back of the head. The snake is then put in a sack I carry slung over my shoulders." Mr. Kaneshiro was out of bed and went through the motion of stalking the snake, using the imaginary two sticks to pin down the creature, much to the amusement and amazement of the ward patients who were watching this demonstration.

"How come you got bitten?"

"Well, I just got careless. I did not hold part of his head in my grasp and just grabbed the neck and the snake snapped back." He was somewhat embarrassed by this admission.

As the doctor walked back to the nurse's desk, the nurse's aide said, "He is quite a character. He makes quite a bit of money by catching the snakes. I heard people buy these snakes at fifteen dollars apiece. Doctor, your salary of nineteen dollars a month is chicken-feed compared to his income," teased the young lady in green and white stripes who was blossoming out into womanhood. There was camaraderie between the physicians and aides. It was pleasant work.

"Talking of pay, I had a funny feeling the other day. You know we delivered Mrs. Seno of a strapping seven and a half pound boy. Her husband is a barber at Block 7. I had a hair cut yesterday and he charged me fifty cents. I do a hundred dollar job for him for nothing and he soaks me fifty cents. Is that gratitude?"

"I should say not. I never saw so many selfish people. Some people are making more money here than they would outside. Board and room free and no taxes to pay. Whatever comes in remains theirs," indignantly replied the young lady.

"Still, there are some good people. A week ago a grateful patient brought us a package of sugar. It was only a five pound package, but I was really thankful. Mr. Okuda is a topnotch baker from Oakland, but he cannot bake any cake without sugar. I'll bring some sugar for him and he can bake a good cake for your birthday, which I know comes pretty soon."

Laughingly she replied, "If I didn't have one coming soon, we d decide to celebrate one next week."

The large recreation hall near the public school was used for theatrical productions, piano concerts, dances, and socials, in addition to basketball games. The many concerts—songfests to give students of the various voice schools a chance to sing before an audience, called *On-shu-kai*—were held in barrack apartments and dining halls. *Joruri*, a classical school of singing appreciated only by the elders would be held in an apartment because the crowd was small. *Utai* of either the *Kanze* or *Hosho* school were in a larger apartment, because the devotees of this school were found in a larger stratum of educated people. But when it came to the new songs: *ryukoka*, and the modified *shigin*, the mess halls were usually used.

A remarkable group from Los Angeles under the guidance of a woman seventy-two years old put on an extravaganza of classical *kabuki* by girls in their teens. This was an achievement in itself as these girls who could scarcely speak Japanese acted in an antiquated language and danced to the music very foreign to their up-bringing. In company of other singers, this elderly teacher chanted all the *joruri* songs apparently from memory, accompanied by a corps of *samisen* players. The rich, gold embroidered costumes had been brought in by this troupe. The girls were superbly trained. It was an astonishing feat. These Nisei girls could hardly understand what they were enunciating and here they were participating in classical drama which could only be seen in the larger cities of Japan and could not be fully interpreted by university graduates. It was all due to the untiring effort and persistence of this remarkable artist and teacher.

Softball teams were organized in every block and a regular league was formed competing for a pennant. *Sumo*, or Japanese wrestling, was another form of athletics organized to sublimate the exuberant energy of the young men and boys.

CHAPTER 30

Segregation of Evacuees

IT SEEMED TO THE EVACUEES THAT THE policy of the Justice Department continually changed and there was no definite, clear-cut program. At first they were told that these concentration camps were for the duration of the war; that they were so kept behind barbed wire fence for their own protection. Then there was this new attempt at segregation of the "loyal" from the "disloyal."

The last definite program by the War Relocation Authority was to release men and women into the midwestern and eastern seaboard states into normal activities of life and to engage in gainful occupations. In most large cities there were WRA officers whose job it was to assist in the relocation of families. These officers performed humanitarian work, a very unsavory task of educating the American public to receive these kin of their current arch enemy as neighbors and fellow workers. These WRA officers were stigmatized as "Jap-lovers" and unless they were men of principle and humanity they would not have lasted at this unpopular work.

Once people are incarcerated and branded as prisoners there develops a complex which is hard to shake off, even when there is no question of criminality involved. The ten foot fence topped with three or four lines of barbed wire that rested on inwardly angulated arms, made escape well nigh impossible. The presence of guards on towers with shotguns and the maneuvering of light tanks on the wheatfields outside could not help but impress the "colonists" that they were unwanted people. There is nothing in a person's life to brighten him and make life worth living unless he is made to feel that he is a useful member of the community and above all, that he is wanted. Contrarily, when he is made to feel like a pariah or a public enemy, he lacks courage, is short of initiative, and feels that life is not worth living.

When the WRA began encouraging people to leave the centers to seek jobs and live in the normal current of American life, the evacuees became dubious of their reception on the "outside." They became cowards and took the line of least resistance which was to sit out the war in the camp.

At the end of August the registration process came to an end. There was going to be a mass reshuffling of the people. Those who preferred to be returned to Japan after the war and those who refused to sign the questionnaires were to be segregated at Tule Lake. Those that answered questions 27 and 28 in the affirmative were to be trans-shipped to other centers. The latter centers were to be closed gradually as relocation progressed. The original inhabitants of Tule Lake showed the greatest number of non-registrants. These people did not register because they were swayed by the pro-Japan element, to be sure, but perhaps a greater blame should be laid at the door of the project director and his staff, for statistics showed that in other centers registration rate was high and in some the record was 100%. The probability of the presence of the pro-Japan element in all the centers was equal to that in Tule Lake. The only conclusion that could be drawn was the lack of human understanding, the attitude of bureaucratic aloofness, and the ignoring of competent advice that was available in the persons of anthropologists who were stationed at each center to make a scientific study of human reactions in such an abnormal environment. The other great reason was a fear in every evacuee that the family might be broken up and the members thrown out into a hostile world if he made a "yes-yes" answer to questions 27 and 28. The wiser of the two alternatives was to refuse to obey and continue cautiously as wards of the government as long as hostilities continued.

In the middle of September 1943, the "loyal" families were again herded into coaches and carried off to any of the nine other centers to make room for the families that preferred to be segregated at Tule Lake for eventual deportation to Japan.

As in all families, there was considerable soul-searching during the registration period and Dr. Murayama held a family council among the four adults.

"Father, let us hear what you will do in this registration. I know you have been talking about it for some weeks among your friends. Under these circumstances each has to decide the way his conscience will guide him." Minoru looked at his father who had grown rather obese in the past thirty years because he liked his liquor and rich food. His face was ruddy. In his youth and in subsequent years he had not changed much, for he was loquacious and loved an argument.

"I was at the mess hall meeting on registration when you delivered your speech. I heard your side of the version and I was proud of your brave stand. Maybe you converted me by that speech for I will sign the questionnaire and follow you wherever you go. I do not wish to have this family broken up under any circumstances. 'The aged should follow the young' is an old Japanese adage. But I am going to make my stand clear even to you, my son, just for my conscience's sake.

"You know that no matter how loyal I want to be to America, I cannot be an American because I cannot be naturalized. Then I must remain Japanese as long as I live. I cannot fight against Japan for that would be treason. Perhaps I am glad that I am old and can neither work nor fight. If I had to choose between the two countries I'd be in an awful dilemma. I am legally bound to Japan, but America has been extremely good to me for nearly half a century. As an honest man what could I do if I were to be pressed to fight one or the other? Perhaps there is only one way; and that is to die. I am sure your mother will second me in that statement."

Lillian was profoundly impressed. Were her own father alive he would have said the same thing. She took hold of his hand and said, "Thank you father, we understand. We'll stick it out together. The war will not last very many years. Peace will eventually come. Some day in the future you will take us to Kumamoto to visit the village in which you were born."

He squeezed her hand. "Well said. I know mama will follow us and so we shall all signify our intentions by answering yes to the two questions. Meanwhile it is better that we keep our mouths shut and not let other people know how we have decided. The people from Sacramento are especially hard-headed. There are really no leaders. It is a shame how gullible they are and cannot think for themselves." He looked at the two women and exhorted them to be cautious about expressing their opinions in their daily talk with neighbors in regard to these questions.

When the segregation movement was taking place, Dr. Murayama was called into the medical superintendent's office. "Dr. Murayama I am glad that you are leaving this center for another. But we'll become short-handed when the doctors pull out. There will be only a few doctors transferring here from other centers and to tide over the short period until we can recruit Caucasian doctors, I want you to remain."

"It is OK with me. If the project director has given his consent I shall be glad to remain and help," he told the superintendent sincerely, for the climate of Tule Lake was to his liking and he did not mind remaining as long as there was an excuse for staying. Thus, the Murayama family remained behind when others pulled out and from other centers many arrived to sit out the war. Dr. Murayama was destined to witness incidents that took place at this transition period, many of which made newspaper headlines.

Dr. Emura was a good surgeon. He realized that what he was today was the result of opportunities offered by American institutions. He never could have attained a semblance of such achievement if he had remained in Japan. There he worked as an apprentice in a dry goods store following his father's economic reversals that had taken place while he was in his early teens, but his burning ambition made him leave the snowy north country for Tokyo. Then he saw better opportunities for education in the country beyond the sea and landed at San Francisco when he was sixteen. He worked the entire curriculum from grammar school to medical school, doing menial housework while he went to school and whatever job that brought money during the summer months. Therefore, he was intensely loyal to America, the country that had given him the opportunity despite the racial discrimination that was encountered in California.

But there was a deep-seated resentment at the treatment received since the war began. As a doctor his interest was primarily the welfare of his fellow countrymen. He was a Japanese National; these people remaining in Tule Lake Center as segregated people were made up of people who asked to be repatriated to Japan or those that refused to sign the questionnaire. Dr. Emura was in a dilemma. The supplicating call of his people for a good doctor in whom they could entrust their lives was very loud and pressure exerted on him to remain in Tule

Lake Center was strong. His sense of duty and conscience would not allow him to desert them. On the other hand he could not answer "no" to the questionnaire and he willy-nilly joined the ranks of the non-registered group.

"Dr. Emura, read this sheet and make up your mind. You are wanted at another center," the assistant project director had him in his office and presented him a printed form.

"But I am needed here and I cannot desert these friends," Dr. Emura protested.

The assistant director adjusted his holster and straightened up in his chair. "Oh, these people will be taken care of all right. Orders are that you are to proceed to Poston at once."

"You mean to say I cannot even go back to my family?" incredulously inquired the doctor.

"That's right. Your family will be sent afterward and we'll see that they will get all the help they need."

Dr. Emura felt that there was no sense arguing. He was a prisoner and was completely at this man's mercy. The wearing of side arms was a symbol of that "Authority" and the adjusting of the gun belt was calculated to remind the evacuee of this relationship and the status of the Japanese. "Well then, there is no other way out. But give me time to think it over." The doctor was confused and could not make up his mind.

The assistant director condescendly declared, "I'll give you an hour" and left the room.

It was then 11 o'clock. Left to himself, Dr. Emura began weighing the pros and cons of the situation. True, he had cast his lot with the non-registrants and decided to dedicate his service and skill to the alleviation of ills and pains of these people. But now he had no choice but to follow another course. That course, too, meant caring for the afflicted of his own people. Either way, at nineteen dollars a month it was evident to anyone that he was not deserting the people for personal gain. He might just as well sign it and proceed to Poston Relocation Center in Arizona. In this act his conscience was clear. The only part he did not like was being ordered around at the point of a pistol. But it was war time. Countless thousands were being sacrificed mercilessly all over the earth in this crazy era of power politics. He read the sheet of paper slowly and signed his name.

At noon the assistant director sauntered in and was wreathed in smiles when he saw the signed order. "Doctor, make yourself comfortable in this office. Magazines are there for you to while away your time. I'll send a tray from the mess hall." He left Dr. Emura for the mess hall to have his own lunch.

Again, Dr. Emura began to review the situation. To be sure he signed the paper of transfer. He would not have to face the center people again, to listen to their supplications for him to remain. But could he in honesty to himself live down the fact that he deserted them? Would he not be troubled in the future by the remembrance of this day when he was cowed and brow-breaten by a burly, swashbuckling man with only a high school education but now made formidable by a black six-shooter? The apparent cowardliness of his behavior was revealed in its stark nakedness to his mental mirror; his *samurai* ancestors would be ashamed of their twentieth century progeny!

He stood up and looked for the paper. It must be someplace in this room because the assistant director left the room bare-handed. Yes, there it was under a book. He picked it up and glanced at it. How to destroy it and leave no evidence behind? He could not get out of the room. There was no fire in the furnace for it was mid-September and heat was not needed during the day time. As a last resort he tore the sheet of paper into hundreds of pieces, put them in his mouth and swallowed them with the glass of water that came on the tray.

When the official returned he looked furiously, high and low, for the signed sheet of transfer order. He glared at the doctor without saying anything. The latter returned the stare and innocently inquired, "May I go now?" Without waiting for a reply he slid out of the office and headed for his apartment and family.

When interchange of evacuees among the ten centers was accomplished, the Tule Lake Center was made up of 6,000 old Tuleans that comprised 35% of the population and the 10,000 malcontents and "disloyals" from other centers. The key positions and responsible jobs were appropriated by the old residents. The newcomers were at a distinct disadvantage in spite of the fact that men of higher caliber could be found among them. When they arrived at Tule Lake they were vociferous in finding fault with camp conditions. They did not mince words in deriding the "spineless" group of men that steered the center, kow-towing to the dictates of the administration.

The authorities anticipated trouble and the military guard was increased to battalion strength and half a dozen light, obsolete tanks were stationed outside the camp in clear view of every incoming train. Of ancient vintage though they might be, the effect on the new arrivals was no different because these iron-clad monsters were capable of spitting rapid-fire bullets. It was rumored that many conscientious Caucasian personnel of the WRA resigned because the center was changing to a genuine concentration camp.

Thus, the new arrivals, branded as "disloyals"—greeted by this martial reception, deprived of the possibility of functioning in capacities of power and responsibility—chafed under ennui, frustration, and belligerency. The bleak, desert-like camp with no water to irrigate and to grow flowers or shrubs around the barracks, was very dirty and uninviting compared to the Arkansas Center where water was plentiful and vegetation abundant. Even the Arizona camps were superior because of the greenery that flourished around the barracks.

The new arrivals were dispersed throughout the center wherever there was an empty apartment vacated by those that had gone to other centers. In some blocks there was a preponderance of newcomers from a certain center, but on the whole there was a great dilution of the transferees. Their bickering, however, found sympathy among the old Tuleans and a general mass meeting was called in each ward. The balloting that followed to elect representatives from each ward returned a great majority of new arrivals and these men were aggressive in demanding improvements. They were duly elected and what they proposed to ask the project director to do met with the approval of practically all residents. For the grievances regarding living conditions were real issues: shortage of ambulances, defective fire apparatus, broken-down plumbing in the latrines, over-crowding, scarcity of jobs, lack of unemployment compensation, and above all, deficiency in the food supplied by the mess halls.

It was alleged that food provided in the mess halls cost only eighteen to twenty cents per person, whereas the WRA regulation called for forty-five cents. Evacuee accountants in the supply department furnished these figures. It was inferred by this group that the Caucasian personnel were disposing of food illegally for private profit in the nearby towns because there was a great demand for many rationed items.

Just about the time that this representative body came into being to conduct all negotiations, a farm truck driven by a minor overturned, resulting in the accidental death of Mr. Kashima, a farm worker. The project director refused to allow a public funeral and cut off the electricity to the center during the service so that the public address system could not function. This action seemed to make the project director a beast without human feelings. The residents got so angry that they became stubborn and belligerent and harsh words were exchanged. So the trump card of the WRA was used and the Military Police stepped in and established martial law in the center. After all, the inmates were helpless and a little diplomacy and human understanding could have brought on peace as in the other nine WRA centers.

As feeling ran high, there was a definite uneasiness among the Caucasian personnel. After repeated conferences, a high barbed wire fence was erected in the wide fire break between the personnel area and the evacuee colony. The hospital and warehouses were in the personnel area. Ingress and egress had to be made through gates guarded by internal security police.

The workers at the farm went on a strike as an aftermath of the Kashima incident and the subsequent unpleasantness regarding the public funeral. From the WRA standpoint the crop had to be harvested. Workers contended that the crop was being sent to other relocation centers and to the open market. The WRA finally brought in workers from Topaz, Utah, to do the harvesting. The warehouse workers were asked to load food onto trucks destined for these strike-breakers. The negotiating committee ordered the warehouse workers not to do the work.

At ten o'clock on the night of November 4, when three trucks of food were taken out after being loaded by Caucasian personnel, young men congregated in the warehouse area. The WRA officials sensed trouble and following prearranged strategy, asked the military to step in. This call marked the first step of two and a half months of martial rule in the Tule Lake Center.

Bill Yano dropped in at the Murayama apartment late one afternoon about the first of November. The doctor was at home and gladly received him, for he had not seen him in months.

"Well doctor, I see you are still here!"

"That's right. But maybe not for long, although it is a secret. How about you? I did not expect you to remain behind in this center. What made you become a 'disloyal' one?"

Bill smiled. "There are many reasons. Foremost is that I am a Japanese National. Legally that is, for I never can shed that name tag. But the more practical reason which made me decide was the consideration and duty I owe to my parents. I am the son they can and must depend on now, for my younger brother is with the army in the 442nd. He volunteered from Chicago. The Americans think of returning from war alive but the Japanese are prepared to die. If one does return, then he is considered extremely lucky. Therefore, in my parents' way of looking at things, George is as good as dead and they will not be shocked if the War Department's notification should come to that effect. It's a fatalistic attitude but one that was nurtured in past centuries. My duty lies with them. Their savings and life work were wiped out. We can not trust what the WRA tells us. If we leave this center and go to others we may be forced out into the cruel, hostile world. Our family may be forcibly separated."

"There have been repeated assurances that that will not be so," interjected Minoru.

"But what can you expect from a government that was heartless enough to carry out this evacuation? Anyway, after much thought I did not register. I am sitting on the fence. Maybe later on I may be allowed to relocate. As long as I have not signed there should be a way out."

"In this uncertain period that may be a cautious approach. Now tell me, are you on the representative negotiating committee?"

"I am not, but I have kept up with the developments," said Bill.

"What really happened when Mr. Myer came to the center? We at the hospital cannot keep up with recent developments because we are kept so busy."

"The gist of the matter is this. You heard of the elected representative body which was to act as a negotiating group? The funeral of the late farm hand, Kashima, showed how undependable and cold-hearted

453

the project director is. Yet he was the person with whom negotiation had to be concluded. Obviously nothing much could be expected. Just then, news that the WRA chief, Mr. Dillon Myer, was arriving at noon was relayed by the janitor to the headquarters of the representative body. This latter body acted fast and had an announcement made at every mess hall that Mr. Myer was going to be interviewed and in order to demonstrate that the center was behind their men, everyone, old and young, should assemble in front of the administration section after the noon meal.

"Probably 10,000 people proceeded to the designated place after their lunch. Not to go was to invite suspicion from fellow block members. I heard the military were ready to march in with tanks, but when Mr. Myer saw women and children he sensed no violence and awaited the appearance of the Negotiating Committee. It took two and a half hours. During this time this great mass of people patiently waited for the outcome of the talks. Time and again the loud speaker quieted the people down. The spokesman made a speech and Mr. Myer talked. Nothing concrete seemed to have come out of the conference. Naturally Mr. Myer backed his man, the project director."

"Then the demonstration of 10,000 people did not bring any immediate result?"

"Evidently not, for the strike is on. The farmers are not working. Evacuees from Topaz, Utah, are said to be coming to harvest the crop. Naturally the crops could not be allowed to go to waste. This is war time. Some ugly rumors are going around the camp regarding the imported labor. Some call them strike-breakers. Others call them 'dogs' and renegades working against their own kind. What I'd like to hear about is the beating of the Caucasian medical director. You fellows at the hospital took a more aggressive direct action, I hear," winked Bill Yano.

"The way I understand from the talk going around is that some of the young men who came to picket the office on that day tried to get into the hospital to induce the workers to join the mob. The medical director shooed them out. Then these men got ugly, returned in force and pushed aside the Caucasian doctor stationed at the door. The medical director was beaten by these young men. I don't think it was planned. Only a spontaneous gang action."

"Could any of them have been identified?"

"Nobody at the hospital knew them. Apparently they are new arrivals at the center," replied Minoru.

"There seems to be a general feeling in the center that the medical director had it coming to him because of his past high-handed dealings with patients. He seemed to have no feeling that is usually a part of a doctor. Usually there are some sympathizers for the victim in a case like this, but I have not heard anyone coming to his defense. He is not the type to work in a camp such as this. Is he that bad?" queried Bill.

Minoru thought for a while. "He was arrogant and outspoken. Maybe talking to Japs did not make him think twice before he opened his mouth. Feelings of superiority, he had. No doubt about that. We did not like him. He was old in his theory and practice. Rank does not make a doctor. A colonel in the medical corps may be a better doctor than a captain, but not always so. He tried to use his rank to dictate to us even in professional matters. We could not stomach that gracefully. And there was a demand from us doctors for his removal."

For several weeks nothing unusual happened to bring the seething turmoil to a head. The cauldron was boiling hot and eventually an eruption had to take place. The center was on a virtual strike. Only food, garbage, and coal trucks were moving. Even these were manned by a fraction of the former crew. Only men passed by the administration could work. The hospital unit was functioning as usual, for it was unthinkable that the sick should be victimized by industrial bargaining. The center people did not try to influence the workers at the hospital.

Then came November 4. Dr. Minoru Murayama was on duty that night at the hospital. Once a week the doctors had to take turns to be on 24-hour duty to attend emergencies and maternity deliveries. Everything was quiet and he was just killing time talking to the ambulance drivers at the dispensary. Suddenly there was a commotion outside. They looked out of the window and about two hundred feet away saw human shadows scuffling under the light near the Caucasian mess hall. Something was raised; it came down and a figure slumped down on the ground.

Ten minutes later a man was assisted into the dispensary. He was the night watchman. By that time clattering tanks that rolled into the camp firing blank machine-gun bullets broke the stillness of the night.

The nurse's aides were on their toes and laid the injured man in the surgical cubicle. There was a ragged laceration of the upper lip which was caught between the blow and the sharp underlying teeth. It was swollen already. Three teeth were loose and blood stained his chin and cheek.

"Miss Yoshida, get the emergency pack out and let us wash the wound. We saw from here what took place out there. The whole camp seems to be in an uproar. What happened, mister?" asked Dr. Murayama as he took his pulse which was regular and strong.

The escort of the injured man replied. "About twenty minutes ago, a Japanese internal security police came across some men loading a truck with boxes of food at the warehouse and challenged them. He had been told to guard the warehouse in particular. A scuffle ensued and in the course of five minutes, tanks began rolling in. Those tanks cannot get moving without warming up. I think it was a trap. MP's with shot guns and police with guns came swarming in and anybody that stood in their way got clubbed. So this watchman was an innocent wayside victim."

Just then there was a knock on the window pane from the outside. Dr. Murayama lifted the window and looked down into the muzzle of a submachine gun handled by a captain. "Open up, we are coming in."

"Miss Yoshida, open the door," ordered Dr. Murayama.

The MP captain came into the dispensary with two MP's similarly armed. "Here he is. We are taking him, doctor!"

"But captain, he is injured. Can't we fix him up before you take him away?"

"That's not my concern. He is my prisoner and he comes with us!" He was almost rude.

Out went the watchman who was knocked down by the butt of a gun because he happened to be in the way of an armed man who was like a bloodhound hot on the scent of quarry. The hospital workers looked at the departing group; everyone was oppressed with foreboding and apprehension. The rough handling was a mere prelude.

Something ominous was going to happen. Maybe a round-up of marked men was being undertaken in the camp. It seemed that the quiet, tense atmosphere of the past four days had finally come to an end of waiting and now there was going to be a show of strength by the party that had might on its side. After all, the project director was certain of American public approval and support, even if the humanitarian WRA director in Washington was contrary-minded and was for a more moderate course, for had not the Metropolitan California papers been needling the WRA for "coddling the Jap prisoners in the concentration camps?" The next day, the *San Francisco Examiner* and also the *San Francisco Chronicle* would be carrying headlines of "Jap prisoners riot in Tule Lake."

The sound of firing and noise of the tanks faded and there was no call for ambulance service. People must have been scared into keeping to their barracks. Even the 11 o'clock shift of nurses did not arrive and somehow the girls and boys on the wards arranged among themselves to work out the extra shift. Dr. Murayama went to bed and slept undisturbed until seven.

CHAPTER 31

Turbulence and Martial Law

IN THE NURSES' QUARTER OF THE MEDICAL
ward, several nurses and Dr. Yamamoto were talking in subdued tones.
Miss Asari, the registered nurse, turned around at the approaching
footsteps. "Where were you Dr. Murayama. We did not see you?"

"Why, I left you at 11 P.M. and had a good night's sleep."

"Well, well. Then you do not know what happened after that? I
think you are the only one that slept last night in this hospital."

"Did something take place last night?"

Miss Asari's face assumed an expression of seriousness and concern.
"At about 2 A.M. we surgical nurses were roused and taken to the
operation room by MP's. There were two cases with scalp injuries. Dr.
Matson, the new doctor, was there to operate. An MP guarded the door
and no orderly was permitted to get in. The only Japanese allowed in
the room were us nurses. Both patients are in the unused wing with
an armed MP on guard. I know one of them, Mr. Hayashida from our
block."

"Ho! and was there anything different transpiring?"

"There is another prisoner in addition to the two injured. He is
also contused and bruised but needed no surgery. You know this hospital
is under the military? No longer is the WRA responsible for our work."
Then turning to Dr. Yamamoto she said, "You tell Dr. Murayama
about the rest."

Dr. Yamamoto who had just finished medical school and internship
before the war started, continued the discourse. "Yes, there is a second
lieutenant at the front office in place of the medical director. There is
no WRA security officer. The setup is completely changed. The lieutenant just told me that until further orders come from above, there will
be no replacement from the center and we have to carry on with what

personnel we have. That means the personnel in this hospital last night. That is all we know now. The cooks were brought in so we'll have breakfast all right."

"Dr. Yamamoto, let's you and I go see this lieutenant. We have to have certain items attended to at once." When the two began walking down the corridor, he said, "How are the girls behaving?"

"Fine. They are taking the grim situation with courage. I know that they will do all right."

Lieutenant Finnegan sat in the office. A young man of about twenty-three, clean-cut and pleasing in his talk and actions, he seemed to be enjoying this assumption of hospital administration.

"I am Dr. Murayama. I heard from Dr. Yamamoto that you are now in charge. Does this mean that we are under the military instead of the WRA?"

"Yes, that is right. I am in charge and I am here to listen to your problems." He shook hands and sat in the revolving chair, smiling.

"First, tell us what happened in the center last night. We heard tanks rolling along and firing now and then."

The lieutenant smiled. "That was just to maintain order. The colony is under control. We foresee no trouble, but patrols are walking the fire breaks and this hospital has become inaccessible. Of course, in emergency sickness your ambulance will fetch the patients, escorted by the Military Police."

Is it true that no shift will be coming to relieve these workers who have worked the past sixteen hours?"

"I have orders to get along with you as you are. No return of workers to the colony until further orders." He seemed to be a man of feeling and was quite apologetic.

Dr. Murayama turned to Dr. Yamamoto, "I am sure the parents of these girls will be wondering what happened. Especially when we are held incommunicado. They will imagine all sorts of things. I think the first thing is to ask the lieutenant to relay to the center that all workers in the hospital are safe. Will you please do that for us, Lieutenant Finnegan?"

"Certainly, I'll attend to that right away. This job is new to me, but I'll do anything I can to help you. Dr. Yamamoto asked me to ensure food delivery and that I'll do too," smiled the young lieutenant as the two doctors took leave. But he was only a lowly lieutenant and

459

not in the department of food delivery. Policy making was left to men in higher rank.

After breakfast, since no janitors were coming, the male orderlies took over the job of mopping the floor. Young Dr. Yamamoto joined in the work. It was like a happy family willingly pitching in to make the best of the situation.

A male orderly returned with a tray loaded with food. The crew mopping the floor turned inquisitive faces. "I took this food to the other wing where the three injured men are confined. The MP guarding the door would not let me in." Everyone looked at each other; a mingled feeling of repression, anger, despair, and resignation was apparent.

"Give me that tray. I'll take it to them!" a young girl of eighteen stepped forward. Miss Terada was usually a quiet, unobtrusive medical clerk and was a recent arrival from Topaz, Utah. Her fellow workers were openmouthed as she strode away with determined steps.

The MP stood in her way. "You cannot enter that room!"

"But this is breakfast!" She looked up into the MP's face which was merely that of a grown-up country boy.

"I have orders to let nobody in or out."

"Order or no order, they are in the hospital. They are, therefore, patients. Who will ever deny patients breakfast? I never heard of such a thing. I am not afraid of you and you can't stop me!" By that time she was past him and into the room.

She only heard behind her back, "And I am not afraid of you!"

In the afternoon of the second day, Dr. Yamamoto went into the kitchen and discovered that food was not delivered and there was only rice and Japanese pickled turnips. For four meals the entire hospital, patients and workers alike, subsisted on rice and pickles. But food was the least of their worries. Everybody's concern was centered on the vital issue of what would transpire within the colony. Prohibited from leaving the hospital, this was a virtual siege. Something could be gleaned from emergency cases that were brought in from time to time, but it was not reassuring enough because even the people in the colony seemed to be keeping to their own barracks.

The hospital employees could live on rice and pickled turnips for several days, but it was not right to have the sick and post-surgical cases subsist on this curtailed ration. The promised food truck had not arrived by afternoon. The two doctors and the responsible nurses convened at the out-patient department for an appraisal of the general situation. There was no Caucasian in the hospital who might act as intermediary, for they were all removed pending solution of the riot. The Japanese were confined to the hospital building. There was no way of contacting either the army commandant of the WRA heads.

Military orders were that no one was allowed out of the hospital buildings. The atmosphere was pervaded with racial feeling, tenseness, and fear. Totally unarmed, the evacuees could be pushed around at will. How to surmount this obstacle, to effect a break-through and appeal directly to the colonel was the problem. Apparently it was impossible for a male to get through the guards to the conference of the Caucasians that was being held in the building across the wide fire break. Nobody could think of a plan.

Dr. Murayama's eyes lit on Miss Terada and a sudden inspiration came to him. No American in his right mind would ever harm a girl. "Miss Terada, will you please undertake the mission to go to that conference room and make a direct appeal to Colonel Austin. In the name of the patients I ask you. I know you can do it."

"Who me! Go across there alone?" She flushed and stiffened for a while. Then she gazed up at the doctor and the trusting faces of her co-workers. Slowly she stood up and weakly said to her fellow clerk, "Let me have your white coat. I'll try."

Everyone's eyes were fixed on the lone figure with the flapping white hospital uniform walking firmly across no-man's land toward the armed guard. She seemed so small and yet loaded with so much responsibility. Dr. Murayama felt like praying. It was a very long five minutes. She emerged and every face relaxed into a smile. But after walking a short distance she turned back to the building she came from. Puzzlement was registered on every anxious face. She soon reappeared and came back to the crowd at the dispensary.

"The colonel promised to have hospital food delivered in time for supper this afternoon," reported Miss Terada. Her face was flushed and she was breathing fast from the exertion and excitement.

"Were you afraid? I can say we were afraid for you," a nurse's aide stood up and embraced her.

"When I got into the room, Miss Stevens came forward. You know the State Department woman who speaks Japanese very well and who was here during the segregation movement. She was in that conference

461

room and she took me by my hands and led me to the colonel. I was no longer afraid of anyone there because I had a friend in Miss Stevens. I stated my mission. The colonel promised that the food will be delivered. Then I thanked Miss Stevens and started on my way back, but then I thought about the message to the center, that we were all safe. I went back to make sure that that message was sent."

At that moment there appeared an imaginary halo about Miss Terada's head, or so it seemed to Dr. Murayama. Heroes are the products of circumstances.

At three o'clock in the morning a ruptured appendicitis had to be operated on. The girl and her parents were too frightened to report to the hospital in time because of the tense atmosphere prevailing in the center. Telephone connections from block managers' offices to the hospital was suspended. All communications had to go through the police and the people at large did not know of such prodecures. Rumors were flying about all the time and uncertainty reigned. Even delivery of food was irregular at the mess halls. It looked as if the WRA was at odds with the army—so it appeared to the hospital employees who became friendly with the lieutenant and non-commissioned officers.

These men were kind. Whether or not they produced the things asked for did not matter much; at least they tried and were sincere in regrets when they failed. Perhaps army rule was to be preferred to the Indian Service trained personnel that constituted the WRA and tried to do things in their accustomed mode of thought and procedure, acquired in their decades of handling American aborigines.

For three days the hospital workers were confined to the area immediately around the buildings. There was no relief, so they did the best they could. Only emergency cases brought in by ambulances were treated at the dispensary and the hospitalized ward patients were attended to as usual.

The stockade, built not far away from the hospital in the Caucasians' section and designated Block 99, was increasing in population daily. Anyone showing any belligerency to the orders of the MP's was summarily arrested and thrown into this enclosure with a ten foot high, meshed wire fence.

Then one afternoon there was a cry, "Come and see, our friends are coming in to relieve us. There must be fifty or sixty. And there is our injured medical director checking the list of orderlies and nurses. Oh! Dr. Emura is rejected! Too bad."

The relief came in and there was great rejoicing as uninhibited teenagers bubbled out their pent-up emotions. "How is it in the center? Anything happening?"

"You know, it's terrible in the center. Not enough food. Milk is rationed and limited to children below seven months. Not enough coal and we have a hard time at night to keep warm," was the unenthusiastic reply of girls as they settled on benches.

"Anyway, I am glad you came to our rescue. Being shut in and in the same uniform all the time was getting us down. But why is it that Dr. Emura and Miss Miyamura were not allowed to come in?"

"The medical director must have a grudge against them. Sometime in the past they must have crossed him. His list was being checked as we filed past him and gave our names. Of course there was no trouble for us nobodies to go past that man. He had smoked glasses to hide his black eyes."

The two friends sipped their cups of tea and were reviewing the power politics within the center. It was November 20 and the clear air of Tule Lake was invigorating, but a continuous fire was a necessity in the apartments.

Bill Yano said, "The negotiating committee was elected by the entire colony. It changed its name several times, but the core of the men in that group is made up essentially of new arrivals from other centers during the segregation movement. The leaders are from Arkansas. Because of their resolutions, they clashed on every issue with the project director and very little headway was made. Only skeleton crews in the food, garbage, and coal truck gangs are maintained. When people are idle they are easily swayed. At first they were behind the negotiating committee 100%, but as days went by they began listening to the more moderate leaders. Now there is a group that is pro-administration and trying to end this paralyzing strike. The fight for power is now intense."

This was the first meeting of the two since the center was placed under martial law. Curfew law was proclaimed and all had to be in their apartments between 7 P.M. and 6 A.M. Going to the latrine within the block was permitted. The fire breaks between wards were patrolled by MP's and jeeps cruised back and forth between blocks to discourage people from sauntering forth at night. Any offender of the curfew law was summarily picked up and thrown into the stockade.

"Who make up this pro-administration group?" asked Minoru Murayama.

"Colonel Austin heads the military. Naturally he is always in consultation with the WRA project director. He virtually declared that the negotiating committee does not represent the majority of the people. The danger of being arrested has driven the two leaders of this group into hiding, but the negotiating committee carries on its work. The opposing group is made up mostly of former Tuleans who were in foremen's positions. They will profit if the strike is ended. The cooperative PX personnel are also among these men. These want to end the strike and get peace re-established. I think there are many who secretly want this peace movement to succeed, but under the circumstances it is unpopular to openly say so among friends. The hope of the colony rests with the good offices of the Spanish Consul who has been here twice to talk to the representatives, but results are not concrete or encouraging."

"Then there is no immediate prospect of this situation getting settled, is there," dejectedly observed Minoru.

"None whatsoever. In the meantime WRA checks are not coming in. Families with little children cannot buy warm clothes and a few children are still barefooted in this cold weather."

"How about the fear of arrest among the adults?"

"That's the point. Nobody knows when he will be picked up by the MP's. Suspicion of being a trouble-maker in the eyes of the army is all the ground that's needed for the stockade, and who but a fellow evacuee spy could furnish such information to the MP's? There is no trial or hearing. I think the morale of the people is at its lowest ebb."

On the night of November 25 at about ten o'clock there was a knock at the door. Answering it, Minoru was confronted by Lieutenant Finnegan. His jeep was waiting in front. He was invited in, but without sitting he said in an undertone. "Early tomorrow morning at daybreak a truck will come for you and your family. I believe you have your boxes ready. Be ready to move. I think it is best that you make preparations tonight without letting other people know."

With that announcement he saluted and slid into the night. The time of his usefulness in the center had apparently come to an end. Probably a Caucasian doctor was coming to replace him. There was quite a discrepancy between a six thousand dollar a year man and a nineteen dollar a month evacuee, but the WRA was not a body to economize.

"Did you hear that, father? We are leaving Tule Lake tomorrow but we cannot bid farewell to friends. Understandably, it is better not to do so. To leave at a time when people's nerves are under such tension, we may be branded *inu* or informers."

"That is too bad, but maybe it is for the best. The boxes are ready. We'll leave the non-essentials behind and travel light. This is a life like the floating water lily. We exist but there is no anchor in life. I wonder where we are heading."

"That again may be a military secret. Anyway we'll be out of California, and we'll be taken to one of the other nine centers."

They went to bed late, but got up at four to make ready. By six o'clock there was a truck driven by the military waiting, and the Murayama family and belongings were piled onto this vehicle. But there was unusual activity going on. Lieutenant Finnegan was cruising by, and in his jeep were Drs. Yamamoto and Emura, for the latter had been reinstated. Soldiers and internal security police were in every block, while the people were ordered to remain in their apartments. A room-to-room search on a camp-wide scale was being conducted to look for contraband, hidden weapons, intoxicating liquor, and rice from which *saké* could be made. Two teams worked from each side of the camp toward the center fire break. A large number of soldiers were stationed in the spaces between blocks to insure that no evacuee could slip back into an area that had been searched.

Minoru heard later that the two leaders of the negotiating committee that had gone into hiding were not apprehended because they were under the floor, but some ninety persons wanted by the internal security police were arrested to swell the population of the stockade.

Under this unprecedented search that kept everyone's nerves taut, the removal of the Murayama family was hardly noticed even by fellow block members. Outwardly, it was like kidnapping. To the Murayamas, it was like skipping the community and there was a tinge of guilty feeling as they took a last glimpse of the ugly block barracks that merged and disappeared in the morning fog.

CHAPTER 32

The Interlude in Arkansas

THE JEROME RELOCATION CENTER WAS quite a contrast to the sandy, invigorating, dry-aired Tule Lake of California. It was a damp cold because this was low delta country; penetratingly cold as there was only wood available for the barrack stove. The camp was in existence a little over one year and quite an inprovement had been effected by the former occupant of the apartment. Shelves were there, crevices in the walls were plugged or covered by narrow pieces of lumber, and a mail box was on the wall near the doorway.

The Murayama family was given quarters in Block 38 because the exodus to Tule Lake was most pronounced from this area. Since the camp was in the delta district of the Mississippi River, drainage was the most important engineering project to make this area livable. Deep, wide ditches criss-crossed the areas, and inhabitants dug small ditches around the barracks to conduct surface water into this lower level and to prevent stagnant pools under houses. The roads between barracks were elevated and surfaced with cinders.

All the ten relocation centers were located in sparsely populated deserts such as in Arizona and Utah, or swampy lands such as in Arkansas. In Arkansas, Minoru immediately felt the release of tension. He could stretch out and sleep for hours if he wanted to. The tempo of life seemed decidedly easy. None of the belligerent and nationalistic, "chip on the shoulder" attitude was found among the people. Call it subserviency if you wish, it was easier to exist and survive the war in a surrounding such as this.

Since the new policy of the War Relocation Authority was to relocate these people in the vast Midwestern States and gradually consolidate the unrelocated evacuees into a few centers, there was no feeling of permanency among the people. Talk of the surprisingly tolerant attitude of the city population and the lucrative jobs in candy factories and other small business made people anxious to go out and investigate. A bonus of fifty dollars per person was even granted for a short while. All those that were cleared by the security office were urged to do so. Ration cards to buy food, just as any citizen received on the outside, were provided by the WRA office. The family could follow or the wage earner could send money to those that remained in the center. However, the WRA was not pushing anyone out.

In the great cities there was an officer and his staff who acted in a liaison capacity to smooth the way for more evacuee relocation. Once a factory or corporation got to know a Japanese employee, there was usually a call for more, because inevitably a good showing was made as each felt he or she was on trial. When a good impression was made it would improve the lot of the thousands of evacuees.

The WRA agents spoke before church gatherings, explaining the circumstances under which these law-abiding citizens were uprooted and what the federal government was now trying to do to restore their confidence in the American Way of Life. They contacted firms that might hire evacuees; looked after housing problems and the hundred and one problems that arose when an unwanted, stigmatized group of people had to be settled. The only factor in favor of the WRA officials was the shortage of workers.

The WRA considered that there was nobody indispensable among the evacuees and held fast to the policy that everyone should again swim in the normal current of life. However, the evacuees felt differently.

"Dr. Murayama, you must have had some exciting experiences at Tule Lake. Compared to peaceful Jerome, there must have been quite a commotion. I don't know whether you are acquainted with the fact that two hundred of our tough Japan-educated young men left this center for Tule. Even while they were here they were led by a few leaders who were very capable and determined. I heard they became leaders at the new place." A neighbor, Mr. Goto, came to pay his respects and remained to gossip.

"Oh, I think I heard rumors to that effect. The Jerome boys, they were called at Tule," replied Minoru.

"That's it. Those boys were not bad. In fact, when they left here a Caucasian official sadly remarked, 'all the good workers are leaving Jerome.' That was an exaggeration, of course, but so it seemed at the time of segregation."

"I see that every day some one is leaving for Chicago or Milwaukee. Do you intend to relocate too?" inquired the doctor.

The man mischievously looked up. "Well, I never had it so good. My three grown-up children are out in Chicago working and I get a money order now and then. Now I don't have to work. My board and room are guaranteed and all I do is improve my artistic education in producing better *kobu*."

"What is *kobu?*" asked Torao Murayama. At this query the man stood up went out and returned with half a dozen objects of quaint handicraft.

"Seeing is believing and the quickest way to sell any merchandise or idea is demonstration. I hope you discern in this object the semblance of a sitting frog. Here is a fruit bowl. This is a vase, and this is a fat, gentle old man."

"Pretty good. Goto-san, how are these made, and why the name *kobu?*"

Looking at Torao, the man continued, "If you wish, you can join me in my next outing and become a member of this ambitious, enterprising artisan society. You will find out that this whole area is covered with trees. Also, if you spend the summer you will discover that thunder storms are frequent. Sometimes you will see six or seven lightning streaks occurring at once in different places. Thunder bolts strike trees and the split trees burn for a while. An irregular tumor on the damaged trees result and as years go by fantastic gnarled lumps form. We roam the woods with saw and ax and leisurely look for specimens up in the branches or down near the roots. We must be careful, for poisonous snakes are plentiful. We saw these portions off and shape and sandpaper the objects so that the end product becomes what we pictured mentally when we first saw the *kobu* on the tree."

"Is there a market for these objects? Maybe we can make a little pocket money." Torao became interested.

"No, as far as I know, no market has been found. There are exhibits about every half year when we compete for prizes. Very favorable comments were made by the few outsiders that came to see the displays," commented the old Jerome resident formerly from Fresno, California.

"We have so much time on our hands that even with poor tools we can bring out the sheen and luster of the wood and shape the *kobu* the way we want.

"But doctor, you are in a different class. Every now and then a doctor relocates to the outside. It is natural for him to do so and the WRA encourages the move. But we do not feel safe when good doctors leave. So there have been petitions with hundreds and thousands of signatures and personal appeals made in the name of 8,000 people to prevent the doctors from deserting us. Yes, we feel deserted. We cannot trust the Caucasian doctors as we can our own. I am not trying to influence you one way or the other; merely to let you know that you doctors are the only group of men we must have remain to the end of this sorry camp life." Mr. Goto was in his mid-sixties, was well-preserved and wiry in his movements. Only a tinge of grey and a slight stoop gave away his age. Years spent in the vineyards and fruit orchards near Fresno after he came over from Hawaii in 1907 gave him the health so often seen in outdoor men.

"Where does one go for banking here? It was convenient to keep on dealing with California banks while at Tule Lake, but I was thinking of transferring at least the checking account to some town bank."

"There is a town called Dermott near here and most people deal with that bank, but the town itself is off limits to us. It is a funny situation. The merchants there are missing out on a very lucrative business opportunity by barring us. On the other hand, there is a small hamlet called Lake Village not far from our railroad station. An enterprising storekeeper made a deal with the project director and he sends his bus to the center to give transportation to shoppers. He is smart, that fellow."

"But why should the town keep Japanese out? Japanese people must be a curiosity to them."

"Well, it all happened this way. Soon after Jerome was being filled with evacuees from the assembly centers of California, a Japanese-American soldier came south to meet his family. He got off the train at Dermott and went to a restaurant to have breakfast. As he was eating a fellow walked in and asked him whether he was Japanese. He answered in the affirmative. That man went out, returned with a rifle and shot this soldier. Luckily, he was a poor shot and inflicted only a grazing wound. For this unhappy incident the town was put off limits to us by the WRA."

"These Southerners are notorious for their backwardness anyway. He must have lost some kin in the Pacific. Similar incidents must have happened all over the country; only the papers have not played them up. Perhaps the War Department is doing its part in preventing any further inquisition of the Japanese in this country. The forced evacuation by the army was plenty bad. You can see how the 100th and 442nd Battalions are reported so often and praised by the army communiques. There must be a connection; the army is trying to atone for its harsh measures of the past," philosophized Dr. Murayama.

There was animation in Mr. Goto's face. "Then, doctor, do you think we can return to the West in spite of the repeated newspaper reports that we would never be allowed there again?"

"Surely when peace returns nobody can stop free travel in this country. Whether or not the small rural communities in California will allow Japanese to rent a home or farm is a difficult matter to foresee. In this democratic country not even the President can dictate to that extent. But if you own a farm in Fresno nobody can stop you from returning there. The roughnecks of the neighborhood, however, can make your life so miserable that you will eventually pull up stakes and sell the land at a sacrifice."

New Year festivity and gaiety was hard to conceive and realize in such bleak circumstances. This was the second cycle. People did not exert themselves to make this day any different. Greetings of "Happy New Year" were the only departure from the routine salutation this morning, and a "Not a very happy one, is it?" was added like an afterthought with a silly laugh.

The Christmas season was more festive in that young people had their parties and sang Christmas carols. There was a very good baritone from Fresno by the name of Seno. His *White Christmas* sung repeatedly at different parties lingered for many months, even in non-Christian ears. The WRA was considerate enough in trying to liven up to the occasion by sending in rice for *mochi*, a rice preparation used at New Year's, but there was not the richness of tenacious starch in this rice.

471

Rice had to be specially raised for this purpose. The resultant *mochi* was crumbly and flat.

Toward the end of January there was a letter from Bill Yano giving the news of Tule Lake.

The strike has finally ended and once more there is peace and normalcy here. The martial law was lifted on January 15. I think you disappeared on November 19, the day of the center-wide search. I heard about your departure when I visited your former block about a week after your abduction. The army was not able to apprehend the leaders of the negotiating committee, but these two men gave themselves up to the FBI rather than to the army on December first. The stockade housed about two hundred people at one time. Many of the young men were sent to the Santa Fe Internment Camp as incorrigibles, but the majority were returned to the colony.

These went on a hunger strike in the stockade for about ten days because of extremely poor food. I heard that several of them got so weak they had to be hospitalized to receive intravenous glucose.

Anyway, I am glad that we have people working for they need the money and none of the nationalistic demonstrations are held in the fire breaks. Intimidation in the blocks has stopped. Before the end of the strike it came to pass that the entire camp was divided into two groups: for or against the strike. Anyone trying to follow a moderate course was under suspicion of appeasement and catering to the administration. He and his family were looked at with suspicion. Life was made miserable in the block where he lived. Even the nurses reporting to the hospital were maligned. Taunts of inu were thrown their way because the hospital operated and the workers were getting paid. The average man was blind and he had no perspective of the situation. He could not see that these nurses were working only for the evacuees' welfare. It was sickening.

What came out of the strike? I am afraid not much could be said for it.

There was a wood-cutting crew from each block. The kitchens, shower room boiler, and individual apartment stoves consumed a huge amount of wood. In the center of each block near the boiler room there were two communal lavatories, laundry, and shower rooms for each sex. Here the chopped wood was piled high for everyone's use. This crew went into the woods that adjoined the camp and cleared the land of its tall timber and underbrush. Eventually a farm to grow vegetables and raise hogs and chickens was on the blueprint of the project. The only danger in this southern forest was poisonous snakes and each working gang was supplied with serum so that an unfortunate victim could be injected on the spot by a trained man in the group. Winter was too wet to carry on extensive chopping while the snakes went into hibernation. But during summer months the reptiles usually slunk away deeper into the woods before the noise and onslaught of human beings.

Spring came early in the Southland. Balmy days followed several days of a delayed Arctic cold wave and it was pleasant to see young shoots of green grass sprout on the roadside. It was then that Mr. Goto dropped in one Saturday evening. "Murayama-san, let us go into the woods tomorrow to gather some *naba*. You will find plenty, especially after the recent rain."

"Do you mean the *naba* that grew on old rotting wood in Japan and in Hawaii on fallen guava trunks?"

"Yes, that is what I mean. Last winter, it was the Hawaiian boys who first began collecting them and then the entire camp caught on. I know the place where we can do our best harvesting."

"All right, I'll be there."

"Bring a gunny sack and get your grandchildren to come too. I am sure they will enjoy the outing."

The next morning Torao Murayama in boots and his older grandchildren similarly shod, followed Mr. Goto to the woods beyond Block 6. That was the side toward the Mississippi River. The ground was wet with recent rain and as they advanced, their boots sank into thick, rotting vegetation and dried leaves. A section of the land a little lower than the rest was a veritable swamp and trees were sparse. Many trees were down, but a large area was impassable because of the perennial surface water after the frequent rains. There was no drainage.

Birds called back and forth and at the approach of human beings their outcry became shriller. A half dozen white, long-legged water fowl took to the air gracefully with their legs tucked under their snowy bodies. Their breakfasting had been rudely interrupted by the "splish-splash" of approaching men. There was little talk among the small band of trudging humans as they cautiously advanced in the water, careful not to step into a hole and get wet.

473

After thirty minutes they reached high ground and many rotting timbers lay here and there. Blackberry vines grew near these fallen logs. Mr. Goto pointed to the saprophytic growth shaped like ear-lobes arranged in straight lines under the logs. In the shade along the crevices and on the non-rotted part of the wood the *naba* were arranged in several layers. Some were already dried and these they avoided. The *naba* was light lavender in color and the young ones were succulent. Torao recognized the vegetation right away as it was the same variety as the one he used to gather in the jungle of Olaa, Hawaii to replenish his hotel larder during the bubonic plague famine when he was a young man. As he was busily harvesting the especially juicy ones from the under surface of a fallen tree, for they grew better in the shaded area, he shuddered when his fingers touched a resting reptile. It moved and slunk away. He saw the four ringed rattle on the tail.

"Goto-san, there are rattlesnakes here."

"That's right, you must probe around first, for they will not bite. They are too sleepy and slow to attack, but it's best to be careful."

The children were warned but they were not afraid and had great fun in gathering this produce of the forest. In no time a half sackful was gathered.

At home this saprophyte was dried in the shade and stored away for future soup and *sukiyaki*. "In Chinatown, this sells for five dollars a pound," someone said.

Before April arrived there was a unique exhibition of snakes in one of the recreation halls. About thirty cages of reptiles were displayed by the enterprising forest-roaming men who hunted these slimy creatures. Most of them were rattlesnakes with ten to fifteen rattles. A few were copperheads, and one was a beautiful coral snake.

Dr. Murayama and his family went to see these snakes. It was not a pleasant sight, but very interesting and educational.

"Daddy, this is the kind grandpa nearly grabbed when we went *naba* hunting the other Sunday. Only it was not so big," said Robert. "Fourteen years old, no wonder its trunk is so large."

"I saw a man who was bitten by one like this at Tule Lake. I wonder how these are captured. Let's find out." He engaged a young attendant and asked, "How do you catch these rattlesnakes? Any trap?"

The young man laughed and said "No, we were taught by the Hawaiian *kibei* boys from Okinawa. Their technique is to have a long pole, seven feet and over. There is a hole about six inches from the tip. A long cord is passed through this hole and the other end is tied or nailed at the tip. At this time of the year the snakes, just out of hibernation, are slow in movement and so the loop of the cord is worked over the snake's head and the cord is pulled tight. This fixes the creature and capture is made."

This method appeared very conservative and now he understood the professional pride of Mr. Kaneshiro of Tule Lake Center who tackled an active vicious *habu* or coral snake in Okinawa and the active rattlesnake in America with two sticks and bare hands many weeks after their coming out of hibernation.

"What do you do with these snakes?" Minoru asked innocently.

"We eat them."

"How?"

"Oh, as you would an eel in Japan. You know what *kabayaki* is? Broil the meat over a charcoal fire and there is nothing like it. Really delicious. We young fellows eat them in this way, but the old people are smoking the meat crisp, almost to a powdery form to be taken as medicine for different sicknesses and weakened conditions. It will last for years in that smoked state."

Many years ago, he recalled, at a get-together in Sacramento, he met an old biologist who had roamed the country for forty years from Alaska to Mexico. He was well educated. What he said still lingered in his ears. "Gentlemen, I am a gourmet. I love the exotics in food and I can tell you that the most delicious food on this North American continent is rattlesnake."

"I think you have something there. The eels in Japan are eaten when people get weak in the hot summer. In August the custom is to eat eels to pep up their system. I too heard that rattlesnake was delicious. I would like to buy one so that I can get a taste of it," said Minoru.

"You are the new doctor, aren't you? I was at the hospital one day and saw you from a distance. It is hard to catch one these days because the continued warm weather has given the snakes more life and they escape into the bush very rapidly. But you can have mine. I'll give it to you because I am soon leaving for St. Louis. I'll have it, cage and all, delivered to you when this exhibition is over."

"Thank you very much. It will give us something to talk about when we get out of this place."

True to his promise, the young stranger ordered a truck to deliver the reptile to Block 38. It was enough to attract attention in this predominantly Hawaiian block. Toward evening, Mr. Fujimoto came. "Doctor, what are you going to do with this snake?"

"I intend to eat it, of course. I heard that rattlesnakes are the best eating on this continent. You people from Hawaii should also eat it so that when you return there after the war, you can say that you had a rattlesnake. People will be impressed, I am sure."

"I think so too. I would like to have a taste of it. I am a good cook. Let me do the cooking for I have manufactured charcoal since I came here. I am doing some of my own cooking at home. I have a small stove to use the charcoal too." Dr. Murayama marvelled at this ingenious man who was a salesman in Hawaii.

"Well, all right. I'll ask you to prepare it for the table, but first we have to kill and skin the creature." He had not thought of this until then.

"Doctor, I'll do it. I am not afraid of snakes. I'll have it all ready when you return from the hospital tomorrow afternoon. Then we can broil it together. In Japan I ate some snakes. I am a gourmet. The exotic is what I am after."

True to his word Mr. Fujimoto had the reptile skinned and it hung from the eaves of the barrack as a large hauser-like rope four feet long. It was white and glistening. "Beautiful, isn't it. I never saw anything so dazzlingly white. Now we can chop it up and start broiling. I have the *shoyu* sauce with proper seasonings for barbecue all made up. We'll soak the pieces in the sauce for a few hours and then later in the evening start cooking." He was all smiles and began dismembering the slippery object. There was a miniature stove fashioned out of a gallon can, salvaged from the kitchen. Charcoal filled another can.

"Where did you get this charcoal? At the PX?"

"No, I made it myself. There are a lot of oak trees in the forest and the hard substance makes first class charcoal. You know one of the joys of this life is good food. I love to prepare it. There is nothing like charcoal and its slow fire to give taste and aroma to any meat. This rattlesnake must be good, because it is like eel and I'll prepare it like I would an eel."

476

So at about 8 P.M. the entire neighborhood became curious about a most unusual, appetizing aroma that emanated from one of its barracks. The people gathered to find Mr. Fujimoto busily turning pieces of sizzling meat over an active, red-hot charcoal flame.

"What is it that he is cooking?"

"Didn't you see the rattlesnake that was in that cage? It's that snake."

"Wow, who's going to eat it?"

"Us of course. They say it will make you strong and healthy," a neighborhood child was explaining the cooking to his friend from the next block. "It will be different and better than the slop we get at the mess hall every day. That smell alone gives you an appetite. I feel somewhat full in my stomach already."

"I don't know. It is hard to swallow that when you think that is a part of that slimy snake. I don't think I can ever gulp it down."

Mr. Fujimoto was already munching on a piece as he was turning the pieces of meat on the meshed wire over the flame. "Oh, this is good. Any of you want a taste of it?" He turned to the watching crowd. A few courageous ones tried.

"I heard that you should not eat too much of it. It is supposed to be very potent and will go to your head. Even a partially blind man will find his vision improved," a woman was commenting to her friend.

"I heard that even an old man will find himself young again. Eat a little every day is the thing to do. Good for all the ills mankind is heir to, so they claim."

"Will you try a piece? Mr. Fujimoto says that it tastes better than chicken," urged the first woman.

"I would gladly, but as you know I am a 'grass' widow. My husband is still at Santa Fe Internment Camp," smiled the second, triumphant that she got her last say.

Dr. Murayama took a piece and slowly chewed on it. It was delectable and luscious. "Friends, I was told that this flesh is the most delicious in the Americas. Maybe some of you know the taste, but I think the majority of you will not again have a chance to try it. Why don't you let your entire family eat one piece each. You needn't tell anyone that the daily food was so bad that you had to eat snakes, because the WRA will not like it. It is a good thing to try something out of the ordinary. You know when a doctor eats it it is not poisonous and ought to be safe. I'll urge every member of my family to eat it too." He laughingly passed around the dish piled high with the blackened meat. "Now take some extra home for those that are not here."

Even after the spectators took home some for their families a large dish was piled high with the black morsels. Lillian said, "If one eats too much at one sitting does it really go up to one's head? Someone said last night that nose bleeds occurred in this center after too much was eaten at one time. Now everybody, don't eat more than four or five pieces a day. In the meantime, I'll distribute these to others less fortunate than we." So it happened all day long that when the mailman arrived or the ambulance driver passed, the dish was offered them.

"Hey mister, have you ever tasted a rattlesnake?"

"No ma'm. Why?"

"If not do you want to taste it? It is very good."

"Why, it is good! They said this is medicinal too. Let me take some home to my poor father. It may help his rheumatism."

Thus it went all day long and Minoru was able to eat a few pieces a day for several days only. Lillian saw to it that he did not develop any nose bleed, but Minoru could not use himself as a guinea pig to test clinically the efficacy of the flesh in the role of rejuvenation.

The hospital was run by an elderly Caucasian practitioner. This soft job was mainly administrative and much to his liking. Because he was not a surgeon he discouraged surgery in spite of the directive from Washington that if there were capable evacuee surgeons any type of surgery was allowed. Under his rule even hemorrhoids could not be removed. Only emergency surgery was allowed. Why he should have taken such an attitude was hard to understand. A realization of personal inadequacy must have been at the root of it. The Nisei nurses' aides and male orderlies were comparable to those in Tule Lake in their dedication and diligence, but as far as the medical personnel was concerned there was none of the aggressiveness, energy, and exhilarating scientific curiosity that characterized the California center because of the undue curtailment of their activity.

At Tule Lake every case of death meant an autopsy investigation for the doctors. The center people willingly signed their consent to such a procedure, because they wanted their doctors to find their mistakes if they made any, to improve their diagnostic ability, and to render better service to the others if they should be unfortunate enough to get sick. A one hundred percent autopsy rate could have been obtained; but there was a limit to doctors' physical endurance. After a while only the instructive cases were studied. Two or three a day was not a rarity. At Jerome an autopsy was an event among the attending doctors. Only rarely was permission granted by the family. It was a reflection on the amount of zeal exhibited by the doctors for a grateful family will usually accede to the request of the doctor.

Chiggers was an ailment new to the California-raised doctors. The other common physical ailments and complaints were of routine variety and of very little stimulation. Thus they spent spare time in softball games or went home to be good fathers and husbands.

Toward May the doctors were asked to convene in the medical superintendent's office. He was always serious and was never known to joke or get into familiar conversation with any of the evacuee doctors. His ulcer was making him a sour man and he constantly wore a scowling expression. This day he was more grave and apparently much agitated.

"I have here a warning that the Mississippi River is rising because the tributary rivers, the Missouri and Ohio, have risen on account of the recent heavy spring rains. When the combined waters hit a certain level there is danger of flood in this low land. The army engineers are keeping vigil at Memphis and we are daily getting reports from them. If the levees break we have to move our eight thousand people to higher ground twenty-five miles away. That is a tremendous job and we must be ready to do the public health work, giving them prophylactic injections and looking after the sanitation of the makeshift refugee camp."

"What is the WRA going to do then?"

"Naturally trucks will be used to transport the evacuees but possessions will have to be left behind. All must live in tents I suppose."

All faces became tense. Each was involved deeply as an evacuee with family and possessions, however small. After being ordered to the Assembly Centers in California with clothing only, the entire evacuee colony was faced with the possibility of losing everything again.

"How long will it take the flood waters to recede?"

The medical director did not even smile and matter-of-factly related:

"About ten years ago, according to the inhabitants of this area, there was a flood that kept this region four to ten feet under water for two months. This information was verified."

"Wow! Then we'll lose everything. Two months under water! Everything will be damaged for good."

"I wish you gentlemen would keep this information to yourself. There is no need to create a panic because we shall be advised in good time what to do. Meanwhile, we have to be prepared medically for this possible emergency."

Fortunately, rains ceased and "The Mother of Rivers" kept her levees intact. The eight thousand evacuees were spared from another heart-breaking experience.

CHAPTER 33

A Visit to St. Louis

DENTISTS IN THE CAMP WERE WELL TRAINED, successful practitioners in Southern California, and were willing to do any kind of work because they were only happy when they produced work that was satisfying in their own estimation. They were artists at heart. They were not allowed, however, to do anything fancy in this center. Cleaning teeth, extracting, and small oral surgery were allowed, but gold work was prohibited even when that metal was supplied by the patient. To prevent such work there was no oven to bake plates. As a consequence some surreptitious activity went on in some barracks but the cost was prohibitive to most of the people. In such cases plates and inlays were sent to the "outside" and were prepared by commerical laboratories or dentists. The prevailing fee was charged.

Minoru needed dental care badly and he decided to seek it outside. He went to the medical superintendent for permission to leave the center to inspect job opportunities as this was the easiest pretext to visit the world beyond the fence.

"I think you will find jobs in different hospitals open to you. The last news was that in Iowa, such openings were plentiful. I'll call up Mr. Murphy of the Leaves Office. He'll attend to the final arrangement for you. Good luck." Evidently the instructions from Washington was to get as many as possible to leave the centers. The medical superintendent was unduly cooperative and was wreathed in a rare smile.

The Leaves Office gave him the necessary papers, arranged with the provost marshal, and supplied him with ration cards for food.

He boarded the north-bound train. The coaches were loaded with soldiers on furlough from the military camps located in the southern states. Minoru could find only standing space on the platform between coaches. He felt self conscious, but nobody seemed to notice him.

Nobody glanced at him with animosity. Above all, the soldiers were most easy going and nonchalant and apparently were not aware of his physiognomy. The eight hour ride to St. Louis was hot and dusty. The train pulled in at St. Louis at ten P.M. and when he was met by his old friend, Mr. Yamamoto, the first sentence after exchange of greetings was "Let's have a glass of beer." The cold beer tasted really refreshing.

St. Louis had grown and improved in the last seventeen years. A new super highway from Forest Park facilitated traffic downtown and the area in front of the Union Station was a change that would delight anyone that had known the drab slum area of bygone days.

The two weeks in St. Louis was an eye-opener. The citizens went about their business as usual in no hurried manner. There was no war hysteria and a normal existence to bolster the home front was in evidence. It bespoke of the greatness of America, the maturity of a nation that could wage a war encompassing the entire world and yet take it leisurely at home.

St. Louis acted as gateway to free America in the eyes of the sixteen thousand evacuees in Arkansas' two relocation centers. Its Japanese population had increased. There were hundreds now in comparison with the bare thirty before the war.

Mrs. Yamamoto introduced a dentist that had relocated from Stockton. He was not yet busy and Minoru had a concentrated ten day treatment and finished his mission in half the expected time. He was told that the Caucasian population accepted this new dentist without any untoward incident. The corner druggist was sympathetic and steered patients to his door. The dearth of dentists was an added factor in his favor and he was sure he was going to become established in no time. When he was graduated from a St. Louis Dental School ten years earlier he had taken the Missouri Board Examination as an experience and passed it before returning to California. He was now lucky to possess a license to practice in St. Louis.

Allen Nagata, a pharmacist from Jerome, was in the city and looking for a job. Minoru sought him out at the YMCA and together they explored the metropolis. They went to a cafeteria and although Minoru was oblivious to anything Allen was perturbed. In a subdued voice he said, "There is a girl looking our way and talking about us."

"Oh, don't be silly. It's nothing derogatory. Perhaps she came from the center of Missouri and is now seeing Orientals for the first time in her life."

"But the way she looks at us makes me feel that she is identifying us with the enemy of the country." Allen became agitated.

"Not at that age. There is no real hate at that innocent age. When I was a student here in this city, my dissecting partner was from the interior of Missouri. He said I was the first Japanese he had met. You see there aren't too many of us in this part of the country."

"But anyway, I am sure I am not comfortable. Let's get out."

They went out as soon as they finished their meal and headed for a shoe store. There were not too many customers and they were waited upon immediately by a young blonde salesman. As he fitted shoes on Minoru, he looked up and seriously inquired, "What nationality are you? Japanese?"

Allen's face underwent a rapid change. The corners of his mouth went taut. "Yes, Japanese in race but we are Japanese-Americans, United States citizens." A sudden realization of the Dermott incident, or an eviction from this store as an unwelcome customer loomed large in his mind.

The blonde's face relaxed and he broke into a smile. "I am a German from the old country, but now enrolled at the Concordia Seminary. It puts us almost in the same boat."

Minoru telephoned and went to the office of John Hobson, classmate and intimate friend, as soon as he was released from the ordeals of being glued to the dental chair. "What brings you to St. Louis at this time of the year?"

"My home now is in the swamps of Arkansas. I came here to have dental attention."

"Then you are in one of the camps down in that ungodly country?"

"Yep. That's what we call home now. Eight thousand of us."

"Well, old man, I think that's a very good thing that happened to you all."

Minoru looked at his old friend who always was in for a joke, but he did not notice any jocularity. Why had he made such a remark? Was it vindictiveness for the sneak attack on Pearl Harbor? It could not be, because in the next breath he was calling his wife on the phone to prepare dinner for a guest.

Was Johnny turning statesman and foreseeing the benefit of dispersement of the Japanese in America over the entire country rather than concentration in the Pacific Coast states? But Johnny was an ordinary doctor and had no such crystal ball view of the future. He must just be swallowing propaganda. Minoru did not answer him. It was easy for Johnny to make such a remark but it hurt very much to be consoled in this manner. For after all, millions, tens of millions of dollars, were lost by his people in the evacuation, and they were at present branded as undesirables and herded in huge corrals. How could there be anything "good" about the whole mess?

"Have you met Dr. Tsuchida? He is professor of parasitology and came after our graduation. He is a nice fellow."

Minoru went over to the pathology department and knocked at Dr. Tsuchida's office. A frail looking man over fifty with thinning crown, horn-rimmed glasses, a nasal apparatus to alleviate his hay-fever, and an ever-present winning smile greeted him.

"Welcome to Washington University, Dr. Murayama. Dr. Hobson just phoned you were coming over." They were like old friends and after sundry talk the professor recounted his experience of the post-Pearl Harbor days.

"When war came I did not know what to do. I was ashamed and at the same time was afraid to stir out of the apartment, let alone show my face at the medical school. So I remained indoors at my apartment. I would have starved. It was a miserable three day hermit life.

"On the fourth day there was a commotion in front of my house on Forrest Park Blvd. Soon there was a loud refrain, 'We want Dr. Tsuchida. We want Dr. Tsuchida' as you would hear on the football field. I feared a mob action and I peeped carefully through the window, pulling the curtain aside a wee bit. To my relief I saw about twenty of my students out there. Naturally I went out and was immediately surrounded. 'Come back to the classes,' they pressed me. 'But I am so ashamed of what my country did to America. I cannot face you in classes,' I apologized. 'That's none of your doing. Come back to school. We need you.' You know they forcefully escorted me to school. Everyone has been considerate and kind and I am doing my best to teach the students parasitology and tropical medicine that will come in handy in the South Pacific and the Far Eastern countries." Minoru noticed moisture in the professor's eyes as he recounted the scene of welcome that he, an enemy alien, received at the hands of his students.

CHAPTER 34

A Reunion of Friends

"MURAYAMA-SAN, HAVE YOU MET MR.
Arata? He arrived from Santa Fe Internment Camp last night with
three other men. I heard that he was from the Hawaiian Islands," said
Mr. Goto as he fell in step with the elder Murayama on the way from
the mess hall after breakfast.

"From Hawaii, eh? Let's go pay him a visit. There were not too
many picked up in the Sacramento area by the FBI when war broke
out, but a few very good friends like Tom Tanaka of Clarksburg got
interned. Maybe he can give us some news of some men we know."
They turned around to the opposite side of the block where a few
barracks were still empty and new arrivals would be there if they were
assigned to this block.

"Good morning. I hear you have come from Santa Fe. This friend
is Mr. Murayama from Sacramento and I am Goto from Fresno. Welcome to Jerome." Mr. Goto was a gregarious spokesman.

"Good morning. Indeed we are from Santa Fe. Being newcomers
we'll be indebted to you in many matters from now on. Please bear
with us." The formal introduction was over and they were seated on
a bench provided by the people of the next apartment.

Seikichi Arata prided himself in remembering faces. A vague recognition of this man from Sacramento was bothering him as the talk touched
many subjects and topics. Yet he could not place this man. Long into
the night he tried to recall where he had seen that face before. It was
not on Kauai; he systematically eliminated all the possibilities on that
tiny island. Could it have been in Honolulu? Possibly, but he could
not be definite.

The following morning he paid a call on the Murayamas. The lady
of the house was in her late sixties and the way she smiled was not al-

together that of a stranger. Of course, he had no recollection of the young doctor and his wife, but the elder couple . . . .

"Mr. Murayama, pardon me if I seem presumptuous. Since yesterday morning when I first met you I have been bothered by a fixed thought. I have met you before somewhere, sometime. I cannot recollect where or when, but again Mrs. Murayama's face is faintly familiar. By chance were you ever in the Hawaiian Islands?"

Torao Murayama smiled, "I have been harboring the same doubt: that I have met you before. I cannot remember too. Yes, we lived in Hawaii for twenty-five years and came to California twenty years ago. We lived on the Hamakua coast while we were there. Yesterday you told us you were from Honolulu, so our chance meeting is unlikely since I did not live in the city."

"Well, I lived the greater part of my life on the island of Kauai at Makaweli Plantation."

Dr. Murayama was sun-bathing on the front steps for it was a lovely spring morning. He was relaxed and lazily listening to the conversation of his elders in the apartment. He suddenly turned around and exclaimed, "You are not the father of Sadao Arata, are you? My friend Sadao Arata was from Makaweli."

Surprised, Seikichi Arata said, "Why yes, Sadao is my son. Then your parents are the Murayamas from Waipunalei. Am I right? Sadao used to talk about you folks. Now I remember. You are the couple that I met at the Yamashiro Hotel. Mrs. Murayama, you and my wife came on the same steamer from Japan. We had a picnic at Waikiki, don't you remember?"

Then the three clasped their hands together. "Of all places to meet thus after half a century! But it is good to live long!"

Almost as a member of the family, Seikichi saw the Murayama's daily and he no longer felt a stranger among the eight thousand people.

Because of the noisiness in the mess hall, meals were impersonal. About once a week Seikichi was invited to enjoy his meal in the homey atmosphere of the Murayamas, followed by leisurely tea-sipping and sundry talk. They loved to talk of their first encounter of the bashful brides which brought a faint blush to the bewrinkled face of the hostess, and of the experiences and exploits of their subsequent lives.

Of course, Arata had more to relate. The war, the internment days in Hawaii and on the mainland, furnished hours of interesting subject matter. The many incidents, the rather intimate knowledge of people—illustrious, notorious, and common—both from Hawaii and stateside, had come to his knowledge. On this topic he was in possession of an inexhaustible fountain of news and gossip.

Prestige, glamor, superiority, and power that camouflage a man in normal society because of social position and material wealth, the intrinsic worth of a man was revealed most brutally in the internment camp. Some measured up to their usual reputation, a few surpassed the estimation accorded by society, but the majority, by and large, were found wanting and disclosed without shame the ugly embodiment of greed and selfishness. That such men stood at the forefront of the Japanese community both in Hawaii and California was the cause of the backwardness and weakness of the immigrant colonies. There was a sad paucity of real leaders. No wonder there was so much internal strife in every community and no real concerted front could be put up and maintained against persecution and bias directed against them by the majority groups.

"Our project director here in Jerome is a very warm and considerate ex-Indian Bureau official. He allows the use of cameras and one is free to take pictures of our life here. Radios are allowed. I know all centers allow radios, but the short-wave variety is prohibited. Still there are short-wave radios in all centers because many good radio technicians are among our boys. The administration knows that these long distance radios are used surreptitiously. But what harm is there in listening to the Tokyo broadcast? We are in Arkansas."

"That's right. This is not a likely place to start a fifth column activity to welcome a landing of the Japanese marines," nodded Arata.

Torao continued, "The insular mind of the Japanese works in a very narrow selfish manner with some. In order to be patted on the head some voluntarily report to the project director that in such a block such a person is listening to Tokyo broadcasts. The director cannot help but act when such information is sent into his office. Looks like we are tightening the rope around our own necks and making life more miserable."

Arata was thoughtful for a while. "I wonder if that is an 'insular trait' as you called it. In all camps a suspicion of 'informer' was directed at some. Many cases were unjust, but some could not be designated any other way, even after months of cool evaluation. In such a camp as this, the danger of falsely accusing one of being an 'informer' is all the more apt to take place."

"You may not know it," Torao took up the train of conversation, "but in many centers violence occurred. At Santa Anita Assembly Center there was a riot after a Korean spy was spotted because of his previous prewar anti-Japanese activity. He was attacked, MP's came to his rescue, and the violence became widespread. Finally tanks rolled into the race track grounds to quell the disturbance." He gulped down a cup of tea and after a few moments to see the reaction of his listener, he continued. "Right in this center, at the beginning of the camp before we arrived, a few of the pro-administration leaders were beaten up. This took place before the segregation movement. A minister and a professional man were the victims of the attack by the *kibei* boys who became incensed by the fawning attitude of this group. The rough-necks were never apprehended."

"It was fortunate that development stopped at mere physical roughening," enjoined Arata.

"Not so exactly. There is a center called Manzanar in California. This was the first relocation center. Most of the people there were residents of Southern California. Struggle for power among the evacuees became very intense. The WRA personnel naturally sided with their stooges, the cooperative pro-American faction. When a few of the leaders got beaten up, the MP's stepped in and harbored them in a building. The mob surrounded this building. Taunts were hurled at the soldiers by teenagers and shots were fired at the crowd by the poorly trained soldiers who could not stand the strain. Four were wounded and one died. These pro-administration leaders were removed from the camp. The apprehended instigators of the mob were taken to a correctional camp in the desert of Moab."

"What became of these leaders?"

"Those sent to Moab, I believe, are now at Tule Lake Center. The leaders who were victims of the riot are now on the outside relocated in the Middle West. The soldiers that fired upon the crowd were exonerated."

"You people of the Pacific Coast states were really unlucky. By contrast, the Hawaiian-Japanese were lucky because, except for us internees, the rest were allowed to carry on as in peace-time and are said to be prospering as never before. I don't think it was the magnanimity of the military that allowed them to remain. I believe it was expediency. When all potential leaders were put behind bars the army was sure it could handle the others in any emergency. The rest were then put to helping the war effort. The American capitalists rooted there for generations and having known our people for many decades had more faith in our loyalty."

"Do you know how we were labelled?" reminisced Torao sadly. "We oldsters are Japanese by nationality anyway and are not allowed to change according to American law and so cannot get angry with the appellation, but the Nisei were really mad and rebellious when the general of the Western Defense said, 'Once a Jap, always a Jap.' In the eyes of the Caucasians there is no difference between a Japan-born or an American-born. Of course an Oriental face remains the same unless there is a mixture of blood.

"The Americans themselves do not seem to realize how much education has molded the young generation in an American way of thinking. Even we, only living in America and not going to school have become Americanized more than we realize. To prove this point, a newly arrived man from Japan cannot follow and understand fully what our children say and do, even if the language barrier were removed. In turn, his talks and actions are sometimes peculiar and outlandish even to us oldsters. Americanization was really an achievement, a 100% success. Take the example of our 100th Infantry Battalion and the 442nd Regiment. Who can say that Americanization has not been a success? The Hawaiian born boys volunteered from their homes, but the stateside boys answered the call from behind the fence. All the more remarkable."

Torao Murayama looked at Seikichi Arata intently. "I heard your grandson was killed in action."

The latter had a momentary far-away look. "I am all Japanese in my thoughts and upbringing when I say this. I do not regret nor feel sorry that he died crossing the Italian river. I met him at Camp Livingston Internment Camp when he came to visit me and I found how matured he was in thought. His death more than anything else has made me resolve to die on American soil."

"How's the rest of the family in Hawaii?" Torao asked to change the subject.

"It is hard to correctly gauge the real situation there. Censorship is strictly enforced and so the truth cannot be told. But a real war-time boom seems to have visited the Islands. This much we were able to find out in the internment camp because there were many apprehended and rounded up a year or more after Pearl Harbor day. Hawaii is a recuperation and recreation area for the combat soldiers in the far-flung jungle battlefronts. My son, Sadao, was cleared by the FBI and army intelligence because he had never been to Japan. He works on contracting jobs sublet by big engineering companies engaged in defense work. Manpower is badly needed and the Nisei are doing their job. Such news is passed by the censors."

April 1945 rolled around and the capitulation of the German Reich put an end to hostilities on one front. Pressure on the Japanese Empire became intensified and the attacks by the B29's on the Japanese homeland itself brought out the truth that the end was near, for there was virtually no counterattack by Japanese fighter planes. Yet the Imperial Japanese Headquarters broadcast the number of B29 bombers shot down and minimized their own losses.

A fight to the finish was proclaimed for the entire population. Women were trained to fight with bamboo spears and pine trees were uprooted to express lubrication oil for the planes. Such news was intended to publicize the fighting spirit of the nation, but at the same time disclosed the fact that its war chest had hit bottom. Evidently the Imperial Headquarters did not realize the effect of such news on their enemy. It was a bravado gesture. The significance of this announcement was not lost on the thinking Issei. The gullible majority still had a blind faith in the Imperial Headquarters' tirade that a terrible reception would be accorded the landing American army as one hundred million were resolved to die defending their homeland.

"Okinawa will fall in a matter of days. General Ushijima, supreme commander of the defending garrison, committed suicide," Torao sadly muttered as if in soliloquy. The boiler room next to the laundry and latrine was a gathering place for the elderly men to play their game of chess and *go* or just talk and argue about anything that was presented. A few cronies had already convened at 9 A.M. The remark was not allowed to go unanswered for the bald-headed Taro Yamada, a Fresno farmer and ultra-nationalist, was sitting nearby. He was bull-necked and stocky in build. Strength emanated from his person but he was not one to think for himself.

"What does that mean? Nothing. The Japanese Navy has a plan to draw the enemy into home waters. This narrow sea between Kyushu and Shikoku will be a place for enemy attack because it is public secret that fortification is not heavy on both shores. It is an entrance to the Inland Sea." He seemed to have read or heard about the high strategy of the Imperial Navy in some magazine for popular consumption.

Torao was not convinced. "What you have said is warfare about the time of the Russo-Japanese War when surface vessels alone exchanged fire. Now war planes have changed everything. Just remember Pearl Harbor. Only air attack destroyed the Pacific Fleet. Airplanes alone sank the two British battleships off Malaya. Even in Okinawa it was attack both by sea and air that paved the way for foot soldiers' landing."

"But Okinawa is a small island. Japan is bigger and cannot so easily get pounded."

"It looks to me," interjected Torao in a slow, sad tone, "that the war should be brought to an end. Negotiated peace if possible. Surrender if necessary." At this Mr. Yamada blew up.

"What are you talking about. Surrender, never. The Imperial Headquarters proclaim that Japan will fight to the last man."

"That may be the words of hard losers, the young officers of the army. They strutted about when the war was a winning one in the beginning. But this retreat after retreat is driving them crazy."

"But what is wrong with fighting to the last Japanese in defense of the homeland?"

"Plenty wrong! From the code of *Bushido* these professional soldiers will commit suicide by *seppuku* and consider that their mistakes can be excused. But what of the millions of non-combatants and future of the race? Should they be sacrificed for the mistakes of the present military caste?"

Torao became heated because this question was a very pressing one and for many long nights he had pondered over the pros and cons of surrender. He realized that American press releases were more accurate. "I believe sincerely that a surrender should be seriously considered by the leaders of Japan. I cannot swallow the Imperial Headquarters, news. That this source of news was always true was a belief that was ingrained in us since our grammar school days. Imperial Headquarters never lie, but who runs this bureau? Nobody but professional soldiers and they can easily twist the news to suit their purpose."

"But I think this is a strategic retreat."

"If so, Okinawa should not have been lost. Okinawa is a part of Japan proper. To lose it after that bitter fight shows that on the field of battle Japan is being pushed around. Present day war, I am told, is not fought with manpower alone, but with superior weapons and you, who have been in America so long, must admit that America can out-produce Japan many times over."

"That may be so, but Japan will never surrender. She had not lost a war yet."

"You must remember, Yamada-san, that in any war or battle, there are two parties. One must lose, by being completely crushed or by surrender. Surrender is nothing new in Japanese history. In the days of feudalism, there were constant wars. There were many defeats and many surrenders."

Mr. Yamada was silent. There was no refutation in spite of his animosity to this man who was presenting arguments for surrender; a concept, he, Yamada, never considered for one moment. He could only add, "You do not know the Japanese in spite of being one. Japan will not surrender."

Torao was sorry for him. He realized how much he might have hurt him by touching upon a sore spot. "Yamada-san. We do not live more than sixty or seventy years and we both will soon fade away. The Japanese race is, however, ever-lasting as long as this earth exists. Like boxing, this round, I am afraid, is a complete loss to the Yamato race, but there are other rounds.

"We both have lived in America for a long time and love America. At this point the two countries are at war, but in the First World War they were allies. Who can say that the two countries will not be friends again or become allies in the future. Above all we cannot allow our race to become wiped out by stupid wars. I am sure there are many statesmen in Japan right now who are thinking of a way out, and perhaps surrender is the only way the allies will allow us to squirm out of this mess." Everyone present was silent and immersed in his own thoughts.

Resettlement of the evacuees in the Midwestern and Eastern States became accelerated as favorable letters came pouring back from the "outside." Even the timid ones began to think more seriously about venturing forth as their cash began to dwindle with each passing month.

Arata tried, through his children in Honolulu, to get permission from the military and naval transport service for passage back to the islands, but without result. After all, civilians did not have much priority and an enemy alien could not expect much under the circumstances. He reconciled himself to the fact that only when the war ended and travel restrictions became relaxed could he hope to return to Hawaii. He would not consider going to the cities as he had no kin living anywhere.

Summer days were terrific. The humid, depressing afternoons were so enervating that the entire center ceased its activity and the inhabitants sought whatever shade they could find in their scantiest clothing. Periodic downpour relieved this unbearable humidity for a little while and the most terrifying electric storms sent shivers through newcomers. Sometimes, three or four lightning flashes against a dark sky occurred simultaneously in different directions. Deafening rumbling and thunder claps were heard one after another. These thunderbolts seemed to have a favorite spot and a certain path to travel in their route of destruction. There was an oak tree four blocks away. Upon this tree, the bolt had struck three times and only certain barracks adjacent to it suffered shock and burnt together with this sturdy monarch of the forest.

Nights were just as bad. High humidity continued far into the small hours of the morning. Everybody tossed in bed and sleep was very fitful. Those families that were able to buy electric fans were fortunate; without this cooling aid life was a virtual hell.

Among the shrubs along the ditches fireflies were abundant. To the children this was a great discovery for they could spend the dusk and evenings capturing these insects instead of fretting at home and being scolded by their elders about nothing. The Issei were making cages to keep these fluorescent insects, a task they did with alacrity and pleasure. In so doing they were able to relive their boyhood experience in native Japan. "To study in the fluorescent light of fireflies" symbolized poverty of their native land, but at the same time spoke for the studiousness and industry of her people. The graduation song of all the schools in Japan was the "The Light of the Fireflies," sung to the tune of *Auld Lang Syne*.

The sultry days of Arkansas were made more unbearable to the older generation of evacuees by the bad news from the Far East. The land of their origin, never before invaded by foreign troops, was now being plastered by heavy bombs and incendiaries. Her flimsy cities went up in flames and thousands of non-combatants of all ages were caught in this inferno of hell and scorched to unrecognizable remains. Even the Imperial Headquarters could not deny the devastation wrought and could only feebly boast of "some" bombers shot down. Their homeland was being reduced to ashes. Their heart was heavy for there were relatives and friends whose fate there was no way of ascertaining.

The center was daily invaded by a different category of soldiers. Their own boys were returning from the battlefields of Europe. War was over and the original 442nd Infantry Battalion and 100th Infantry Unit were being replaced by new men. The veterans were back. From honor to evacuee camps! The irony was there, but not a stinging one; for the nation recognized the mettle of the Nisei and showed how wrong the entire program of evacuation had been in the first place.

The older generation, who could not become citizens no matter how much they tried, saw in these bemedaled sons and grandsons the fulfilment of their dreams and felt pride that was unbounded. The fate of Japan was a nebulous one, but the future of Japanese as Americans in America was glorious. The entire American press toed the line of the War Department in singling out the exploits of the Japanese-Americans in Europe as combatants and in the South Pacific as interpreters and translators assigned to the front line. It fell to the lot of these bilingual soldiers to read and translate the captured documents of the enemy and render fluid the war tactics at the front line.

The atomic bombs over Hiroshima and Nagasaki and the surrender on the 10th of August followed in rapid succession. Minoru hurried back from the hospital when the siren blew at 2 P.M., for this signal had been arranged beforehand to announce the end of war. He wanted to be with his parents when this epoch-making news of surrender and end to the war became a fact. When he walked into the apartment his mother and father were silently alone.

His mother looked up with anguish in her eyes. "Is it true that Japan has surrendered?"

Minoru sat down beside her and held her hands. "I am afraid it is true, mother." There was a sudden burst of tears followed by an uncontrollable sobbing for about five minutes. He held her tight without saying a word; he felt the violent vibrations that shook her body. His father stood up, walked to the window and silently gazed out at the delta landscape steaming under the August afternoon sun. The siren kept blasting away for nearly an hour.

Some months ago when Italy capitulated, Minoru remembered, there was an article in the *New York Times*. A roving reporter cruised around the Italian section of New York and found it like a dead city. There was no light in the shops and no gaiety on the streets. It did not mean that these people were not glad that the war ended in favor of the Allies, for most of them were against Fascism and Mussolini. They were only sad to realize that their native Italy had so ignominiously crumbled like a deck of cards.

His father returned to his chair. "Mother, let us have some tea." A routine activity brought her out of her despair. She wiped her tears and began to boil water on the electric plate. "We expected this event to come, didn't we? But it is shocking just the same. I only hope there will not be a revolution of the die-hards to prolong the misery of the common people."

"What will the army and navy people do?"

His father was thoughtful. "I think they will follow the wish of the commander-in-chief who is the Emperor. In the Japanese armed forces the soldiers owe their allegiance to the Emperor alone."

"Then why did you say you feared a revolution? By that you mean, Japanese fighting Japanese?" asked Minoru.

His father went on to elaborate. "That is right. The armed forces as a whole and the men in command will acquiesce to the Imperial command to lay down the arms. But the younger officers may not view the situation in the same light and resolve to carry on the fight. After all, these officers were trained and imbued with the spirit never to surrender. All have weapons you know. And it will be just as easy to train them on their own buddies if they believe in a certain principle."

"That will be bad. The country will certainly be reduced to ashes."

"But I think even the young, fanatical officers will come to their senses. When the truth of the Imperial desire for peace becomes understood, they too will follow the order to cease fighting."

"I hope so. Of course, the real peace terms must await signatures, I suppose."

Torao was again in deep thought. "To avoid any ill feeling, talk freely among the younger generation, but I advise you to keep your mouth shut when you discuss the surrender among Issei people. There are many who cannot believe the truth. They must be given time to adjust to the new development."

With the end of the war and the gradual return to normalcy the closing of the relocation centers was inevitable. No matter how much the life of being a government ward appealed to some, there could be no more easy life. The relocation center was intended for the duration of the war. Besides, the Pacific Coast states were now open to free travel and return of the evacuees.

The problem of the War Relocation Authority was now to pave the way for the Japanese return and acceptance on the part of Caucasian community in Washington, Oregon, and California. For those that found jobs and homes in the cities of the midwest there was no problem, but the sentiment in the towns and villages in California was strongly against the return of these people that had been ousted as a war measure.

At Hood River, Oregon, the sixteen Nisei names were removed from the county honor roll. These Japanese-American soldiers were born and raised locally and drafted into the armed forces along with their friends, but were not considered fit to grace the honor roll. There were many homes to which the Nisei returned as soon as the restriction to travel was lifted. Before they could repair the damage to the house resulting from neglect or vandalism, ruffians from cruising vehicles poured volleys of lead into the house to show their displeasure at the Japanese return. Incendiary fire started and burnt some houses to the ground as soon as news got around that the legal Japanese owners were returning from camp. The good news did not make news and was not reported, but these outbreaks of violence made sensational headlines.

The War Relocation Authority sent their men into these areas to speak at churches, Rotary meetings, and Lions clubs to educate the people to facts. It was not an easy task. Obstacles were met everywhere. However, there were friends of the Japanese in towns and farming areas. These men and women were courageous enough to work with the officials to provide hostels to accommodate them on arrival and help resettle them to jobs as opportunities turned up. The scarcity of workers, especially on the farms, was a great blessing and families were rapidly dispersed to the rural area from which the migratory workers from Oklahoma and Arkansas had suddenly bundled their belongings and were on their return trek. These people had been driven out of the "dust bowl" in the thirties and sought opportunities in the West. Many settled permanently as independent farmers, but an equal number were shiftless and irresponsible and left the ranches without help when the fruits were ripening for market. Therefore, the Caucasian farmers were forced to employ Japanese or suffer an irreparable loss. It was not entirely a broad-minded gesture.

Dr. Minoru Murayama heard that one of his colleagues had returned to Sacramento, but met with a very chilly reception. He was not extended the privileges he had enjoyed at the hospitals prior to the war. It incensed him so that he opened an office in Los Angeles instead. The delta district of the Sacramento River where Minoru had practiced was not being resettled by the Japanese. The Oakies and Mexicans had permanently replaced them as tenant farmers. It seemed to him that the ties that bound him to California had been severed by the evacuation. He had to deliberate well before he set out on a new life. The War Relocation Authority was duty-bound to transport an evacuee to a desired place of resettlement. For the Hawaiian evacuees, as soon as a ship was available, there was going to be free transportation to the islands by the Navy. Any other evacuee who wanted to join this group was to be processed and, if the reasons were valid, was allowed to board this ship.

The fate of the Murayamas was decided one evening when Seikichi Arata called to while away a few hours. "What are you planning to do? Returning to Sacramento?"

"That is a problem we are talking among ourselves. The pros and cons seem to weigh equally. To settle in the Midwest, a medical license of that state must be first obtained. On the other hand, return to California will mean an uncertain reception and a poverty-stricken clientele. I cannot look forward very much to non-Japanese patients for I know feelings are against us. Very few are returning to the Sacramento delta area where I did my work."

Arata was grinning now. "Maybe you ought to return to the land of your birth. Go back to Hawaii. The islands are very, very prosperous now. People have money as never before because of the war-time boom.

There is an opportunity for quite a few more good doctors in Honolulu."

"This is something to really think about, and I believe this entire family can get free transportation to the islands."

"Then I'll write Sadao that you will return to Hawaii permanently. I know he will be awfully glad."

"Thank you. We'll discuss it and very likely apply for a return to the islands."

The Murayamas were excited. The old were unable to sleep for the nostalgic memories of their youth and the children tossed in their beds for the adventure in an unknown land. To Minoru it was a solution to his future and he became light-hearted. To Lillian it was a great relief to realize that there was to be no more of this communal life without privacy, an end to this squalid, primitive existence, and a new hope to build for future security and comfort even at a belated start.

CHAPTER 35

The Return to Hawaii

POST WAR LOS ANGELES WAS TEEMING WITH people that had been engaged in the airplane industry and other war time efforts. The Little Tokyo around First Street was occupied by Negroes that had migrated from the South and were remaining as permanent residents. The Japanese returnees from the relocation centers were housed in several hostels to meet their immediate shelter needs. They did not take long to find jobs as these were plentiful if not too choosy. Accustomed to monthly stipends of sixteen or nineteen dollars, a gardener's wage of a dollar or more an hour was astoundingly attractive. They were all engrossed in furiously making up for lost time and wasted months.

From the Arkansas Center the Murayamas and Seikichi Arata traveled on the railroad tickets furnished by the WRA to Los Angeles. It was an almost unnatural sensation to feel free, to be able to do what one wanted, to go places without restriction. There was no shut-in feeling, but the feeling that someone was watching you, that somebody kept track of your doings and you had to account for them later, could not be shed. Minoru was keenly aware of this new sensation of self-consciousness. It must be akin to a religious conversion to a "thou shall not" cult, but without the ecstasy of such a new discovery in one's emotional life. For there was no great joy in this newly found liberty and freedom of action. Minoru labelled it "a prisoner complex," but kept this appellation to himself.

People from other centers of Arizona, Colorado, and Wyoming were assembling at this Santa Ana Army Airfield Camp for the same purpose: awaiting transportation to Hawaii. Many families that had gone out to Chicago, Denver, and Milwaukee were converging daily to this camp for this long-awaited opportunity of returning from exile, and the total numbered about three hundred.

As there were several days of waiting, the WRA official organized a conducted tour of Los Angeles and suburbs. To Seikichi Arata this was the only glimpse of free America. What he had witnessed in his three years sojourn was through the meshes of fences and the windows of train coaches. He was led from one camp to another, being let off trains to stretch his legs on deserts, farmlands away from human dwellings, and the salt beds of the Great Salt Lake. His destination was always army camps or relocation centers which were built in vast wastelands or sun-parched deserts. If ever there were greens it had to be malaria-ridden swamps of the Mississippi Delta. America as seen by these people was by no means flattering.

The people at Santa Ana were the first to board the ship. The next day a train pulled in and disgorged three hundred and twenty men, women, and children on the wharf. These had come from Tule Lake Center. There were thirty unattached single men, and the rest were women and children. On the third day a train arrived from Crystal City, Texas, bearing one hundred and seventy persons. These people comprised family groups. The husbands had formerly been interned at Santa Fe and the families joined them from the relocation centers or directly from Hawaii.

The last special train from Texas had a baggage coach and from this the belongings were strewn on the wharf. The new arrivals were busy identifying their baggage when forty Nisei soldiers appeared and began helping them carry the baggage up the gangplank to assigned cabins and dormitories. These veterans of the 100th and 442nd Battalions had been awaiting transportation at different California camps after their return from Italy, when they were suddenly ordered by the War Department to board this ship to journey back to the islands, acting as intermediaries in carrying out army orders with the least friction. They were there to quell any riot or mutiny should that arise among any of the passengers.

Sergeants Aoki and Goto were the ranking members of these veterans. Sergeant Murata found his father and brother among the returnees and many soldiers discovered their language school teachers among the passengers. It was a joyful reunion to all and precluded any friction. It had been arranged beforehand that irrespective of early or later arrival, families with infants and children were assigned cabins on A and B decks and the rest placed in the large dormitories.

The *Shawnee* was a United States Army transport of about eight thousand tons displacement and used to be a regular plyer between New York and the Carribean Islands. She was old. The outer hull was made of steel, but the whole interior was of wood and the danger of fire was constantly present. The promenade section of decks A and B were turned into dormitories in which three-decker beds were installed to accommodate as many soldiers as possible. The large smoking room at the prow was converted to an officer's mess. The kitchen was located at the stern and the regular mess hall for the troops was located adjoining it at the very end of the ship. Long tables about four and a half feet high, arranged in parallel rows, constituted the sole equipment and there was no chair or bench. The soldiers had taken their meals standing up and on this trip all adults and children above six had to eat in this large mess hall. The little ones naturally could not make use of the high tables and so found nooks in the hall where they squatted and hurriedly gulped down their food. All mothers with children below six were to take their meals in the officer's mess and so were comfortably seated. But this mess room was the former smoking room at the front of the ship and all food, dishes, and trays had to be transported back and forth by KP's from the kitchen. The kitchen was two decks below at the opposite end and their being no elevators, the KP's had to go up and down on almost perpendicular stairways. The order to have as many as possible eat in the regular mess hall was easily understood. Nobody was allowed to carry food to seasick persons in the cabin. The only exception was the really ailing ones certified by the doctor.

As soon as the people from Crystal City, Texas, arrived, there was a meeting of the representatives from each group and the order came from Captain Eudy of the United States Army to elect a spokesman for the entire group and foremen for the different tasks. Dr. Okimura became the spokesman to represent the passengers.

Dr. Murayama was elected medical and sanitary officer and was given a more or less free hand by Capt. Glasgow of the U. S. Army Medical Corps. To be self-sustaining, sixteen cooks, a few bakers, and one hundred fifty kitchen help to do the menial work had to volunteer. These KP's peeled potatoes, washed pots and pans, and did the policing of the dining hall and kitchen. They also carried the food to the officer's mess hall. Military Police were supplied from the passengers. These men patrolled the decks because of the ever-present fire hazard. Careless disposal of cigarette butts might spell fire, the untidiness of the decks could bring down the ire of the ship's captain, and above all the children running up and down the decks and stairways had to be supervised to forestall broken bones and worse calamity. Janitors had to tidy up the ship twice daily.

The ship slipped out of the Wilmington Harbor at 4 P.M. The entire night and the next day found the ship rolling and pitching. Very few were up and only a handful turned up at the kitchen either to work or eat.

At about ten o'clock there was a loud speaker announcement. "Dr. Murayama, please report to Captain Eudy's office." Minoru was a good sailor and he was able to answer the summons immediately. In the room the captain and Sgt. Goto sat without a smile. The sergeant had been a language instructor at Camp Snelling, Minnesota. The captain was a young man of about twenty-eight with a phlegmatic temperament found among many men of responsibility. He did not crack a smile and seemed deeply perturbed.

"Mr. McDuffie, the chef, reports to me that your men are on strike and the kitchen crew did not report to work. Mr. Goto tells me you seem to be the only one that could be consulted as to how to deal with the situation."

Minoru had met this chef the previous day. The name of McDuffie was familiar to all Honolulu residents because it had been associated with the detective bureau so long. If this man was a brother to the famous detective then he was not altogether a stranger. He felt sorry that this man had been let down.

"Captain, I do not think this was a strike. It only means that on this rough trip most of the people are really seasick and cannot report to duty. Besides nobody will eat anything."

The captain was still adamant. "Regulations call for the preparation of two and a half meals a day "

"Even if the food has to be dumped overboard?"

"That is right. We must follow regulations even if the fish are the only ones to benefit from the cooking. The ship is dirty. The janitors have not done their cleaning yet."

"They too are too seasick to do any work."

"Doctor, I confess I do not know how to handle these people. My work has been to transport troops and I have made countless trips in the Pacific. But civilians are something new to me. My orders are to treat civilians the same as the military. That means that anyone not obeying my orders will be considered recalcitrant. These Nisei soldiers are here to maintain order and anyone not cooperating will be thrown in the brig. This is the ordinary military way and the only method I employ. What may I do?" The captain was almost sullen. Sergeant Goto did not say a word and was glum.

"Captain Eudy, let us have this entire day to get accustomed to this rough rolling and pitching. I hope by tomorrow many of us will be able to stir about. Even if the sea is still rough I am sure you will have full cooperation as soon as the people understand your position and what you are up against. This spokesman method is not an effective one. My suggestion is for you to call together the representatives that were elected last evening and tell them what you just disclosed to me. I am sure you will get cooperation."

The captain turned to Sergeant Goto and the inquiring glance was answered with a nod.

The next morning the Nisei soldier at the broadcasting room called the names of the representatives and announced that a very important meeting was to be held at the officers' mess by Capt. Eudy. He did not have any difficulty in making himself understood as Sergeant Goto interpreted the orders. With understanding of the situation the foremen went into a huddle, made a list of the really seasick workmen, and found substitutes to get the complete roster required by the captain.

Meanwhile the sea became a little calmer, but the large swells continued, for a December Pacific Ocean is far from being pacific. Still, the number of people on the decks increased. Feeling better, they emerged to get fresh air and looking at the ocean they noticed a change in the color of the sky and a deeper blue in the undulating billows. Their spirits soared for their homeland was nearing. They sat on the benches of the outer deck basking in the sun, with gazes fixed on the horizon. Cloud banks of white assuming bizarre contours along the distant horizon made these exiles wonder what lay beyond. Past the age of romantic notions and day-dreaming, it was a rare occasion to feel so youthful as to indulge in day dreams. Bereft of material wealth after four years of prison camp, during which time they were pressed by the simple primitive needs for mere existence, they were now lazily cruising along like the well-to-do to a definite objective without care of worry.

For three years, their roamings had been a "military secret" and they did not know whither they were transported. Now this ship was steaming for Honolulu. What reception would they meet at their destination? Let that be answered when that day comes. For the time being, concentrate and picture an animal, a building, or a battlement in the mass of clouds above the distant horizon. A childish game, but a treat to be a child again. To be tossed about by the waves of war had been very fatigueing.

Seikichi Arata was also out sitting on the bench with Y. Asasaki, a language school teacher in Honolulu. As they were exchanging news of Santa Fe after Seikichi had left that camp for Arkansas, a master sergeant came along. Seikichi abruptly stood up and asked, "Sergeant, do you by any chance remember Edward Arata of Company A who died in Italy? I am his grandfather and should like very much to hear about his last days."

Sergeant Aoki extended his hand, "My name is Sgt. Aoki and I remember Edward very well. There is a fellow of Company A here and he can tell you better I think. Hey, Hank, come here," and he beckoned to a youngster who was comfortably strumming a ukulele at the stern. "This is Ed Arata's grandfather. I think you belonged to his squad. He wants to hear about how he fought and died."

Henry Sato's face became taut. It was painful to think of the less fortunate buddies who were left behind on foreign soil. It was a torture to review in words the battle, especially to a kin of the deceased and in a language in which he was not too fluent. He turned aside and in so doing looked at Mr. Asasaki, "Why teacher, how are you? I am Henry Sato!"

"Oh, let me see. You are Sato from McCully St. I would not have recognized you. You have grown so tall and husky. I congratulate you on your exploits in Europe. We are all proud of what you did and thankful for the result it may bring to us all."

"I knew you were interned with all the leading Japanese at the outbreak of the war, but I did not know you were on this ship."

"Yes, the majority of the internees went back by way of Seattle about a month ago. There are about thirty of us stragglers on this ship. By the way, this is Mr. Arata from Alewa Heights. Mr. Arata, this is Henry Sato my former pupil."

It was now easier for Henry to face his buddy's grandfather for he had a friend to help him out in case of language difficulty or when he could not express a sentiment in the right sort of way. "Ed and I were in the same squad of Company A. I remember him talking about you when he visited you at Camp Livingston, Louisiana, while we were training at Camp Shelby, Mississippi. So you see, I know something about you because we soldiers, in moments of waiting on maneuvers and on the eve of battle when there was nothing but small talk to kill time, talked about home. We talked of the pleasant things of the distant past and places far away from the actual scene where we were caught like flies in a spider web. We talked about our parents, grandparents, brothers, sisters, and friends. Anything and everything. We told the same stories over and over. Somehow that kind of talk soothed our nerves.

"Ed was a happy boy and kept up our morale in many ways. He could sing and he could entertain us with the ukulele. He was corporal and was always at the lead with the sergeant. It was that way at the Volturno River. The Germans were entrenched and had all points zeroed. Our advancing units were mowed down by the accurate artillery and machine guns from prepared nests. We were beaten badly and were forced to fall back. We reformed and during the middle of the night we crossed the Volturno River. At daybreak we found ourselves poised with the other Caucasian units on each side on the northern bank. From that point we began a furious attack up a hill at Dragoni. The Germans were in machine gun nests on top of the hill overlooking our advance. The slope of the hill was terraced to plant grape vines. We deployed and sought whatever cover there was as we climbed slowly from one terrace to another, trying to hide ourselves behind the stumps and green branches of grape vines. But the Germans could pick us out from above and volleys of machine gun fire plastered us whenever we stirred. Ed was hit by this fire. Through the head. It was an instantaneous affair.

"When the machine gun nest was destroyed by a buddy who threw a grenade, the hill became ours and we collected the wounded and killed. I then saw how Ed had met his death. A bullet through his temple. He rests there in the military cemetery in Italy."

Seikichi Arata was able to visualize the battle scene as Henry described the charge up the Dragoni hill. As he looked out on the undulating waves, he could picture the American soldiers scurrying from one grape vine to another, but always onward and upward. The reddish dirt and the cluster of green fatigue uniforms that darted here and there; the rat-tat-tat from above resulting in a cloud of dust on the hillside, were duplicated on the billows by white spray that crested the waves. Seikichi was content and satisfied; his grandson had come to a warrior's end. Nothing more could be asked.

"Mr. Sato, thank you very much. I am glad to know the details and am happy that he went as he did. Let an old man thank you for the association my grandson was privileged to have with you and I hope you will find happiness in the future."

Mr. Asasaki took over the conversation, "Henry, there must have been more in your outfit from my school. Give me some news about them."

"We are going home in dribbles. As soon as replacements arrived we were sent back. Many are back in Hawaii already. On this boat there isn't any other Makiki boy. But about fifteen left our outfit when we were training at Camp Shelby to take further language lessons at Camp Snelling in Minnesota. All the good students at Japanese School were picked for this type of duty. I was not so bright as you remember, and so was overlooked and continued in the infantry. Those boys went to the South Pacific and also to India and Burma as interpreters for the American and Allied armies."

"Then as a language school teacher I am glad that I have contributed something in a small way to the war effort, although I was interned as an enemy alien," smiled Mr. Asasaki.

"Of course you have and in a big way. No Caucasian soldier could have taken the place of the Nisei interpreters in the Pacific. They contributed much to the shortening of the war. I did not learn much of the Japanese language, but at least I learned something of the history and the spirit of the Japanese people under you. During the bayonet charge in the mountains of France when we went to the rescue of the Texas boys, someone yelled *Banzai* and you know, we all understood and joined the battly cry and yelled *Banzai* as we charged. I think this was the only *Banzai* charge in the American army."

507

Two days of idyllic comfort befell the passengers of the homecoming ship. Then at ten o'clock, December 9, there was a loudspeaker announcement, "Dr. Murayama report to Captain Eudy immediately."

There in the office of the transportation commander sat the captain, Captain Glasgow, Sgt. Goto, and Captain Sorensen of the *S. S. Shawnee*.

Capt. Eudy began the discussion. "We just made an inspection tour of the ship and find that it is very dirty."

Minoru could not suppress a smile. He was thinking about the decrepit condition of this wooden ship of a half a century vintage. Why make so much fuss about cleanliness when it could not become spick-and-span no matter how much scrubbing was applied?

Captain Sorensen was offended when he saw the smile, "This is no laughing matter. I never saw such a dirty ship. Why, it has not been swept in two days. The lavatories are dirty, especially the women's. As it is right now we may not be allowed to enter the harbor. As sanitary officer you must clean up the ship." To this tirade there was nothing to say.

"I'll do my best," and he sought the foremen of the janitors. As he guessed, the directive had not reached them through the negligence of the spokesman.

To the two janitor foremen he explained the condition and the wrath of the captain and had them round up men for immediate action. He then took to the air. "Ladies and gentlemen, tomorrow we shall be landing at Honolulu. It is a great day for us. But we may have to anchor off port and not be able to dock because the quarantine officers may not allow this ship in the harbor. The captain of transportation, the ship's doctor, and the captain of the ship made an inspection tour of the ship this morning and the verdict was that there never was such a dirty vessel afloat. Especially mentioned was the unmentionable state of the women's lavatories. We have a reputation of being a very clean people. Let us not spoil this good name. It will be a tragedy if we are not allowed to steam in tomorrow and be greeted by our relatives who are sure to be waiting on the dock. Let us get together and scrub. Let the porcelain of the lavatories become snowy white. There will be another inspection in three hours."

The whole ship became active. Conspicuously, women took the

lead. Sedate wives of school principals became the most aggressive workers, exhorting others to pitch in and meet the deadline. In two hours the ship was ready for inspection.

The captain was much pleased after the second inspection tour and invited Dr. Murayama for a bottle of *Coca-cola* in his office. He saw that this assignment of civilian transportation was now almost an accomplished fact, and it was much easier than what he had feared.

That night everyone had a fitful sleep. The morrow was December the tenth and an odyssey of three to four years was coming to an end, when the *S. S. Shawnee* would calmly steam into "Fair Haven" of the Pacific, Honolulu.